Female Experience

Female Experience brings together contributions from three generations of female psychoanalysts writing about their own experiences of working with female patients and questioning the specific determinants of female sexuality and gender identity which have become central in psychoanalytic debate. The authors represent a cross-section of different theoretical orientations (Kleinian, Freudian and Independent) and also draw on varied professional backgrounds.

The individual chapters cover different phases of the female life cycle, overarching themes of relationships, mourning, female creativity and the obstacles to it. The authors deal specifically with female bodily representations, phantasies, desires, sexual abuse, eating disorders, childbearing, perinatal loss and postnatal depression, and primitive exchanges between mother and baby in their manifestations in the female to female psychoanalytic encounter.

Beginning with Freud, psychoanalysts have questioned the constraints of gender as manifested with transference and countertransference within the therapeutic process. However, explorations have focused on cross-gender alliances. The contributors to this book present detailed material pertaining exclusively to the analytic relation between women. The insight this book gives into the female analyst's special way of listening to and understanding women's preoccupations serves to illustrate why British analysts have made such a huge contribution to the psychoanalytic gender debate in recent years.

The editors are both full members of the British Psycho-Analytical Society and the International Psychoanalytical Association.

Joan Raphael-Leff is Professor of Psychoanalysis at the Centre for Psychoanalytic Studies, University of Essex, and a psychoanalyst in private practice specializing in the emotional aspects of reproductive issues.
Rosine Jozef Perelberg is Honorary Senior Lecturer in Psychoanalytic Theory at the University of London and a psychoanalyst in private practice.

Contributors: Enid Balint; Catalina Bronstein; Dana Birksted-Breen; Marion Burgner; Alicia Etchegoyen; Paola Mariotti; Maggie Mills; Rosine Jozef Perelberg; Dinora Pines; Joan Raphael-Leff; Joan Riviere; Valerie Sinason; Deborah Steiner; Maria A. Tallandini; Jane Temperley.

Female Experience

Three Generations of British Women Psychoanalysts on Work with Women

Edited by Joan Raphael-Leff and
Rosine Jozef Perelberg

Foreword by Juliet Mitchell

London and New York

First published 1997
by Routledge
11 New Fetter Lane, London EC4P 4EE

Simultaneously published in the USA and Canada
by Routledge
29 West 35th Street, New York, NY 10001

Typeset in Times by
Ponting–Green Publishing Services, Chesham,
Buckinghamshire
Printed and bound in Great Britain by
Creative Print and Design (Wales), Ebbw Vale

British Library Cataloguing in Publication Data
A catalogue record for this book is available from the
British Library

Library of Congress Cataloging in Publication Data
Female Experience: Three Generations of British Women
   Psychoanalysts on Work with Women / edited by Joan
   Raphael-Leff and Rosine Jozef Perelberg.
      Includes bibliographical references and index.
      1. Women and psychoanalysis.
      2. Women–psychology.   3. Female psychoanalysts
      4. Women–Mental health.
      I. Raphael-Leff, Joan.   II. Perelberg, Rosine Jozef.
RC451.4.W6F44   1997
616.89'17'082–dc21   96–40328

ISBN   0–415–15769–2 (hbk)
ISBN   0–415–15770–6 (pbk)

Contents

Contributors

Enid Balint, who died in 1994, was a training analyst and leading figure in the British Society since the 1960s. Before this as London organizer of the Citizen's Advice Bureaux she became extremely interested in studying the interaction between partners, seeing a marriage as 'entity rather than two separate individuals' and in 1948 founded the Family Discussion Bureau, later to become the Institute of Marital Studies based at the Tavistock Institute of Human Relations. In the early 1950s Enid joined her husband, Michael Balint, in his exploratory work with general practitioners and together they developed an internationally renowned training method to sensitize doctors to an awareness of the 'unnoticed happenings' and psychological aspects of interaction with their patients. In 1980, Enid was made an Honorary Fellow of the Royal College of General Practitioners. She continued to conduct research and demonstration groups until well into her eighties, and a book of her collected papers *Before I was I – Psychoanalysis and the Imagination* (edited by Juliet Mitchell and Michael Parsons) was published by Free Association Books in 1993, in her ninetieth year.

Dana Birksted-Breen is a training psychoanalyst of the British Institute of Psycho-Analysis. She obtained a *licence-ès-lettres* at the Sorbonne, Paris and a PhD in social psychology at Sussex University. She qualified as a psychoanalyst in 1980 and has been in full-time private practice since then. Her main publications are *The Birth of a First Child: Towards an Understanding of Femininity* (Tavistock Publications, 1975); *Talking with Mothers* (Jill Norman, 1981, and Free Association Books, 1989); *The Gender Conundrum: Contemporary Psychoanalytic Perspectives on Femininity and Masculinity* (Routledge, New Library of Psychoanalysis, 1993). She won the 1995 Sacerdoti Prize for her paper 'Phallus, Penis and Mental Space' given at the IPA Congress in San Francisco (published in the International Journal of Psychoanalysis, 1996, vol. 77, Part 4).

Catalina Bronstein is a full member of the British Psycho-Analytical Society and a member of the Association of Child Psychotherapists. She studied medicine and qualified as a psychiatrist in Buenos Aires, Argentina. In

London, she trained as a child psychotherapist in the Adolescent Department of the Tavistock Clinic and did the psychoanalytic training at the Institute of Psycho-Analysis. For the last ten years she has been working at the Brent Adolescent Centre, at the Centre for Research into Adolescent Breakdown and in private practice. She is Honorary Senior Lecturer at the Psychoanalysis Unit of the Department of Psychology, University College London and teaches at the Tavistock Clinic, in other psychotherapeutic organizations and abroad.

Marion Burgner was a training analyst and full member of the British Psycho-Analytical Society where she taught on the theory and practice of psychoanalysis. Before training to be a psychoanalyst she read English literature at the University of London and then psychology. She also qualified as a Child Analyst at the Hampstead Clinic, and continued working with children and adolescents for many years both at The Anna Freud Centre and Brent Consultation Centre. In addition, she supervised registrars and medical students in the Department of Psychological Medicine at University College Hospital, London. She worked in a Project at the Tavistock Clinic offering psychoanalytic psychotherapy to those who are HIV-positive or suffer from AIDS, and from 1990 was also involved in a research project at The Anna Freud Centre offering treatment to young adults who have suffered breakdown. Throughout her professional life, Marion Burgner was invited to address many national and international conferences, and published and taught widely both in the UK and abroad. She died prematurely in October 1996.

Alicia Etchegoyen is a full member and child analyst of the British Institute of Psycho-Analysis. She is also Physician in Charge of the Children's Department at the London Clinic of Psychoanalysis, Consultant Child and Adolescent Psychiatrist and Clinical Director of the Perinatal Mental Health Service at the Chelsea and Westminster Hospital. Publications include papers on the analyst's pregnancy, infant observation and child care.

Paula Mariotti trained as a doctor in Italy. She is a psychoanalyst, and a full member of the British Psycho-Analytical Society. For several years she was Honorary Consultant at the London Clinic of Psychoanalysis. Her main commitments at present are to her family and to her psychoanalytic practice.

Maggie Mills read Jurisprudence and Psychology at Oxford. As a full-time academic, she ran a peediatric research unit in a London teaching hospital, classified films and videos for children for many years and published research findings on parental mental health, family relationships and women's issues. Ten years ago she retrained as a clinical psychologist and works now as a psychotherapist in the NHS and with Mellow Parenting, a group intervention project for under-resourced families. She is training as a psychoanalyst in the British society and, currently, is writing a book about violence in the home.

Juliet Mitchell is a writer and psychoanalyst in private practice in London. She is a full member of the British Psychoanalytic Society and has recently been appointed Fellow of Jesus College, Cambridge University. She is also a distinguished Visiting Professor at Cornell University, USA and Visiting Fellow at the Social Science Research Unit, London University. Her books include *Psychoanalysis and Feminism, Woman's Estate* and *Women: The Longest Revolution* and editions of the writings of Jaques Lacan, Melanie Klein and Enid Balint.

Rosine Jozef Perelberg is a full member of the British Psycho-Analytical Society. After gaining a PhD in social anthropology at the London School of Economics she trained at the British Institute of Psycho-Analysis and has been, since 1989, an Associate Editor of the New Library of Psychoanalysis. She is Honorary Senior Lecturer in Psychoanalytic Theory at University College London. Previously she worked for many years in the NHS and as a senior psychotherapist and family therapist at the Maudsley Hospital, Institute of Psychiatry and Marlborough Family Service. Since 1990 she has been working at the Anna Freud Centre on a research project offering subsidized analysis to young adults who suffered breakdown. She has written and taught widely on the theory and practice of psychoanalysis, gender issues and violence, both in England and abroad. In 1991 she was co-winner of the Cesare Sacerdoti Prize at the International Psychoanalytical Association Congress in Buenos Aires for her paper 'What Can You Possibly Learn From Babies?'

Dinora Pines is a training analyst and supervisor of the British Psycho-Analytical Society. Before teaching she worked both in hospital clinics and in general practice, so her experience with women patients has been extensive and very varied. Her clinical experience has also been with male patients so that the dynamics of the couple are born in mind. Dr Pines lectures extensively abroad both in Europe and the United States. In addition she is well-known in the former Soviet Union for her public lectures and clinical seminars. Her collected papers, entitled *A Woman's Unconcious Use of Her Body*, were published by Virago in 1993.

Joan Raphael-Leff is Professor of Psychoanalysis at the Centre for Psychoanalytic Studies, University of Essex. She is a full member of the British Psycho-Analytical Society and has served on the Committee of the Independent Group of Psychoanalysts. Over the last twenty-one years since qualification she has specialized in private practice devoted to reproductive issues, and has published some fifty professional articles in the field and two books – *Psychological Processes in Childbearing* and *Pregnancy – the Inside Story*. Previously, as a social psychologist she worked for the Medical Research Council's Social Psychiatry Unit at the Institute of Psychiatry, and as a senior psychotherapist at the Marlborough Day Hospital. Between 1985–1991 she served as Deputy Editor of *The British Journal of Psychotherapy*, and is currently English Language Editor of *International Psychoanalysis*, voice-piece of the International Psychoanalytical Association. She is on the steering Committee of the Royal Society of Medicine Forum for Maternity and the Newborn, Marcé Society and the Association for Infant Mental Health, UK, and was external adviser to the Anna Freud Centre's Under Fives Project. She is also Honorary Senior Lecturer at University College London and has taught and conducted workshops for primary health care workers and psychotherapists in many training institutions in England and over five continents abroad.

Joan Riviere was born in 1883 and although she had no university training, became proficient in German while living in Germany at the age of seventeen. This stood her in good stead when, after an unsatisfactory analysis with Ernest Jones and a brief analysis with Freud (who thought her a 'real power'), she embarked on translating Freud's papers into English and from 1922 until 1937 held the position of Translation Editor of the *International Journal of Psycho-Analysis*. In 1919 she was a founder member of the British Psycho-Analytic Society, and thereafter took an active part in training activities and and served with Ernest Jones, Alex and James Strachey on the 'Glossary Committee' deliberating on the translation of Freud's technical terms into English. In 1935 she was sent to Vienna as an envoy from the British Society to present views on female development in a series of exchange lectures. She attended all the Controversial Discussions and worked closely with Melanie Klein for two decades, jointly published several books with her and original papers of her own on psychic processes and mechanisms. These were published by Karnac in 1991 as *The Inner World and Joan Riviere – Collected Papers 1920–1958*, edited by Athol Hughes. Joan Riviere continued seeing patients until her death in 1962.

Valerie Sinason is a consultant child psychotherapist at the Tavistock Clinic and a consultant research psychotherapist at St George's Hospital Medical School and the Portman Clinic. She has lectured and published widely both nationally and internationally on the subjects of learning disability and sexual abuse. Her books include *Mental Handicap and the Human Condition* (Free Association Books, 1993), *Understanding Your Handicapped Child* (Rosendale, 1994), *Treating Survisors of Satanist Abuse* (Routledge, 1994) and Memory in Dispute (Karnac, 1997, forthcoming). She is also a poet (last collection *Night Shift* (Karnac 1996).

Deborah Steiner first trained as a child psychotherapist at the Tavistock Clinic. She completed the training in psychoanalysis at the Institute of Psycho-Analysis in 1987 and qualified as a full member in 1992. She currently works part-time as an analyst in private practice and part-time as a child psycho-therapist in the NHS. She contributed *Understanding Your One-Year-Old* and *Understanding Your Six-Year-Old* in the series *Understanding Your Child* published by the Tavistock Clinic in 1992. Other publications include 'The

Internal Family and the Facts of Life', *Journal of Psychoanalytic Psycho-therapy*, 1989, vol. 4 no. 1.

Maria A. Tallandini qualified as psychoanalyst in 1985 at the Italian Psycho-analytical Society and is a member of the British Psycho-Analytical Society since 1991. Her major interest is the reciprocal influences during development between affects and cognition. As associate professor, she taught Developmental Psychology at Padua University from 1973 until 1990. At present she teaches Genetic Epistemology at Trieste University and also holds a part-time lectureship at University College London. Her research work has dealt with the development of social representations in children. She has recently carried out research on children's drawings at the Winnicott Research Unit (Cambridge) with the aim of evaluating the influence of maternal depression on children's graphic representations of their own family. She is also a member of the Anna Freud Young Adult Research Group that is engaged in analysing the psychoanalytic process with young adults patients who find the transition to adulthood difficult.

Jane Temperley read Modern History at Oxford and then trained in the USA as a psychiatric social worker. She was formerly Principal Social Worker in the Adult Department at the Tavistock Clinic, with a particular interest in marital work. She is especially interested in Klein's position both in the controversies about female psychosexual development and in the history of British psychoanalytic views on the subject. She qualified as a psychoanalyst in 1975.

Foreword

In England, psychoanalytic training and practice have always been remarkably sexually egalitarian with women not only being equal in numbers to men
but also holding top administrative positions and, especially in the persons
of Melanie Klein and Anna Freud, advancing the major theories since Freud.

Psychoanalysis in Britain grew to strength only after the First World War
and, more particularly, in the latter part of the twenties when Ernest Jones
invited Melanie Klein to Britain where she subsequently established herself.
This was a period of substantial changes in psychoanalytic theory, changes
that had issues of femininity and women at their centre. Most obviously there
were the debates about the construction of female sexuality that flourished
from the mid-twenties until the mid-thirties when the first exchange lecture
between the disagreeing camps of London and Vienna was devoted to female
sexuality. More elusive but probably more important, were the post-First
World War theories of the death drive, primal anxiety and masochism that
reoriented the focus from the father of the castration complex to the mother
of pre-oedipality. This was the fertile ground from which Object Relations
theory sprang with its clinical and theoretical emphasis on the infant–mother
relationship. These two strands – the concern with female sexuality and the
concentration on very early mental processes, desires and affects – can be
felt to have come together in Freud's suggestion that women analysts were
perhaps in a privileged position to understand women as their female patients
did not take refuge behind a transference to the father which had, in Freud's
own case, kept the earliest psychological formations of femininity hidden.
One could say, then, that women analysing women has a crucial place in the
whole development of psychoanalysis.

In Europe generally the new and open practice of psychoanalysis benefited
from the release of energy and creativity of middle and upper middle class
women following the emancipatory gains of feminism and of women of
almost all social classes working during the First World War. Having had, in
the tradition of pre-war practice, a lower level of secondary education than
her brothers, Anna Freud was able to train as a psychoanalyst and pioneer
child analysis and analytical oriented educational programmes in Vienna and

ultimately in Second World War England. Melanie Klein initiated her theories and practice of a psychoanalysis of infancy in Budapest, Berlin and finally London. Women brought what have classically been considered women's interests of the profession and these were of the greatest importance for its subsequent development.

A particular feature of the situation in most European countries favoured women becoming psychoanalysts. Medical schools until recently discriminated quite massively against women; the absence of a medical requirement for training as a psychoanalyst was both a passive and an active advantage for women. Continental Europe and England followed Freud's recommendation that lay analysts should be equally trained and share the same status as medically qualified ones. Quite a number of the first women analysts were in fact medical doctors, but an important number were not. Lay analysts brought a wide range of cultural interests that had flourished in the absence of a particularly career-focused prior training. Subjects hitherto (and still today) thought of both as unconscionably non-scientific and (the two of course are not unconnected) as associated with femininity – dreams, the emotions, imagination and fantasy – were the stuff of psychoanalysis. On the Continent, before the efflorescence of Nazism it was also a profession open to Jews. In England it remained so. The diaspora brought important women to Britain and to the centre of the psychoanalytic world whereas those that left for the United States could only practise as analysts if they were doctors like Karen Horney and Helene Deutsch. The absence of a medical ruling opened the doors to the wide-ranging creativity of women and England was a double beneficiary, receiving both medical and lay Jewish immigrants in addition to its continuing strong indigenous tradition.

Both numerically and intellectually from the time of *Studies in Hysteria* (1895) women patients have been crucial for psychoanalysis. It is curious therefore that with the importance of women analysts, of women patients, of the subject of female sexuality and, above all, of the focus on the maternal transference in Object Relations theory in Britain there has not hitherto been much work on the implications of women analysing women. In part this may be because sexual differentiation in the pre-verbal infant is not of enormous psychic importance; it may also be because a number of eminent male analysts either have taken an interest in female sexuality (Ernest Jones) or, more importantly, been able – unlike Freud – to accept and theorize from the position of the pre-oedipal mother (Winnicott, Bion).

The interest in women analysing women was first taken up by Baruch and Serrano (1988) in a book of interviews with women analysts. Enid Balint, who was interviewed in that volume, opens this. Her paper, though in some ways it reverses, in fact also echoes Freud's problem: where Freud's women patients hid their primary homosexuality behind the paternal transference, Balint's women patients deploy their heterosexuality in marriages and affairs to conceal that their main aim is to satisfy their mothers/analysts. The problem for Freud was the problem of 'Dora' in 'a fragment of a case of hysteria' whose revulsion/attraction for her suitor/father masked her fascination with his wife/her mother. Balint proposes that if her patients can find adequate, non-sexual ways of caring for the mother then it will be possible for their heterosexual choice to be unified and more satisfactory. The question seems to be one of the quantum of sexuality in the primary relationship to the mother. It may well be that if there is too much sexuality in the primary relationship then the outcome may be not homosexuality but hysteria – as in Dora's case. The difficulty is to demarcate between what is accepted as normal femininity and what as pathological hysteria. If all infants – male and female – start psychic life in a primary relationship to the mother (Melanie Klein's 'primary femininity') a subsequent turning to the father makes heterosexuality always a precarious substitute. This is uniquely true of humans because our premature birth makes us more utterly dependent for far longer than other comparable mammals, allowing time not only for learning but for an accentuation of ambivalence as the object that is needed is also the object that deserts. In much pyschoanalytic theory it is this ambivalence that allows the girl to leave her mother and seek her father as a more satisfying object. However, in Object Relations theory, human beings are driven, like other primates, by instinct, to natural heterosexuality; the weight of the turning to the father is placed not on the psyche but on biology. This problem has been solved in two ways: either it is postulated that human society with its prolonged maternal dependence and biology with its instinctual heterosexuality are at irreconcilable odds for the woman or that the female psyche more or less adjusts to social prescription and biological reality. In fact, as Joan Raphael-Leff's work on generativity initiates, it is possible to trace a complex and paradoxical interweaving of psychic, social and biological. Where Freud considered that biology was the bedrock beneath which psychoanalysis could not penetrate, work specifically from women analysts with women patients suggests that, it not penetrated, then at the very least the biology of male and female and of procreation must be encompassed in an imaginary unity which privileges neither one at the expense of the others.

REFERENCE

Baruch, E. and Serrano, L. (1988) *Women Analysing Women*, New York: New York University Press.

Juliet Mitchell
March 1996
London

Acknowledgements

On behalf of all the readers of this book we would like to thank the *International Journal of Psycho-Analysis* for kind permission to reprint several papers (chapters 1, 6, 7, 12) and *Free Associations* for chapter 14. We are also most grateful to those two fine women, Jill Duncan and Paula Lavis, librarians at the British Institute of Psychoanalysis, for all the help and interest they has extended.

On a professional level, we have been inspired by the many lucid thinkers in our Society and acknowledge the analysands whose candid expression of their innermost feelings contributes to greater understanding of gender issues.

On a personal level, our thanks to the contributors to this book for their belief in the project despite long delays. And to our families for their committed support for our work which involved not only enthusiasm for our ideas but also taking on responsibility for practical arrangements in daily life, and for their bemused tolerance when we were caught up in our intense exchanges, electronic and otherwise, at the most inconvenient hours.

Prologue

Joan Raphael-Leff

THE BOOK

Female Experience attempts to do what, to our knowledge, no book has done before – bringing together contributions from three generations of female psychoanalysts in the British Psycho-Analytical Society, writing from within clinical experience with women and girls, and questioning specific determinants of female sexuality and gender identity which have become central to our thinking. The conception for this book arose out of a desire to celebrate the rich multilayered tapestry of female theorizing within the British Psycho-Analytical Society. The authors represent a cross-section of different theoretical orientations (Kleinian, Contemporary Freudian and Independent) and membership status (from candidates to training analysts) over a time span of more than sixty years. The idea was initially floated in the early 1990s with a call for papers in our internal *Bulletin*. In addition we specifically approached female analysts who have a special interest in treating women, commissioning papers. Sadly, two of our contributors, Enid Balint and Marion Burgner, have since died, but their work lives on in this book. As space restrictions forced us to limit ourselves to only one 'golden oldie', after much deliberation between papers on female development by some of the 'grand old ladies' – Marjorie Brierley, Anna Freud, Sylvia Payne, Melanie Klein, Paula Heimann and others – we chose one of Joan Riviere's papers as illustrative of the intellectual fermentation of its era.

Our orbit inevitably encompasses female bodily representations, phantasies and desires; and specifically female experiences of childhood trauma, sexual abuse, eating disorders, childbearing, lactation, perinatal loss and postnatal depression. Topics covered pertain to various phases of the female life cycle, with overarching themes of revitalization of intrapsychic relationships within the therapeutic matrix and countertransferential reverberations of unconscious facets in the female to female psychoanalytic encounter. Although in clinical work, these fifteen analysts use interpretative systems guided by different organizing principles, some shared themes recur across theoretical divisions:

- A psychoanalytic stance of tolerating incoherence and the state of not-knowing while continuing to believe in the existence of meaning.
- The hope of helping the analysand to break out of lifelong self-employed constrictions through recognition of the inevitability of ambivalence and uncertainty.
- Preoccupation with past and current obstacles to development of female creativity.
- Exploration of nebulous manifestations of revitalized primitive ties, often expressed in concrete or psychosomatic form.
- Transformation of anachronistic repetitions through insight, and utilization of the real (female to female) analytic exchange to develop new forms of relating.
- A belief in the need to work through losses entailed in each of life's transitions and the importance of mourning as a means of processing experience, incorporating excluded portions of psychic reality and reaching inaccessible aspects of the self.

While each contributor has written from the area of her expertise, informed by her own theoretical tradition, the chapters are unified by their format. One common denominator is a 'story-telling' mode of presenting detailed clinical material which unfolds in the analytic relation between women. Highlighting women's preoccupations, this narrative includes the unverbalized thoughts of the analyst as well as her special way of listening to and understanding the fine detail of interwoven internal and external, conscious and unconscious realities elaborated in the past and here and now.

THE BRITISH SOCIETY

In many ways, our Society has been unique among psychoanalytic institutions in its agreement to differ. From its inception, women have played a strong role, contributing to the scientific life of the Society and its training courses, and holding central officer posts on committees. Since 1913, of the twenty presidents in our Psycho-Analytical Society, five have been women (Sylvia Payne, Hanna Segal, Pearl King, Anne-Marie Sandler and, currently, Irma Brenman Pick). Unlike many trainings elsewhere which insisted on previous medical experience (largely debarring female applicants), from the start 40 per cent of members of the British Society came to psychoanalysis from a medley of backgrounds – a broad range of liberal professions and different disciplines contributing to the atmosphere of cross-fertilization in our Society. This is reflected in the many diverse subjects covered in members' publications over the past eighty years. For instance, topics between 1926 and 1936 included psychoanalysis and design in the plastic arts; fetishism and art; the effect of the film on the mind; the psychology of clothes; of toys; and of children's games; social change; anthropology; linguistics;

mythology; drug ritual and addiction; criminality; nursery education; the meaning of sacrifice; eye diseases and emotional states; bewitchment; eating disturbances; stammering; Shakespeare; virginity and ritual defloration; unconscious motivation of attempted abortion; emotional dimensions of alcoholism; menstruation; impotence; and creativity.

Furthermore, as reflected in this book, the variegated nature of our membership has been *cultural* as well as multidisciplinary. Although the original founding members were British-born, their personal analyses took place in Vienna, Berlin or Budapest. Thus, from the first, structuralization of British psychoanalytic experience was embedded in a geographical and emotional network that extended beyond these island shores. Building on lively exchanges of ideas with other European analysts it opened the Society's doors to candidates and analysts from abroad (initially refugees from war-torn Europe; later exiles of conscience from South Africa, and *émigrés* from Asia, the United States, Canada, Latin America, Australia and New Zealand) which again increased the diversity.

ATMOSPHERE OF DEBATE

The British Society is also unique in accommodating a triologue between at least three theoretical schools of thought. Historically these different formulations grew out of an atmosphere of debate. In the early 1920s two 'hot' issues came into prominence – the first being *psychoanalysis of children*, which, Freud commented in 1925, had become 'the main subject of psycho-analytic research' (quote in Young-Bruehl, 1988, p.133). In London, Susan Isaacs had already instituted disciplined child observation in her nursery school (Isaacs, 1930); Mary Chadwick was already seeing children in therapy, and Nina Searl, Sylvia Payne, Alix Strachey and others declared an interest in child analysis; Melanie Klein was analysing children beginning with her own in Budapest, then in Berlin, and Hermine von Hug-Hellmuth and Anna Freud were treating children in Vienna.

Increasingly, with presentation of child cases, differences of technique began to emerge between Klein's view (1926) equating play with free association thus permitting interpretation of unconscious phantasy and anxieties, and that of Anna Freud, for whom play was a mixture of unconscious symbolic expression and enactment of day-to-day events, involving modifications of the analytic stance (such as analysing daydreams and drawings and an educational/explanatory approach) necessitated by the immature ego, and pre-emption of transference by ongoing parental relationships (A. Freud, 1926, 1927).

In parallel, beginning with Abraham's catalytic account of 'Manifestations of the female castration complex' (1920) (which anticipates themes such as envy of maternal fertility and transgenerational transmission of psychosexual values), and in response to Freud's 1905 and later (1923, 1924, 1931) essays,

a flurry of papers were written focusing on *female libidinal development*.
Interest in this topic was not confined to the consulting room. By 1930 the
suffrage mass-movement towards 'sexual revolution' was 100 years old. The
interpretative discipline of psychoanalysis offered a new tool for uncovering
unconscious sources of female devaluation intrapsychically and in culture.

With growing awareness of theoretical divergences between psychoanalysts in London and Vienna, exchange lectures were arranged in the mid-
thirties to facilitate communication on 'hot' issues. Disputing Freud's
'phallocentrism', two envoys were sent to present British views on female
sexual development – Ernest Jones (1927, 1933, 1935) followed by Joan
Riviere (1929 (reprinted here as Chapter 12), 1936) – corroborated by
evidence from female British psychoanalysts such as Sylvia Payne (1935),
Marjorie Brierley (1932, 1936), Melanie Klein (1928, 1932), Susan Isaacs
(1927), Nina Searl, Mary Chadwick, Sybille Yates, Karin Stephen, Alix
Strachey, Merrell Middlemore and others from their work with female child
and adult patients.

The lively debate during that period hinged on *awareness of the vagina*.
Throughout the decade, Freud upheld an exclusively monistic view for both
sexes – 'not a primacy of the genital, but of the phallus' – and although at first
he admitted ignorance of the 'corresponding processes in the little girl' (1923,
p.143) primary masculine sexuality won the day: '[T]he little girl is a little
man' (Freud, 1932). Like the boy, she was deemed aware only of the male
genital until discovering her own 'castrated' state. Then, disillusioned with her
non-phallic mother she switches to love for her father, and by giving up
('phallic') masturbation, paves the way to changing her erogenous zone from
clitoris to vagina, and to replacing penis envy with desire for (his) baby.
Femininity is thus *reactive*, constructed on a masculine foundation, and the
wish for a baby is a secondary compromise formation. Klein (1928, 1932) and
others argued for primary femininity and awareness of female genitalia (and
innate heterosexuality) – depicting the penis-wish not as narcissistic, but a
libidinal/sexual desire to receive the (paternal) penis. Outside London, in 1922
Karen Horney (1924, 1926) also took umbrage at the application of male
standards, attributing the notion of female deficiency and 'inferiority' of female
genitals to 'masculine narcissism' (of sexist theoreticians). Later (1932, 1933),
she ascribed male 'dread of women' and denial of the vagina to fear of the
archaic mother, stressing womb envy and social denigration of mothering.

Publications from that period sparked each other off, crisscrossing Europe
and becoming more polemical as various points were argued back and forth.
Positions crystallized between female analysts supporting Freud's view of
the girl's late discovery of her own vagina (Jeanne Lampl-de Groot, 1928;
Helene Deutsch, 1925, 1930) and those who claimed innate unconscious
knowledge of internal genitals. The latter included evidence of early vaginal
masturbation from direct observation of little girls (Josine Muller, 1925) or
even earlier activation of vaginal impulses during pleasurable suckling
(Brierley, 1936). In this view, the girl's phallic phase was treated as a

defensive, secondary construct (Jones, 1935), and it was assumed that for both sexes 'the undiscovered vagina is a vagina denied' (Horney, 1932, 1933), denied 'from motives of anxiety connected with the imaginary dangers of copulation' (Brierley, 1934, p. 26). These analysts held the view of original femininity (Jones, 1927) repression of which relates to a girl's fear of her rivalrous mother's retaliative attacks on her reproductive organs (Klein, 1932).

As Juliet Mitchell (1974) pointed out, the debate ended in impasse as it slid into biologisms, whether sociological (Horney) or psychologistic (Deutsch), stressing innate disposition as opposed to Freud's emphasis on the cultural meaning of gender. However, the adaptive 'civilizing' process, expressed as repression of the qualities of the opposite sex, paradoxically was prescriptively depicted by Freud too, in isomorphic anatomical (clitoris, vagina, penis) terms. From our vantage point today, we may wonder whether the debate on female sexuality fell into obscurity partly because the under-pinning theoretical differences involved an intrinsic challenge, personally dangerous and testing to the integrity of female analysts themselves. How in the face of internalized norms could they maintain self-reflective awareness, challenging 'phallacies' of vaginal orgasm, masochism or passivity without being branded infantile or disturbed? Freud's pronouncement on this subject may have contributed to unease: 'We shall not be very surprised if a woman analyst who has not been sufficiently convinced of the intensity of her own wish for a penis also fails to attach proper importance to that factor in her patients' (1940, p.197). Today, as then, theoretical differences abide and each of the contributors to this book has her own tacit answer to Ernest Jones's question: *'Is woman born or made?'*

By the 1940s, the debate broadened as divergent developmental theories and issues of technique were debated within the British Society itself in the famous wartime discussions (for transcripts see King and Steiner, 1991). These are usually posed as a rivalrous duel between Melanie Klein (who had left Berlin to settle in London in 1926) and Anna Freud (who, following interrogation by the Gestapo had arrived in June 1938 together with Sigmund Freud and other leading Viennese analysts). However, many analysts contributed to these 'controversial discussions' including Susan Isaacs, Paula Heimann, Joan Riviere, John Rickman and Winnicott on the one hand and Barbara Low, Dorothy Burlingham, Melitta Schmideberg (Klein's daughter) and her husband, Barbara Lantos, Kate Friedlander and Hedwig and Willi Hoffer on the other. Between these two theoretical factions was a group of people searching for common ground, among whom were Marjorie Brierley, Sylvia Payne, Ella Sharpe and a male contingent including Ernest Jones, John Bowlby, Michael Balint and William Gillespie. (Members of this 'middle' group later became known as 'Independents', since, while accepting basic tenets of classical psychoanalytic theory and technique, each member had his or her own eclectic mixture of theoretical influences (see Gregorio Kohon,

1986; Eric Rayner, 1991 on the Independent 'school')). And far from drab, these wartime discussions were lively, erudite, acrimonious at times, but colourfully flamboyant. (Anne Hayman has recently reminded me that female analysts of that era wore elaborate hats to the Society and members of each 'camp' sat on opposite sides of the room.)

Through the ensuing discussions, metapsychological differences underpinning theoretical positions crystallized. 'Kleinian' emphasis was on innate sadistic impulses directed against phantasized internal objects, and the oedipal conflict (predated to early infancy) was seen as primarily aggressive rather than libidinal and fraught with paranoid anxieties about parental retaliation for (imaginary) envious attacks, initially against the babies and paternal penis inside the mother's body (for later development of Kleinian concepts see Elizabeth Spillius, 1988; Robert Hinshelwood, 1994). This view of the infant preoccupied with internally derived phantasy figures differs greatly from the Freudian emphasis on defences (further elaborated by Anna Freud) against external dangers, and internal objects as introjected representatives of reality, including parental identifications that constitute the superego which pave the way to relinquishment of oedipal desires (for Contemporary Freudian developments of these concepts see Sandler, 1987; Sandler *et al.*, 1992). Clearly, the issue of these two seemingly irreconcilable paradigms of infancy was not academic but the basis of divergent schools of thought. One outcome of these heated discussions was the so-called 'gentlemen's agreement' (signed by three forceful women!) whereby ideological divergences were recognized and a tripartite division was instituted to ensure a balance in matters of political power and issues of training.

THE TRIALOGUE

A formulation of the fifties depicted theoretical differences as 'one-body' (solipsistic), 'two-body' (interactive), or 'three-body' (oedipal) psychologies (Rickman, 1951). I suggest that the continuing debate may be imagined as a 'trialogue' around a father, a mother and a baby. Historically, the power structure between dramatis personae altered as the oedipal father as first representative of authority gave way to primacy of the mother–child relationship. Within the British school of Object Relations, classical valorization of independence and autonomy was reframed within the new focus on pre-oedipal attachments and lifelong interdependence or 'mature dependence' in Fairbairn's term (1946). His and Klein's respective foci on the initial phase of life threw the intrapsychic life of the infant into prominence, she privileging the baby's innate primary phantasies (1932), he, initial lack of differentiation and 'state of identification with the object' (Fairbairn, 1941, p. 48) and internalization of the unsatisfying object as a defensive measure (Fairbairn, 1943). It was in London that the mother, too, had her centre-stage debut, albeit her shift to centrality was reflected differentially in each of the three theoretical groups. In the Freudian story attachment was 'anaclitic' as, following meeting of physiological needs, the child was gradually wooed away from autoeroticism into object relations. In the Kleinian story, too, orality was dominant. The mother was depicted from the infant's point of view, as an internal 'object', an appendage of 'the breast', or a numinous body to be possessed. Conversely, Independents emphasized the *actuality* of the relationship, seeing the infant as actively pursuing 'primary love' (Michael Balint, 1952), mutuality and identity of interests between mother and baby (Alice Balint, 1939) and feeding as secondary to attachment (John Bowlby, 1956).

This is one area where the 'trialogue' between the three groups has resulted in cross-fertilization. Increasingly, despite differences, the emphasis has come to be on the *dyadic* nature of construction of intrapsychic reality. This began with Winnicott's famous statement to the Society at one of the Wednesday Scientific Meetings: 'There is no such thing as a baby [without a mother]' stressing not only her physical care but 'holding' and graded introduction of the external 'shared world' and its explication (Winnicott, 1952). Whether the neonate is seen as initially 'undifferentiating', 'symbiotically merged' or engaged in projections, henceforth, a common theme permeating the British Society is of evolution of selfhood (Rickman's 'onebody' relationship or Winnicott's 'capacity to be alone' (Winnicott, 1958) as an *outcome* of dyadic intersubjectivity and introjection of the emotionally containing and metabolizing presence of the (m)other and her capacity for 'reverie' (Wilfred Bion, 1962; see too Daniel Stern, 1985; Peter Fonagy, 1995). Priliveging maternal primary care has therapeutic ramifications.

Some American psychoanalysts have studied differential effects of female mothering (Chodorow, 1989) on individuating boys who must 'disidentify' with the primary care-giver (Greenson, 1968) and girls who remain embedded in a network of affiliation and connectedness (Jordan *et al.*, 1991), leading to an orientation not of autonomous morality but of contextual concern (Gilligan, 1982). In recent years, partly influenced by neonatal research and attachment studies, the early relational matrix is being expanded to include the father, not only as protector of the dyad and symbolic cultural intercedent between mother and baby, but as a primary (pre-oedipal) figure in his own right, discriminated by four weeks (Yogman, 1982).

Elsewhere I have suggested that psychoanalytic theories are inextricably rooted in the nature of baby, mother and father envisaged. Likewise, that different views of infantile endowment predicate different types of prescribed parental care, and by metaphorical extension, dictate *different approaches to the psychotherapeutic relationship*, emphasizing separateness and boundaries, an intrapsychic focus or bi-directional relational exchange (Raphael-Leff, 1986, 1993).

THE PSYCHOTHERAPEUTIC RELATIONSHIP

As psychoanalysts, we constantly grapple with difficulties inherent in expressing unconscious phantasies and grasping glimpsed representations of self and desire; we are aware too of ways in which cultural metaphors and tacit assumptions about psyche and soma shape and curtail possible meaning. In our work, we are undoubtedly influenced by each analysand's idiosyncratic presentation – presence, tone, silences, singularity of semantic connotations and non-verbal communications; his or her notions of sexuality and unconscious gender transmissions; and non-verbal bodily presentations and representations. Likewise, the work is inflected by personal determinants of our own which inevitably affect interpretation of exchanges within the consulting room.

In his papers on technique, Freud posed the analyst's 'evenly suspended attention' as counterpart to free association (1912), thus establishing analysis as *a relation*. The exchange is marked by an ambiguous symmetry – analysand's *transference* of earlier reactions into the consulting room as s/he 'yields to the compulsion to repeat which now replaces the impulsion to remember' (Freud, 1914, p.151), and analyst's *countertransference* – a dialectic of two unconscious systems of 'highly explosive forces' necessitating a 'threefold battle' waged in the latter's mind 'against the forces which seek to drag him down from the analytic level; outside the analysis, against opponents . . . [and] against his patient's overvaluation' (1915, p.170).

The view of countertransference as the analyst's internal resistance and pathological reactions to the patient's influences on his unconscious feelings has undergone a multitude of sea-changes in the British Society, being regarded as the totality of the analyst's *transference* to the patient (M. Balint, 1933), or outcrop of an ambivalent relationship which includes 'hate in the counter-transference' (Winnicott, 1947). As we shall see in the chapters of this book, most British psychoanalysts today agree with Paula Heimann's formulation that far from being an impediment, the analyst's emotional responses can serve as *a useful 'tool'*, an 'instrument of research into the patient's unconscious' (Heimann, 1950, p.74). Acting as the patient's 'auxiliary ego' the analyst asks himself: 'Why is the patient doing what to whom?' using transference interpretations to reinstate 'the past in the present' (Heimann, 1956, p.305). In parallel, the analyst's exploration of countertransference takes place, empathically asking what s/he is feeling, why and why now (Little, 1951) thereby utilizing unconscious understanding (Ella Sharpe, 1947) through 'neutrality' that allows this 'affective response' to tap into unconscious pre-verbal material (Pearl King, 1978). Other Independents invoke the analyst's 'negative capability' to remain in a state of uncertainty and 'complete unknowing' (Coltart, 1992, p. 7) maintaining a creative process of oscillating fusion and differentiation (see Milner, 1987) that allows for primary process type apprehension of the more primitive sensations in countertransference. But is the analyst medium or (sexed) participant?

Theoretical viewpoints vary as to the *source* of countertransference – whether stemming from the patient's or analyst's contribution and/or repetition of past relationships. Kleinians have tended to attribute countertransference to the patient's communication and unconscious expression of intolerable feelings (Bion, 1962), often involving projective-identification and non-verbal pressure on the analyst to act (Betty Joseph, 1983). Agreement exists that these seductive or aggressive invasions into the analyst's mind can be potentially overwhelming when projected by patients who were themselves targets of parental projections (Hanna Segal, 1977), at times uncomfortably dovetailing with the analyst's own vulnerabilities (see Irma Brenman Pick, 1985). The cyclical process of absorption, recognition and interpretation of 'normal countertransference' alternates between states of empathic introjective identification (during which the patient represents 'the damaged objects of the analyst's own unconscious phantasy' or 'a former immature or ill part') and reprojection through interpretation (Money-Kyrle, 1956, pp. 360–361). Contemporary Freudians recognize countertransference as a broad spectrum of reactions to the patient's attempts to 'actualize' self–object interactions (Sandler, 1976). Some Independents regard the analyst's feelings as a product of the reciprocity of exchange – transference and countertransference as two parts of an 'illusory (single) system' (Symington, 1983), an empathic experience resembling the primary mother–infant 'transformational object' situation (Bollas, 1987). Across theoretical orientations all agree that while countertransference is an inevitable part of the therapeutic process, it yields greater insight only through the analyst's self-knowledge and capacity to maintain internal freedom both to experience and to scrutinize feelings arising in the context of a specific patient.

GENDER AND THE ANALYTIC PROCESS

In his paper on 'Femininity' Freud remarks: 'When you meet a human being, the first distinction you make is "male or female?"' (1932, p. 113). Beginning with Doolittle's famous quote about his discomfort – 'I do *not* like to be the mother in the transference, it always surprises and shocks me a little. I feel so very masculine' (Doolittle (H.D.), 1974, pp. 146–147) – psychoanalysts have been invited to grapple with subtle constraints of gender manifested in these transactional patterns, within the consulting room as outside it. However, this area has remained largely unexplored.

Although in recent years there has been some interest in the impact of gender on the therapeutic exchange, its focus has been mainly on cross-gender issues. The few exceptions looking at females with females have emphasized countertransference overidentification and 'maternal' overprotectiveness (Bernstein and Warner, 1984), the analyst's defensiveness against homosexuality, paternal transference, competitiveness and prolonged regression (McDougall, 1986; Bernstein, 1991), inhibition of sexual material and gender-related blind spots (Kulish, 1986), and patient issues of closeness and distance with the maternal object, and sexualization of the transference (Lester, 1990). One study of American analysts found a broad range of themes supporting the influence of the female analyst's gender (Kulish, 1984). An international study based on interviews with senior female analysts (including four from the British Society) reveals a wide diversity of responses with only a few female analysts discussing the potential effects of the sex of the analyst (Baruch and Serrano, 1988). From her own study of early women psychoanalysts, Nancy Chodorow (1989) comments that self-reflection too is culturally shaped, suggesting that rather than being 'gender-blind', the generation of older analysts experienced a different salience of gender as a social category, splitting public/theoretical and domestic/personal interpretations, or (like Judith Kestenberg, 1980) emphasizing the 'three faces of femininity' – motherhood, eroticism and career/intellectual development.

In our own book there is some reiteration of these themes, especially evocation of primitive maternal transference and tendency for deep regression in the female to female analysis. It is my contention that as this book attests, female therapists working with female patients also experience a host of *countertransferential resonances* arising out of a common bodily sensorium, shared primary imagery, as well as meshing or clashing polyphonous psychosexual representations. And, professional differences notwithstanding, we also share a position in culture.

One difficulty arises from blurring the distinction between the neutrality of the analyst of whatever sex which allows for development of transferential phenomena, and the ineffable influences of the (non-neutered) sex of the analyst on the nature of the therapeutic process. The latter case has been well illustrated in documentation of unavoidable effects of the analyst's pregnancy, in terms of reactivation of each patient's most significant infantile conflicts (Lax, 1969), envy of fecund woman or foetus, sexual curiosity, sibling rivalry, etc. (Raphael-Leff, 1980, 1993; Lazar, 1990) and countertransferential effects (Mariotti, 1993; Etchegoyen, 1993). Likewise, in my clinical judgement, women with certain presenting problems, such as reproductive issues, (male) sexual abuse as a child, or loss of mother before puberty, highlight the specificity of seeing a female therapist.

Not surprisingly, for those who work within an object relations framework resting on assumptions of intersubjective exchange, issues of gender inevitably do come to the fore as increasingly psychoanalytical conceptualizations are formulated as a function of conscious and unconscious *dialectical* processes originating in the intimate encounter between (sexed) individuals. On the other hand, there is many an analyst within the British Society who, like Glover (1940), would adhere to a belief that his or her sex is immaterial to the analytic process, on the assumption that the analysand will treat as interchangeable any 'hook' on which to hang the transference.

AN OVERVIEW OF THE BOOK

Given the originary encounter with a female body, we have chosen to begin exploring some of these ideas within the context of the 'primitive tie to the mother'. The book opens with a chapter by Enid Balint noting that in their relationships, women want to relate in terms of a primitive mother–girlbaby bodily 'mutual concern'. Revealing her own responsiveness, she describes the difficulty experienced by a female analyst analysing women who feel they have been unable to bodily satisfy, or be satisfied by, their early depressed mothers. This chapter is followed by Maria Tallandini's exposition of manifestations of the intense wish-fear for merger within the female to female therapeutic couple. In addition to her illustrative case history she reviews the literature on influences of the therapist's gender on treatment. Rosine Jozef Perelberg illustrates perceived dangers inherent in primary female mother–daughter differentiation, and a female analysand's use of bodily enactments to bypass verbal memories. The chapter focuses on the difficulty in thinking/relating when the past is thus eradicated. Catalina Bronstein describes a girl's profound hatred of her mother's femaleness and the effect of early relationships on her struggle with her sexual identity and search for an ideal mother–daughter relationship in homosexuality. Marion Burgner's chapter describes work with an adolescent with bulimia nervosa who felt she and her mother 'lived inside each other's skins'; the premature ending of the analytic treatment simultaneously reveals both 'clamouring, needy infant' despairing of help and a 'triumphantly sadistic child' destroying it. The last chapter in this section, by Dana Birksted-Breen, describes some of the feelings aroused in a female analyst while working with an almost entirely silent anorexic patient. This paper, too, focuses on the wish for and fear of, fusion with the early mother, use of anorexia as a drastic means of attempting to establish a body separate from mother's, and silence as a refusal to take on identity.

In the second part of the book, we look at ways in which primitive mother–infant experiences are reactivated during childbearing. It begins with Dinora Pines who traces the relevance of early psychic development to pregnancy and abortion and ways in which women make use of the fertile body to express emotional states of mind. In her chapter entitled 'Creativity and fertility: the one-parent phantasy', Paola Mariotti focuses on the experience of analysing a woman for whom the compulsion to idealize an exclusive relationship with mother prevents her from developing her own creativity. These themes carry over in Deborah Steiner's chapter. She looks at the primal relationship in terms of difficulties a mother may have in differentiating between her own infantile experiences and those of her infant – and the impact of such a *folie à deux* on analysis in a female to female therapeutic situation. In her chapter on postnatal depression based on work with women not often seen in an analytic consulting room, Maggie Mills explores how persisting systems of infantile belief and defensive idealization of the archaic mother can be reformulated in the context of a woman-to-woman therapeutic relationship. Finally, examining the impact of perinatal loss, Alicia Etchegoyen brings an example from child analysis to illustrate the transgenerational effect of an unmourned dead baby in the mother's mind on her daughter's well-being, and ways in which the powerful emotional undercurrents of such cases can affect those working with them.

In the final part of the book we focus on 'femininity' and the female to female psychoanalytic process, beginning with a paper by Joan Riviere written in the midst of those heady days of intellectual fermentation discussed above. While dated in some ways, in others it is remarkably fresh, focusing on an issue she defines as 'masquerade' – the coquettish seeking of reassurance assumed by intellectually able women to hide possession of father's penis, as a placatory act to allay anxiety and assuage the guilt of having sadistically castrated him and deprived mother in the process. The tacit implication rests on a symbolic equation between using her mind and the (stolen) penis. This ties in with a theme in my own chapter (Joan Raphael-Leff) of difficulties which arise from conflation of creativity and procreativity leading to an inability to sublimate. Proposing the concept of 'generative identity' as a specific aspect of gender identity, I explore disturbances which seem more readily rectified in the context of a female to female therapeutic relationship. Jane Temperley questions whether the Oedipus complex is bad news for women, and like so many other contributors, focuses on themes of gender acquisition, identification, the painful exclusion denoted by separateness, and a female patient's attempts to control the female analyst as evidence of omnipotent phantasies of living in her archaic mother's body. Finally, our book ends with a lively chapter by Valerie Sinason bringing material from her work with learning disabled girls and women, seen individually or in a therapeutic group, where, by means of words and non-verbal communications, preoccupation with gender-linked issues such as body representation, sexuality and procreation are graphically explored.

REFERENCES

Abraham, K. (1920) 'Manifestations of the female castration complex', in *Selected Papers on Psycho-Analysis*, London: Hogarth, 1949.

Baker-Miller (1984) 'The development of a woman's sense of self', *Work in Progress*, 12, Wellseley Stone Centre Working Papers Series.

Balint, A. (1939) 'Love for the mother and mother love', in *Primary Love and Psychoanalytic Technique*, ed. M. Balint, London: Tavistock, 1952, pp. 91–108.

Balint, M. (1933) 'On transference of emotions', in *Primary Love and Psychoanalytic Technique*, London: Tavistock, 1965.

—— (1952) *Primary Love and Psychoanalytic Technique*, London: Tavistock.

Barnett, M.C. (1966) 'Vaginal awareness in infancy and childhood of girls', *J. Amer. Psychoanal. Assoc.* 14:129–141.

Baruch, E.H. and Serrano, L.J. (1988) *Women Analyse Women – in France, England and the United States*, New York: New York University Press.

Bassin, D. (1982) 'Woman's images of inner space', *Int. Rev. Psychoanal.* 9:191–205.

Benedek, T. (1959) 'Parenthood as a developmental phase: a contribution to libido theory', *J. Amer. Psychoanal. Assoc.* 7:389–417.

Bernstein, D. (1990) 'Female genital anxieties, conflicts and typical mastery modes', *Int. J. Psychoanal.* 71:151–167.

—— (1991) 'Gender specific dangers in the female/female dyad in treatment', *Psychoanal. Rev.* 78 (1): 37–47.

Bernstein, A. and Warner, G.M. (1984) *Women Treating Women: Case Material from Women Treated by Female Psychoanalysts*, New York: International Universities Press.

Bion, W.R. (1962) *Learning from Experience*, London: Heinemann.

Bollas, C. (1987) *The Shadow of the Object*, London: Free Association Books.

Bowlby, J. (1956) 'The effects of mother–child separation', *Brit. J. Med. Psychol.* 29:48–73.

Brenman Pick, I. (1985) 'Working through in the countertransference', *Int. J. Psychoanal.* 66:157–166.

Brierley, M. (1932) 'Problems of integration in women', *Int. J. Psychoanal.* 13:433–448.

—— (1934) *Trends in Psycho-Analysis*, London:Hogarth, 1951.

—— (1936) 'Specific determinants in feminine development', *Int. J. Psychoanal.* 17:163–180.

Butler, J. (1993) *Bodies that Matter – On the Discursive Limits of 'Sex'*, London: Routledge.

Chasseguet-Smirgel, J. (1976) 'Freud and female sexuality: the consideration of some blind spots in the exploration of the "dark continent"', *Int. J. Psychoanal.* 57:275–286.

Chodorow, N. (1978) *The Reproduction of Mothering – Psychoanalysis and the Sociology of Gender*, Berkeley: University of California Press.

—— (1989) 'Seventies questions for thirties women:gender and generation in a study of early women psychoanalysts', in *Feminism & Psychoanalytic Theory*, New Haven, CT: Yale University Press.

Coltart, N. (1992) *Slouching Toward Bethlehem . . . and Further Psychoanalytic Explorations*, London: Free Association Books.

Deutsch, H. (1925) 'Psychology of women in relation to the function of reproduction', *Int. J. Psychoanal.* 6:405–418.

—— (1930) 'The significance of masochism in the mental life of women', *Int. J. Psychoanal.* 11:48–60.

Doolittle, H. (H.D.) (1974) *Tribute to Freud*, New York: McGraw-Hill.

Etchegoyen, A. (1993) 'The analyst's pregnancy and its consequences on her work', *Int. J. Psychoanal.* 74:141–150.

Edgecumbe, R. and Burgner, M. (1975) 'The phallic-narcissistic phase', *Psychoanal. Study Child* 30:161–180.

Erikson, E.H. (1950) *Childhood and Society*, New York: Norton.

Fairbairn, R. (1941) 'A revised psychopathology of the psychoses and psychoneuroses', in *Psycho-Analytic Studies of the Personality*, London: Routledge, 1952, pp. 28–59.

—— (1943) 'The repression and the return of bad objects', in *Psycho-Analytic Studies of the Personality*, London: Routledge, 1952, pp. 59–81.

—— (1946) 'Object relationships and dynamic structure', in *Psycho-Analytic Studies of the Personality*, London: Routledge, 1952, pp. 137–151.

Fonagy, P. (1995) 'Playing with reality: the development of psychic reality and its malfunction in borderline personalities', *Int. J. Psychoanal.* 76: 39–50.

Freud, A. (1926) 'Introduction to the technique of child analysis', in *The Psycho-Analytical Treatment of Children*, London: Hogarth, 1955.

—— (1927) 'The theory of children's analysis', in *The Psycho-Analytical Treatment of Children*, London: Hogarth, 1955.

Freud, S. (1905) 'Three essays on the theory of sexuality', *S.E.*7:125–243.

—— (1912) 'The dynamics of transference, papers on techique', *S.E.* 12: 97–108.

—— (1914) 'Remembering, repeating and working-through (further recommendations on the technique of psycho-analysis II)', *S.E.* 12: 145–156.

—— (1915) 'Observations on transference-love (further recommendations on the technique of psycho-analysis III)', S.E. 12: 159–171.

—— (1923) 'The infantile genital organization of the libido', *S.E.* 19:141–153.

—— (1924) 'The dissolution of the Oedipus complex', *S.E.* 19:173–182.

—— (1925) 'Some psychical consequences of the anatomical distinction between the sexes', *S.E.* 19:243–258.

—— (1931) 'Female sexuality', *S.E.* 21:225–243.

—— (1932) 'Femininity', in *New Introductory Lectures on Psychoanalysis*, *S.E.* 22:112–135.

—— (1940) 'An outline of psycho-analysis', *S.E.* 23:141–207.

Galenson, E. and Roiphe, H. (1976) 'Some suggested revisions concerning early female development', *J. Amer. Psychoanal. Assoc.* 24: 29–57 (supplement – female psychology).

Gilligan, C. (1982) *In a Different Voice*, Cambridge, Mass.: Harvard University Press.

Glover, E. (1940) *The Technique of Psychoanalysis*, Baltimore: Wilkins & Wilkins.

Greenson, R. (1968) 'Dis-identifying from mother: its special importance for the boy', *Int. J. Psychoanal.* 49:370–374.

Heimann, P. (1950) 'On counter- ʌsference', in *About Children and Children-No-Longer: Collected Papers 1942–1980*, eds P. Heimann and M. Tonnesman, London: Routledge, 1989.

—— (1956) 'Dynamics of transference interpretations', in *About Children and Children-No-Longer: Collected Papers 1942–1980*, eds P. Heimann and M. Tonnesman, London, Routledge, 1989.

Hinshelwood, R.D. (1994) *Clinical Klein*, London: Free Association Books.

Horney, K. (1924) 'On the genesis of the castration complex in women', *Int. J. Psychoanal.* 5: 50–65.

—— (1926) 'The flight from womanhood: the masculinity complex in women as viewed by men and women', *Int. J. Psychoanal.* 7:324–329.

—— (1932) 'The dread of women', *Int. J. Psychoanal.* 13:348–360.

—— (1933) 'The denial of the vagina', in *Feminine Psychology*, ed. H. Kelman, New York: Norton, 1993.

Isaacs, S. (1927) 'Penis–faeces–child', *Int. J. Psychoanal.* 8: 74–76.

—— (1930) *Intellectual Growth in Young Children*, London: Routledge & Kegan Paul.

Jones, E. (1927) 'The early development of female sexuality', *Int. J. Psychoanal.* 8:459–472.

—— (1933) 'The phallic phase', *Int. J. Psychoanal.* 14:1–33.

—— (1935) 'Early female sexuality', *Int. J. Psychoanal.* 16:263–273.

Jordan, J., Kaplan, A.G., Miller, J.B., Stiver, I.P. and Surrey, J.L. (1991) *Women's Growth in Connection: Writings from the Stone Centre*, London: Guilford Press.

Joseph, B. (1983) 'On understanding and not understanding: some technical issues', *Int. J. Psychoanal.* 64:191–198.

Kestenberg, J.S. (1956) 'Vicissitudes of female sexuality', *J. Amer. Psychoanal. Assoc.* 4:453–476.

—— (1968) 'Outside and inside, male and female', *J. Amer. Psychoanal. Assoc.* 16:457–520.

—— (1980) 'The three faces of femininity', *Psychoanal. Rev.* 67:313–335.

King, P. (1978) 'Affective responses of the analyst to the patient's communication', *Int. J. Psychoanal.* 59:329–334.

King, P. and Steiner, R. (1991) *The Freud–Klein Controversies 1941–45*, London: Tavistock/Routledge.

Klein, M. (1926) 'The psychological principles of early analysis', in *Love, Guilt and Reparation and Other Works 1921–1945 by Melanie Klein*, London: Hogarth, 1981.

—— (1928) 'Early stages of the Oedipus conflict', *Int. J. Psychoanal.* 9:169–180.

—— (1932) 'The effects of early anxiety-situations on the sexual development of the girl', in *The Psycho-Analysis of Children*, London: Hogarth.

—— (1945) 'The Oedipus complex in the light of early anxieties', *Int. J. Psychoanal.* 26:11–33.

Kohon, G. (1986) *The British School of Psychoanalysis – The Independent Tradition*, London: Free Association Books.

Kulish, N.M. (1984) 'The effect of the sex of the analyst on transference', *Bulletin of the Menninger Clinic* 48:93–110.

—— (1989) 'Gender and transference: conversations with female analysts', *Psychoanalytic Psychology* 6:59–71.

Lampl-de Groot, J. (1928) 'The evolution of the Oedipus complex in women', *Int. J. Psychoanal.* 9:332–345.

Lax, R. (1969) 'Some considerations about transference and countertransference manifestations evoked by the analyst's pregnancy', *Int. J. Psychoanal.* 50:363–372.

Lazar, S. (1990) 'Patients' responses to pregnancy and miscarriage in the analyst', in *Illness in the Analyst*, eds H. Schwartz and A. Silver, New York: International Universities Press.

Lester, E.P. (1990) 'Gender and identity issues in the analytic process', *Int. J. Psychoanal.* 71:435–444.

Little, M. (1951) 'Counter-transference and the patient's response to it', *Int. J. Psychoanal.* 32:32–40.

McDougall, J. (1986) 'Eve's reflection: on the homosexual components of female sexuality', in *Between Analyst and Patient: New Dimensions in Countertransference and Transference*, ed. H. Meyers, Hillsdale, NJ: The Analytic Press, pp. 213–228.

Mahler, M., Pine, F. and Bergman, A. (1975) *The Psychological Birth of the Human Infant*, London: Hutchinson.

Mariotti, P. (1993) 'The analyst's pregnancy: the patient, the analyst, and the space of the unknown', *Int. J. Psychoanal.* 74:151–164.

May, R. (1986) 'Concerning a psychoanalytic view of maleness', *Psychoanal. Rev.* 73: 579–597.

Milner, M. (1987) *The Suppressed Madness of Sane Men*, London: Routledge.

Mitchell, J. (1974) *Psychoanalysis and Feminism*, Harmondsworth and New York: Penguin.

Money, J. and Ehrhart, A. (1972) *Man and Woman, Boy and Girl*, Baltimore: Johns Hopkins University Press.

Money-Kyrle, R. (1956) 'Normal counter-transference and some of its deviations', *Int. J. Psychoanal.* 37:360–366.

Montrelay, M. (1993) 'Inquiry into femininity', in *The Gender Conundrum: Contemporary Psychoanalytic Perspectives on Femininity and Masculinity*, ed. D. Breen, London: New Library of Psychoanalysis.

Muller, J.A. (1925) 'A contribution to the problem of libidinal development of the genital phase in girls', *Int. J. Psychoanal.* 13:361–368.

Parens, H., Pollock, L., Stern, J. and Kramer, S. (1976) 'On the girl's entry into the Oedipus complex', *J. Amer. Psychoanal. Assoc.* 24:79–107.

Payne, S.A. (1935) 'A conception of femininity', *Brit. J. Med.Psychol.*15:18–33.

Person, E. (1985) 'The erotic transference in women and men: differences and consequences', *J. Amer. Acad. Psychoanalysis* 13: 159–180.

Raphael-Leff, J. (1980) 'Psychotherapy with pregnant women', in *Psychological Aspects of Pregnancy, Birthing and Bonding*, ed. B. Blum, New York: Human Sciences Press.

—— (1986) 'Facilitators and Regulators: conscious and unconscious processes in pregnancy and early motherhood', *Brit. J. Med. Psychol.* 59:43–55.

—— (1991) *Psychological Processes of Childbearing*, London: Chapman & Hall.

—— (1993) *Pregnancy: The Inside Story*, London: Sheldon Press (New York: Jason Aronson, 1996).

Rayner, E. (1991) *The Independent Mind in British Psychoanalysis*, London: Free Association Books.

Richards, A.K. (1992) 'The influence of sphincter control and genital sensation on body image and gender identity in women', *Psychoanalytic Quarterly* 61:331–351.

Rickman, J. (1951) 'Number and the human sciences', in *Selected Contributions to Psycho-Analysis*, London: Hogarth, 1957.

Ritvo, S. (1989) 'Panel: current concepts of the development of sexuality' (reported by S.Vogel), *J. Amer. Psychoanal. Assoc.* 37:787–802.

Riviere, J. (1929) 'Womanliness as a masquerade', *Int. J. Psychoanal.* 10: 303–313.

—— (1936) 'On the genesis of psychical conflict in earliest infancy', *Int. J. Psychoanal.* 17: 395–422.

Sandler, J. (1987) *From Safety to Superego*, London: Karnac Books.

Sandler, J. (1976) 'Countertransference and role-responsiveness', *Int. Rev. Psychoanal.* 3: 43–47.

Sandler, J., Dare, C. and Holder, A. (1992) *The Patient and the Analyst – The Basis of the Psychoanalytic Process* (revised), London: Karnac Books.

Segal, H. (1977) 'Countertransference', *Int. J. Psychoanal. Psychother.* 6:31–37.

Sharpe, E. (1947) 'The psycho-analyst', in *Collected Papers on Psycho-Analysis*, London: Hogarth, 1950.

Spillius, E. Bott (ed.) (1988) *Melanie Klein Today: Developments in Theory and Practice*, vols I and II, London: Routledge.

Stern, D. (1985) *The Interpersonal World of the Infant: A View from Psychoanalysis and Developmental Psychology*, New York: Basic Books.

Stoller, R.J. (1976) 'Primary femininity', *J. Amer. Psychoanal. Assoc.* 24:59–78 (supplement – female psychology).

—— (1985) *Presentations of Gender*, New Haven, CT: Yale University Press.

Sweetnam, A. (1996) 'The changing contexts of gender between fixed and fluid experience', *Psychoanalytic Dialogues* 6:437–460.

Symington, N. (1983) 'The analyst's act of freedom as agent of therapeutic change', *Int. Rev. Psychoanal.* 10: 407–413.

Tyson, P. and Tyson, R.L. (1990) *Psychoanalytic Theories of Development: An Integration*, New Haven, CT: Yale University Press.

Winnicott, D.W. (1947) 'Hate in the countertransference', Chapter 15 in *Through Paediatrics to Psycho-Analysis*, London: Hogarth, 1982.

—— (1952) 'Anxiety associated with insecurity', Chapter 8 in *Through Paediatrics to Psycho-Analysis*, London: Hogarth, 1982.

—— (1958) 'The capacity to be alone', in *The Maturational Processes and the Facilitating Environment*, London: Hogarth, 1965.

Yogman, M.W. (1982) 'Observations on the father–infant relationship', in *Father and Child*, eds S.H. Cath, A.R. Gurnitt and J.M. Ross, Boston, Mass.: Little, Brown, pp.101–122.
Young-Bruehl, E. (1988) *Anna Freud*, New York: Summit Books.

Part I

The primitive tie to the mother and its manifestations in the transference and countertransference

Introduction to Part I

Rosine Jozef Perelberg

It was in 'Group psychology and the analysis of the ego' (1921) that Freud defined the concept of 'primitive tie' as a type of identification where a distinction between self and object has not been firmly established. It is an *unconscious* process, that takes place in *phantasy*. In the early modalities of identification mental processes are experienced in bodily terms such as ingesting or devouring. Already in his work on 'Mourning and melancholia' (1915b) Freud had discussed the role of incorporation whereby the individual would identify in the oral mode with the lost object; the constitution of the internal world was made through identifications. In the 'Wolf Man' (1918, see also Wolheim, 1984) Freud discussed the shifting identifications in the primal scene, which go towards constituting the individual's character.[1] If in Freud's topographical model of the mind the emphasis is on the conflict between the drives, where the object may appear to be accidental, in the structural model, the object becomes 'theoretically crucial' (Baranes, 1993, p. 172). Freud thus progressively concentrates on how it is that the external is 'taken in' and is constituted into psychic reality. The concept of a 'primitive type of identification' became relevant in his discussions on female sexuality in that he postulated the little girl's primitive attachment to the mother. To quote Freud:

> Everything in the sphere of this first attachment to the mother seemed to me difficult to grasp in analysis – so grey with age and shadowy and almost impossible to revivify – that it was as if it had succumbed to an especially inexorable repression.

> (1931, p. 227)

In 'Female sexuality' (1931) Freud indicated the fear the little girl has of being *devoured* by her mother. The importance of the 'pre-oedipal'[2] relationship with the mother has been more fully discussed since Freud's time (for example Deutsch, 1925, 1930; Brunswick, 1940; Chasseguet-Smirgel, 1964; McDougall, 1964). More recently interest in the nature of female identity can be found in the works of Ethel Person (1974), Irene Fast (1979) and Jessica Benjamin (1988) in the USA as well as in the works of Janine

Chasseguet-Smirgel (1964), C. Luquet-Parat (1964), Maria Torok (1964) and Joyce McDougall (1964) in France. The powerful character of the primitive maternal imago is experienced by children of both sexes. Both boys and girls desire to be the object of their mother's desire: both would like to give her a baby.

Marie Langer (1989) has suggested that it is at *this* level that one can find an explanation for the stress on matriarchy in early attempts to outline the history of society. Matriarchy thus becomes a myth arising from the personal history of every individual. In the beginning there is an all-powerful mother who nourishes the infant. The father then makes his appearance as the embodiment of the law, interrupting that duality (p. 196).

In England, psychoanalytic work from an early stage started to concentrate on primitive states in infancy and progressively attention was paid to the impact of these primitive states in the transference. Klein's work brought an emphasis on the relationship between the infant and the maternal body. The little girl's earliest anxiety is of 'having the inside of her body robbed and destroyed' (1930, 1932) as she believes her mother's body contains every-thing that is desirable, including the father's penis. As a consequence the little girl is filled with hatred towards her mother and wishes to attack and rob the inside of her body in turn. Melanie Klein's views on this early relationship between mother and baby had an impact on some of the early writings on femininity in the British Society, such as the work of Joan Riviere (1929) and Sylvia Payne (1935).[3]

The idea that the psychoanalytic situation reproduces the early mother–infant situation has been explored since by many other authors such as Balint (1952). The functions of the original maternal environment as being empathic (Kohut), mirroring (Winnicott), facilitating (Mahler), containing (Bion) or being able to mentalize (Fonagy) are seen as being re-enacted in the analytic situation. Progressively psychoanalysts from all the groups in the British Society, inspired by the works of Winnicott, Brierley and Bion, have emphasized the connection between primary affective development and object relationships. Winnicott believed in a state of primary identity between the little girl and her mother: 'this primary identity can be a feature from very early, and the foundation for simple being can be laid (let us say) from the birth date, or before, or soon after' (1971: pp. 80–81).

For Winnicott, affective development has to include the *mother's affects* and her capacity to tolerate, sustain and relay affective messages to the baby, in a way which allows the baby to integrate them. Winnicott postulates a primary identification with the mother for both sexes. In the earliest years it is the mother who provides the infant with a reflective and containing environment which allows the infant to go on being. When this containment does not take place, mental and emotional functioning are not facilitated and development in the internal relationship between subject and object is arrested.

More recent emphasis has been given to the role of the father as interposing himself on the imaginary mother–infant dyad (Lacan, 1966), and as representing the beginnings of the cultural order (Lévi-Strauss, 1949/1969). In the mother, the child sees a mirror of herself. It is the father who interposes himself between the dyad, thus presenting the child with the experience of the relationship between the couple. The denial of this third object is one of the tenets of the modern understanding of perversion (see Chasseguet-Smirgel, 1984; Britton, 1989). The impact of the absence of the father, either literally or emotionally, for the child's emotional development has been discussed and understood in terms of not helping the creation of the internal boundaries in the relationship between mother and child and inserting the child in a chain of reciprocity which requires the presence of the third object (Limentani, 1991; Stoller, 1975; Burgner, 1985; Gaddini, 1974; Schachter, 1993; Campbell, 1995; Fonagy and Target, 1995).

THE PHALLIC MOTHER AND THE EMERGENCE OF FEMININITY

An imago present in this early relationship is that of the phallic mother which Freud first introduced in his paper on Leonardo da Vinci (1910). In this paper Freud discussed Leonardo's phantasy of a bird-woman with a penis who beats in the mouth of a child. It is in the discussion of this phantasy that Freud, for the first time, establishes the equivalence between the breast and the penis. In 1922 Abraham suggested that the spider in dreams represented the bad sadistic mother, possessor of a penis.

In her review of the literature Kulish (1984) indicated that in his writings on perversion Freud stressed that the little boy has the phantasy of a woman with a penis in order to deal with his fear of castration (1927, 1940). Later Stoller (1975), Greenacre (1968) and Glasser (1979) emphasized the importance of this phantasy. All these authors stressed the relevance of the environment in the construction of phantasies such as that of a seductive mother and an absent father (Limentani, 1991).

In my clinical practice I have found that the phantasy of a phallic, all-powerful mother is commonly present for both men and women.[4] A patient of mine, a young single woman, expressed a derivative of this phantasy in her daydreams. At the beginning of her analysis she reported the violent daydreams she had while she masturbated. She imagined scenes of enormous aggression in love-making with a man. In these daydreaming states she had the phantasy that *she* was both male and female and thus not needing a sexual partner. Her aggression was encapsulated in these daydreams and she could not find a creative alternative for it. Several years of analysis allowed her to work through her feelings of guilt towards both her mother and father for finding each lacking and for her wish to be more successful than them. This allowed a process of mourning to take place, enabling her to give up the phantasy of being all-powerful and *both* male and female. She was then able to take on a position which allowed her creativity to be expressed through painting.

There are several images which tend to express the phantasy of the phallic mother or a combined primitive couple, such as vampires, sharks, piranhas or werewolves. In one session a woman who struggled with her masculine and feminine identifications told me the story of a werewolf, derived from a film she had seen, where a woman at the time of a full moon transformed herself into a wolf. This had first happened when she had been raped and had killed the man who had raped her. This story seems to contain some of the primary phantasies I have been discussing such as the imago of the phallic, all-powerful castrating woman and the primal scene as the scene of a murder, a sadistic encounter between a rapist and a murderer.

The imago of a phallic mother is present in the women discussed in this book, like the image of the ugly hunchback brought by Mrs Y (Chapter 1), the imago of the monster in Cara's dream (Chapter 5) and the sadistic all-powerful queen in Maria's analysis (Chapter 3).

HYPOTHESIS: THE CORE CONFLICT AND BODILY SYMPTOMS

One of the hypotheses at the basis of this book is that a same gender therapeutic relationship (i.e. female patient and female analyst) may be an aid in the re-enactment of aspects of an early relationship between mother and infant. I am not assuming that there is a *replication* of this relationship in the sense of the present being isomorphic with the past, since over time changes occur in the meanings and functions of conflicts (Sandler, 1988; Sandler and Sandler, 1994), and other layers of experiences and phantasies are added.

It is perhaps not surprising that so many women's struggles to turn away and separate from their mothers involve a bodily symptom. I have come to understand many of the bodily experiences of some of the women whom I have seen in my clinical practice as representing attempts to have a body and a sense of self that is separate from the mother. At the same time these symptoms seem to represent an aspect of the relationship with the mother which has not been properly internalized. I think that the aspect of the mother which has not been internalized is the mother as a protector against the child's own destructive phantasies (like in the story of the woman-werewolf killing the man).

These bodily experiences may range from severe symptoms such as anorexia or ulcerative colitis to vertigo, asthma, eczema or states of anxiety such as insomnia and gastric disturbances. I have found that symptoms may present themselves as a solution to the conflict between longing for and fear of fusion with the mother. Glasser has suggested that this is the conflict at the core of perversions, but which I think may have a wider relevance, being found at the core of each individual's relationship with their mother (see Pines, 1982; Burgner, in this book; Laufer, 1993; Breen, 1993). This has a specific relevance for the little girl who, according to Irigaray, 'has the mother, in some sense, in her skin, in the humidity of the mucous membranes, in the intimacy of her most intimate parts, in the mystery of her relation to gestation, birth and to her sexual identity' (1989, p. 133). S. Felman (1987) has suggested that the mother (or the mother's image) stands for the first object of the child's narcissistic attachment (an object and an image of the child's self love, or love for his own body – for his own image), inaugurating a type of mirroring relationship. Laufer (1993, 1984) has extensively discussed the relevance of the little girl's identification with her mother's body and how this functions as an organizer which lays the foundation of her future relationship to herself as a sexual woman (see also Pines, 1982).

In her analysis of the literature on female sexuality Breen has pointed out the conflict between those psychoanalysts who stress a more positive, 'biologically based experience of femininity' and those who define it in terms of a lack (a positive femininity), indicating that some other authors stress the existence of both. If one postulates that natural biological differences are both culturally and psychically reinterpreted, however, one might potentially find a solution for the debate. Breen herself argues for 'an understanding of femininity which encompasses both an unconscious representation of a lack and an unconscious representation of its "concentric" aspects' (1993, p. 37).

It is thus not by chance that several of the chapters in this part of the book focus on anorexia, although other bodily symptoms such as ulcerative colitis or other forms of attacks on the body such as self cutting are also present. In these cases it is essential for the analyst to keep in mind what Brierley pointed out all these years ago, 'that the processes of introjection and projection are psychic processes which must be distinguished from concomitant phantasies and bodily efforts to cope with concrete objects' (1936, p. 174). I suggest that these are attempts to attack thoughts, feelings and desires which by definition occur in the mind, through the body.

What we have considered throughout the book is whether an analysis with a female analyst allows for an identification with a primitive maternal imago to explode more vividly in the transference. At times this may lead to impasses in the analysis, and perhaps this is because the 'as if' so necessary for a therapeutic alliance is broken and a patient may become more deluded about being in a real fusion with the mother.

THE EFFECT OF THE SEX OF THE ANALYST ON THE TRANSFERENCE

Many writers have argued that the sex of the analyst has no major influence on the development of the analysis (Glover, 1955; Greenacre, 1959; and Chasseguet-Smirgel, 1964). If bisexuality is a characteristic present in both sexes, it should be possible, in the transference situation, for both the femininity and the masculinity of the analyst to be the vehicle for the expressions of their patients' sexuality. In 1920, however, Freud was the first to point out the relevance of the gender of the analyst when treating a case of a female homosexual who developed a negative transference to him. Later, in 1931, he also emphasized the importance of women analysts as being able to have more access to the pre-oedipal transference in female patients. He said:

> It does indeed appear that women analysts – as, for instance Jeanne Lampl-Groot and Helene Deutsch – have been able to perceive these facts more easily and clearly because they were helped in dealing with those under their treatment by the transference to a suitable mother substitute.
>
> (1931, pp. 226–227)

I think that the belief of the relevance of the gender of the analyst–patient pair is present in the training of psychoanalysts, as it is recommended that the first training case should be of the opposite sex of the analyst, as the identification might not be as powerful. Obviously this is a complicated issue. As Kulish has pointed out in her review of the literature (1984); 'to isolate one aspect, in this case the sex of the analyst, from such a complex, multidetermined phenomenon as the transference is to run the risk of distortion and superficiality' (p. 96). She also raises an important question for writers who put forward the notion that female analysts promote a specific type of transference; whether there is an 'active' process that takes place on the part of the analyst or whether one is just talking about the fact that the analyst is female (p. 100). As Raphael-Leff points out (in this book) representations of gender also reside preformed in the mind of each clinician, and like all pre-conceptualizations, inevitably colour our views of our patients (p. 255).

Many analysts have agreed that the sequence of material presented in the transference may reflect the sex of the therapist, early pre-oedipal material being more frequently identified in the analysis with female analysts. Glover (1955), Blum (1971), Pines (1993) and Balint (Chapter 1 here) also point out in their work with female patients that there are specific issues that arise in the transference to female analysts. Pines believes that 'a woman analyst's physical capacity to be a mother appears to facilitate the transference of primitive feelings arising from partial maternal deprivation' (p. 24). This is in contrast with the transference to male analysts which often tends to be reported as presenting itself in an erotized pseudo-heterosexual way (see Lester, 1993).

Karme (1979) has suggested that a possible reason for an emphasis on a maternal as opposed to a paternal transference to female analysts is related to the fear of a phallic mother and suggests that maternal transference reported by male analysts is of the pre-oedipal mother. However, Kulish (1984) feels that there is no evidence to support these points. In a later paper she reports the results of interviews with seventeen senior female analysts who mostly felt that the analyst's gender particularly affects the *sequence* of the emergence of the material and that female analysts might pull pre-oedipal material into the transference more quickly.

In all this, one must not lose sight of the eminently oedipal configuration of the analytical situation. Chasseguet-Smirgel has pointed out that in analysis the analysand is offered a womb, a potential for regression, but in the setting itself with its framework and rules the limits are also indicated, in the same way as the father separates the mother and the child (1986). She prefers to discuss the issue in terms of how the femininity of the analyst – whether male or female – affects their professional practice. I would suggest, however, that the presence of a female analyst facilitates the phantasy that Chasseguet-Smirgel has called the archaic Oedipus complex, a smooth universe, without obstacles, representing the mother's insides to which one would have free access (1986, p. 30).

TRANSFERENCE AND COUNTERTRANSFERENCE

The other aspect which needs to be taken into account when examining the mutual impact of gender in the analytic process – not present in the American discussion – is the countertransference of the analyst. This is a dimension present in every chapter in this part of the book.

In the British School the inclusion of the analyst's affective states in the sessions – the understanding of the countertransference – became increasingly part of the central analytical task. It is in the process of holding, containing and transforming feelings that cannot be elaborated by the patients themselves that the analytic work is carried out. Klein had already suggested that there are 'pre-verbal emotions . . . [which are] revived in the transference situation . . . [and which] appear . . . as "memories in feelings"', which are reconstructed and put into words with the help of the analyst (Klein, 1937, p. 316).

A group of analysts have addressed themselves to specific modes of communication present in analyses that impinge on the analyst in the countertransference. Starting with Heimann (1950), this line of enquiry has been developed by Money-Kyrle (1956), Bion (1967a, 1967b), Racker (1968), Grinberg (1962), Joseph (1975, 1984), Segal (1977) and Brenman Pick (1985). For these authors the countertransference became a way of gaining access to patients' unconscious communication. In the analytic situation it is the analyst who has to be able to take in and reflect on her patients' feelings and desires and return them in a more digestible form. Sandler (1976) has coined the term 'actualization' to indicate the patient's attempts to re-establish with the analyst an early object relationship. This approach combines an experience of the transference as actualized in the consulting room as well as a comprehension of the unconscious phantasies. To my understanding this actualization is not only of wished-for patterns of relationships, but also of experiences which were not previously understood.

In the British Society, the understanding of the countertransference has become the main area of work from which the understanding of feeling states in the analytic session is derived. This has marked a shift in terms of a stress on the emotional quality of the experience in the analytic process. In 1977 Limentani stated that 'the success or failure of an analysis could in fact be said to rest on the degree of affective changes which take place during its course.' I think that Limentani's statement relates affect and meaning.

This is the way in which I also understand Bion's formulations. There is an equivalence, for Bion, between emotions and knowledge. He writes: 'Before an emotional experience can be used for a model its sense data have to be transformed into alpha elements to be stored and made available for abstraction. In minus-K the meaning is abstracted, leaving a denuded representation' (1962, pp. 74–75). By thinking about emotional experiences and by understanding them, the mind comprehends meanings. All knowledge is assumed to have its origins in primitive 'emotional experience'. The incorporation of feelings into the psychic sphere, in early life, presupposes the experience of having had a care-giver able to reflect on the mental states of the infant, able to be both a witness of and a participant in a child's emotional development. When this process does not take place, there may be emotional arrest and a disavowal of the need for the object.

THE CHAPTERS

The various chapters in this part of the book share an approach to the way in which, in the analytic process, aspects of the internal world, parts of the internal self-representation, are projected on to the analyst and re-enacted in the transference. The analyst is invited to take on these different aspects and re-enact these different roles to the patient who will then 'take on' other aspects. The process is characterized by the fluidity with which these various parts present themselves, although in the cases presented in this part, because of the severity of the psychopathologies, there is a tendency for some interactions to become more fixed and to last for a long period of time. In several cases one can identify different stages in the process. All the chapters are also concerned with understanding the pre-verbal states which can be apprehended in the understanding of the transference and counter-transference.

Enid Balint's paper is concerned with the 'dark continent' of a woman's early attachment to her mother. Balint is referring to Freud's discussion of the little girl's prolonged attachment to her mother (Freud, 1925, 1931) and presents two women patients who had not been able to identify with their mothers, although they did manage to establish sexual relationships with men. Balint points out that these women's preoccupation remained with women whom they attempted to care for. In their analyses this was expressed by these women's wish to satisfy their analyst; one in an erotized way, whilst in the other the relationship with the mother was represented in a frozen way, unintegrated into the patient's ego. It 'seemed a foreign body frozen and untouchable inside her'. Balint suggests that in both women there was a denial of castration and an undervaluation of their husbands as representing their fathers. Balint does not think her patients are latent homosexuals but are rather driven by a wish to keep their depressed mothers alive. She further puts forward the idea that a woman needs to feel that she was satisfied by her mother's body as an infant in order to feel that her own body satisfied her mother. The early relationship between mother and daughter is thus expressed in the experience of the body itself and the way it is represented.

In my own chapter I examine some of the problems raised in the analysis of Maria, a patient who has to adhere to a version of reality that emphasizes processes in her body as opposed to processes in her mind. This assumed a concrete dimension in the two accidents she suffered on the two first anniversaries of the start of her analysis. I suggest that my patient's experience of these two accidents and the way she brought them into the transference revealed her beliefs about her internal primary relationships to her objects. Both accidents became a screen on to which she projected her beliefs about relationships in her life, more specifically her beliefs about her early catastrophic relationship with her mother and her beliefs about sexual intercourse as a violent and catastrophic encounter. It is because any encounter between two people is potentially violent, sexual and murderous that Maria had to retreat into a timeless world where people did not exist as whole persons and thus were unable to differentiate from each other. The analytic process presented her with an impossible dilemma: to be in a relationship with me implied the risk of this violent and dangerous encounter; not to be, however, meant remaining trapped in a two-dimensional, timeless world. This patient also adhered to a representation of herself close to the somatic and her various experiences in the analysis for a long time took the pathway of her body.

Tallandini discusses a patient for whom the basic conflict is between the wish for merger with a pre-oedipal mother on the one hand and the terror of it on the other. It was only after some time in the analysis of her phantasies of a state of fusion that oedipal wishes made their way into the transference allowing the previous symbiotic and eroticized relationship with the mother to be recognized. Her patient, a 26-year-old married woman, had retained an erotic longing for her mother as well as a wish to have an exclusive relationship with her, denying hostility, envy and rivalry towards her mother. Tallandini discusses how in the analysis there is a collusive silence about the gender of both analyst and patient which serves as a defence against any experience of separation.

Burgner discusses the analysis of a 17-year-old bulimic girl who had attempted suicide. In her analysis Cara expressed her conviction that bingeing and vomiting were her only possession, the thing that she felt that she did for herself and to herself, separately from a mother who was experienced as intrusive and invasive. It was also an omnipotent attempt to avoid any feelings of need and therefore of abandonment. Cara experienced no sense of separation from her mother, that they were bound to each other through crazy and addictive sexuality. She was caught in the conflict between her struggle to separate from her mother on the one hand and a yearning for a state of no-separation from the breast/mother/analyst. In the analysis Cara brought to the transference this sado-masochistic relationship with both her parents. In this, like in other accounts in this book, the analyst's counter-transference was an important source of information on the patient's affective states, and one which allows for pre-verbal states of mind to be understood in the analytic process. Burgner suggests that what are palpable in the transference are primitive, pre-oedipal relationships.

In her chapter Birksted-Breen also discusses the case of an anorexic patient in terms of the anorexic wish for and fear of fusion with her mother. She points to the lack of a transitional space in the relationship between mother and daughter in early stages of her patient's development. She suggests that in anorexic patients there is a disturbance in the area of symbolization which does not allow for this space to be developed. In the early stages of the analysis the patient brought to the transference this desire for fusion with the mother–analyst. Interactions between patient and analyst had a sense of rhythm in which the analyst identified a sort of rivalry as to which of the two was more needy of the other. At the same time they could also alternate in terms of which of the two was a never satisfied infant or a voraciously demanding and never satisfied parent. If, on the one hand, the patient wanted the analyst to understand her completely without needing to explain herself to her analyst, she felt, on the other hand, intruded upon when the analyst did understand her. In this, like in other narcissistically vulnerable patients, it is their own sense of self that the patients feel they are ultimately protecting.

Bronstein discusses the analysis of a 17-year-old adolescent who, through her various attempted suicides, had been attacking her own femaleness. She was isolated, living in an imaginary world. Rachel disliked everything about herself and this led her to self-cutting. This adolescent's homosexuality was understood by the analyst as representing a search for an ideal mother–daughter relationship. Differences for this girl were experienced as a concrete fight between parts of herself. Any experience of the analyst as separate and female were filled with acute paranoid anxiety. The analyst was also able to identify that it was her 'heterosexual femaleness' that was most threatening to her patient. Within a Kleinian framework Bronstein suggests an early hatred by the little girl for her mother. She also raises, however, the importance of the mother's early response to her daughter, her possible difficulty in accepting her baby's projections as well as her denigration of femininity. The role of the real environment is emphasized, like the mother's pregnancy when Rachel was 4 months old and her daughter's sexual abuse from childhood through to her adolescence. In adolescence, her attacks on her own body came to represent attacks on her mother's sexual body. Rachel developed a belief in a male 'double' who, by becoming an embodiment of her projected badness, represented an attempt to protect herself. In the various aspects of herself which were projected on to him Bronstein suggests that what had to be maintained was a dyadic relationship which prevented the appearance of a triangular relationship.

All the chapters in this part incorporate certain central themes:

- The setting includes a female patient and female analyst.
- A core conflict present in the analyses is between a longing for fusion with a pre-oedipal, idealized mother, on the one hand, and a terror of this mother on the other.
- Pre-verbal and pre-oedipal experiences are centrally brought to the transference.
- There is a recurrence of bodily symptoms as vehicles for the expressions of conflicts.
- The use the analyst makes of her countertransference feelings in order to understand the analytic process.

NOTES

1 I would like to suggest a distinction between the concepts of 'identification' and 'identity'. Identification is a process that takes place in the System Unconscious and is thus the stuff of phantasies. Throughout his work Freud postulated the fluidity of identificatory processes, especially in relation to the primal scene. I suggest that 'identity', in contrast, is an attempt that each individual makes to organize these (by definition) conflicting identifications in order to achieve an illusion of 'unity'. It is only this illusion which allows an individual to make the statement 'I am this' (and not that). I think that names, for instance, tend to perform this symbolic function in contemporary societies. I have developed this distinction between 'identification' and 'identity' further in another paper (Perelberg, 1997).

2 One should note that from the analyst's perspective there is no such thing as a pre-oedipal mother because any mother–child relationship presupposes the existence of the father. The term is thus used as shorthand to express the perspective of the patient's phantasies and experiences. The analytic encounter takes place by definition within a triadic constellation, because the third element – whether the father or the analytic process – is present in the conceptual framework of the analyst. In an earlier work, where I discussed feminist writings in the field of psychotherapy in the 1970s and 1980s (Perelberg, 1990) I pointed out the misleading emphasis on the mother–daughter relationship at the exclusion of the father. I then said: 'However, it is that very triangle that makes the relationship between mothers and daughters possible: there can be no mother and daughter unit without the existence of a father' (p. 37). Another aspect that tends to be

neglected in the literature that emphasizes the early experience between mother and infant is the role of oedipal sexuality. Lebovici has pointed out in a recent interview that the woman/analyst who appears in the psychoanalytic literature is represented in terms of the 'good breast' or the 'bad breast' and never in terms of the 'woman's breast'. The erotic relationship with the breast disappears (in Baruch and Serrano, 1996).

3 Some of these views on early infancy, however, have been challenged and viewed as an attribution of sophisticated mechanisms to the mind of the infant: the innate character Klein attributes to unconscious phantasies; her reduction of all mental life to unconscious phantasies (thus flattening the distinction between thinking, memory, perception and phantasy) and her belief in constitutional knowledge. Klein was also criticized for her neglect of the role of experience in the constitution of the unconscious phantasies. These challenges to Kleinian theory were raised by Glover, Foulkes, Brierley and Anna Freud (in King and Steiner 1991); also Yorke, 1973 and Hayman, 1989. Klein's work, however, through its emphasis on the early relationship between the infant and her mother, has had an important impact in contemporary psychoanalytic thinking . I think, however, that it is only with Bion that a Kleinian theory of thinking will be developed, with an emphasis on the role of the environment and the interaction between internal and external reality (1962, 1967a, 1967b). This line of work has been further developed in the works of Segal (1996) and Britton (1989, 1995) in their establishing a relationship between mental space and triangulation.

4 The relevance of this imago will be further discussed in the Introduction to Part III of this book.

REFERENCES

Abraham, K. (1922) 'The spider as a dream symbol', in *Selected Papers on Psycho-Analysis*, London: Maresfield Reprints, 1979.

Balint, E. (1952) *Primary Love and Psychoanalytic Technique*, London: Tavistock.

Baranes, J.J.(1993) 'Devenir soi-meme: avatars et status du transgenerationnel', in *Transmission de la Vie Psychique Entre Generations*, eds R. Kaes, H. Fainberg, M. Enriquez and J.J. Baranes, Paris: Dunod.

Baruch, E.H. and Serrano, L.J.(1996) *She Speaks, He Listens*, London: Routledge.

Benjamin, J. (1988) *The Banks of Love*, New York: Pantheon Books.

Bion, W.R. (1962) *Learning from Experience*, London: Karnac Books.

—— (1967a) 'Differentiation of the psychotic from the non-psychotic personalities', in *Second Thoughts: Selected Papers on Psycho-Analysis*, London: Maresfield Library.

—— (1967b) 'Attacks on linking', in *Second Thoughts: Selected Papers on Psycho-Analysis*, London: Maresfield Library.

Blum, H.P. (1971) 'On the conception and development of the transference neurosis', *J. Amer. Psychoanal. Assoc.* 19: 41–53.

—— (1973) 'The concept of erotised transference', in *J. Amer. Psychoanal. Assoc.* 19: 41–53.

Breen, D. (1993) 'General introduction', in *The Gender Conundrum: Contemporary Psychoanalytic Perspectives on Femininity and Masculinity* , London: Routledge and the Institute of Psycho-Analysis.

Brenman Pick, I. (1985) 'Working through in the counter-transference', in *Melanie Klein Today*, ed. E. Spillius, vol. 2, London: Routledge in association with the Institute of Psycho-Analysis, 1988.

Brierley, M. (1936) 'Specific determinants in feminine development', *Int. J. Psych-oanal.* 17: 163–180.

Britton, R. (1989) 'The missing link: parental sexuality in the Oedipus complex', in *The Oedipus Complex Today: Clinical Implications*, eds R. Britton, M. Feldman and E. O'Shaughnessy, London: Karnac Books, pp.83–101.

—— (1995) 'Psychic reality and unconscious belief', *Int. J. Psychoanal.* 76: 19–23.

Brunswick, R.M. (1940) 'The pre-oedipal phase of the libido development', *Psychoanalytic Quarterly* 9: 293–319.

Burgner, M. (1985) 'The oedipal experience: effects on development of an absent father', *Int. J. Psychoanal.* 66: 311–320.

Campbell, D. (1995) 'The role of the father in a pre-suicide state', *Int. J. Psychoanal.* 76 (2): 315–324.

Chasseguet-Smirgel, J. (ed.) (1964) 'Feminine guilt and the Oedipus complex', in *Female Sexuality*, London: Maresfield Library, 1985.

—— (1984) *Creativity and Perversion*, New York: W.W. Norton.

—— (1986) 'The archaic matrix of the Oedipus complex', in *Sexuality and Mind: The Role of the Father and the Mother in the Psyche*, New York and London: New York University Press.

Deutsch, H. (1925) 'The psychology of women in relation to the functions of reproduction', *Int. J. Psychoanal.* 6: 405–418.

—— (1930) 'The significance of masochism in the mental life of women', *Int. J. Psychoanal.* 11: 48–60.

—— (1965) *Neurosis and Character Types*, New York: International University Press.

Fast, I. (1979) 'Developments in gender identity: gender differentiation in girls', *Int. J. Psychoanal.* 60: 443–455.

Felman, S. (1987) *Jacques Lacan and the Adventure of Insight*, Cambridge, Mass.: Harvard University Press.

Fonagy, P. (1991) 'Thinking about thinking: some clinical and theoretical considerations in the analysis of borderline patients', *Int. J. Psychoanal.* 72 (4): 639–656.

Fonagy, P. and Target, M. (1995) 'Understanding the violent patient: the use of the body and the role of the father', *Int. J. Psychoanal.* 76: 487–501.

Freud, S. (1910) 'Leonardo Da Vinci and a memory of his childhood', *S.E.* 11: 59–137.

—— (1915a) 'On narcissism: an introduction', *S.E.* 14: 69–102.

—— (1915b) 'Mourning and melancholia', *S.E.* 14: 237–258.

—— (1918) 'From the history of an infantile neurosis', *S.E.* 17: 3–122.

—— (1920) 'The psychogenesis of a case of homosexuality in a woman', *S.E.* 18: 147–172.

—— (1921) 'Group psychology and the analysis of the ego', *S.E.* 18: 67–143.

—— (1923) 'The ego and the id', *S.E.* 19: 3–66.

—— (1925) 'Some psychical consequences of the anatomical distinction between the sexes', *S.E.* 19: 248–258.

—— (1927) 'Fetishism', *S.E.* 21: 149–157.

—— (1931) 'Female sexuality', *S.E.* 21: 225–243.

—— (1940) 'Splitting of the ego in the process of defence', *S.E.* 23: 271–278.

Gaddini, E. (1974) 'Formation of the father and the primal scene', in *A Psycho-Analytic Theory of Infantile Experience*, ed. A. Limentani, London: Routledge in association with the Institute of Psycho-Analysis, 1992.

Glasser, M. (1979) 'Some aspects of the role of aggression in the perversions', in *Sexual Deviation*, ed. I. Rosen, Oxford: Oxford University Press.

Glover, E. (1955) *The Technique of Psychoanalysis*, New York: International Universities Press.

Greenacre, P. (1959) 'Certain technical problems in the transference relationship', *J. Amer. Psychoanal. Assoc.* 7:484–502.

—— (1968) 'Perversions: general considerations regarding their genetic and dynamic background', in *Emotional Growth*, vol. 1, New York: International University Press.

Grinberg, L. (1962) 'On a specific aspect of countertransference due to the patient's projective identification', *Int. J. Psychoanal.* 43: 436–440.

Hayman, A. (1989) 'What do we mean by "phantasy"?' *Int. J. Psychoanal.* 70: 105–113.

Heimann, P. (1950) 'On countertransference', *Int. J. Psychoanal.* 31: 31–34.

Irigaray, L. (1988) 'Interview', in *Women Analyse Women*, eds E.H. Baruch and L.J. Serrano, New York: New York University Press.

—— (1989) 'The gesture in psychoanalysis', in *Between Feminism and Psychoanalysis*, ed. T. Breman, London: Routledge.

Joseph, B. (1975) 'The patient who is difficult to reach', in *Melanie Klein Today*, ed. E. Spillius, vol. 2, London: Routledge in association with the Institute of Psychoanalysis, 1988.

—— (1984) 'Projective identification: some clinical aspects', in *Projection, Identification, Projective Identification*, ed. J. Sandler, London: Karnac Books, 1988.

Karme, L. (1979) 'The analysis of a male patient by a female analyst: the problem of the negative oedipal transference', *Int. J. Psychoanal.* 60: 253–261.

King, P. and Steiner, R. (eds) (1991) *The Freud–Klein Controversies 1941–45*, New Library of Psychoanalysis 11, London: Routledge and the Institute of Psycho-Analysis.

Klein, M. (1930) 'The importance of symbol formation in the development of the ego', in *Love, Guilt and Reparation and Other Works*, New York: Delta Books, 1975.

—— (1932) 'The effects of early anxiety-situations on the sexual development of the girl', in *The Psychoanalysis of Children*, London: Hogarth and the Institute of Psycho-Analysis, 1975.

—— (1937) 'Love, guilt and reparation', in *Love, Guilt and Reparation and Other Works*, New York: Delta Books, 1975, pp. 306–343.

—— (1946) 'Notes on some schizoid mechanisms', in *The Writings of Melanie Klein*, vol. 3, pp. 1–24, London: Hogarth, 1975.

Kulish, N.M. (1984) 'The effect of the sex of the analyst on transference: a review of the literature', *Bulletin of the Menninger Clinic* 48: 93–110.

—— (1986) 'Gender and transference: the screen of the phallic mother', *Int. Rev. Psychoanal.* 13: 393–404.

—— (1989) 'Gender and transference: conversations with female analysts', *Psychoanalytic Psychology* 6 (1): 59–71.

Kulish, N. and Mayman, M. (1993) 'Gender linked determinants of transference and countertransference in psychoanalytic psychotherapy', *Psychoanalytic Inquiry* 13: 286–305.

Lacan, J. (1966) *Ecrits*, Paris: Seuil.

Langer, M. (1989) *From Vienna to Managua: Journey of a Psychoanalyst*, London: Free Association Books.

Laplanche, J. and Pontalis, J.-B. (1985) *The Language of Psycho-Analysis*, London: Hogarth and the Institute of Psycho-Analysis.

Laufer, E. (1993) 'The female Oedipus complex and the relationship to the body', in *The Gender Conundrum: Contemporary Psychoanalytic Perspectives on Femininity and Masculinity*, ed. D. Breen, London: Routledge in association with the Institute of Psycho-Analysis.

Lester, E.P.(1993) 'Boundaries and gender: their interplay in the analytic situation', *Psychoanalytic Inquiry* 13: 153–172.

Lévi-Strauss, C. (1949/1969) *The Elementary Structures of Kinship and Marriage*, Boston: Beacon Press.

Limentani, A. (1977) 'Affects and the psychoanalytic situation', in *Between Freud and Klein*, London: Free Association Books.

—— (1991) 'Neglected fathers in the aetiology and treatment of sexual deviations', *Int. J. Psychoanal.* 72: 573–584.

Luquet-Parat, C. (1964) 'The change of object', in *Female Sexuality*, ed. J. Chasseguet-Smirgel, London: Maresfield Library, 1985.

McDougall, J. (1964) 'Homosexuality in women', in *Female Sexuality*, ed. J. Chasseguet-Smirgel, London: Maresfield Library, 1985.

Money-Kyrle, R. (1956) 'Normal counter-transference and some of its deviations', in *The Collected Papers of Money-Kyrle*, Aberdeen: Clunie Press, 1978.

Payne, S. (1935) 'A conception of femininity', *Int. J. Psychoanal.* 15: 18–33.

Perelberg, R.J. (1990) 'Equality, asymmetry and diversity: on conceptualisations of gender', in eds R.J. Perelberg and A.M. Miller, *Gender and Power in Families*, London: Routledge.

—— (1997) 'Masculinity, femininity and the phallus', paper presented at the UCL Conference 'Psychoanalytic understanding of sexuality and aggression in border-line young men', University College London, autumn 1997.

Person, E. (1974) 'Some new observations on the origins of femininity', in *Women in Analysis*, ed. J. Strouse, New York: Grossman, pp. 250–261.

Pines, D. (1993) 'The relevance of early psychic development to pregnancy and abortion', in *A Woman's Unconscious Use of her Body*, London: Virago, pp. 97–115. Also in *International Journal of Psycho-Analysis* (1982) 63: 311–318.

Racker, H.(1968) *Transference and Countertransference*, London: Karnac Books.

Riviere, J. (1929) 'Womanliness as a masquerade', *Int. J. Psychoanal.* 10: 303–313. Also this volume, Chapter 12.

Sandler, J. (1976) 'Countertransference and role-responsiveness', *Int. Rev. Psychoanal.* 3: 43–47.

—— (1988) 'Introduction to the first plenary discussion', *Bulletin of the European Psycho-Analytical Federation* 31: EPF, Barcelona.

Sandler, J. and Sandler, A.-M. (1994) 'Phantasy and its transformations: a contemporary Freudian view', *Int. J. Psychoanal.* 75 (2): 387–394.

Schachter, J. (1993) 'A young man's search for a masculine identity', *Bulletin of The Anna Freud Centre* 16 (1): 61–72.

Segal, H. (1977) 'Countertransference', in *The Work of Hanna Segal*, London: Karnac Books, 1986.

—— (1986) *The Work of Hanna Segal*, London: Karnac Books.

Stoller, R.J. (1975) *Perversion*, New York: Random House.

Torok, M. (1964) 'The significance of penis envy in women', in *Female Sexuality*, ed. J. Chasseguet-Smirgel, London: Maresfield Library.

Winnicott, D. (1971) *Playing and Reality*, London: Tavistock.

Wolheim, R. (1984) *The Thread of Life*, Cambridge: Cambridge University Press.

Yorke, C. (1973) 'Some suggestions for a critique of Kleinian psychology', *Psychoana. Study Child* 26: 129–158.

Chapter 1

The analysis of women by a woman analyst

What does a woman want?

Enid Balint

Strachey (1961, p. 244), in a footnote to his introductory remarks to Freud's 1925 paper on female sexuality, quotes Ernest Jones as saying that Freud said: 'The great question has never been answered – what does a woman want?' Freud's most important additional contributions to the subject of female sexuality concerned the little girl's pre-oedipal attachment to the mother which, he said, was stronger and of longer duration and richer in content, and left behind many more opportunities for fixation and character formation, than he had previously realized (Freud, 1925, 1931). He stressed also that the girl's sexual aims in regard to the mother are active as well as passive and contain a wish to give her a baby as well as to bear her one and that she fulfils them in indirect ways. Freud also admitted that we know less about the sexual life of little girls than of boys, and that the sexual life of the adult woman is a 'dark continent for psychology' (Freud, 1926, p. 212). In spite of much recent research into this subject, this is still largely the case. In this chapter I shall concentrate only on the many obscure aspects of a woman's attachment to her mother which are a part of this 'dark continent'. These need to be clarified if we are to understand more about her sexual life and approach the question 'what does a woman want?'

The problem of what brings the powerful attachment to the mother to an end has often been discussed. It involves more than a simple change of object (i.e. from mother to father) and often ends in hate of the mother, which may last throughout life although it is usually carefully over-compensated for in adult life. In Lampl-de Groot's (1928) important contribution to the subject, she gives clinical material to illustrate the immense difficulty a little girl has in giving up her possession of her mother and changing from possessing her to having her solely as a loved object to be identified with. The little girl feels that the possession of her mother can only be maintained if she, the girl, is not castrated, but has a penis. It follows therefore that if the little girl cannot give up the possession of the mother, she denies castration and either forms no relationships with men at all and keeps her mother as her most important possession, or, while secretly denying castration, forms relationships with men with whom she is frigid but still remains inwardly attached to her mother.

In my experience, however, as I hope to show, such women are not necessarily frigid. They never identify with their mothers or with any mature woman, but, in spite of this, can establish satisfactory relations with men in many ways. However, the men are never really at the centre of their lives; their real preoccupation remains with women and how to care for and satisfy them; but on the condition that their own bodies are for men: they do not give or get any direct physical bodily satisfaction with women; they wish to care for them but at a distance. Lampl-de Groot speaks of one of her own patients who wished to become an analyst, not so that she could identify with her, the analyst – but so that she could get rid of the analyst's analyst (a man) and thus take his place by herself becoming the analyst's analyst (a man), and thus care for her in a non-sexual or sexually inhibited role.

Helene Deutsch (1946) describes the woman's struggle to get away from her mother while at the same time showing an intensified and anxious urge to remain under her protection. She also sees the attachment to the mother as continuing in adult life, and says that:

> In all the phases of woman's development and experience, the great part played in her psychologic life by her attachment to her mother can be clearly observed. Many events in that life are manifestations of attempts to detach herself, attempts made in thrusts, and the woman's psychologic equilibrium and eventual fate often depend on the success or failure of these attempts.
>
> (Deutsch, 1946, p. 16)

Deutsch thinks that if the little girl cannot detach herself from her mother successfully she will continue in adult life to need a considerable amount of tenderness and motherly protection and find life unbearable without it. In the analyses of the women on which I base this chapter, this wish is shown as having been reversed; namely, these women avoid motherly protection and wish instead to give it to other women and perhaps enjoy it vicariously.

This problem first came to my notice during the analysis of two women patients who, although dissimilar in most ways, seemed to present similar features in the transference and also in their relations to men. In both analyses the work apparently went well; they did not make me feel frustrated or inadequate. In fact, I often felt I was doing well with both of them, particularly during the hour itself. During the work some of their conflicts in relation to men were made conscious and some resolution of them took place. However, one area of work was repetitive and unfruitful; namely that in relation to their mothers. Although they spoke about their mothers, little unconscious material came to light, either in fantasy or in memories, and little change occurred in their feelings about or their attitude to their mothers, or to me. Furthermore, although each patient presented very different (almost opposite) transference patterns, in neither analysis did these problems vary from day to day.

My feelings of unjustified satisfaction during the sessions put me on my guard and I gradually came to see this as a major technical problem. It appeared that both patients wished to satisfy and please me but since their wish was acted out it was difficult to analyse: in one it was eroticized, in the other not. Both patients felt in different ways that coming to analysis regularly and producing dreams and free associations satisfied me – who was seen as the mother, seldom as the father – and thus their major problem was solved day by day. In addition, as this desire was satisfied in the transference their relationships with me became less tense and artificial, although on the whole their unconscious relation to objects remained the same. I was doubtful whether they would ever be enabled to introject their mothers – or if they had done so, to identify with the introjects in a way which would enable them to give up their peculiar distant, though intimate, satisfaction from trying to please and care for them, and come to value men in a wholly satisfactory way.

Both these patients were married women with children; both had lovers; both were referred to me because of 'marital problems'; both liked their husbands and thought that they were nice, good, even interesting men, but both were cool and critical of them while being capable of being warm, intimate, and loving with their lovers, with whom they had good relationships – not only sexual. Neither saw her lover as superior to, or even nicer than her husband. There was plenty of evidence to support the hypothesis that they were in the sexual phase dominated by the oedipal complex which should present no particular problem to the analyst. For instance, they denied that their mothers were satisfied by their fathers or had ever had satisfactory sexual relationships with them. In this way they denied their envy of their mothers, or hostility to them. They both also denied feelings of guilt because of their relationships with their fathers, although they admitted to fantasies about being given babies by them, and of being preferred by their fathers. Both valued their vaginas, but there was evidence of a denial of castration and an avoidance of penis envy. Both patients were girlish in their appearance and manner, although one was in her forties and one was in her thirties, and it seemed as if neither could really show herself to be a fully adult woman who could be satisfied genitally by her own husband, that is, by her children's father. They could, however, as they had in fantasy with their own fathers, have their husbands' babies and be mothers of their children. They denied guilt but could have no pleasure from their husbands. One of them concentrated on pleasing (erotically to begin with, and later in a more caring way which was only sometimes a reaction formation against hostile feelings); the other one on utterly failing to please – their mothers and me. Their mothers were more important to them than their husbands although they could give pleasure to and receive pleasure from men if they were not their husbands. They appeared to have less severe superegos than I at first suspected and were thus able to enjoy some relationships in spite of their hostility to their mothers. Both these women had older brothers with whom they had been intimate when they were young, and perhaps they had thus to some degree solved their oedipal problems by transferring some of their sexual strivings from their fathers to their brothers, thus diminishing the hostility and guilt they felt towards their mothers at the oedipal level.

During the first few years of the analyses I worked with these ideas to which both patients agreed in an unconvincing way, with little protest (although one as I will show became confused) but the work did not change their attitudes to their mothers or to me. Their analyses remained repetitive. One patient's attachment to me was based on an aim-inhibited sexual drive and a hope of overcoming my hostility, and the other on a hopeless attempt to be near to me which sometimes involved a search for a penis with which to do so.

I will now give some material about the two patients separately before coming back to theoretical considerations.

Early in her analysis Mrs X acted out her wish to satisfy and please me – the mother analyst – in a teasing erotic way, secretly imagining that I was satisfied each time she entered my room. She thus identified with a penis; I was related to as an external object and simultaneously as one who could be identified with (Freud, 1923). She dreaded touching me but entering my room symbolically represented entering my body and giving me pleasure and so set her free to have pleasure with her lover. She was anxious when she left my room, which she did with the greatest care and tact. She never touched me and lay on the couch as if she were not really supported by it. She told me that she hated men when they withdrew after intercourse, and was sad and never happy after intercourse because she would have to wait until the next time before she was needed by a man again. He would be indifferent to her for the time being and would go to sleep. She wanted to be wanted all the time, to be the need-satisfying object for her lover, which was easy (because she had a vagina); and for women, which was more difficult as her vagina was no good to women. In spite of this the task was not felt to be hopeless or impossible. Early in her analysis she had many lovers, as she thought that I would be aroused and stimulated and amused by stories of them as her mother had appeared to be by her childish sexual games. She never for a moment risked my envy as it was always made abundantly clear to me that men did not really matter to her, which was in a way true. However, she herself enjoyed her relations with men in a rather offhand way. When later in her analysis Mrs X realized that her sexual aims in relation to women were unrealizable, I was given up as an external sexual object and she began to get in touch with an early, more primitive, repressed introjected object who was felt to be truly feminine and for whom she could feel concern. This object represented her nanny who had looked after her from the age of 2½ years until she grew up and withdrew from her. The patient had been truly dependent on this nanny, who had been strict and thus felt to be caring and dependable. The patient had identified with the caring nanny and was herself able to look after – that is, to care for – her when she in turn was ill. A relationship of mutual concern had developed between them. The nanny had responded to the patient's care, unlike her mother, who had not. It may be significant that until this nanny's arrival the patient had been looked after by a series of nannies and that her mother had breast-fed her with frequent interruptions for test weighing. She was given the breast, taken off it, put back, and later given a bottle to supplement.

Freud (1923) discussed the problems which arise when the ego's object identifications are incompatible with one another and said that this may result in a disruption in the ego. Mrs X was saved this disruption, perhaps because she did not introject her mother but kept her as an external sexual object. The nanny was therefore the only real feminine introject and her individual with this introject was kept apart and secret. Soon after the identification with and relation to the nanny was remembered, the mother (as well as myself) was given up as a sexual object and the patient then tried to care for, and love, her mother in a non-exciting, non-sexual way. The mother then withdrew from her. The patient responded by resorting again to attempts to please her mother erotically. She tried to hide her emerging femininity; became very thin and started to dress like a boy. When this too failed, she behaved like a stupid hysterical girl, making scenes in public, once more hiding her maturity and her pleasure in being able to relate to her husband and children. Following this episode Mrs X went through a period of grief and hopelessness in the analysis until she accepted her mother's rejection and started liberating herself from her. She then slowly began to change: she dressed like a woman and let me see how much she loved and valued her husband. During this time she seldom related to me as she had before but started to show her care and love for me, which I saw now not as a reaction formation but based on her emerging ability to come to terms with reality. The transference mani-festations changed from time to time but on the whole she related to me as she had been related to by her nanny. She also stopped treating her husband as she felt her mother had treated her and her father, as inferior beings and objects needing continual sexual stimulation.

The second patient, Mrs Y, was aged 43 when she came to analysis. Her mother had died a few years before the beginning of the analysis. The mother had probably been a lifelong depressive. This was revealed by her diaries which, although in the patient's possession, were only read by her after many years of analysis when some resolution of her problems had taken place. The diaries described her mother's struggles to make a close relationship with my patient, her only daughter, and to be able to hold her close when feeding her. This the mother failed to do and in order to bear the strain of feeding her baby at all she had smoked cigarettes and read continuously during the feeds.

Mrs Y had few memories of her early relationship with her mother but the analysis soon uncovered memories of early relationships with her brothers and father. When she was very young her older brother, John (which was the name of her lover), cared for her, although later he became the main object in the oedipal phase. Her relationship to her mother was unreachable. She was represented in dreams as a frozen, icy box or coffin or an unreachable bare room. This part of her inner world was not related to her other love objects – nor was it integrated into her ego – and seemed a foreign body frozen and untouchable inside her.

Mrs Y had been told that analysis was a painful treatment and she thus knew that if she was upset and hurt I was a good analyst and was doing my job properly. I would therefore be happy, so she was content. Although I was seen as an ugly hunchback she did not mind; in fact, her hostility and envy of me was thus diminished. I was felt to be near to her when she was upset and she felt adequate so long as this situation continued. According to the patient her brothers and her mother and father were all intelligent and she was the stupid member of the family. However, during the analysis she felt that if she understood me and I was willing to work with her she could not be so stupid after all; otherwise I would be bored with her. To her stupid meant castrated.

However, she could not bear it if I showed her the oedipal conflicts expressed in her dreams, not when her dreams and associations led us to her earlier experiences with her mother. Still more difficult was it for her when I linked the conflicts of these early years with the conflicts she was having in her present life with her husband and with her lover. When these interpretations were made she got confused, felt attacked, and could not understand me. In spite of this she continued to give me dreams and associations in which her present life was connected with her past and with the frozen, isolated part of her inner world which represented her mother. I tried to help her feel sorrow and her need to warm her mother, but this also made her feel that I was attacking her and was angry with her; and that I too would therefore become distant. She could not accept or really understand the meaning of my words; they became part of the isolated, frozen past. One day, however, she dreamt about her search for a penis and went to buy one at the chemist's shop. With this she could warm up her mother: she was then able to remember some of her mother's clothes, the contents of her cupboards and the books on her shelves; these representations of her mother gradually became familiar objects, and not part of the frozen mother inside her. When these became loved and grieved over she began to take her memories of her mother out of cold storage.

Mrs Y always dreamt profusely and usually wept when telling me her dreams; however, one day she came into the room looking happier than usual and told me that she had a truly marvellous dream – quite different from the usual ones.

It was about a piece of marvellous velvet, the most beautiful material, texture, colour, she had ever seen; but it was not hers. It was Hope's (the name of a friend of hers). Here the patient wept. She, the patient, could not have the velvet, or touch or stroke it, unless she were Hope – and she was not. 'But still', she said, 'it was a marvellous dream. I never imagined such beautiful stuff.' She then spoke about her mother and soon realized that the velvet represented her mother's body. She went on to speak about her father's attitude to her mother when she (the mother) was 'blue' (her phrase – I did not yet know the colour of the velvet which was first said to be golden, but later became a lovely blue colour like her mother's eyes). Father could do nothing for mother and so when she was depressed he used to go to his shed and mend his boat. The patient then wept again, and spoke about hopelessness. No one could cure or soothe or stroke her mother – only Hope could stroke her. Later in the same session Mrs Y spoke about her lover who often stroked her but did not touch his own wife; nor could she let her husband touch her.

The meaning of this dream was, of course, over-determined: it proved a turning point in the analysis which for some time became centred on the theme of hopelessness. This was connected with not being able to help or care for or satisfy mother, or to get near to her. I, the analyst, was no longer seen as the angry hunchback, and gradually the frozen isolated part of the patient, the unloved frozen mother, receded. Mrs Y later began to form relationships with women and she cared for an old, angry woman whom she tended before she died. Later still she was able to let her husband leave her. This involved being able to release him and let *him* give up the hopeless relationship with her and his hope of pleasing her. She is still in analysis and is discovering what it is like to be a woman and to be able to relate to the world – which involves giving up her relationship with unhelpable people – and to be able to receive help from the analyst.

Theoretically the question is: was Mrs Y's inability to accept and give satisfaction to her husband based on the early failure with the depressed mother who fed her? Did she in this way act out and preserve her relationship with her mother, so that her husband had to relate to her as she had related to her mother and was not allowed to warm her or leave her? Or were her strivings based on a later structure, the result of her oedipal wish to have her father and give up her attachment of her mother? Her relationship with her husband enabled her to postpone the acceptance of her failure to revive her mother, and her relationship with her analyst enabled her to deny her failure to be nourished by her. She had first to feel the hopelessness and then give up centring her life around it before she could give up her hostility and fear and perhaps reach the depressive position, thus making reparation possible.

THEORETICAL CONSIDERATIONS

I have presented material to illustrate some of the difficulties encountered by a woman analyst when analysing women patients whose mothers were either depressed or withdrawn. These patients' main preoccupation is with the satisfaction of their mothers without giving up their pleasure in their genitals with which they satisfy men. They enjoy and value their vaginas but not their total femininity. This dual aim (the satisfaction both of their mothers and of men) necessitates: (a) a denial of castration; (b) the undervaluing of husbands, who represent fathers; (c) a particular form of relationship with the women who, they feel, do not have the sexual pleasure they have. They have a horror of touching these women but want to render them harmless and to warm or stimulate them.

My thesis is that a state of primitive concern is one factor in the structure of human relationships and can be reached during the analysis of some patients once their defences against their hostility, their reaction formations to their aggressive tendencies, and a period of hopelessness are overcome. Their early primitive emotional feelings can then be used in mature object relationships.[1]

It is open to question whether these patients should be thought of as latent homosexuals. In my opinion they should not because, although they are preoccupied with women, this is more because of their love and fear and pity for their mothers and their wish to keep them alive, than because of their libidinal drives, which are directed towards men.

In the analysis, these patients have first to accept that they cannot satisfy their mothers sexually: they then internalize them (if they have not already done so) and feel love and concern for their introjects. Lastly, they have to go through a period of hopelessness and grief because their love and concern are useless to their mothers. They do not then turn to another woman to satisfy sexually, but find other women to care for and love. I do not see this as connected mainly with guilt feelings. They can also then form loving and not only sexual erotic relationships with their husbands. It should once again be noted that these women do not turn to women for sexual or body satisfaction. They relate to women as love objects – and objects for mutual concern – but not mainly as drive-satisfying objects.

These patients illustrate the technical difficulties inherent in the analysis by a woman analyst of those women patients whose preoccupation it is to satisfy a depressed mother while having sexual lives of their own. I have tried to show how difficult it is to follow the threads of their instinctual life and how these run parallel with the ego's struggle to maintain its object relationship. The analyst has to understand the conflicts appropriate to the oedipal and pre-oedipal phases and see how they relate to the primitive object relationships in which the origins of mutual concern can be traced. In the patients I describe the instinctual drives do not deviate but their failure to satisfy their mothers is acted out in their relationships with their husbands and lovers, who are kept as necessary but only partially satisfying objects, and with their analysts whom they feel they can satisfy for ever. I have emphasized these patients' needs to care for their mothers and not what I assume to be the earlier need to be cared for by them.

Before summarizing this chapter I want to make an attempt at some generalizations, in order to give a partial answer to the question in my title – 'What does a woman want?' I am (I think rightly) afraid of generalizations because I believe they tend to blur the clinical material on which they are based and inevitably omit many important issues, but perhaps it is appropriate at this stage to try to make some.

I suggest that women want, in their relationships both with men and with women, to use that primitive structure in human relations, namely the capacity for mutual concern. Owing to its primitive nature it can only be satisfactorily expressed by the body itself, or by feelings in the body based on inner representations of the body and by body memories. The vagina is that part of a woman's body which is felt to be the most important area with which to express mutual concern with men (this does not exclude the use of the rest of her body). However, in her relation to women she is at a loss to know how to express it unless she has herself introjected and identified with a woman's body which satisfied her and which she felt she satisfied when she was an infant. I assume that if she was satisfied by her mother's body she rightly felt that her own body satisfied her mother. I do not think it is adequate to think in terms of identification with parts of a woman's body or of the environment created by the mother. Furthermore, I suggest that unless a woman can experience mutual concern with women her relationship with men is likely to be impoverished and men may be undervalued and not experienced as objects for mutual concern.

SUMMARY

1 Some technical problems connected with a woman's attachment to her mother in adult life can be hard to detect by a woman analyst in the analysis of women patients, but if not detected can hold up treatment and the analysis can become repetitive.

2 This tendency shows itself in many ways. For instance, the most important part of the session can be the way the patient comes into and leaves the analyst's room, and the verbal communication is meaningless unless the real meaning of entering the room is understood.

3 The patient's feeling that the analyst looks to the patient for satisfaction and is excited by her has to be understood not only in terms of a wish to satisfy the mother and the analyst, but also as the method the patient adopts in order to keep her own femininity, and prevent the mother from being too envious of her as the possessor of an exciting, excited vagina, which she feels her mother does not have and which is useless in relation to her mother.

4 This can be understood as a form of latent homosexuality but arguments have been put forward to suggest that the heterosexual strivings are primary and are not a defence against homosexuality. The wish to care for the mother arises partly because she (the mother) was depressed or withdrawn

when they were young, and partly because of the hostilities of the oedipal phase. These women are able to do so after some analysis because there was some early object who cared for them and once the reaction formations against hostility have been overcome.

Such patients do not repress their heterosexual drives and the pleasures their vaginas can give to men. In spite of this they can be seen to centre their lives around their mothers and to choose their husbands in order to repeat a pattern that they had with their mothers, in which they, like their mothers, cannot be satisfied. At the same time they secretly satisfy other men, not their husbands. It is possible that this also repeats the pattern which they had as children when they satisfied their brothers. In consequence the lives of these women are split into two apparently disconnected parts in which women are valued but unsatisfied and unsatisfiable, and men are undervalued but some are satisfied and satisfiable.

NOTE

1 John Klauber made a valuable contribution to this chapter when I read it to the British Psycho-Analytical Society and gave me permission to refer to his ideas. He restated the underlying problem as being connected with the way the judgements of the ego impose themselves on the drives and with the important role played by the ego in coming to terms with the realities of the mother's character. This in turn he saw as depending on the basic health in the child which can survive the bad parts of its early experiences and eventually utilize the good parts for mature object relationships.

REFERENCES

Deutsch, H. (1946) *The Psychology of Women, Vol. 1: Girlhood*, London: Research Books.
Freud, S. (1923) 'The ego and the id', *S. E.* 19: 12–59.
—— (1925) 'Some psychical consequences of the anatomical distinction between the sexes', *S. E.* 19: 248–258.
—— (1926) 'The question of lay analysis', *S. E.* 20: 183–258.
—— (1931) 'Female sexuality', *S. E.* 21: 225–243.
Lampl-de Groot, A. (1928) 'The evolution of the Oedipus complex in women', *Int. J. Psychoanal.* 9: 332–345.
Strachey, J. (1961) Editor's note on 'Some psychical consequences of the anatomical distinction between the sexes', in S. Freud, *S. E.* 19: 243–247.

Chapter 2

Female to female

The symbiotic loneliness

Maria A. Tallandini

> Ultimately each one of us experiences only one conflict in life which
> constantly reappears under different guise.
> (Rainer Maria Rilke: letter to Comtess M., 10 March 1921)

A common experience in the treatment of female patients is meeting with a
variety of feelings all of which end with complaints of a state of deficiency,
incapacity, and helplessness. This common set of feelings has different
origins and reasons. Torok (1964) points to the peculiarity of these states of
mind in women and suggests that they relate to the nature of their sex.
Frequently in the analysis of women we find that women think they have this
experience of an inner void, an absence of power, an inability to stand up for
themselves, because of their s˙x

I will present the case of a patient who had all the correlates of a sense of
incapacity, neediness, inhibition, anxiety, depression, but who did not relate
any of these symptoms to being a woman. I see these difficulties as related
to her sense of incompleteness, lack of omnipotence, and her desperate
resistance in acknowledging separation from the mother and therefore of
mother's relationship with the father.

Breen (1993) has rightly pointed out that 'masculine' and 'feminine' refer
to the way in which each individual deals with the recognition of that
difference. I intend to show how the process of individuation (Mahler *et al.*,
1975) can prove to be a strong obstacle in acknowledging the presence of the
third. This difficulty is repeated inside the analytic situation and the same
gender of analyst and analysand can be of help in the reproduction of the
maternal transference and fusional state, but can also make it more difficult
to move forwards.

Mahler *et al.* (1975) described the process of separation-individuation
during the first three years of life. In their view this process allows the
individual to acquire the capacity for autonomy and independence. On this
subject Mahler says:

> the term symbiosis ... is a metaphor. ... It describes that state of
> indifferentiation, of fusion with mother, in which 'I' is not yet differentiated

from the 'not I' and in which inside and outside are only gradually sensed as different. Any unpleasurable perception external or internal is projected beyond the common boundary. . . . *The essential feature of symbiosis is hallucinatory or delusional somatopsychic omnipotent fusion with the representation of the mother and, in particular, the delusion of a common boundary between two physically separate individuals.* (my italics) (pp. 44–45)

The symbiotic phase, in all its aspects, needs to be elaborated before giving way to the presence of a real separation-individuation.

I shall present a patient who appeared to stay in the symbiotic phase expressing in the transference love and hate for the omnipotent and fusional mother. This patient denied the existence of the third in order to keep her illusion of omnipotent fusion with the mother intact. This fusion implies the possession of the mother and mother's satisfaction.

What influence does the gender of the analyst have on the psychoanalytic encounter when both components of the couple are of the female gender and the primary conflict they have to face is a specific female conflict? This question becomes further complicated and puzzling because, in the analytic situation, the sex of the analyst is supposed to be 'obliterated' by thoughts, fantasies, and emotions projected by the patient on to the analyst. Moreover, the analyst is supposed to be above his or her biological and cultural background and stands in complete neutrality before the patient's material.

More recently this claim has been widely disputed, e.g. by Sandler (1976) and Blum (1971), who see the transference as influenced by the reality present within the analytic situation. Others (Gill and Hoffman, 1982) see the actuality of the therapist's personality and the patient's view of it as a way to build upon and define the transference itself. In this context the analyst's gender assumes a role that shapes many aspects of the transference. Freud (1912) repeatedly questioned the absence of gender in the unfolding of the transference. He observed (1915) that male patients had a greater tendency than female patients for a hostile transference to him. He thought this was due to his being male. Freud (1931) also believed that some transference resistances in his analyses of women were a result of his sex. He suggested that the sex of the analyst may make a difference in the intensity of certain transference feelings since pre-oedipal maternal transferences were more prominent in analyses conducted by female analysts.

Gender differences in psychoanalytic treatment have only recently become the focus of clinical research and exploration. A number of observers (Person, 1985; Meyers, 1986; Moldawsky, 1986) have explored differences within the four possible gender dyads and have found that initial transference, transference sequences, and the relative length and intensity of various transference manifestations are indeed influenced by the gender of the analyst.

Kirshner *et al.* (1982) conclude that vulnerability to gender-related feelings and stereotypes is more pronounced in younger and less experienced therapists. Person (1983) thinks that the female patient's conscious choice of a female rather than a male analyst is motivated by a variety of factors, including a fear of sexism, a wish to avoid secrecy due to shame, and the desire for a role model.

Despite the salience of oedipal issues in the female–female dyad, pre-oedipal issues are frequently even more central. Gornick (1994) notes that a female analyst will both evoke in her patient and expect of herself qualities of maternal aptitude and caretaking associated with the female gender role, which result in a pull towards a relatively greater regressive therapeutic experience and a loosening of boundaries for both therapist and patient. Meyers (1986) observes that, for patients of either gender, pre-oedipal maternal transference is more easily established with female as opposed to male therapists. Because the gender of the female therapist and female patient repeats the original mother–daughter dyad, it creates the potential for 'some of the most archaic, dangerous, and potentially healing conflicts within treatment' (Bernstein, 1991). There is a pull towards regression and relatively fluid boundaries for both analyst and patient; regression to a pre-ambivalent symbiotic-like state as a defence against envy, competition, and rivalry.

Gender is an issue that deeply influences transference and counter-transference. This influence can support the analytic work (Chasseguet-Smirgel, 1984) or vice versa can be reason for difficulty and impasse.

Very little empirical research has been carried out on the influence of the psychoanalyst's gender upon different aspects of the psychoanalytic process, such as quality of the transference, content of material, and sequence of developmental conflicts during the course of treatment.

Kulish and Mayman (1983) have conducted an interesting analysis on verbal reports given by psychotherapists about analytically oriented psychotherapy. Therapists were interviewed about two of their cases, preferably one male and one female. The interviews were conducted over a period of two years, at four and six month intervals. The aim was to detect the emergence of a specific transference during the therapy. This research is particularly interesting because it takes into account the countertransference and its gender connection. The material provided by the psychotherapists was evaluated separately by two judges who interpreted the transference material without knowing the evaluations expressed by the therapists. The results supported some views already found in the clinical material, namely that patients have a strong inclination to develop an initial transference consistent with the therapist's gender; in the presence of an opposite gender dyad, therapists, especially female therapists, have a strong bias against perceiving themselves in the opposite gender role. Perhaps therapists encourage the development of gender consistent transferences.

Kulish and Mayman conclude that the therapist's gender, the aspect of reality that the patient unquestionably knows, exerts a strong pull upon the patient who initially perceives the therapist in terms consistent with that reality. Equally, the therapist begins to process the patient's material in terms of his/her own gender. These results apply to psychotherapy; currently there is no data on psychoanalytic treatment. It is possible that the gender bias is less influential in long term treatment.

I will present the case of a patient where the female gender of the analyst seems to have deeply influenced the process of treatment.

Mrs R

Mrs R asked for analysis at the age of 26. Her motivation was a generalized discomfort and a situation of crisis with her husband that has lasted for some years. She was working as a teacher and was married to an academic at the start of his career.

When Mrs R came for consultation, she reported being withdrawn and apathetic in all spheres of her life, without any push for new developments. Professionally she was reducing her work to embrace only passive situations, too fearful to stimulate or propose new projects. Like many other women (Torok, 1964), she was renouncing all creative activities.

With dark hair, cut very short, a slim figure dressed in an untidy way, she gives the impression of being rather shabby and unkempt. I thought that she could even be not very clean. Her movements are slow, hampered, stiff, as if she dreaded being looked at. Her body expresses a deep lack of comfort. She speaks slowly, in a deadpan voice, without emphasis, expressing uneasiness, her difficulties in dealing with day-to-day life. Her marriage is on the verge of collapse.

Her words give a picture of a childhood and adolescence under the sign of women's presence. She is the third of six children, five girls and a boy. The brother was born two years after the patient and, eight years later, the youngest sister arrived on whom Mrs R focused all her hostility because she felt she took her place.

The mother was the domineering figure in the family. Mrs R describes her in an adoring tone of voice in which is present nostalgia, loss, and in which, from time to time, a note of bitterness appears. Mother is beautiful, clever, always extremely busy. She organizes the house, the children, and helps her husband in the trade that provides them with a good standard of living. Mother expresses very clearly her domineering position: she makes it explicit that the house in which they live is *her* family house, and that *she* comes from a higher social class than her husband. Mrs R recounts this with conviction and it is immediately evident that the father is a weak figure, never centre stage. He was allowed to bring up the boy, while mother stayed with the daughters. The mother did not mind showing her power inside the family and towards the father. She often imposed her will and her opinion was prevalent. For example, she prohibited father's relatives from access to the house, whereas she allowed her own relatives to actually live in the family home. She hosted two old aunts in a separate part of the family home, and a sister who only left when, in her forties, she married. This aunt participated in the childhood of nieces and nephew and has kept strong links with the family ever since.

In this matriarchal world, the male figures are faded, almost non-existent. Father is never prominent and seems to avoid any engagement. The home is mother's and Mrs R accepts her authority even if, in doing so, she might alienate her sisters. She recognizes her mother's authority and does not hesitate to pass on her sisters' secrets, breaking her alliance with them.

The focus of her attention, the centre of her world, is mother, her object of love.

The parental economic situation, good for many years, suddenly collapsed. The mother did not hide her anger towards her husband and openly accused him of weakness and ineptitude. Mrs R recounts all this without any sympathy for him. Even now, at the beginning of analysis, she still shares her mother's opinion which is unquestioned and impermeable.

The crisis was precipitated by two tragic events which cast some doubt on Mrs R's conviction about the general set-up of the family. While Mrs R was on holiday with sisters and brother, father suddenly died. The tragic news did not reach them at their holiday resort due to a failure of communication, and when they returned home they found the house locked, nobody there. The mother had been unable to bear staying at home by herself after this tragic event and left, careless of what her children, upon returning, would experience. One year later, the mother was affected by cancer. She did not struggle against her illness, and the patient assisted, impotent and angry to her death.

Mrs R's attachment to her mother has never ceased, nor has her sexual aims towards mother, and her longing for an exclusive relationship that keeps the rest of the world at bay. Lample-de Groot (1928) indicated the immense difficulty a girl has in giving up possession of her mother and changing from possessing her to having her as a loved object to be identified with. But, while Lampl-de Groot thinks that the little girl feels that the possession of her mother can only be maintained if she, the girl, has a penis, it seems to me that the material from my patient indicates the endurance of a belief that her mother has a penis, who is so powerful that she (Mrs R) castrated her father who is humiliated and deprived of any power.

It follows that she cannot form any relationship with men. She could get involved with men or marry, but as soon as this did happen she put her husband into a humiliating position. These women are so deeply attached to the mother that any possibility of an independent relationship is forbidden. The absence of the father makes separation from the mother impossible as it is only his presence that makes separation necessary (Chasseguet-Smirgel,

1984). The real preoccupation for such women remains with women and how to care for and satisfy them (Balint, 1973). This position does not result in a homosexual relationship as this would be a great disappointment. These patients want to deny mother's lack of a penis in order to recognize the importance of their own vagina. The most important issue is the fact that attachment with the mother has the general characteristic of achieving the complete fulfilment of the wishes of both.

Helene Deutsch (1946) has described the woman's urge to remain under mother's protection. She also sees this attachment continuing throughout adult life. If the little girl cannot successfully detach herself from her mother, she will continue to need, even in adult life, a considerable amount of tenderness and motherly protection and will find life unbearable without it (Deutsch, 1946). These women regard a partner more as a protector than a person with whom they can share an equal adult relationship (Pines, 1982). In this way they can deny the existence of the male and of his penis. To recognize it is to inflict an unbearable offence on the mother as it would mean recognizing her as being female. This would be equally unbearable for the patient herself as it would signify losing her capacity to satisfy her object of love through her vagina.

One of the characteristics of Mrs R was that she denied any possible satisfaction of her mother from her father. She remembers her indifference towards her father's death. She thought immediately she would *dedicate* herself to her mother. As E. Balint (1973) points out, she denied hostility, envy, and rivalry towards her mother. In her married life Mrs R never wanted to take any responsibility in her home and she refused to have children. Only inside the analysis did her hostility towards her mother surface, considering mother as a traitor because of her link with her father.

THE DESERT OF THE SYMBIOSIS

Mrs R began the analysis showing a very strong resistance. She lay immobile and tense, with no words even to answer my tentative smoothing of her difficulties. After several sessions, she brought a dream: 'A flame was attacking my face. I was terrified. What will I find here? I feel you are terrible. . . . I made another dream in which you were a sweet and good person, bringing a bunch of flowers.' She is telling me her fear that the analysis could burn and dissolve her mask, revealing both her hate and her love towards the analyst representing here her maternal image. But more than that, she is terrified that analysis could make her external face vanish, and reveal the fragility of her image. The dream could refer to 'losing face' and the consequent shame.

To 'lose face' would mean to acknowledge the existence of another continent, the male one, and women as a different part of humanity, lacking a penis. In fact, in her illusory representation of the powerful mother, there is a denied awareness of this difference. Mrs R wanted to have a female analyst for reasons she did not specify at the beginning of the treatment but that appeared later to be a choice that could collude with her internal fragile illusion. She chose a woman as her analyst because women were the only humans who were 'real' to her (Shainess, 1983). Nevertheless, analysis is seen as a terrible danger because it could make the reality clear.

The first two years of her analysis are characterized by obstructionism. Mrs R speaks a lot but it is a monologue in which the voice of the other, the analyst, has no room. She recounts intimate feelings and thoughts but uses them to exclude the analyst. Any intervention from the analyst seems to put a stop to a river of sounds. Mrs R becomes suddenly silent, and then again begins to speak, as if nothing had happened. Only after some years of analysis does she tell me that at the beginning she would not acknowledge my presence; I was a person at a great distance, of whom she was frightened. Later on she thought she was speaking in front of a mirror, or as if she was in an echoing grotto, as if nobody was there but, at the same time, somebody was. There was a looming shadow from whom she had to shelter. She could not understand anything. She was feeling alone and at the mercy of her emotions. The narcissistic situation prevails; the patient regresses in this unreal world where her omnipotence is kept intact.

My words fall on empty space; they are incomprehensible: 'I feel as if I were at the theatre, without knowing what the play is.' The interpretation of her wish to exclude me but also the great pain of having to face her fears alone finally find a breach. For the first time, she listens to my words. She tells me that analysis for her is a continuous battle – she leaves each session exhausted. And she asks me: 'And for you?' For the first time she can notice my presence as a different human being.

Her narcissistic retreat gives way to a strong ambivalence. She feels as if I am ambushing her when she comes to the session. She projects her aggression on to the analyst who is seen as a persecutory object, and as a hated mother. The patient protests about the time of the sessions, their length. 'How can you think that I can talk about myself within the confines of *your* schedule?' The couch, the analysis, myself, are a mother deeply loved but also hated because of mother's betrayal. The betrayal is not the fact of going with a man in itself, but showing through this choice the existence of another sex, different from the female one. In this way the mother shows the lack of a penis in the little girl, and how the little girl's vagina cannot satisfy mother's needs.

Mrs R remembers that she was the favoured one, always afraid of losing her privileged position. She never confronted her mother, and only aimed to have her approval; for this reason she was always at mother's side, against siblings and father. This complete dependence was, of course, accompanied by aggression and acute ambivalence, always on the verge of losing her mother's love, with the consequent collapse of her internal *and* external world. The early erotic tie to her mother is prevented from emerging inside the analysis through the mobilization of her anger (McDougall, 1964).

The wish to possess her mother's body and, at the same time, her curiosity about it, appears in a memory from her childhood.

> We used to go to the seaside during the summer and I remember my pleasure in touching the sand with my body and watching the naked women. My mother didn't put on her swimming costume, she was always completely dressed. I loved to watch these naked women. When I was 6, 8 years old, other children used to go to watch the women getting undressed through the cracks of the bathing huts. At the time I was asking myself if my mother was like these other women.

She would have liked to do the same but was held back by her mother's disapproval and anger.

She feels I disapprove of her. I realize that my gender was not brought into the analytic setting either by her or by myself. This aspect of reality has been kept collusively silent; both I and my patient are bound up by our manifest sex (Kulish, 1986) which is being used by both of us as a way of strengthening the defences so that we cannot see beyond it.

Symbiosis with mother gives her a safe haven, she feels protected and omnipotent. At the same time she is perpetually in danger of intrusion from the external world and prisoner of the dyad. Her wish for autonomy appears and is a reason for conflict. She brings a dream: 'There was a war, riots, I was sat in a corner and a soldier was holding a pistol to my forehead. He was threatening to kill me. I was frightened of dying.'

The war, the riots, are the changes that are beginning to happen in her mind. I am the mother who menaces her if she goes beyond the symbiotic stage and allows herself autonomy, and the analyst-mother who menaces her, pushing her towards autonomy and therefore death.

In her fantasy, the wish for independence and autonomy has the effect of calling up her mother who, as warden, will not let her free herself. At the same time, the situation of symbiosis and omnipotent claustrophobia make her wish for mother's death. Mrs R feels that her wish for autonomy was responsible for her mother's death.

TOWARDS INDEPENDENCE

After the fourth summer break, Mrs R returns with different insights. She remembers how difficult it was for her to share her mother's attention with her sisters and how dramatic the youngest sister's birth had been for her. She still sees this event as the means of diverting mother's attention away from her, rather than as evidence of her mother's relationship with her father. Leaving the symbiotic state means to recognize her hostility towards me-mother, who is too busy to dedicate all my/mother's time to her. She protests against it and expresses her feeling of danger: 'All dependencies are dangerous.'

In this context she brings a dream: 'Somebody died at home. There was a very sad and desperate child who did not want to play.'

She considers the death of her mother to be the result of her step towards autonomy. Mrs R wants to get rid of me as she wanted to get rid of her omnipotent mother, but she feels her wish was responsible for her mother's death and eventually will be for mine. Bernstein and Warner (1984) summarized several cases of female patients seen by female analysts in which images of the analyst in the transference alternated at times between phallic mother and oedipal father or became condensed into one intrusive figure. They suggest that the sexualized homosexual transference which develops initially with certain of their female patients is pre-oedipal, as a defence against deep, early longings for the mother perceived as unavailable. Her hostile wishes and the fear of their consequences are expressed in an image of a statue that is disintegrating. This image represents her internal mother who is now seen from another perspective.

After five years of analysis, Mrs R begins to express fantasies about my personal life and notices sounds coming from other parts of the house. This process proceeds through dramatic steps, as illustrated in this dream:

> I was in a wood with many trees, I was with my aunt [her mother's sister], her daughters, my sisters. A big black dog hurled itself upon me, using its teeth. He was pulling me around. My relatives tried to tear me away from its mouth but they did not succeed. In the end, the dog bashed me against a tree. It was unclear if I died or not.

She is frightened of recounting this dream in which she projects aggression towards me and sees me as this terrible dog, a persecutory father figure who takes her away from her female world (all the people present in the dream are female), attacking her peaceful and safe environment.

In another brief but significant dream, there is a woman who put her hand on Mrs R's heart. The hand is in fact inside her body and tears away her heart. This woman is again a condensed image of herself, myself, and her mother. Myself/mother are pulling out her heart, making her aware of separation and, therefore, of differences. After this dream Mrs R did not come to the following session, too frightened to show her aggression. When she comes back she does not deny her insight about this dream, she acknowledges her difficulties and the necessity of putting some distance between us.

TO BE IN LOVE

The following year Mrs R begins to be able to recognize her feelings of love towards me and, at the same time, her existence as an autonomous person.

> I have such intense feelings during the session. I see myself as one of my students [her students are 15–16 year olds], in love with their peers. I am very ashamed. It seems to me my body is too present here. I would like to be here only with my head. When I used to come back from school I would find my mother waiting for me. In the evening she was often so tired that she fell asleep. I liked to stay near her and watch her. My siblings used to go out to play in the courtyard. I preferred to stay near her.

The emergence from the symbiotic state permits Mrs R to look at her sexual feelings towards her mother. Only after this step is she able to speak of her periods, of her body, of her vagina. She is no longer only 'part of', she is a woman who recognizes her femininity.

After this discovery and after she recognizes her similarity to, *not* her complementarity with, the mother, she is able to bring her father into the analysis, with his positive connotations. Her father was not boring or heavy, he was able to stand up to her (Mrs R's) protests and tantrums; in a family argument he was able to address the central point of any question. I become her father's figure in an oedipal context.

'My little nephew is going to school this year. He has so many expectations. He will inevitably be disappointed.' Her nephew is herself, and her expectations, which she knows will be disappointed, are towards me-father who is now also an object of desire and competition with her sisters. 'I dreamt last night I was fighting with my sisters and, in the end, I decided to go away and stay with my father.'

The feelings of her betrayal towards her mother are nevertheless very strong:

> One of my students is lazy, unable to concentrate. I had a dream in which I was reproaching him for being, as I said, lazy and inattentive. He told me that the reason for his difficulties came from his mother's death. He told me that his mother died in 1980, and so I told him that both my parents were dead. [And she continues] I think I am this dazed child. Today I couldn't prepare my lectures because I felt very confused.

At this point, Mrs R has an insight and her body jerks: 'What happened to me in 1980 was not my mother's death, it was my wedding. . . . I would like to be a turtle, to clutch myself inside my carapace.'

Her wedding is seen as the definite death of her mother. Mrs R's wish for a man is seen as responsible for it. Her powerful mother who could satisfy her needs and whose needs she was able to satisfy, would disappear because she was acknowledging different needs and looking outside the dyad in which love and satisfaction could come only from a mother provided with her father's penis.

After years of analysis, Mrs R recognizes that her difficulties with her husband began when she refused to have intercourse with him and she decided to go away with a group of women. She expected to find satisfaction with them by excluding the presence of a male figure and paying this tribute to her mother. Nevertheless the oedipal wishes were present:

> I had a dream in which my father was answering a telephone call. I was a girl, 7–8 years old, and I was admiring him. At a certain point of the conversation, my father said his surname, but in fact he said my husband's surname.

The oedipal components, i.e. her love and desire for her father, appear evident in this dream in which her father is taking her husband's place. However, the fear of losing and disappointing her mother had made her deny these wishes towards her father. These had been allowed to appear again only when she could proceed in her differentiation process. Differentiation meant, in this case, seeing the similarity between mother and daughter.

DISCUSSION

I have presented material to illustrate some difficulties encountered by a woman analyst when analysing a female patient, where the patient uses the symbiotic relationship to deny her eroticized relationship with her mother, in this case not a homosexual relationship but a fantasized heterosexual relationship that permitted her to deny the father's presence.

McDougall (1964) supported the idea that the wish for a penis is also seen as expressing the wish to repair the mother and remain the object of her desire. What can be seen in Mrs R is her giving to the mother the father's attributes for the same purpose, i.e., to remain the object of mother's desire.

Limentani (1991) notes the absence of the father from the material on his work with sexual deviants which he describes as a 'lack of internalization of the father'. Although my patient was not a sexual deviant, the complete absence of the father figure in the clinical material until the last stage of the analytic treatment seems to indicate a splitting and a denial of this figure that can be better considered as a refusal to accept the representation of the father (Breen, 1993) in accordance with the refusal to accept the parental relationship (Britton, 1989).

Mrs R was stuck in, or she had regressed to, a pre-oedipal position in which she excluded the presence of her father, castrating him and giving her father's penis as a splendid gift to her mother. In this way, she could further two aims: (1) she substituted the mother for the father, and (2) she hoped to obtain a mother to whom she could give satisfaction because she (the patient) owns a vagina. Thus her experiences of helplessness and deficiency are not linked to being female because through her vagina she could express her power over her mother. This fantasy was accompanied by the illusion of being in complete fusion with the mother, and the result was the exclusion of any male figure; males were simply denied as an entity.

Mother provided for all Mrs R's needs but, for the same reason, she (mother) held all rights and all the power. She was the feeding mother but also the devouring mother who would permit no distraction from her and required an absolute fidelity. Mrs R had reduced her life to nothing in order to obey this dictate, having to hide her wish for independence and an autonomous life.

The crisis came when the death of the father brought into focus mother's affection and dependence on him, showing the importance of the male figure for her mother. The patient found herself completely deprived of her illusory power because, tragically, the mother died soon after the father, as if life did not have any importance for her without him.

Only after having allowed herself out of the fusional state did paternal transference come into the treatment.

This process has been acknowledged by other analysts dealing with a female therapeutic couple. In particular, paternal or masculine images are more tied to the reality of the therapist's gender and are less likely to be experienced with a female therapist (Kulish, 1984; Karme, 1979).

The reality components of the setting can influence the way in which transference develops (Sandler, 1976) and gender is an important organizing factor both for the patient and the analyst (Kulish and Mayman, 1993). The female gender of the therapeutic couple presents a danger of regression to both analyst and analysand but the analytic situation in itself can be used as a protector (Chasseguet-Smirgel, 1984).

It seems that in this case the patient's basic conflict, the wish-fear for merger, may have been enhanced by the analyst's gender which made such conflict more intensive and persistent. From another point of view the reality of the analyst's gender may have facilitated transferential fantasies that needed to be elaborated. Only after a thorough analysis of her fusional state could Mrs R allow herself to recognize her oedipal wishes towards her father and free herself from the symbiotic and eroticized relationship with her mother.

REFERENCES

Balint, E. (1973) 'Technical problems found in the analysis of women by a woman analyst: a contribution to the question "What does a woman want?", *Int. J. Psychoanal.* 54(2): 195–201. See also Chapter 1 of this book.

Bergman, A. (1982) 'Consideration about the development of the girl during the separation-individuation process', in *Early Female Development: Current Psychoanalytic Views*, ed. D. Mendell, New York: S.P. Medical and Scientific Books, pp. 61–80.

Bernstein, D.H. (1990) 'Female genital anxieties, conflicts and typical mastery modes', *Int. J. Psychoanal.* 71 (1): 151–167.

—— (1991) 'Gender specific dangers in the female/female dyad in treatment', *Psychoanal. Rev.* 78 (1): 37–47.

Bernstein, D.H. and Warner, G.M. (1984) *Women Treating Women*, New York: International Universities Press.

Blum, H.P. (1971) 'On the conception and development of the transference neurosis', *J. Amer. Psychoanal. Assoc.* 19: 41–43.

Breen, D. (1993) *Gender Conundrum*, London: Routledge, Institute of Psycho-Analysis.

Britton, R. (1989) 'The missing link: parental sexuality in the oedipus complex', in *The Oedipus Complex Today*, ed. J. Steiner, London: Karnac.

Chasseguet-Smirgel, J. (1981) *Female Sexuality*, London: Virago.

—— (1984) 'The femininity of the analyst in professional practice', *Int. J. Psychoanal.* 68: 465–475.

Deutsch, H. (1946) *The Psychology of Women*, London: Research Books.

Freud, S. (1912) 'The dynamics of transference', *S.E.* 12: 97–108.

—— (1915) 'Observations on transference love', *S.E.* 12: 157–171.

—— (1931) 'Female sexuality', *S.E.* 21: 221–243.

Gill, M.M. and Hoffman, I.Z. (1982) 'A method for studying the analysis of aspects of the patient's experience of the relationship in psychoanalysis and psychotherapy', *J. Amer. Psychoanal. Assoc.* 30: 137–167.

Gornick, L. (1994) 'Women treating men: interview data from female psychotherapists', *J. Amer. Acad. Psychoanal.* 22 (2): 231–257.

Karme, L. (1979) 'The analysis of a male patient by a female analyst: the problem of the negative oedipal transference', *Int. J. Psychoanal.* 60: 253–261.

Kulish, N. (1983) 'Gender and transference: conversations with female analysts', *Psychoanalytic Psychology* 6(1): 59–71.

—— (1984) 'The effect of the sex of the analyst on transference', *Bulletin of the Menninger Clinic* 48: 95–110.

—— (1986) 'Gender and transference: the screen of the phallic mother', *Int. Rev. Psychoanal.* 13(4): 393–404.

Kulish, N. and Mayman, M. (1993) 'Gender-linked determinants of transference and countertransference in psychoanalytic psychotherapy', *Psychoanalytic Inquiry* 13(2): 286–305.

Lample-de Groot (1928) 'The evolution of the Oedipus complex in women', *Int. J. Psychoanal.* 9: 332–345.

Lester, E.P. (1985) 'On eroticised transference and resistance', *Int. J. Psychoanal. Psychother.* 11: 21–25.

—— (1993) 'Boundaries and gender: their interplay in the analytic situation', *Psychoanalytic Inquiry* 13(2): 153–172.

Limentani, A. (1991) 'Neglected fathers in the aetiology and treatment of sexual deviations', *Int. J. Psychoanal.* 72: 573–584.

Mahler, M., Pine, F. and Bergman, A. (1975) *The Psychological Birth of the Human Infant*, New York: Basic Books.

McDougall, J. (1964) 'Homosexuality in women', in *Female Sexuality*, ed. J. Chassequet-Smirgel, London: Virago (1981).

Meyers, H.C. (1986) 'Analytic work by and with women: the complexity and the challenge', in *Between Analyst and Patient: New Dimensions in Countertransference and Transference*, ed. H.C. Meyers, Hillsdale, NJ: The Analytic Press, pp. 153–176.

Moldawsky, S. (1986) 'When men are therapists to women: beyond the oedipal pale', in *New Psychoanalytic Visions*, eds T. Bermay and D. Cantor, Hillsdale, NJ: The Analytic Press.

Person, E.S. (1983) 'Women in therapy: therapist gender as a variable', *Int. Rev. Psychoanal.* 10: 183–204.

—— (1985) 'The erotic transference in women and men: differences and consequences', *J. Amer. Acad. Psychoanal.* 13: 153–180.

Pines, D. (1982) 'The relevance of early psychic development to pregnancy and abortion', in *A Woman's Unconscious Use of Her Body*, ed. D. Pines, London: Virago (1983).

Raphling, D.L. and Chused, J.F. (1988) 'Transference across gender links', *J. Amer. Psychoanal. Assoc.* 36(1): 77–104.

Sandler, J. (1976) 'Countertransference and role responsiveness', *Int. J. Psychoanal.* 3: 43–47.

Shainess, N. (1983) 'Significance of match in sex of analyst and patient', *American Journal of Psychoanalysis* 43(3): 205–217.

Torok, M. (1964) 'The significance of penis envy in women', in *Female Sexuality*, ed. J. Chasseguet-Smirgel, London: Virago (1981).

Chapter 3

'To be – or not to be – here'

A woman's denial of time and memory

Rosine Jozef Perelberg

INTRODUCTION

It was in the middle of the fourth year of her analysis that Maria raised the question of 'to be here or not to be here'. It followed an interpretation I had formulated addressing what I felt was the central dilemma for her at that time. I had said that as she allowed herself to get more in touch with her murderous and violent feelings towards me, she had to paralyse her body and experience it as incapacitated, because she was terrified of becoming out of control. I said that she felt tortured by this conflict. To be here in the session with me was to get in touch with feelings that she felt could have dangerous consequences for both of us since she feared she would feel like committing murder; not to be here, however, was to condemn herself to feeling trapped by these feelings and beliefs about herself for ever.

Since the very beginning of this analysis, now in its eighth year, I have been consistently struck by the two-dimensionality that followed my patient into the consulting room. In her two-dimensionality the past is eradicated, a sense of time and history which is so central for the constitution of the subject is also lost.[1] My patient's world has to be repetitive so that the experience of differences is avoided: differences between past and present, male and female, inside and outside, love and hate, her and me. The past was privileged as opposed to the present and future. This past, however, was presented in a reified, stilted way, through repetitive and predictable accounts which contained no enlargement or new information. It had no depth and was simply presented as the opposite of now; events and sequences of events had no place. From that perspective I would like to suggest that my patient has 'screen memories', as opposed to memories (Freud, 1899). What differentiates the two is the process of condensation and overdetermination that is present in the selection of these memories. In his editorial introduction to the work Strachey indicated that the use that Freud makes of this notion is that in which 'an earlier memory is used to fit a later event' (p. 302), as well as one in which an earlier event is screened by a later memory. I will indicate my understanding of the way in which my patient makes use of her screen memories to cover both the past and the present, holding on to an experience of time that stresses trauma instead of history.

When my patient came to analysis there was a specific moment in her life – an unhappy love relationship in her early twenties – to which she repeatedly returned. If, on the one hand, this process represented an attempt to understand something which had until then been unintelligible, it also had a defensive function. The account of her history was reduced to this point, the underlying phantasy being that there was no past that had preceded it and that thirty-five years had not gone by since then. Her stereotyped accounts surrounding this event served both as a screen for later events, including her experience of her analysis, and as elaborations of early childhood experiences.

It is within this framework of a lack of historicity, where events have to be presented as frozen and encapsulated in a stilted way, that I have understood Maria's two accidents since she started her analysis. On the first anniversary of beginning her analysis Maria had an accident on a motorbike whilst on holiday; on the second anniversary she had a crash whilst on holiday abroad in which her car was completely destroyed.

Granel (1987) has discussed the unconscious processes that precede, accompany and follow accidents. They show that 'in many cases the situation preceding the accident is characterised by an unbearable state that cannot be worked over in the form of a representation. The unsolvable drama of the internal world is replaced by real drama (accident)'. Having an accident is an attempt to 'give form to the unformable'.

Since the accidents Maria has consistently attempted to relate her various feelings and experiences to them. My hypothesis is that the accidents have also become another screen on to which her beliefs about her life are projected. Granel has contrasted repetitive traumatophilia with analytic historicization which introduces a different perspective of temporality. I think that the accidents have expressed Maria's experience of the analysis itself as a major catastrophe in her life.

Bion (1970) considers that all processes of development inevitably involve catastrophic change. Such change is a configuration of circumstances linked together by violence, disorder and invariance. A 'new configuration' or a 'new idea' can only appear with disruptive force. The analytic attempt has been that of creating a narrative, a story, out of the enclosed and ritualized presentation of sameness.

The tension in this analysis has been that of engaging in a conversation in which it is very important for Maria to adhere to a specific version of reality – one which emphasizes accidents and processes in her body as opposed to her mind – and still have a sense of a working alliance that allows the therapeutic task to be carried out. I feel that I have had to undertake a double task. Whilst I formulate interpretations to Maria that seem to powerfully challenge her views of herself, I must, at the same time, understand that for her to stick to her views is akin to being able to remain alive. She is terrified that to experience herself in a relationship with me is to submit to my version of reality. As her mode of relating is so basically dominated by projections, she can only find in the other repetitions of herself. The tension in the analysis has thus been between my acceptance of her experiences, necessary for containment, and my retaining my own experience as an analyst. Sometimes this has proved almost impossible as interpretations would be followed by an attack of fury, an experience of a crash taking place in the consulting room in which I would feel as crushed as her car had been. I would suggest, however, that it has been our endurance of this contradiction between our views that has allowed her analysis to take place. The analysis has thus, paradoxically, been able to contain the unbearable, which is for her the traumatic experience of differences and the faint beginnings of an experience of becoming. Whilst I progressively attempted to formulate to myself my own thoughts about Maria, I also had consistently to communicate to her my understanding of how unbearable the process was for her. I will illustrate how these experiences have been manifested in the history of the analysis and how patterns have developed in the transference to me.

In the following section I will give a brief account of Maria's history and her idiom in the analysis.

BACKGROUND INFORMATION

Maria was in her early fifties when she came for her first consultation. She had a basic problem in establishing relationships and felt analysis could help her with that. In the previous five years she had experienced many physical ailments which included back pain, a stiff neck and stiffness in the jaws and legs. She had also had bleeding colitis. At that first consultation I already had an experience of a part of her 'not being there' and enquired about it, in an attempt to verify her experience of herself. She felt that since her relationship with Alex she had disconnected herself, a part of her never 'being there' again.

Maria is an attractive woman, with blonde hair and dark eyes, and appears much younger than her age. She was born in a Spanish-speaking country and is the eldest of three children, her sister being two years younger and her brother five and a half years younger. She remembers feeling jealous when her sister was born and thinking that her mother loved the new baby best. She feels that, throughout her childhood, her mother was never available to her, being a withdrawn and cold woman, unable to show affection either emotionally or physically. Progressively in her analysis we have had access to a deep terror of her mother. She has vague memories of her mother leaning towards her, screaming at her and trying to throttle her. Maria turned to her father from very early on, seeking his love and support, but was bitterly hurt by the realization that her mother always came first for him.

Her rage soon turned against herself and she started to attack her own body. This became an expression of her rage, loneliness and feelings of being unloved. Later on she experienced various illnesses and pains in her body and found that it was a way of engaging her mother into worrying and looking after her. The psychic pain began to be more systematically bypassed and to be transformed into bodily complaints. It was also a way of battering the body which she felt was so unloved by her mother.

Her attempts to leave home when she was 18 years old failed, and she returned to live with her parents. She fell in love with Alex, a Frenchman on holiday in her country. At the time she read in the newspaper about a man in the States who had raped and killed several women and said that she could well understand that someone could feel like that. Progressively in her analysis her terror emerged that she might have done something to this man she loved, and it became clear that her breakdown was also a way of protecting him.

She very much wanted to believe that this man could have saved her, but he became very angry with her and finally gave her up. She described her heart as broken. This became the point in her life she constantly returns to in her analysis, repetitively describing it in detail, almost in slow motion. Yet, very little extra content or information is given each time. My basic experience remains that fundamentally it is a most painful and terrorizing reality that Maria is trying to make sense of. Any interpretation I formulate to her about the present is immediately related back to that period in her life. She describes how she then 'disconnected' herself and experienced herself as becoming like the withdrawn, cold, hated mother of her childhood.

She finished college and embarked on a successful career. When she started analysis she registered for a course which would give her a university degree, which she succeeded in getting.

She told me at the first consultation that during the previous winter she had stayed in bed for six weeks. Her friends had become very worried about her, thinking that she was depressed, but she said she was actually *frozen* due to the coldness in the school where she worked. This concrete bodily experience indicates my patient's emphasis on her body as the locus for her experiences. The extended descriptions of her physiological and physical states became the stuff of which the sessions were made for years to come.

THE ANALYTIC PROCESS: THE PATIENT'S IDIOM

Throughout the first year of analysis Maria had a special idiom in which she expressed herself. The first sign of her presence was her deep cough, while still coming along the street, her long ring of my bell, her heavy steps climbing up the stairs while still coughing. She was consistently five minutes late and, when in the room, embarked on long monologues that made me feel very drowsy, sleepy and almost hypnotized. At times I felt bombarded by her in ways that felt intolerable.

An important clue that these feelings were related to something the patient was projecting onto me was expressed in the second dream she brought to analysis, a month into treatment. There were three women and a huge block of concrete suddenly fell on top of them. The women were completely flattened and then started to rush about crazily. Maria said it looked like a cartoon. She said it was a dream but it did not feel like a dream. She then said that perhaps this was what had happened to her when she was 18. In this session we talked about her experience that this had not felt like a dream because it was so integral to the way she felt – that she had lost her feelings and her three-dimensionality and had become flattened. It was also her experience of feeling disconnected from herself in the present, and of her way of relating to me, of flattening me in the sessions. I could then also understand the experience of having concrete inside my head.

The dream which 'had not felt like a dream' took on another layer of meaning, expressing a terror that she was going to be 'hit' by the analysis and would not be able to cope. Retrospectively this was also a prognostic dream, a description of what was going to happen both to herself and to the analytic process. Perhaps, too, the three women represented herself, her mother and the analyst, all flattened out of recognition.

During the first year of analysis some important themes emerged, which we worked on very slowly in the following years. We had access to these themes primarily via dreams which functioned as markers of what was happening for her in the analysis: her consistent lateness (which had a multitude of meanings), her rage towards her mother, her phantasy of violence in sexual intercourse, her sexual identity, her rage towards everybody (including me), her perceptions of her physical body (which included both her fear and rejection of her femininity and of the babies she might have been able to produce) and, ultimately, overriding all these previous themes, her beliefs of how dangerous it was to experience any feelings (either positive or negative) towards me.

In spite of a great deal of material slowly surfacing, the quality I had experienced in the first consultation remained – 'a part of her was not there'. She would not consciously remember things from one session to the next. I gradually learned to trust my experience that I could tell something about her state of mind by tracking my own feelings. I would suddenly feel more alert and we would then have a more vital exchange. This would usually last for about five minutes, reaching twenty-five minutes in only one specific session. It never lasted more than half a session in that first year. Some years later she was to refer to how she could remember how in that first year her heavy eyes just wanted to close.

She let me know, at the end of that first year, that she was feeling more alive. She had started to buy newspapers, something she had never done before in her life, and was also starting to do jobs in her house which she had completely neglected for years.

After the first summer break we increased from four to five sessions a week. Four weeks after the end of the break she had an accident on a motorbike while away on a holiday. During the following year this accident and the damage it did to her body became central to her analysis. She experienced a range of physical pains and related them to the accident. Her repetitiveness was relentless. My patient's sense of being misunderstood and not heard was profound. She spent most sessions on a raging crusade against almost everybody.

THE LANGUAGE OF ACCIDENTS

A year after the motorbike accident and two years after starting analysis, Maria was involved in a car crash whilst on holiday abroad in which a van hit her car at a junction. She told me that her car was a 'write off '. It is not possible for a non-medical analyst to assess the physical impact the accident had on Maria. My hypothesis, however, has been that the accidents have functioned like a screen on to which she has projected her own, condensed version of her history. The analysis has attempted to recover the unconscious processes that these accidents both express and may mask.

During the next year Maria became progressively worse, both in her state of mind and in her bodily symptoms. The GP sent her to many specialists for investigations but no one could find any evidence of physical illness. Her rage towards everybody for not being able to understand what was happening to her made her unreachable. She felt fragmented and persecuted. All the specialists consistently said that her problems were psychological in origin and she was infuriated since she said she was experiencing 'real' pain. In the sessions I was in despair about my capacity to make contact with her.

After the Easter break in the third year of her analysis, Maria came back with twitches in her body. Her body would be overtaken by a tremor, every twenty seconds or so. The atmosphere in the sessions was of absolute terror and despair. We both felt she was capable of violent behaviour either against me or herself at the time. Throughout that whole period I sat with her in the sessions, talking to her about her feelings about being with me. My experience was of profound precariousness. If I said too much, the risk was that she would actually attack me; if I left her too much on her own she might feel so despairing and abandoned that she could kill herself.

Eventually she managed to tell me about her fear that she would have to destroy my consulting room and throw all the furniture (and me) through the window. In the next session she told me about a film that she had seen the previous day. It was about twin brothers in the East End of London. They came from a working class background and had been very well looked after. Yet they had done terrible things, mugging people, murdering and raping. It made her feel she was like that because she too came from this sort of background and yet she had these terrible thoughts. She was shaken by violent tremors as she told me this.

She then said that similar twitching had preceded the breakdown she had twenty years ago because she had been unable to tell Alex all her thoughts about him at the time. My response was that she was telling me now how frightened she was of having violent feelings towards me. It was a precarious moment in the session. I thought that she was also feeling frightened of me – the twin brothers were *both* violent – and I said that she was perhaps frightened not only of her own violent feelings but that I might have them too. As soon as I said this she started to cry terribly, with great sobs; she gradually calmed down, but the twitches continued. She went back to talking about the pain which had preceded the twitching twenty years ago. I said I thought that she blurred emotional and physical pain and that she attempted to bypass emotional pain with physical pain.

A few weeks later she talked about her battles with her mother and how even now her mother did not accept that she (Maria) might like different things from her. I spoke to her about her experience that there was a battle with me about realities. She has a story about herself which is the story of the pains in her body and the accidents she has suffered. She wants to tell me about the pain in her back, in her skull, her jammed head, her twitching. She feels that at least in her ailments she is alive. She said that I had said this to her before. It was on the same day as James, her osteopath, had been spot on, although he usually was spot on. She did not feel I was usually spot on about her ailments, although I was usually right about everything else. She felt I was an expert, but not on her ailments. I said that perhaps she did not feel there really was anything else, so in effect she made me an expert on nothing. The following day she came saying she had thought a lot about the previous session. It had felt clear like a maths class, QED.

This was followed by a session on a Monday to which she came very excited. She felt her memory was starting to come back. She woke up and remembered a tune, something she had not been able to do for ages. She had gone to a party over the weekend and danced twice for the first time in many years. She was, however, twitching more. I related the twitching to her feeling excited and her anxiety about feeling too excited.

In the Friday session I again had a feeling of being bombarded by her which became almost intolerable at one point. I talked to her about how she wanted to show me what it felt like to be assaulted by a woman who was so entrenched in her own reality that nothing she could say or do would make an impact on that woman. She immediately related to what I said, saying that this was what it had felt like to be with her mother. She cried, making deep sobbing noises. A later material that she brought to the session allowed me to say to her that she experienced her twitching as the concrete experience of her contact with me, where she felt both excited and attacked by me. By the next session, the twitches had stopped.

After the summer the sessions took on a different quality. I felt that she was more able to be present in the sessions. She was twitching again, although it was much less severe and there were many fewer twitches. At one session she told me about her experience with Alex twenty years before, about being overwhelmed by her sexual feelings towards him and not knowing what to do with them. She talked about her confusion at the time between emotional and sexual feelings and the tremors preceding her breakdown. I felt it was possible to say to her then – perhaps that was the reason she felt she had to retreat emotionally, that she was afraid, if she became emotionally connected to me, she would experience uncontrollable sexual feelings; perhaps her current twitching was her experience of that, of a sexual connection with me.

She came to a session telling me how much she had enjoyed the film *Cinema Paradiso*. We were able to establish in that session not only that she felt she had to keep her anger out of the sessions, but her loving feelings too, just as in the film all the kissing scenes had been censored. She started to cry, saying that she had not thought of that and I was being so understanding. She could not handle it. She could feel herself becoming angry with me. She sobbed and talked again about something she had told me a couple of years before but which had been left untouched. She had to feel angry with me otherwise she would want to hurt my genitals because I had been so nice to her.

It was a painful moment in the session. She cried, saying it was so upsetting. She wanted to be nasty to me, to shake me. She felt that was what her mother used to do to her. She then had a memory of an expression on a woman's face. It was contorted and she remembered seeing a couple by a door. She did not know whether they were making love or whether it was rape. I said that for her they were the same; this made her frightened of any contact between us. I felt it was also difficult for her to talk about this because it made her feel it was so real. She was much calmer as she left.

As the fourth and fifth years of her analysis proceeded, Maria was progressively more able to be *psychically* present in the sessions. This was, however, paralleled by an increasing experience that her body was getting worse. She spent long periods in bed and only got up to come to her sessions (in the afternoon). I then addressed myself to this conflict – that as she was able to allow herself to get in touch with her thoughts she had to paralyse her body, experience it as incapacitated, because she was so terrified otherwise of being out of control. There followed a dream where she saw herself being held down by many people as she was wild and screaming, attempting to murder someone. I said that as she allowed herself to get more in touch with her murderous and violent feelings towards me, she had to incapacitate her body because she was terrified of becoming out of control. I said that she felt tortured by this conflict. To be here in the session with me was to get in touch with feelings that she felt could have dangerous consequences for both of us since she feared that she would feel like committing murder; not to be here, however, was to condemn herself to feeling trapped by these feelings and beliefs about herself for ever. She replied: 'To be here or not to be here, that is the question.' Then she started to cry saying she would rather do something to herself than hurt me.

She remembered a dream, where she had stuck a knife into an adder, which she explained was the only poisonous snake in Britain. She remembered that she saw one when she went to the zoo with her parents and they spent some time together in the snake house. Other associations led me to interpret her fear of the poisonous strength of her rage and her capacity to provoke other people to attack her; she was terrified of what she could provoke in me. This was an image of a primal couple, who were both lethal. I then said that this was what she believed happened in this room, that it was like the snake house. On the following day she came back feeling very disjointed although she also said she felt it was because she wanted to forget the previous session. She then started to cry and said it was very upsetting to think about what she must have put me through all these years. How must it have been for me to be with her in this room? In a subsequent session she said she felt I had helped her to remain alive.

Perhaps as an illustration both of current themes and of some progression within the analysis, it would be helpful to give some material from a recent session.

Maria arrived and told me excitedly that she had been to a performance of the opera 'Turandot' on the previous evening. She spoke graphically of the cold sadistic Queen and of the sacrifice of the slave girl who was tortured and then killed herself to protect her beloved prince Calaf. What was most striking in her spontaneous account, as opposed to the frozen, retentive communications for most of her analysis, was the liveliness with which she said: 'I felt that the Opera was telling my story, that I was the cruel Queen and that the self-sacrificing slave girl was the part of the Queen that she could not acknowledge as belonging to her.' In essence, I felt that Maria was telling me that there was not just a cold sadistic part of herself but a loving and devoted part that she was struggling to reach. My response to her was: 'You know, I think you are also telling me how frightened you are of owning that part of yourself which feels enslaved to me.' Maria's answer was: 'When you talk to me in this way I feel that I could cry for a million years.'

This then is the focus of our current work in the analysis: her struggle, in the transference, between sadism and revenge, as opposed to hope and even love.

SOME CLINICAL AND THEORETICAL REFLECTIONS

I would like to discuss two main issues in relation to this analysis:

1 The connection between the screen memories, accidents and the avoidance of time.
2 The language of the body: hysterical symptoms or traumatic events?

The connections between screen memories, accidents and the avoidance of time

When Maria started her analysis she repeatedly told me about the tragic love affair that she felt had changed her life. There was not much, initially, in the factual story. He was from France, on a holiday in her country. They had met, fallen in love and she had felt unable to respond to his sexual interest in her, driving him away. Her despair about it lay in the fact of not being able to let him know how much she desired him, behind the frozen facade she had presented. For a long period in her analysis her accounts of the tragic story in her live were stereotyped, repetitive and monotonous (frozen, containing none of the passion she was referring to), with no new information.

Maria's narrative had a familiar rhythm that I recognized from my readings about rituals in traditional societies, where stories have to be repeated in exactly the same way, where changes, by definition, cannot occur. The function of the formalized and repetitive type of communication expressed in rituals is not that of understanding the world, but that of hiding it (Bloch, 1977). The experience of familiarity with Maria's way of communicating with me helped me to understand that this was, fundamentally, Maria's attempt to freeze something about her life that she had not understood. She presented herself with an internal world that was repetitive, timeless, where the repeated accounts functioned as a screen for experiences. The analytic task was that of reintroducing a historical dimension – a dimension that allows the individual to have a sense of herself over time. In a session Maria commented that many people had told her that she looks younger than her age but that *somewhere* she knows that she is growing old. Then she added: 'It is like the portrait of Dorian Gray! In my attic I am growing old!'

In 'Beyond the pleasure principle' (1920) Freud interpreted the game of his grandson with the cotton reel as the child's attempt at mastery of his mother's absence. Terry Eagleton (quoted by Dirmeik, 1992) suggests that the 'fort-da' game can be understood as the first glimmerings of a narrative,

the shortest story one can imagine: an object is lost and then recovered. But then even the most complex narratives can be read as variants on this model: the pattern of classical narrative is that of an original settlement which is disrupted and ultimately restored.

(in Dirmeik, 1992, p. 13)

In her discussion of the same paper, 'Negation', Tonnesman (1992) also stressed Freud's formulation that thinking begins 'when the omnipotent control over the subjective object is shattered'.

The absence of a narrative is, by implication, an attempt to deny separation, the comings and goings and diachronical time, and to reify synchrony. A disruption of this framework is experienced as a catastrophe that has characterized Maria's analytic encounter with me – an encounter that threatens to interrupt the sense of timelessness and leads to fragmentation. My attempts to introduce organization (via the work of interpretation and construction) were experienced as terrifying and had to be defended against through thoughts and phantasies of violence. The analytic work, by the very constitution of a sequence of sessions, weeks, holidays, becomes an attempt to introduce a series of narratives incorporated into a broader one.

For much of the time, Maria attempts to deny the relevance of the analytic process for her. Thus, especially during the first few years, she would not remember what we had talked about in sessions. Interpretations would either be confirmed in terms of her saying: 'this was exactly what had happened when I met Alex, thirty-five years ago' or 'this was exactly what I had been thinking on my way to the session today.' I felt that such responses had a number of functions. It was an attempt, continuously and firmly, to expel me from her field of experiences, disavow the analytic process and the passage of time. I had, at the same time, an awareness that what she said was also true. Bollas (1987) has coined the term 'transformational object' for the analyst's role in gaining access to and transforming that which is known but has never been capable of thought and words by the patient. I have found Bollas's work relevant, especially in the process of understanding this patient's reaction when I thought I was saying something new to her. Her reply that she already 'knew' what I was talking about was true, and was not just a wish to undermine the analyst.

In any analysis one is bound to find layers of material pointing to different stages of the patient's development. It is fundamental for the analyst to distinguish between these different layers otherwise the analysis may be hindered by a lack of historicization for the patient. In the case of Maria this seemed to be of particular importance, as the patient herself tended to crush and condense her history. I think that at least two dimensions of time unfolded during her analysis. At the beginning of her treatment, the moment in her life she returned to repeatedly was the love affair in her late teens. She remembers that her mind *then* became filled with violent and frightening thoughts and she was afraid she would end up by harming her boyfriend. In the analytic process, Maria has struggled with the terror that this was also what was going to happen between us. The two accidents Maria suffered during her treatment became the concrete representation of the damage that can happen in the encounter between two people, of the destructive violence of the couple. As the analysis progressed, however, it also became clear that this was her belief about her early relationship with her mother. My suggestion is that these different time dimensions – pre-genital relationship with the mother and primal scene – not only became condensed into one but later crystallized into a specific content in the relationship with her boyfriend. Essentially I am talking about deferred action, i.e. that different stages were relevant to her in the structuring of her phantasies (see also Sandler and Sandler, 1994).

In the analytic process, my patient 'actualized' her earlier experiences. Sandler (1976) has coined this term to indicate the patient's attempts to re-establish with the analyst an early object relationship. This approach combines an experience of the transference as actualized in the consulting room as well as a comprehension of the unconscious phantasies. To my understanding this actualization is not only of wished-for patterns of relationships, but also of experiences which were not previously understood.

The language of the body: hysterical symptoms or traumatic events

Since Breuer and Freud's statement that hysterics suffer mainly from reminiscences (1893) and Freud's work 'Remembering, repeating and working through' (1914), the idea that psychic conflicts can be expressed in ways other than words has been familiar in psychoanalysis. Originally, Breuer and Freud related hysteria to the re-experience of the original psychic trauma. Freud was still, however, emphasizing the importance of having access to the past in the psychoanalytic process, whereas psychoanalysts today would also emphasize the communicative role of that which cannot be put into words, such as symptoms and actions present in the psychoanalytic process (see, for example, Limentani, 1966). The importance of that which is beyond verbalization, either in somatization or in enactments, was thus suggested in the psychoanalytic literature very early on and has been discussed by most analysts dealing with a variety of symptomatic presentations present in hysterical, psychosomatic and psychotic patients. Verbal processes are bypassed and conflicts are expressed in non-verbal ways: *memories are represented in symptoms.*

Some psychoanalysts have dealt with specific kinds of symptomatic presentation in their patient. McDougall (1974, 1982, 1989), for instance, distinguished between hysteria and psychosomatic illness, suggesting that whilst in hysteria the body 'lends itself' to the mind, in psychosomatic illness 'the body does its own thinking' (1974, p. 441). The symptoms in the latter function as signs rather than symbols and follow somatic rather than psychic processes. The lack of the capacity to experience psychic pain in such patients has been noted by Sifneos (1977), De M'Uzan (1974) and Fain and Marty (1965). In hysterics, McDougall suggested, the symptom tells a story. She thus follows Freud's suggestion in the 'Project' that hysterical symptoms follow primary process mechanisms because they are created by ideas and memories.

An attempt to find a diagnostic formulation for my patient poses several problems. Over the years, in discussion with colleagues, a variety of diagnoses have been suggested, I think simply because she fits a variety of them. Several of her symptoms, for instance, tell a story, and seem to bear the imprint of her relationship with her mother, like the pain in her leg, which she relates to a fall from a horse and being underneath it; her mother said 'it was nothing' and still sent her on a trip abroad against her will. I often wondered about her various descriptions of feelings in her skull as expanding and contracting, and have an image of a baby who is shaken and whose head is banged against something. The ulcerative colitis, in contrast, seemed to function more as a sign, and cleared up very early on in her analysis (see Jackson, 1978 for a discussion of the various attempts at distinguishing between different formulations of somatic symptoms). Rosenfeld (1978) has written of the existence of 'psychotic islands' embedded in psychosomatic symptoms, and this idea also seems relevant to the understanding of this patient. In the sequence of her analysis, it seems that the apparent amelioration of Maria's psychosomatic complaints (ulcerative colitis) was succeeded by an explosion of symptoms, spread out in various parts of her body, which paralleled a breakdown in her psychic functioning.

Maria obviously presented a way of functioning very close to the somatic, with complicated descriptions of what she felt happened in her body. At the same time, however, she was able to give associations which sometimes indicated a slightly higher level of mental representations. Thus, it was not the whole of Maria's personality that had been caught up in a somatized and ritualized framework. A part of her was not, otherwise there would be no language to talk *about* herself, and she would only be able to *be* it. I would have found no way of communicating to her. A statement by Wittgenstein comes to mind: 'If lions could speak, we could not understand them.' Communication with a completely different system of thought is not possible; if Maria had a completely different system of beliefs, I would not have been able to communicate with her at all.

In Maria's analysis what has allowed me to formulate my understanding of her has been the transference framework and my attempt to trace her thoughts, behaviour and symptoms in the relational context in which they were expressed (Marty *et al.*, 1963). The analytic task has consisted of the expansion of the chains of associations which insert the various phenomena in the context in which they occurred. This also implies that, for a long time, the emphasis of the analysis was on the form and *functions* of the patient's communications rather than on the content of the material. The relevant material to be understood thus included all the various symptomatic manifestations Maria brought to the analysis, from the various pains she complained of, to her twitches and the dramatic centrality of her accidents.

Maria fears that to experience herself in relation to me is to become imprisoned in a violent world and to succumb to what she experiences as my wish to take her over and tear her to pieces. The dilemmas for the transference are obvious, and she attempts to deal with her terror of me by carefully watching and regulating how much she can actually interact with me at each session. If there is an obvious sado-masochism implied in frequently keeping me waiting, and in the process of relentlessly letting me know of the minutiae of the functioning of her body and of the various other professionals she has seen, I feel that the main function of all this is not to attack me, but to defend her very survival.

Conceptually, I understand my patient's thoughts of violence as attempts to deal with an object that is experienced as terrifying and dangerous, and as an attempt to create an equilibrium where she neither feels too separate from nor too overwhelmed by this object. I feel, however, that when the analyst formulates interpretations – of whatever kind – she is *inaugurating* something for the patient, independently of the content of the interpretation. The analyst introduces differentiations and separations into a territory previously more chaotic and undifferentiated. The theories present in the analyst's formulations are thus not there, present in the mind of the patient, available to be uncovered, but become constructions made by both the analyst and the patient in the analytical process. In metapsychological terms, I think that the analyst is, in this process, helping to construct the patient's preconscious. The understanding of the analytic process as a process of construction cuts across the dichotomy of whether one is dealing with a deficiency or lack or a disruption related to trauma: 'all are dysfunctions of the preconscious system' (see Aisenstein, 1993).

In her analysis my patient has relentlessly and sadistically projected on to me her rage at feeling unloved as well as her terror of me. At the same time, she cannot experience differentiation because this means being in touch with an inner reality where the stress is on violence and murderous encounters between two separate people. She has attempted either to contain these contradictory experiences in a relationship with her own body which has thus been characterized by violence and fragmentation, or to project them outside, as in her experience of the two accidents (which are also violent encounters). She has persisted in encountering an external world that she feels is dangerous and violent towards her. Her analysis has consisted of a slow process through which we have attempted to understand her profound terror of both fusion with and differentiation from me since she feared she could only find in me a mirror of her self.

SUMMARY

In this chapter I have examined some of the problems raised in the analysis of a patient who has to adhere to a version of reality that emphasizes processes in her body as opposed to those in her mind. Such an adherence assumed a concrete dimension in the two accidents the patient suffered on the first two anniversaries of the start of her analysis. I have suggested that my patient's experience of these two accidents and the way she brought them into the transference revealed her beliefs about her internal primary relationships to her objects. I have also suggested that her experience of the accidents may be conceptualized as an attempt to emphasize a sequence of bodily experienced traumas instead of historicization. Both accidents became a screen on to which she projected her beliefs about relationships in her life, more specifically her beliefs about her early relationship with her mother and her beliefs about sexual intercourse as a violent and catastrophic encounter. It is because any encounter between two people is potentially violent, sexual and murderous that Maria had to retreat into a timeless world where people did not exist as whole persons and thus were unable to differentiate from each other. They were maintained as part objects, in the same way she felt herself to be a collection of bits which are in pain and suffer. Thus the various parts of her own body become the containers of profound and prolonged pain, stripped of psychological meaning. The analytic process has presented her with an impossible dilemma: to be in a relationship with me implied the risk of this violent and dangerous encounter; not to be, however, meant carrying on being trapped in a two-dimensional, timeless world. I have suggested that it has been the endurance of this paradox in her analysis that has allowed the analytic process to take place. The analysis has thus been able to contain the most unbearable: the progressive experience of differences.

NOTES

1 This constitution, for Freud, is characterized by a movement towards differentiation: between pleasure and unpleasure, between the various agencies (id, ego and superego), between the internal and external worlds, between self and other and, finally, between the sexes and the generations (in the oedipal constellation). In psychoanalytic terms, the acceptance of an order based on the differentiation between the genders and the generations and on the incest taboo introduces the individual to an experience of renunciation and mourning (Cosnier, 1990). This is the source of identifications and thus of the foundation of psychic reality (Freud, 1917). The relinquishment of the experience of the permanent possession of the object is also central to Klein and her followers in the formulation of the depressive position (Klein, 1948; Segal, 1973, 1991; Britton, 1992; and Steiner, 1992). This is a universal requirement, present in all societies. As Lévi-Strauss has suggested, together with the incest taboo, and as corollary of it, it is the differentiation between the sexes and the generations that inserts the person into an exogamous system of exchange (1947).

    The anthropologist Edmund Leach (1961) has suggested that the myth of Cronus indicates that the creation of time institutes the world of differences. In classical Greece, the sexual act itself provided the primary image of time. This means that the body, bodily differences and the history of one's desires are taken into the psychic sphere, giving an individual a sense of temporality and existence.

2 Money-Kyrle has suggested a theory of stages in representational thought that goes from a stage of concrete representation (where no distinction is made between

the representation and the object represented), through a stage of ideographic representation, as in dreams, to a stage of conscious and predominantly verbal thought (1968, p. 422).

REFERENCES

Aisenstein, M. (1993) 'Psychosomatic solution or somatic outcome: the man from Burma', *Int. J. Psychoanal.* 74: 371–381.
Bion, W.R. (1970) *Attention and Interpretation*, London: Tavistock.
Bloch, M. (1977) 'The past and the present in the present', *MAN* 12 (2): 278–292.
Bollas, C. (1987) *The Shadow of the Object: Psychoanalysis of the Unthought Known*, London: Free Association Books.
Breuer, J. and Freud, S. (1893) 'On the psychical mechanism of hysterical phenomena: preliminary communication', *S.E.* 2: 3–181.
Britton, R. (1992) 'The Oedipus situation and the depressive position', in *Clinical Lectures on Klein and Bion*, ed. R. Anderson, London: Routledge in association with the Institute of Psycho-Analysis.
Britton, R., Feldman, M. and O'Shaughnessy, E. (eds) (1989) *The Oedipus Complex Today: Clinical Implications*, London: Karnac Books.
Cosnier, J. (1990) 'Les Vicissitudes de l'identité', in *Devenir 'Adulte'?* eds A.-M. Alléon *et al.*, Paris: PUF.
de M'Uzan, M. (1974) 'Psychodynamic mechanisms in psychosomatic symptom formation', *Psychotherapy and Psychosomatics* 23: 103–110.
Dirmeik, F. (1992) 'Comments on "negation"', presented to the British Psycho-Analytical Society, unpublished.
Fain, M. (1992) 'La vie opératoire et les potentialités de névrose traumatique', *Revue Française de Psychosomatique* 2: 5–24.
Fain, M. and Marty, P. (1965) 'A propos du narcissisme et de sa génèse', *Rev. Franc. Psychanal.* 29: 561–572.
Freud, S. (1899) 'Screen memories', *S.E.* 3: 303–322.
—— (1909) 'Analysis of a phobia in a five-year-old boy', *S.E.* 10: 3–149.
—— (1914) 'Remembering, repeating and working through', *S.E.* 12: 145–156.
—— (1917[1915]) 'Mourning and melancholia', *S.E.* 14: 237–258.
—— (1920) 'Beyond the pleasure principle', *S.E.* 18: 3–64.
Granel, J. (1987) 'Considerations on the capacity to change, the clash of identifications and having accidents: their interrelations', *Int. Rev. Psychoanal.* 14: 483–490.
Jackson, M. (1978) 'The mind-body frontier – the problem of the "mysterious leap"'. Paper presented to the Psychiatric Section of the Royal Society of Medicine. Unpublished.
Klein, M. (1948) 'On the theory of anxiety and guilt', in *Envy and Gratitude and Other Works 1946–1963*, New York: Delta, 1977.
La Fontane, J.S. (1978) *Sex and Age as Principles of Social Differentiation*, London: Academic Press.
Leach, E.R. (1961) 'Two essays concerning the symbolic representation of time', in *Rethinking Anthropology*, London: The Athlone Press.
Lévi-Strauss, C. (1947) *The Elementary Structures of Kinship and Marriage*, Boston: Beacon Press, 1969.
Limentani, A. (1966) 'A re-evaluation of acting out in relation to working through', *Int. J. Psychoanal.* 47: 274–282.
McDougall, J. (1974) 'The psychosoma and the psychoanalytic process', *Int. Rev. Psychoanal.* 1: 437.

—— (1982) 'Alexithymia: a psychoanalytic viewpoint', *Psychotherapy and Psycho-somatics* 38: 81–90.

—— (1989) *Theatres of the Body*, London: Free Association Books.

Marty, P., de M'Uzan, M. and David, C. (1963) *L'Invéstigation Psycho-Somatique* Observations Cliniques, Paris: PUF.

Money-Kyrle, R. (1968) 'Cognitive development', *Int. J. Psychoanal.* 49: 691–698. Also in Meltzer, D. (ed.) *The Collected Papers of Roger Money-Kyrle*, Pertshire: Clunie Press, 1978.

Rosenfeld, R. (1978) 'The relationship between psychosomatic symptoms and latent psychotic states', presented to the British Psycho-Analytical Society, unpublished.

Sandler, J. (1976) 'Countertransference and role-responsiveness', *Int. Rev. Psycho-anal.* 3: 43–47.

Sandler, J. and Sandler, A.-M. (1994) 'Phantasy and its transformations: a Contemporary Freudian view', *Int. J. Psychoanal.* 75 (2):

Segal, H. (1973) *Introduction to the Work of Melanie Klein*, London: Hogarth and the Institute of Psycho-Analysis.

—— (1991) *Dream, Phantasy and Art*, London: Routledge.

Sifneos, P.E. (1977) 'The phenomenon of "alexithymia"', *Psychotherapy and Psychosomatics* 28: 47–57.

Steiner, J. (1992) *Psychic Retreats* (The New Library of Psychoanalysis), London: Tavistock/Routledge.

Tonnesman, M. (1992) 'Comments on "negation"', presented to the British Psycho-Analytical Society, unpublished.

Chapter 4

Maternal ties in an adolescent's struggle with her sexual identity[1]

Catalina Bronstein

I would like to explore in this chapter the intense psychological conflict experienced by an adolescent girl (whom I will call Rachel) in her struggle to accept herself as a woman. I am going to look specifically at how Rachel's early relationship with her mother was already disturbed by intense hostility, eventually resulting in her rejection and early disavowal of her own gender and in an identification with her male brother whom she felt was her mother's desired child. Her hatred towards her mother was, I think, directed to her awareness of her mother being *female* like her and her consecutive hatred of anything female. The disavowal of her gender, that is her rejection of her own reality, left this girl in a state of psychic fragmentation.

Not unlike Freud's (1924) description of how, in psychosis, the 'rejected piece of reality constantly forces itself upon the mind', the physical changes that occurred in puberty were experienced by this girl as bringing back a reality (her femaleness) that had been rejected, threatening her precarious defensive organization with the reintrojection of intense hostile feelings towards her mother and herself as a woman like mother. This was concretely experienced by Rachel in the feeling that she had a mother who sadistically 'pushed' femaleness into her, making her 'accept' that she herself was also a sexual woman. In this case 'need' and 'dependence' were equated with masochistic 'submissiveness' and seen as a dreaded intrinsic characteristic of the female condition.

I intend to explore this girl's search for an ideal mother–daughter relationship through her homosexuality and to show how the awareness that her partner was 'just a woman' led to panic and intense despair as it confronted her again with her reality as female. Rachel was left then feeling that only suicide or the symbolic killing of herself through a change of identity were the only possible solutions left to her.

CLINICAL CASE: RACHEL

Rachel was initially referred by her doctor to our Walk-in-Centre[2] at the age of 17, after her sixth attempted suicide. After a series of interviews with a member of staff she was referred to me for five times weekly analysis, to be funded by the Centre for Research into Adolescent Breakdown.[3] Her parents were also seen and initially agreed to the referral.

Rachel described herself as 'homosexual'. She felt that most of her difficulties were caused by her parents' rejection of her homosexuality. She was very depressed; she hated being herself, and she could not stand her own name and surname ('they were not chosen by me'). She disliked her appearance intensely and this often led her to attack herself with a pair of scissors, cutting her arms and thighs. She experienced her mind as being divided into parts and that she was driven mad by the fights between these parts. She often felt on the verge of killing herself.

Background

Rachel's parents, Mr and Mrs B, were both immigrants. When Rachel was 4 months old her mother became pregnant and gave birth to a boy (Tim). Another boy was born when Rachel was 4. Both parents came from disturbed personal backgrounds and both had had close relatives who had committed suicide.

Rachel had a very traumatic childhood. There seemed to be a lot of violence in the family, mostly enacted by Mr B who used to hit his wife as well as the children. Mrs B was described by Rachel as passive and masochistic, allowing herself to be hit and never standing between the father and the children; indeed she often told Mr B when the children had done wrong, thus inciting him to punish them. This caused Rachel and Tim to address their parents as 'the parrot' and 'the ogre', never as Mum and Dad. Rachel developed a very intense hatred of her father. However, she felt that until the age of 4 she had had a good relationship with him, and remembered with longing a photograph taken at that age in which she was sitting on father's lap, while Tim was on mother's. She could not remember ever having experienced any physical closeness to her mother. Mrs B said that as a baby, Rachel could never be left alone and had had screaming fits whenever she left her.

According to Rachel, she and Tim lived in a world of their own, a magical world where they became very dependent on one another. They were always 'flying away' on a 'magic carpet', away from what they called 'the monsters downstairs'. She remembered that when the next brother (John) was born, she had wanted to name him after her teddy bear but her mother had said indignantly that babies should not be called after teddy bears. On holding her brother for the first time, she had dropped him on the floor. From then on, she seemed to ignore him and John never participated in their games.

> Tim and I were always flying off on our magic carpet. John didn't seem to matter; he would try to join in but as he was a baby we would push him out or pretend he had just fallen off the magic carpet. We felt we were in charge.

Rachel said she had always been convinced that she had great powers and felt this was confirmed by a visit that God made to her when she was 5 years old. She felt her gaze was very powerful and would stand staring intensely at her father until he reacted, usually by hitting her. She related numerous episodes, in which she had felt herself to be the victim of an incomprehensible violence, in being hit and punished by father, often with mother inciting him or looking on.

When Rachel was 7 years old, her mother decided to study and the children were looked after by a male relative who sexually abused Rachel until the age of 11. The sexual abuse was never described in full but it appeared to involve masturbation and there was once an attempt at anal penetration, which was prevented by Tim's coming into the room. This relative convinced Rachel that if she did not allow him to touch her, or if she told her parents, he would make the whole household and her parents disappear. She believed in his magical powers and did not disclose the abuse until she was 16.

Rachel said it had never occurred to her that she was not a boy until she went to junior school. As a child she saw herself as the 'eldest boy'. She felt that she and Tim were twins. Puberty, with its unavoidable physical changes, brought a major crisis. The denial of reality was now more difficult to sustain as she had to contend with a changing body that permanently exposed her to being a woman. She felt her breasts had started to develop at the age of 10 or 11 and were 'enormous'. Menarche occurred at the age of 12. She hated her body, mainly her breasts. Mother was experienced as contributing to the rejection of her daughter's femaleness. Rachel said her mother refused to acknowledge that her breasts were growing and did not want to buy her daughter a bra until she was much older. Mother was reported as always saying 'Why didn't I have three boys?' At the same time pressure was being put on her to get married soon, and suggestions were made in connection with some young men whom her mother felt might be suitable.

Since puberty, Rachel had felt driven into states of despair during which she attacked herself with scissors. Her first suicide attempt was at the age of 12 when she swallowed washing-up liquid. The other attempts were with medicines such as sleeping pills and paracetamol.

Rachel had felt sexually attracted to women since puberty. She felt a great admiration for one of her teachers whom she thought wonderful. She also became very attached to a school-friend and felt deeply betrayed when this girl rejected her. At the age of 15 she slept in the same bed as her female cousin who touched her breasts and genitals and made her feel 'fantastic'. It seems that around this time she was also bingeing and vomiting and her periods stopped for nine months. At the age of 16 she developed a very close relationship with a male homosexual teacher at school and found the strength to reveal that she herself was 'gay'. This seems to have been experienced by her parents as a declaration of war and brought on a high degree of violence at home which culminated in an episode in which Rachel (without 'knowing why') attacked her mother with a knife. Her father interposed himself and got cut instead on the hand. Rachel was temporarily taken into care, though she later decided to go back home.

The analysis

Her internal world

Rachel's experience of differences was that they always felt potentially catastrophic. Differences were linked to split parts of herself fighting each other. She felt she was divided into four parts, all rowing with one another. The first part, she called 'neutral'. Then there was a part representing 'the past'. The 'third' part wanted to cry and felt bad and needed help; this was the 'dangerous one' in that she felt it led to a world of dreams, of extreme passivity, of fusion with the object. The 'fourth' part was the one that 'kept her going', for example it stopped her from stepping in front of a car, told her she should get on with things, not be a wet. This part could be very cruel but was 'necessary, vital for her survival'. This fourth part was experienced as sadistically bringing in some sense of reality. The 'past' brought a lot of hatred and the 'neutral' one could not be explained, but I felt it was there to prevent a lethal triangular relationship between the other ones.

Her experience of sexual differences leading to intercourse was similarly dangerous and needed to be denied. She lived most of the time in a dreamy state in which she was not herself. She had two main structured daydreams which she felt took over her life. One was with 'Jan', her imaginary girlfriend, the partner with whom she could have very satisfactory sexual experiences and who was the one present in her mind while masturbating. She spoke about her in such a convincing way that most of her friends thought she did exist. However, 'she knew' that Jan did not exist. The other daydream that took over her mind involved a homosexual artist (whom I will call Sam and who belonged to a pop group called 'Queen'). She could either identify with him and feel she was 'him' or at other times she could identify with the one 'chosen by him' as the object of his love. This latter identification with Sam's 'loved one' was via the repetition of an imaginary scene in which she was a 4-year-old girl sitting on Sam's lap. Sam was her father and would provide her with love and care and material things as well.

The identification with 'him' operated when she experienced herself as an adult. She would call herself 'Samantha' and move between knowing she was daydreaming, and a delusional state in which she would speak like him, sign school tests under that name and buy many things she could not afford, only realizing at the counter that she did not have his money. It was then that she felt she was going mad and it was only by denigrating herself that she felt she could recover some sense of reality. Dreams, daydreams and delusions were very difficult to differentiate as she moved from one to the other.

Rachel resorted to self-accusation ('you are stupid, an idiot, can't you see he is not real?', etc.) or, at other times, to attacks on herself in order to introduce some sense of reality. This left her feeling devalued and hateful, and she was forced to go back to her world of dreams in order to recover some sense of goodness, thus creating a vicious circle in which sado-masochism led to a disavowal of reality which in itself led to further sado-masochism.

She described it as 'My Obsession': 'I need it because it is part of me and that is what I spend many hours on.' She said she had a mirror with 'Queen' printed on it and would spend long hours looking at it until one day her father got furious and accused her of being only interested in looking at this pop star and smashed her mirror.

Sam is my father and my fourth part says it is rubbish but I do believe he is my father. I have been with him for years but I got worried the other day when I saw I was doing something, it was getting out of control. [She had signed a school test with his name and only realized it when the teacher questioned her.] When I was younger I would tell myself that he would come and pick me up in half an hour and would wait by the door. . . . I think I look like him. It was incredible that three years ago everybody would say Oh! You look exactly like him!

At times she felt Sam was becoming very possessive and turning into a persecutory hateful 'Double' who would not leave her in peace. At other times, however, her anxiety was linked to the possibility that Sam might be destroyed or disappear. Rachel panicked at the thought of Sam's possible disappearance as she felt that this imaginary father was the only one to protect her from her own destructiveness.

Rachel was unable to sleep at night as she felt she could hear noises coming from her parents' bedroom suggesting that her parents were having sex. She described it as a sort of rape in which her mother would accept her father's violent intercourse. She resorted to wearing headphones at night and listening to loud music but she could still feel hearing them, so she would leave her room and start shouting and banging things so as to let her parents know that she was aware of what they were doing.

Rachel felt a compelling need to harm herself, to scratch her arms with scissors, to attempt suicide, and also to provoke father's hatred so that he would attack her. It is relevant to note that, even though she was given the opportunity to leave home and stay with foster parents, she rejected it. At one point, in describing her father hitting her, she said she had wanted him to go on hitting her until he killed her.

She also suffered from terrifying repeated nightmares, one of which was seeing herself trapped in a closed room filled with mirrors and seeing her own reflection repeating itself to infinity. Her reflections represented herself at different ages and they were all laughing at her. She could not escape and felt driven mad by this mocking laughter that would grow louder and louder, until she woke up shaking with terror.

Rachel had not been aware of having any particularly strong feelings towards her mother until later in the analysis. She was conscious of a deep hatred towards her father but could not understand why she had tried to kill her mother.

Transference and countertransference

Rachel came to her sessions quite regularly, but there were many times when she phoned me from a tube station far away from the consulting room, saying she did not know how she had got there. The distorted perception of her own reality was matched by a gross impairment in her perception of time. In the sessions Rachel would frequently lose all sense of time. She would merge with her male 'Double' and be with him or 'become him', excluding me completely. At other times I was to become 'him' and was to be incorporated in another more fusional dream in which she was a tiny little girl floating down the river on a leaf. She would get into this dreamy state, which was very powerful, and I often found myself struggling to keep in touch with some sense of reality as this had a very hypnotic effect on me. When she was 'with him', still managing to keep an awareness of me as a separate object, she would become very anxious and often experienced me as wanting to spoil and take away the sense of well-being she had achieved. I would then carry all the envy and jealousy of this idealized relationship in which she sometimes had, and at other times was, the ideal object. My interpretations were then experienced as dangerous, as forcing her to accept a reality that she felt was damaging. It would bring her back to what I believed was an intense longing for the maternal object as well as the murderous feelings and the despair that went along with it. On the other hand, when she left the sessions in a dazed state she felt here too that I was leaving her in a dangerous and potentially destructive state of mind. She would then go to the Thames and sit there for hours wondering whether to jump in, death being idealized by her as the absolute denial of separateness and the absolute enactment of destructiveness.

The denial of the passage of time was necessary in order to deny the changes that affected her body, her female development into a mature woman, and the powerful feelings of love, need and hatred that this process evoked. The experiences of me as 'separate' and 'female' were seldom acknowledged. Those moments were filled with acute paranoid anxiety. She felt claustrophobic, desperately needing to get out, and she had to sit on a chair as she could not lie down on the couch. She felt that I was trying to drive her mad, usually believing that I wanted her to become heterosexual, to 'force' her to give up who she felt she was. It often seemed to me that she was struggling with an impossible task. As a woman, I could elicit homosexual feelings in her which she experienced as a threat and which greatly disturbed her, probably because of the incestuous connotations of a possible sexual relationship with me. But I think it was my 'heterosexual femaleness' that was more threatening. She then felt trapped and forced into what she experienced as a sado-masochistic relationship. She would become very anxious, would have to leave the couch and sit up, would experience me as mocking or extremely critical of her, usually laughing at what she felt was her fat and ugly appearance. At these times it seemed to her that I was 'pretending' to care and to help her to own a reality about her own femaleness in order then to devalue and attack her. In the same way, she felt I wanted her to need me and become dependent on me, only so that I could dismiss her and leave her. Therefore, any awareness of needing me, such as during weekends and holidays, aroused extreme anxiety. Becoming and/or being with the Queen–Father was the only safe solution to her anxiety.

I could often experience the impact of her mistrust and anger towards me as well as of her desperate necessity to get my help and her despair at not knowing whether she would be taken over by her wish to kill herself or injure herself after the sessions. I often worried about the possibility of her killing herself, mainly during weekends and holidays. There were many times when I felt threatened by her behaviour. At other times it was her distress and fear of madness that prevailed in the sessions, as well as a profound sense of pain when she became more in touch with what she was doing to herself.

Clinical material

After a year in analysis, in the first session back after a holiday (which coincided with her father's trip abroad), Rachel reported that she had been very depressed: 'It has been an awful month. Things went very wrong. I didn't do anything, didn't have a job, didn't even read anything; just stayed at home and cut myself again' (mainly her thighs). She said she had desperately wanted to come and see me, she had counted the days, one by one, before she could return.

Sam also left me! What happened is that I decided to write a novel about him and a girl like me. But I thought it would be too boring, for Sam to be such a good, wonderful father, so I kept changing him into somebody horrible and mean and selfish. He didn't want to see me around and pretended I wasn't his daughter. He would tell everybody I was just a relative. And then I wanted to come back to Sam but I couldn't. I think I have spoiled him forever. I tried to practise some driving but I just couldn't because I felt all the cars were coming to swallow me up.

The next week she spoke about her anxiety over food. Whenever she ate the food her mother had prepared she felt like vomiting. She felt her mother wanted to possess her. She had to get away. Anxiety about what I wanted from her prevailed in the sessions.

On Friday she brought a dream she had had the night before:

> I was on a train, going on a very long journey. My mother was at the front of the carriage and I went and sat down with her. I knew that Paul was at the rear of the carriage [Paul is one of the male homosexual teachers whom she idealizes and with whom she identifies herself, and the person who in reality helped her disclose her own homosexuality to other teachers]. Apparently I got on the train with my mother and just sat beside her. But at a certain moment I walk down to the end of the carriage and sat down with Paul. My mother became furious and after a while came to where we were sitting and started to scream at Paul, accusing him of having AIDS, shouting that he had an infectious disease and was spreading it all over the place and that he should be locked up, and that maybe he should die. I felt so furious with her that I got up and started pushing her, wanting to throw her out of the train. There was a terrible struggle. After a while Paul came up to where we were fighting. His presence was terribly important. He did not need to say anything; just by his being there I knew I should not throw my mother out of the train. I then went back to sit with Paul, and it was as if there were a cinema screen in front of my eyes and I could see both myself and Paul sitting down beside me.

Rachel described the dream as if she were still in it. She was very passive and detached throughout the session and only at the very end of it could I make some contact with her.

The dream appeared to be part of the reality and the session seemed to be experienced as a dream. I felt I had to take this up before I could make some contact with her. I said maybe she felt I wanted to separate her from the dream, just as she felt her mother had tried to separate her from Paul.

She replied that her mother had always wanted to separate her from Paul. 'Everybody is against me being with Paul. But, if it is not Paul, it is Sam.' She went on to describe how sometimes Sam takes over and the enormous impact this has on her life.

> When I get on a train I have to sit next to an empty seat so Sam can sit beside me. I have long conversations with him while we travel together. I realize people look at me because sometimes I forget they can't see him and I end up speaking in a loud voice. I hate it when somebody comes and sits on the seat next to me where he is. I have to get up and find two seats somewhere else.

She then added that it was terribly unsafe to tell anybody about her phantasies. 'I am going to be left with nothing.'

I said she was anxious lest, in feeling abandoned by me, she might be left not just with nothing but with actually murderous feelings. At the same time she did not seem to experience these feelings here, because she became very detached from what she was talking about as if it did not belong to her. I said that it is mainly her phantasy of being with Sam that prevented her from feeling anything towards me in the session.

Rachel was by now speaking in a very passive, detached way. She said Paul had told her how to deal with family rows, 'Just back out, leave it.' Sometimes she knows she can't do that and she goes on and on with the fight. 'If Paul had not been there in the dream I would have killed her.'

I took up, on the one hand, her feeling that if she were not so detached in the session she would not be able to stop herself from attacking me; but also her fear that I would attack her, by trying to take away or destroy this ideal Queen–Father, which she felt was what enabled her to keep good aspects of herself.

I think this illustrates Rachel's need to re-create Sam's image (or Paul in the dream) to prevent her from killing her mother. Sam (or Paul) contained the split part of herself that was capable of good, loving feelings towards her mother. But because of that, he also contained the dangerous disease, AIDS, that is, the need for the object, the need for help (AIDS=help). AIDS seemed to condense the ideas of Need and of Sexuality, both becoming killers. The mother in the dream appeared to contain Rachel's projected hatred at being left alone by me at the weekend (probably to be with a man instead of staying with her). At that point, the only solution to her murderousness was through an identification with a man who had no need for a woman but who, in his identification with a woman and need for a man, contracted the killer disease (Paul was actually dying from AIDS). I think Rachel's dilemma was that she felt that both her need for a woman and her need for a man ended in death.

The following Monday she arrived ten minutes before the end of the session, looking extremely anxious. She sat down on a chair as she was unable to lie on the couch. She stressed that she was feeling awful and the whole weekend had been dreadful. She had cut herself again. She could not understand 'time'. She had got all the times muddled in her head today. She knew, of course, that the session was at 2.20 p.m., but she still could not understand time. She had gone to her lessons at 10 o'clock that morning but they had not started until 12.00.

I said that time did not seem to make any sense to her. Probably, when she felt she most needed me, at the weekend, she could not have a session. That may have made her feel desperate and very angry.

She said she felt very angry indeed. On Sunday she had wanted very badly to see M (the school counsellor whom she saw for a year prior to her referral to us). She thought M would have forgotten all about her by now. She had just come from a bookshop, where she had wanted to throw all the books around. She felt she was too near to doing so. She had then started accusing her mother of nagging her, not understanding. She had wanted to kill her mother. She said that, with certain people, she did not experience any rage.

I thought she was telling me that at the weekend she had felt enormous hatred towards me that had ended in an attack on herself, and she was probably protecting me now by coming late, when, at the same time, she had wanted to discard and attack all knowledge, because this included the knowledge of 'time'.

Rachel left, very distressed, and it was only on the Tuesday that she could describe what she had felt during the weekend.

On Tuesday she told me that in the course of the weekend she had started hating herself. She could not stand her body, the way it looked. She had spent the whole weekend bingeing and vomiting. She felt fat and horrible. What had triggered this was an imaginary 'scene' in front of the mirror which had occurred on Saturday morning. This phantasy involved Sam, Peter (a colleague of Sam's in real life) and Ann (Peter's real-life girlfriend). Ann is an actress who appears in TV advertisements. Rachel said that she had felt at times very jealous of Ann. (I think it is important that she could not discriminate between envy and jealousy and she was right in saying she was jealous, in that she was not just expressing envy of the woman who appeared to be feminine and seductive but also her hatred of having to share her.) The row in her mind started because she accused Ann of having no brains, of being stupid and incapable of thought. She accused her of just being beautiful and caring only about her body and wanting to be slim. Peter had started to defend Ann and accused Rachel of attacking Ann, saying he would tell Sam about it. Rachel became terrified of what Sam would think of her attacks on Ann. She had then started to attack herself. She said she couldn't talk to me about this very much because I – 'being slim' – would never be able to understand.

Some months later Rachel was thrown out of her home by her father. She had returned home late one night and her father started shouting at her. She had answered back and this had triggered a more violent response from her father. He started to hit her. Rachel's mother tried to interfere and got between them but Rachel 'accidentally' punched mother's face. Rachel was aware that at one point she had just wanted her father to kill her.

After leaving home, Rachel became involved with her first real girlfriend. She had had many 'crushes' on girls who she felt were 'wonderful' but, as readily as she fell in love with them, she would drop them for somebody else. She felt that with this girl it was different. However, after some days, she became panicky and experienced a tremendous anxiety about breaking down. She felt she was going mad and that it had to do with this girl (Susan). She could no longer bear Susan. Susan wanted to be with Rachel, she had become too demanding, clinging, she 'has even sent me flowers! And Susan just wants to be with women and does not like being with gay men. I just can't stand this!' Rachel was very angry; she felt deceived in that she had thought Susan was tough but 'in the end she sounds just like a woman!'

Rachel needed a man to protect her from the hostility triggered by this clinging sexual woman; at the same time there was no peace with a heterosexual man either. Her Sam-phantasy was experienced as not helping her in the way it used to. She started searching for the ideal non-sexual woman. She experienced this conflict as intensely maddening and it worsened during the second analytic summer break. After the break she reported she was dreaming about becoming somebody else: 'I want to be somebody else, I want to have a different body, a different face, different hair.' She felt she had to get rid of herself and also, probably, of the awareness of the parental intercourse that had conceived her and named her. The only other solution which did not involve an actual suicide was what she decided to do: she gave birth to herself by changing her name and surname and triumphantly stated she now no longer needed me.

Discussion

I am mindful of the many difficult and traumatic circumstances surrounding this girl's life which cannot be fully explored in this chapter, such as the culture clash both for her parents and herself, the importance of mental illness in the family, and the effect of a violent upbringing, together with the impact that the sexual abuse had on her.

I will start by looking at one aspect of this material, that is, Rachel's hatred of the sexual woman, which represents the sexual mother-analyst and includes Rachel's hatred for her own femaleness.

Melanie Klein, in her early works, develops the idea of an early Oedipus complex which sustains the child's phantasy of a combined object (hostile mother containing hostile penis). This phantasy is based on the child's projection of destructive sadistic impulses that turn the breast into a bad persecutory object. Spillius (1994, pp. 328–329) summarizes Klein's views, stating:

> She [Klein] thinks the infant feels the mother's body to be the source of all good (and bad) things, including the father's penis and in phantasy the child attacks the mother's body both out of frustration and in order to get possession of her riches. . . . Combined with phantasies of projecting sadism into the mother, anxiety about attacks on her body means that her body is felt to be dangerous.

In 'Notes on some schizoid mechanisms' (1946, p. 11) Klein describes an aspect of projection that is related to the 'forceful entry into the object and control of the object by parts of the self'. This, according to her, leads to introjection being also felt as a forceful entry from the outside into the inside and this 'may lead to the fear that not only the body but also the mind is controlled by other people in a hostile way'. Spillius (1994, p. 330) adds that

> Klein thinks the girl has a lasting fear of damage to the inside of her body because of the sadistic attacks she has made on her mother, and that this is for girls the counterpart of castration anxiety in boys.

This raises the question as to what role the child's and mother's gender play in their early interaction and, specifically in relation to this girl, what were the elements that prevented her from a successful working through of the Oedipus complex that would have enabled her to identify herself with her mother in her sexual capacity.

Here we would probably have to include the mother's early reactions to her daughter, together with the baby's projections of her hatred, and her wish to control, and intrude into, her mother's body. I think we should not only consider the mother's possible lack of 'reverie' – that is, the mother's possible difficulty in accepting the baby's projections and making them tolerable for the infant to reintroject (Bion, 1962) – but also the mother's experience of her own femaleness, and therefore her reaction to having had a baby daughter. (E. Welldon suggests that the object relationship that the baby has with its mother and her acceptance and acknowledgement of her baby's sex from birth are crucial in the establishment of the child's core gender-identity (Welldon, 1988, p. 45).) Here we should perhaps take into account the girl's envy of mother's capacity to produce babies with father, as well as her jealousy and intense feelings of exclusion. This leaves open the question as to whether Rachel's hatred of her mother carrying another baby might possibly have been reinforced by her mother's projection of her own devalued aspects into her child. Therefore her identification with mother's femaleness may imply the introjection of overwhelming hatred that cannot be integrated with more loving aspects of the self.

Rachel's mother could be experienced as recognizing her daughter as a woman, but only in order to 'force her into becoming like her'. This meant for Rachel a woman who would masochistically submit herself to a man. Rachel's anxiety intensified when she recognized in herself her wish to be killed by her father, her wish to provoke his rage, and the way in which she enacted this with herself, by cutting herself. In this context, the experience of 'need' and 'dependence' was equated with this masochistic 'submissiveness'. Mother's need of father was seen in this light. Here one might remember this girl's dream in which 'AIDS' became so dangerous and her contempt for her female homosexual partners when they became dependent on her. Therefore, to be a woman was felt by Rachel to occupy a denigrating position, to be unlovable. It was as if her mother were saying 'You should be like me, but if you are like me, then you mean nothing to me.'

Mother's pregnancy when Rachel was 4 months old must have contributed to the girl's sense of rejection, both from the effect of her own projected hostility and of mother's search for another baby who Rachel felt could provide her mother with what she could not. Rachel's feelings of hatred towards the mother containing a baby, which was making her feel completely abandoned, might already have been linked to her experience of mother as female – like her. There may have been a stage when Rachel felt she was giving her mother the new baby (Freud, 1931; Langer, 1951) as well as a wish to have a baby herself like her mother, as when her periods stopped for nine months after her first homosexual encounter.

It seems to me that she was unable to work through her hatred of the limitations imposed by her state of immaturity and her need of a mother who did have a real capacity to become pregnant by father. It is likely that, through identification with the 'twin' brother, she could maintain the denial of sexual differences and sexuality altogether, thus enabling her to turn to her father in a loving way. Inasmuch as she could identify herself with mother's desired baby, she could preserve some good loving feelings towards the parents, because, at the same time that she felt she was the desired baby, she could magically deny (through the self-sufficient magic carpet) that 'she' was a 'baby' needing a mother. The next baby boy, though, together with the very painful traumatic episodes in childhood, such as the physical and sexual abuse, may have increased the need to resort to an omnipotent denial of sexuality. Mother's statement that babies could not be named after teddy bears brought home the feeling that she could not give her mother a baby, that she was herself a baby.

The sexual abuse may have been felt by her as a further rejection by her mother who was now leaving her exposed to a male sexual attack. The good, loving feelings she had preserved towards her father through her identi-fication with the mother's loved baby were destroyed by the hostility triggered by the 'heterosexual' man. One could see this in her attempt to repair and recover a good, loving father in her wish to write a novel during the analytical holidays (which coincided with her father's trip abroad). But the Sam–Father figure became nasty when he became the 'relative' who, through sexual abuse, spoiled her relations with men forever.

Puberty presented this girl with a 'new' reality. Her body became the permanent reminder of her femaleness, of her similarity to mother's body – that is of mother's sexuality – and, at the same time, of sexual differences. According to Laufer (1993) the attacks on the body could represent the attacking of a body containing the mother's sexual body. It seems to me that it was through her body, as reflected in the mirror (or in persecutory dreams), that she was 'sadistically' reminded of the mother's sexuality and forced to reintroject the hatred that that induced. According to Laufer (1994), adoles-cents perceive their own bodies as the source of their anxiety, and the hatred provoked by the body compels them to attack it. Laufer states that the special intensity that makes the anxiety seem so unbearable is related to the identification of the adolescent's body with that of the parent's body of the same gender as themselves. 'The fantasy is that of being forced, by their body to become the mother or father, . . . being taken over by the parent's body and forcing them to be like them' (Laufer, 1994, p. 8).

As in childhood, recourse to splitting and projective identification with a male Double (now homosexual) was needed to preserve some sense of goodness, which in itself was very precarious, and left her exposed to the feeling that she could be driven into a mad and maddening state if the different split parts of herself came together (therefore her need to keep her 'four' parts separate). This maddening state was felt as being overwhelmingly taken over by destructive feelings that would lead her to kill the mother through her own death. There was then a search for a man (Paul–Sam) who might protect her from a destructive mother–daughter relationship (McDougall, 1979).

At times, not even the Double could protect her from her murderousness; and he could also be spoiled, and turn into someone nasty, mainly when her need and longing could not be denied, in a similar way to Rank's (1914) description of how the Double becomes the embodiment of the projected badness. Rank places the emphasis on the persecution by the Double which has become now an independent entity.

One can see in Rachel how the Double is actually, in the beginning, the one who protects her from her hatred towards the mother and from the mother (her real feminine double). The Double therefore contains the projections of the male (and probably idealized female: Queen), asexual, good, loving and lovable aspects of herself. Whatever the permutation of the 'Him–Her' couple, it must always be a dyadic relationship which denies the existence of the triangular relationship:

1 Four-year-old girl with homosexual father (representing a man who does not desire a woman).
2 Four-year-old with homosexual man (who represents the woman 'Queen': therefore female homosexual couple which excludes men but is kept safe in that she is only a girl).
3 If she sees herself as an adult, she becomes Him/Her as projected on to the cinema screen, once she has disavowed the female desiring and needing (and therefore hateful and hated) part of herself (the wish to throw her mother out of the train).

This last possibility is also experienced when she looks at the mirror holding the figure of the man–Queen. She feels enormous pleasure – and relief – when looking at the combined male–female her. According to Rank

we find in our material that the Double is often identified with the brother. . . . The appearance for the most part is as a twin and reminds us of the legend of the womanish Narcissus, for Narcissus thinks that he sees in his image his sister who resembles him in every respect.

(1914, p. 75)

Rachel's narcissistic identification with her brother seemed to be an identification with an idealized aspect of herself (the combined self-sufficient her) by which Rachel could then deny her origin and give birth to herself.

In the transference, Rachel could very rarely acknowledge my own separateness and femaleness. This was the only way she could return to a session. Any feeling of becoming dependent on me provoked more self-destructive behaviour in order to re-establish her sense of omnipotence (Laufer, 1994).

O'Shaughnessy (1989, p. 141) describes similar difficulties in a child who had a brother when he was 13 months old and how, according to her, 'the projective identification that aims to separate and attack the sexual parents fractures a combination'. She links it with Klein's (1952) notion of combined figure as characteristic of the earliest stages of the Oedipus complex. According to O'Shaughnessy,

> the objects of fracture are in any case distorted by unretrieved projections, but through their fracture and further projections their heterosexual procreative qualities are destroyed and the patients have, instead, pathological sexual objects – distorted, incomplete and broken open.

She links this to the father then being seen as sadistic, and the mother often becoming weak and openly masochistic. She goes on to describe how, because of their lack of an internal good object, 'these patients feel little capable of bearing singleness. They must be in a state of projective identification with another object' (p. 149).

At weekends, and even more during long breaks, the Double became insufficient to contain Rachel's hatred in her awareness of a sexual me–couple that left her out. Splitting and projective identification seemed unable to contain all the jealousy and envy provoked by the sexual mother–me who is experienced as having 'no brains' to say 'no' and 'wants' to engage 'masochistically' in intercourse while devaluing and looking down on her excluded daughter. Rachel's perception of her own female body is met with the same hatred and is similarly despised. I think the homosexual relationship represented a combination of the hatred followed by denial of the mother's heterosexuality plus the longing and need for a woman who could make her feel that she had what would satisfy the mother. But this same need filled her with hatred and the homosexual relationships would break down when she experienced the other woman as containing the 'need' which she so much hated within herself and which she believed was intrinsically represented by the female body. The reintrojection of this female part of herself that contained all her hostility made her feel acutely anxious after the homosexual act and needing to withdraw in order to retain some sanity. Homosexuality was, then, a compelling 'solution', which repeatedly broke down because of the repeated realization that the other was 'just a woman', like herself.

NOTES

1 An earlier version of this chapter was presented at the 11th Conference of the European Psychoanalytical Federation, 8 April 1995.
2 Brent Adolescent Centre, 51 Winchester Avenue, London NW6.
3 Centre for Research into Adolescent Breakdown is a charity offering five times weekly psychoanalysis to disturbed adolescents. It works jointly with the Brent Adolescent Centre.

REFERENCES

Bion, W.R. (1962) *A Theory of Thinking in Second Thoughts: Selected Papers on Psycho-Analysis*, London: Karnac, 1967.
Freud S. (1905) 'Three essays on the theory of sexuality', *S.E.* 7: 135–243.
—— (1920) 'The psychogenesis of a case of homosexuality in a woman', *S.E.* 18: 147–172.
—— (1924) 'Loss of reality in neurosis and psychosis', *S.E.* 19: 186.
—— (1931) 'Female sexuality', *S.E.* 21: 225–243.
Klein, M. (1946) 'Notes on some schizoid mechanisms', in *Envy and Gratitude*, London: Hogarth, 1980.
—— (1952) 'The origins of transference', in *Envy and Gratitude*, London: Hogarth, 1980.
—— (1955) 'On identification', in *Envy and Gratitude*, London: Hogarth, 1980.
Langer, M. (1951) *Motherhood and Sexuality*, New York: The Guilford Press, 1992.
Laufer, M.E. (1993) 'The female Oedipus complex and the relationship to the body', in *The Gender Conundrum*, ed. Dana Breen, London: Routledge in association with the Institute of Psycho-analysis, New Library of Psychoanalysis.
—— (1994) 'Active and passive identifications and the relationship to the body in adolescence' (unpublished).
Limentani, A. (1979) 'Clinical types of homosexuality', in *Sexual Deviation*, ed. I. Rosen, Oxford: Oxford University Press.
McDougall, J. (1979) 'The homosexual dilemma: a clinical and theoretical study of female homosexuality', in *Sexual Deviation*, ed. I. Rosen, Oxford: Oxford University Press.
O'Shaughnessy, E. (1989) 'The invisible Oedipus complex', in *The Oedipus Complex Today*, ed. R. Britton, M. Feldman and E. O'Shaughnessy, London: Karnac Books.
Rank, O. (1914) *The Double*, London: Maresfield Libraries, 1971.
Spillius, E. (1994) 'Developments in Kleinian thought: overview and personal view', *Psychoanalytic Inquiry* 14 (3): 324–364.
Welldon, E. (1988) *Mother Madonna Whore*, London: The Guilford Press.

Chapter 5

Analytic treatment of an adolescent with bulimia nervosa

Marion Burgner

This analysis, which ended prematurely after one year, was of an adolescent girl with incapacitating symptoms of bulimia and vomiting. Cara, aged 17 years, telephoned the Centre (Centre for Research into Adolescent Breakdown, where adolescents are treated in five times weekly analysis) saying she had heard of the availability of intensive treatment. She expected, in fact demanded, that analysis be on immediate offer for her and such an omnipotent expectation was characteristic of Cara's approach to the world. Instant gratification of wishes was paramount, and it was unthinkable for her to envisage delay, whether imposed by others or herself. Perhaps the main reasons for the persistence of such peremptory demands for immediate satisfaction lay in her inability to tolerate anxiety or, indeed, any other affect, as well as a hopeless conviction that she was beyond help. Certainly the emotional climate, as it emerged in the transference, was undeniable – that within this adolescent there was a clamouring, needy infant who despaired of my capacity to sustain and help her; but there was also a triumphantly sadistic child who felt compelled to destroy what I offered her.

Cara was seen for six assessment interviews by a colleague at the Centre, Dr A, before she was referred on to me for analysis. A slight, extremely thin girl, with frizzy hair and carefully applied layers of make-up, she was provocative and seductive in her dress and dramatic, histrionic and demanding in the presentation of herself and her problems. Dr A found her both irritating and likeable, and was left feeling very worried – responses that continued to be experienced by me during the analysis. Tears rolling down her face, Cara said she wanted to die and that she could not rid herself of this idea; the year before, when she was 16, she had taken thirty-eight dramamine tablets. Earlier suicide gestures from latency onwards were revealed during the analysis. During the assessment, she underplayed the centrality of the addictive bingeing/vomiting cycle in her life. Family therapy had been attempted by her and her parents for some months and was dismissed as useless, as was her brief treatment by a psychiatrist. Such dismissal of therapeutic help is, of course, very common in this type of disturbance.

At the time she was studying for university entrance examinations and had the offer of a place at a prestigious music college. During the analysis, she postponed entry to college and held down a boring office job which she aggrandized beyond recognition. Friends were few, and boyfriends often only took her out once; her social life was sterile and repetitive, without enjoyment. Her parents had come separately from South America in their late teens, met and married in England when they were both young; she was born some years after the marriage and was their only child. Mother had suffered from depression probably from Cara's birth if not before, and had become dependent on alcohol and other substances from Cara's eighth year. The mother was an intrusive presence from Cara's first contact with the Centre; father was initially less overtly involved but later his interference was more subtle and destructive. The parents endeavoured to deal with their acute ambivalence towards their daughter by uniting in their attacks on the analyst and on the process of analysis.

Cara adulated her mother, seeing her as attractive and flamboyant, while father was viewed as just the opposite – shabby and insignificant. In the one interview I had with the parents, I was struck by the discrepancy between them and by their shared acrimony and destructiveness. The mother came in as if dressed for a party, with false hair piled high, false long eye lashes and heavy make-up, while father, soberly clad, looked thin and careworn. The battle between the parents crackled sporadically in my presence and it seemed that, in their continuing sado-masochistic onslaught on each other, honours were evenly divided. It became clear that the event the parents most feared was that their daughter would be seduced away from them by me and that the three of them would no longer be able to share the destructive and incestuous excitement contained in Cara's disturbance. The parents would monitor their daughter's every move, force her on the weighing machine, lock the kitchen so that she could not get at the food, lock the lavatory to prevent her vomiting, though then she would vomit secretly into plastic bags; she would flaunt her thin body at them and they grabbed at her protruding bones beseeching her to eat so that menstruation would return. The shared excitement between the three of them was maintained in consistent attack and counter-attack.

In my first brief meeting with Cara to discuss practical arrangements about starting analysis she was reasonable, placatingly charming and careful not to show me the extent of her problems. At the beginning of the analysis, I found her pseudo-sophistication, her triteness of phrase, and her conventional cleverness rather irritating, though she was nevertheless quite likeable. She seemed so often to be echoing the way her mother might think and speak rather than to have thoughts and feelings of her own, and the mother's presence within her and in the consulting room was palpable right from the start. Cara demurred about using the couch since she wished to see my face and monitor my responses, though she eventually agreed to lie down.

Cara was a very lonely, isolated girl and it is relevant that the first incident of bingeing and vomiting occurred when, at the age of 16, she felt utterly alone and abandoned by her parents and acquaintances. In the first week of the analysis she talked of her friends predictably abandoning her because she had nothing to offer them and how they became bored with her as, of course, she feared I would as well. She felt there was no fun in her, and I silently thought that she was right about this, that beneath her dramatic, hysterical facade, she was a pathetically bleak and joyless girl. She said she had once had sexual feelings for a boy when she was drunk at a party, and she described how she could have transitory and excited feelings with a boy she might encounter on holiday in the sun. In fact, she was unable to have feelings for a boy, concentrating solely on her effect on men; 'my interest is only in their interest in me,' she said. I shared with Cara my impression that she was so terrified of fun feelings, sexual feelings, and indeed any other feelings getting out of control that she had to minimize *all* feelings; it was only her bingeing that was allowed free expression and then she immediately re-established control by vomiting. This bingeing/vomiting pattern was an excited focus for her and it took on a life of its own with the beginning of analysis, increasing in frequency and intensity. Undoubtedly, she hoped to replicate with me the repetitive, annihilating scenes between herself and her parents and to involve me in their shared, mostly unspoken, panic that she would eventually kill herself. She was able to talk of how her parents were terrified for her but could not accept my understanding that the three of them shared a terror of her death.

She described to me how she would greedily eat for an hour until she was full to the top and then, once her parents had left the house, make herself vomit for a further hour. She added that she would continue eating and not bother to vomit, were it not for the fact that she would grow very fat. The bingeing and vomiting certainly had a number of important psychic meanings for her, as we came to understand during the analysis. One such meaning was the concrete way in which Cara experienced her quarrelling parents as fixed characters in her internal world whom she continuously tried to attack with her massive intake of food and subsequent expulsive vomiting. Of importance too was Cara's narcissistic conviction that the bingeing and vomiting were her very own possession, done for herself and on herself. A further psychic determinant was concerned with the feelings she experienced, particularly panic and rage, when she felt unwanted and abandoned, whether by analyst, parents or acquaintances. When I interpreted, after one weekend break, the rage she expressed with the binge and the ensuing internal calm she sought with the vomiting, Cara responded: 'when I am hollow and empty, then I am alone and sometimes quite calm.' I could then link this illusory calmness with her extreme vulnerability, her feeling that to accept me as part of her internal world was dangerous since she then exposed herself to abandonment; whereas, if she destroyed me, there was no further loss to be feared and she maintained her omnipotence. After the first six weeks of analysis, there was a long weekend break of four days. She talked of 'needing my parents to be with me because of their vigilance, otherwise I would stuff and vomit every two hours. It is like bacteria inside me which I cannot control.' Plainly, the internal parents were experienced as consuming her. Equally plainly, she was frightened about the first distinct break and about her capacity to retain the analyst as a benign internal object or as somebody to be destroyed.

Cara described herself as always having been given absolutely everything she wanted, but unhappy at school, adding that the girls ganged up on her. She volunteered that she had begun to steal when she was about 10. Her stealing was a distinct precursor of the bulimia and vomiting and probably expressed much of her disturbance in pre-puberty and early adolescence. She stole consistently from the age of 10 until 16, possessions from other girls at school, stationery from school, and money from mother. She would amass these articles and buy quantities of make-up with the money; little of this was used but it was all thrown together in carrier bags in a useless mess. The analogy is plain to see: her envy of what other girls and mother had was enormous but everything she stole from them was useless; it gave her no pleasure whatsoever. Similarly, the food she crammed into herself, whether of gourmet quality or junk food, was equally valueless and was made into a vomited mess; similarly too, what I gave her in sessions was experienced as useless, and messed up by her and her parents. But the stealing had another dimension too: falsehood and double-dealing were familiar to Cara in terms of family behaviour, and any superego introjection that had taken place was of a delinquent parental morality. The entire analysis carried the hallmarks of secrecy and deceit. But the ultimate and pervasive deceit was the parents' omnipotent conviction that, if only their daughter was restored to them from the analyst, they would make her well.

For Cara and her father I was not only invested with the power 'to take their baby away', as father phrased it; I was also, in their paranoid world, a powerful analyst who threatened the sexualized relationship compulsively shared by the three of them, and whom they felt compelled to destroy. When she began analysis, Cara was sometimes still bathing with her father, occasionally also with her mother; sometimes she crept into bed between them to watch a late-night film. She remained adamant that this was perfectly natural behaviour for a 17 year old though, describing her father's passionate embraces after she had attempted suicide, she did observe: 'I could have been his wife not his daughter.' Cara and her parents were determined to perpetuate the erotic, incestuous ties between them and they were equally determined that I should not interfere. However, there was never really an oedipal rival in Cara's world, only the effect of triangulation; she was sexually number one for father *and* for mother. She characterized herself as 'a pawn, as glue between my parents, without me they would fall apart.' I added that they were glued together in a closed system where they had no need of others and certainly felt they had no need of me. In effect I came to stand for all three of them as the external superego who threatened to interfere with their perverse, gratifying relationship.

We came to understand during the analysis that the only way Cara felt able to experience herself as separate from her internal objects was to destroy them in this compulsive cycle of bingeing and vomiting. But with her retreat to this polymorphously perverse state, not only were internal relationships annihilated but her adolescent body was also in danger of being destroyed. Just as Cara felt herself 'addicted' to the bingeing and vomiting, character- izing it as 'a yearning' not to be denied, she often expressed the fear that she would 'become addicted' to me, 'dependent and never wanting to leave'. Similarly, with mother, she often had no sense of separateness; she felt they lived inside each other's skins, sharing their craziness, addictiveness and spurious sexuality. When I interpreted her anxiety about being engulfed and swallowed up by her mother, Cara vehemently contradicted me, assuring me that was what she really wanted – to be engulfed; indeed, this issue of being engulfed or separate was absolutely essential to her disturbance and to the transference. I was experienced both as the desired occupant inside her body as well as its constant persecutor who had robbed her of her autonomy and sexuality and greedily taken it over for myself. In her quarrels with her mother, the latter would scream at her that she (Cara) would only get better when mother and father were dead. In talking about the possibility of the parents' deaths, Cara said she would never accept it; she felt so close to them that she would simply go on pretending it had never happened.

As the first summer break approached, Cara expressed her oppressive fear that she would become so much worse that committal to a psychiatric hospital would be inevitable. Her veiled threat to kill herself became linked with the whole issue of control over me; of her overwhelming feelings of rage that she could not stop me from taking a holiday, from giving up my control of her. She described a book written by a 'hippy girl who had to tear herself away from her father' and we talked about the tearing that continually occurred inside and outside of herself – her vomiting, whereby she attempted to tear her father out of her and herself away from father, and the excitement of her parents tearing her away from me and from each other. She complained that her parents kept constant surveillance over her; both in her flat (she had moved temporarily to a flat in her grandmother's house) where her father was doing repairs at each of the windows in turn so that he constantly looked in on her, and in the local food shops, where she felt that mother, by following her around, had made a public exhibition of her daughter's craziness, drawing attention to all the food she bought. I interpreted how she seemed to have three parts to herself at present: the caring part, the wish to feed and look after herself; the destructive, murderous part that stuffed herself and everyone inside her; and the controlling part that vomited everything and everybody out but had nonetheless failed to control me and stop me from leaving her for the summer break. I enlarged on these aspects of herself in terms of the feelings of triumph, envy, rage and, finally, utter despair. Cara then spoke of her feeling that I was leaving her to do everything on her own and that she did not trust me to return to her. I interpreted her anxiety about acknowledging her dependence on and need of me, and her response was that this really was the trouble – weekends were very bad, she could not rely on me too much because separations increased her bad feelings and her symptoms. We could then explore her anger as well as her desolation and despair about weekends and holidays. One of the problems, as Cara saw it, was that she would never be able to 'wean' herself from me, that she would be dependent on me and addicted to me forever.

The next period of eight months was to see her gradual and systematic destruction of the analysis. In retrospect, I think she could not tolerate having to postpone her need for immediate gratification from me. When we resumed after the summer break, Cara quickly gave me to understand that she was torn between going home and 'relaxing' (bingeing and vomiting) and coming for her session first. She became more overtly denigrating and tormenting, triumphantly seeking to replicate the sado-masochistic battle with her parents, wanting me to be as 'servile as mother, obeying my every whim'. In the final weeks of the analysis when she was constantly missing sessions, I understood that Cara was driving past the top of the street, omnipotently looking down the hill at the consulting room where I was available to her for her session, and then continuing on to her flat for her triumphant binge and vomit. Then I could interpret her panic about being lovingly and angrily involved with me and how she had to rush home instead to a passionate involvement with herself and a displaced, destructive onslaught on me. To this Cara brought a phantasy that I sat in my consulting room during her non-attendance, 'crying your eyes out', as distraught and terrified for her as her parents were. As I explored this and also mildly disclaimed any such feelings, Cara angrily and crisply retorted that she refused to accept what I was saying: 'it can't be so because if it were, there would be no point in my staying away.'

There were moments, however, when she could acknowledge her emptiness and desolation. As she said: 'the trouble is you are only available for fifty minutes a day and I need somebody inside me all the time, therefore it has to be myself.' The paradox was plain to see: object constancy, in the sense of the self-representation maintaining an affective relationship with the specific internal object representation was impaired and essentially she could only relate to objects in a functional part-object way; when they were physically present, they satisfied her needs and wishes: when they were no longer there, she was compulsively forced to fall back on her self as the narcissistic object.

As her paranoid feelings in relation to her body and to her internal objects gained in momentum, the bingeing and vomiting became even more compulsive, as did taking quantities of laxatives, forty tablets at a time. Cara focused on her physical complaints – sweating, hair loss, stomach cramps, swollen legs, fatigue. For the first time since she had begun her analysis some six months before, Cara missed a session. The next day she woefully told me that, on the way to a meeting of Anorexics Anonymous, a meeting she had intended to substitute for her analytic session at her parents' suggestion and her own agreement, she had crashed her car into an oncoming car. Cara had often talked in a taunting way about the effectiveness of other treatments, but this was the first time, at least as far as I knew, that she had tried to seek an alternative to analysis. My endeavours to explore the crashing of the car as an anniversary enactment of her previous suicide attempt as well as an expression of her despairing conflict over whom she would destroy and whom she could allow to survive, may have helped her temporarily, but she was quick to come back and tell me her father thought I was talking crazy rubbish. She missed another session the next week and returned to tell me analysis was making her worse and she was going to stop. My response was directed to the two occasions when she had missed sessions and had taken drastic action – crashed her car, and decided to stop her analysis; perhaps these two actions were related to her dilemma over whether to keep us intact and working together or to destroy us.

The content of some sessions highlighted not only the denigrating attacks on me but also the ways in which Cara successfully kept herself from understanding what was happening in her internal world. When I suggested that fantasy and reality sometimes confusingly overlapped, Cara recounted what had happened that day at work when she had told another girl about the scintillating weekend she was going to have, even believing this account herself – about the planned visit of many friends, the fun they would have together, and the mess they would leave behind. I interpreted the sadness and loneliness contained in this fabrication and in her losing me over the weekend and I took her back to the mess she experienced inside and outside herself. She complained that the men at work treated her like a child despite the enormous effort she made to wear the dressy clothes of a career woman in her thirties and how, notwithstanding these clothes, she failed to feel grown-up. I suggested that she was trying very hard to keep her body as a child's and that the discrepancy between her body and her adult fantasies made her very confused and unhappy. So far so good, but she became angry when I went on to point to the excited sexuality that was palpable in the bingeing, vomiting, taking laxatives and defecating; that her sexuality was not hidden, only disguised. She attacked me for not making her better, not providing her with somebody special who would love her; instead, she said, she simply felt crazy inside her head and grotesque on the outside of her body. Indeed she often felt she was her 'parents' crazy baby'.

The external situation worsened concurrently with the internal one. She gleefully contributed to horrifying, hysterical scenes between herself and her parents, ensuring that they visited her flat, saw the chaos she created and the bowl containing the vomit from the previous twenty-four hours. She described how she would weigh herself before the hour-long binge and afterwards vomit for a similar time into a large bowl, carefully judging whether the amount vomited corresponded to the amount eaten; weighing herself several times during the vomiting, she could only stop once her weight was the same as before the binge. This enactment took place two or three times daily. Cara elaborated that when she was at her ideal weight of 6 stone, she felt 'fragile and helpless', a person everyone was concerned and caring about, whereas with an extra 2 pounds she felt – delusionally – 'oafish and clumsy'. She indignantly refuted my comment about her confusion as to whether her body felt masculine or feminine. There was confusion too in the speed with which her feeding switched from pleasure to attack; she aggressively stuffed the food into herself and then scratched and damaged her mouth and the back of her throat in her frenzied efforts to vomit up the food inside her. While she attacked her body mercilessly, it continued to be experienced as persecutory; gratification was transitory, the addictive abuse of her body in an attempt to substitute for a relationship invariably failed.

Cara's provocative style of dress was remarked upon at the diagnostic stage. There were occasions when she came to sessions looking like a high-class prostitute. 'Female attributes' (breasts and hips) were an abomination for her; and while she claimed that she wanted 'a penis right in there', she could also acknowledge that she was 'absolutely terrified of it'. She reflected that sex repelled her while in fantasy she yearned for it; and the fantasy was enacted with an asexual, imaginary object with whom she danced in a light-headed haze after bingeing and vomiting. Cara herself made the link between giving up masturbating and her bingeing: 'when I stuff, my whole body shakes with excitement.'

She became increasingly frightened about the damage she was doing to her body, fearing that 'my sexual organs will atrophy'. But any satisfaction she might have felt in the analysis receded when juxtaposed against 'the excitement of my feast'; she left carrier bags full of food in the waiting room, knowing throughout the session that the overwhelmingly superior excitement could be master-minded by her afterwards, and that our analytic interaction was a pale shadow of what was to follow when she was alone. She reflected that the trouble was she could not find in herself 'a yearning from' the food; she brought herself up short to say she had not meant 'yearning' but another word which she could not now remember. I interpreted her confusion between *yearning* and *weaning* and how she yearned to be continually at the breast with the accompanying unseparated relationship with the analyst/mother. Her intolerable loneliness and despair, her feeling that it was impossible to share with me what was happening in her inner world, were all consistently explored, but I felt that her closed, repetitive system of autoerotic grati-fication might well prove too powerful an adversary to the analysis.

As the analysis slowly but inexorably ground to a halt with a pattern of increasing non-attendance, she became more frightened at the extent of her involvement with me. She feared she was 'falling apart', becoming like a crazy, blackened drug addict she had seen begging in a New York street some years before. She also stayed away since she was terrified that her badness would run amok and cause me to disintegrate. At times she barely differentiated herself from me in the possibility of our joint disintegration; such fragmentation was characterized by her as tantamount to going crazy. She brought a theme from a futuristic space film in which there was a female monster who beguiled people by allowing them the wish-fulfilment of turning her into whomever they most desired, whereupon the monster retaliated, extracting all the salt from their bodies and turning them into a heap of nothing. This Cara felt she did to me when she stayed away from sessions and that it was a question of her power and control over me that was at stake. As we explored this, I could interpret that there was also something else at stake – namely, her terror and envy of my monster-like power over her – and this brought us to her pervasive wish to be totally dependent on and unseparate from me.

Cara now experienced me as the firmly lodged, persecuting, internal object and she could barely bring herself to attend sessions. Finally, when she came for one session in response to my contacting her yet again, I told her we had to terminate. I explained that I could not continue on her terms of an illusory analysis characterized by her elective absence from it, though I emphasized I was willing to continue if she came regularly. I carefully interpreted her excited destruction of the analyst during her absences, either in collusion with her parents or in the bingeing and vomiting sequence, and her excited, fantasizied triumphing over me enacted in her internal scenarios. I suggested to Cara that a major characteristic of her analysis and indeed of her relationships was this sado-masochistic emphasis on mutual destructiveness. While I felt Cara had been put somewhat in touch with her excited interaction in our work together, she had also managed to keep this characteristic split off and encapsulated in her bingeing/vomiting symptom. Thrice daily enactment of these primitive phantasies were, at that time at any rate, far too gratifying in an autoerotic context; the analytic relationship proved intolerable for her.

It is important to emphasize my countertransference responses during the analysis. In my work with Cara, I was frequently aware of feelings of anger, rage, impotence, guilt, disappointment, responsibility for her disturbance, to name but a few; I was also experiencing some of what she could not and dared not allow herself to feel.

I must also mention the recurring doubt I felt about the possibility of successfully treating this adolescent, entrenched as she was in the family environment; it had become clear to me that analysis did not stand much of a chance unless Cara was able to live consistently apart from her parents.

DISCUSSION

I think Cara was one of the adolescents encountered in analytic work for whom the prospect of psychic separation involves such primitive anxiety that it presages annihilation; separation anxiety thus takes on the terror of annihilatory anxiety. Analysis reveals that such adolescents have not had adequate expectable experiences of appropriate relationships within the developmental phases. Instead, what seems to happen is minimal, if any, neurotic conflict and ensuing *distortions in development*. By this I suggest that there have been difficulties of an impacting nature from infancy onwards and quite often virtually no oedipal experience, conflict or resolution, since the parents – particularly the mothers – of these adolescents are invasively and permanently present in their children's internal and external lives. In turn, these children cannot tolerate the ordinary developmental process of becoming separate and, greedily yet with overpowering hostility, have to retain the parental objects as part of their inner world. Thus, these develop-mental distortions, continuing from infancy onwards, culminate in stasis around adolescence, in a foreclosure in development. In fact, what appears to be a surfeit of adolescent disturbance is, in essence, a pseudo adolescence, just as the preceding developmental phases have also carried that 'as if' hallmark. Disturbance is palpable in the *primitive* (pre-oedipal) nature of their enactments to the self and others.

These developmental distortions become organized in the breakdown in adolescence, obviously not the first severe disturbance in the person's life, and are particularly evident in their incapacity for psychological separateness from the parents, in the chaos of their internal object relations and affects and in faults in psychic structuralization.

Cara ended her analysis with the central dilemma apparently unresolved; the question remained of how could she become psychologically separate from her parents and her analyst without destroying them and herself in the process. Suicide attempts seem to occur frequently in adolescents who can neither negotiate separateness nor an entry into young adulthood. Perhaps her awareness, on leaving analysis, that she had not annihilated me was of limited but continuing help to her. She accepted my participation in her referral to an in-patient anorexic unit, though she discharged herself after a few weeks, and she then made a half-hearted attempt to return to analysis.

Over the next four years she asked for two interviews. In the first, she told me that she had moved away from her parents and had a boyfriend, but wanted admission to a different hospital to deal with her 'habit' which was as compulsive as ever. Her refrain throughout the interview was on the uselessness of the many and varied treatments offered to her so far. She was in touch with her own destructiveness towards all therapy and its practitioners but ineluctably compelled to put such destruction into operation. She struck me then as quite inaccessible to further therapeutic help; and I was certainly neither analytically nor personally comfortable with such awareness since failure was a prominent feature in the accusatory transference and in my counter-response.

Some two years later she came to see me again. Now aged 22, she looked very different from our last meeting. Her weight and appearance were normal, and I learned that menstruation had returned. She was neither attacking nor provocative and she was no longer preoccupied with suicidal thoughts. Her professional success pleased her; she was buying her own flat and lived quite apart from her disturbed parents. While they were still locked together in their sadistic quarrelling, Cara seemed more separate from them, saying that the more she stayed out of their lives, 'the more they would just have to get on with it and with each other'. This last comment was indeed an advance on the sexual triangulation so carefully and erotically fashioned by the three of them against their experience of my threatened incursion during her analysis.

She went on to tell me of her distress at the ending of a two-year relationship and of the recent beginning of a new attachment, fearing that her 'addiction' might now prove an encumbrance. She wanted me to resume therapy, though not analysis, with her because she still felt compelled to binge and vomit once daily (unlike the two or three times daily during her analysis).

I referred her to a colleague and she started therapy with him. I know little of this therapy, except that the bingeing and vomiting were reduced further to once a week; also, there ensued a stormy, promiscuous time and an abortion which left her very depressed. But depressive affect, that is *experiencing* feelings rather than eruptive, unpremeditated action against the self, is an advance in the treatment of such young adults. Doubtless, this abortion was linked to the issue of her ending her analysis with me as well as to the future, premature ending of her therapy. When her analyst left London, I understood that she had decided to seek further therapy, but now three times rather than once a week. So, a decade later she was still trying to make some order in her internal and external worlds. I do not think she could have continued with this endeavour without that minimum of separateness which she had accomplished by the age of 22 when adolescence as a developmental phase was, more or less, over for her; there was then an alternative for her to the previous foreclosure with which we had initially struggled in her analysis and which she was enabled to continue working on after the analysis ended.

Chapter 6

Working with an anorexic patient

Dana Birksted-Breen

There exists an extensive literature, though perhaps more psychiatric than psychoanalytic, on anorexia nervosa, the syndrome which includes the relentless pursuit of thinness and the preoccupation with food as a way of life (Bruch, 1974).

Some authors have focused on the oral symptom – not eating – which they view as a defence against greed and the wish for oral impregnation (Berlin *et al.*, 1951, for instance); others emphasize the disturbance in body image as does Crisp (1973) who states that 'the disorder is primarily one of the psychological meaning of body weight with reference to puberty and not to food and its direct relevance in terms of mother', Freud, in a very early paper (1895) makes a link between anorexia nervosa and melancholia, focusing on the loss of appetite. The Kleinian perspective points to the paranoid fears of being poisoned, sometimes connected with the mother's projection into the child of her own wishes (Menzies-Lyth), or the depressive fear of endangering the good internal objects.

Tustin (1984) points out the connections with autism and suggests that the anorexic turns away from the extreme sensations of the ecstasy of food and rage when the food is not there. The French authors Kestemberg *et al.* (1972, p. 11) were particularly impressed by the perverse and masochistic components and felt that their patients were 'dying of pleasure' (my translation).

In recent years anorexia has also been considered from the angle of the family as a system (Minuchin *et al.*, 1978; Palazzoli, 1978), and of the mother's psychopathology (Weinreich *et al.* (1985) talk about the mother's devaluation of her daughter's attempt to be an adult; Sours (1974) of her narcissistic use of the child to maintain her grandiose self).

Most attempts at understanding have tried to incorporate the fact that anorexia nervosa is a disturbance which is found typically in adolescent girls and would therefore, at least in part, be a way of dealing with conflicts which beset the girl in her development (for instance oedipal conflicts). In this connection one would want to explore possible predisposing factors in the girl (for instance, stronger introjective processes in girls, as hypothesized by Klein), and the nature of the mother–daughter relationship which Grunberger, for instance (1964, p. 76), describes as essentially 'frustrating to both of them because neither is a satisfactory object for the other'. Male anorexia, which is much rarer, has been considered in terms of a feminine identification (Falstein *et al.*, 1956).

Sours (1974) finds it useful to distinguish two groups of anorexics. One group comprises anorexics who, under increased instinctual pressures of adolescence, experience the resurgence of oedipal feminine wishes leading to regressive solutions; the other group comprises anorexics who show structural ego defects related to failure in early separation and individuation; they are slightly older and more disturbed than the first group.

Jessner and Abse (1960, p. 302) summarize the breadth of the disturbance as follows: 'anorexia nervosa, with its hysterical, phobic, obsessive, psychosomatic and psychotic features and suicidal tendencies, seems to condense the potential pathology of adolescence.'

There is a general feeling of reluctance and pessimism about the possibility of treating anorexics with psychoanalysis, because anorexics do not see anorexia as a problem, hence there is difficulty in forming a therapeutic alliance, and because of the repetitive and deeply suicidal nature of the pathology. On the whole, anorexics arouse powerful reactions of anger and disappointment, sometimes in the wake of rescuing phantasies, in those closely involved in their treatment.

A number of people have been impressed, as I have, by the anorexic's wish for, and fear of, fusion with her mother (Bene, 1973; Spillius, 1973; Bruch, 1974; Boris, 1984; Sprince, 1984; Hughes *et al.*, 1985). It is on this aspect of anorexia nervosa that I wish to focus in this chapter and I will now develop this line of thought and its ramifications, as I see it. From this perspective, anorexia can be seen as a girl's attempt to have a body separate from her mother's body, and a sense of self separate from her mother, the pathological nature of this attempt arising from the very lack of achievement of such separateness prior to adolescence. The anorexic is caught between the 'terror of aloneness' (Sprince, 1984) and the terror of psychic annihilation. Whereas the wish and fear of fusion with the mother could lead in the boy to sexual perversion (Glasser, 1979), in the girl it could lead to finding a way of having a body different from the mother's body, as if maturing into adulthood is experienced as becoming the mother (Hughes *et al.*, 1985). In the extreme it would mean doing away with her body altogether. The wish to be fused, the refusal to take and the attack on the representation of the mother's body through self-starvation are given fuel by feelings of envy. As with perversions, 'normal' adulthood and, in this case, femininity, are denigrated in favour of a different way of life and body appearance (including masculine elements).

Boris (1984, p. 319) discusses fusion in terms of the lack of a 'not me' and 'not you' space. Making use of Winnicott's idea of the transitional object

(1971), he says: 'the transitional space is like a buffer, a neutral zone, between two bodies (as if a demilitarized zone) which makes room for the play of imagination and the apprehension of reality – both.' The anorexic has failed to maintain those boundaries and hence that space.

I have also been struck by the experience in the transference and counter-transference with anorexic patients, from a purely phenomenological point of view, of the lack of a space between patient and analyst. One might think of this as the lack of a third term – the father who disrupts the phantasy of fusion. I am using the term 'father' here as one talks about 'the breast' not the actual organ or the person, but the father as representing the Other, and the space between mother and infant without which there will be no symbols, no words. I am suggesting, therefore, that there is in anorexia nervosa a disturbance in the area of symbolization connected with this lack of space. Here I have in mind something along the line of Segal's (1957) concept of 'symbolic equation'. In anorexia nervosa the food is felt actually to be the mother rather than representing her care. Piaget (1954) describes the early stages of mental life when the part is equated with the whole; here it is the food, only a part function, which represents the whole. Sohn (1985) and Boris (1984) both point out that envious belittling comes into reducing the mother to this function. Furthermore, at this level of 'symbolic equation' (Segal, 1957) type of functioning of the anorexic, the maturation of her body is felt to be taking a bit of her mother's body away from her, rather than developing a body which symbolizes adulthood and motherliness. In the sessions, the analyst's words do not symbolize care but are felt to be the milk, or nipple or penis which literally makes her fat, pregnant, sleepy, poisoned, etc. Projection, envy, the lack of needs being met appropriately and the consequent need for total and omnipotent control of the object, can all contribute to this lack of transitional space and hence hinder the development of the capacity for true symbolization.

If a person's identity is constructed in language (Lacan, 1977) then perhaps the refusal to talk, so characteristic of anorexics, is also a refusal to take on an identity (as female) and a refusal to be defined (as adult). The anorexic girl is continually attempting to achieve a separate identity in the face of this lack of differentiation, but not the one which is structured for her and she maintains a state in which she is in phantasy both fused with mother and not like her.

I wish to illustrate these points and some of the determinants of this state of affairs through the description of the first four years of the analysis of one anorexic patient, Denise. I have found the features I describe to be present in other anorexic patients. There are, of course, aspects of anorexia nervosa which I will not be discussing here (for example, the somatic delusion, the obsessional feature or the sexual fears). My aim in this chapter is to illustrate what I feel to be a central type of object relationship of the anorexic patient to her analyst and hence to her primary objects.

I will divide the material from this one analysis into three phases. The first phase was characterized by her wish to be merged with me in order to deny need, and slowly gave way to a second phase when she could accept greater separateness from me and begin to communicate more verbally but during which she was repeatedly trying to destroy her own wish and attempt to become an 'ordinary' adult woman (out of intolerance for her feelings of envy). It is relevant here to say that in this perspective one can perhaps understand why she, like many anorexics, needed to be outstandingly successful scholastically, that is in her own child sphere, until reaching a professional training level when she could no longer function. (I am aware that the excellent school performance of many anorexics is usually interpreted as compliance with the parents' wishes, and this may well be a factor too.) During the third phase, anxieties about loss and death which had been defended against by the anorexic state of mind were released.

Denise is in her twenties. She has been overtly anorexic since her early teens. Denise comes from a French-speaking country where she pursued architectural studies, the profession of her mother and father. Denise had just come out of the anorexic unit of a hospital in her home town when her father took up a contract in London. Denise, who did not wish to go back to her studies, came with the family. She was 6 stones 5 pounds when she went into hospital. Her weight increased to 7 stones 9 pounds in hospital but went rapidly down again when she came out. Denise had been amenorrhoeic for years. When she moved to London her doctor arranged that she would go for regular appointments to one of the teaching hospitals. A few months after this she started analysis with me, following the long-standing advice of this doctor. Denise was then 23 years old.

Denise arrived fifteen minutes early for her initial consultation with me. She struck me as being tiny, like a child. She was wearing cord trousers, a shirt and running shoes, and I though her gait was that of a boy. There seemed to be a disproportion between her head, which took up a lot of space because of a mass of reddish curly hair, and the rest of her, which seemed to shrivel away progressively. She had an enigmatic faint smile on her inscrutable face and she made me think of one of the Marx Brothers – Harpo; this was before I found out that she too was almost dumb. Interestingly, the only comparison she has herself made to date was with another silent comedian, Marcel Marceau, when she described feeling in the previous session like his act in which he pretends to be wearing a mask with a permanent smile while his face is intermittently struggling to get through.

In this first consultation, I invited Denise to tell me something about herself and why she had come to see me. She was silent and tense and eventually said, 'this isn't going to work.' She seemed to be struggling with herself about whether or not to get up and leave. I tried to encourage her to talk, but again she said, 'there is not point in this.' I took up how she was showing me the difficulty which had brought her here, that she wanted to be helped but then she felt in despair because she couldn't let another person try to give this help. She was silent and eventually said she found it humiliating. We struggled along like this until the end of the time I had allocated to her. I then said that I would like to help her find out what her difficulties were about and gave her the times of the vacancy I had. (In offering treatment I had to rely on the more traditional psychiatric consultation which she had had with the consultant who referred her for psychoanalysis.) She said: 'I think you'd better keep that vacancy for someone else.' I said she felt she wasn't worth it. She looked tense and upset. As she walked out she said she didn't think she wanted to come again. I said I thought she should at least come tomorrow and we could discuss it further. Denise has been coming ever since, though for a long time I would never take it for granted that she would keep coming. Months later she said to me: 'you asked me why I wanted to come ... *they* think I'm coming because of anorexia, *I*'m coming because I don't like what I am, what I do, what I think.'

In the first phase, lasting over eighteen months, Denise hardly spoke. In a typical session she arrived early. She did not look up when I came to collect her from the waiting room. She lay very still on the couch with her hand covering her face. Her fingers are cyanosed. She could remain entirely silent for up to three sessions running. When she did talk she rarely made more than one to three statements. These would be very brief and usually highly ambiguous or even incomprehensible. The tone of her voice was also often ambiguous, so I couldn't be sure of her mood. Usually she did not respond to what I said. She left without looking at me or saying goodbye, banging the door when she was angry.

I felt that Denise wanted to be merged with me, that I should know things about her without her having to tell me and, most of all, that I should get it absolutely right. To talk meant acknowledging that she needed something from me and that I had something she hadn't got. She said on one occasion: 'I'm being very generous when I talk because that increases the difference' (between us, she meant). The very use of words meant acknowledging the presence of two separate people who have to use a common language to understand each other, and I sometimes had the fantasy that she and I were buried in a tomb of silence for eternity. Denise often used the pronoun 'you' to refer to something she was feeling or thinking, as if she and I were one person.

There was a phase where she came closer to acknowledging some regressive wishes, holding the sleeve of a large woolly sweater against her face as a child might hold a blanket for comfort. She reacted by becoming severely anorexic. She told me that she wanted to have the strength not to eat anything. She felt hungry and the soles of her feet were cold and her head ached, but she had to prove that she was strong. She said that she can only eat if she has got a reason to eat. If she tells herself that there is a reason for keeping a certain weight, then she is justified to eat, but then she thinks it is just a trick so that she can eat, and then she can't eat. I took up how much she hated needing someone or something outside herself in order to keep alive, how she wanted to feel she depended on no one. She replied, 'I could say to myself, in order to keep alive, you need something or someone, eat you silly fool – then I think I'm just giving myself an excuse and I can't eat.'

In a later session, referring to her parents' commenting on some food she was eating, she said, 'they always point out that I'm not infallible and then I smash a cup.' And I know how tactful I must be in pointing out her progress if it is not to be totally smashed up. She once told me of her admiration for a friend of hers who was killed in an expedition, her admiration for the fact that she could deny her own comfort and safety to the point of death, that not even death would make her renege her ideals. In fact, anything short of death means imperfection.

Denise never told me what she would be doing or had done during weekend or holiday breaks, but she did describe one holiday, two years later, which well expressed the state of omnipotent self-sufficiency and of fusion with an ideal breast, which she withdrew into:

> Two summers ago, when I was in Norway, the last week we went to this island with a hill in the middle. We were the only people there for a whole week. It was hard, pushing one's way through the forest, but it was great. the last night I went to sleep and thought, I'm the only person who knows how to live, and in 24 hours I'll be back in London and I won't be able to do anything.

And, as after most holidays, she very nearly broke off treatment. In fact she broke off treatment with the doctor at the hospital with whom (I now found out as he wrote to me) she had been having 'psychotherapy' concurrently with her analysis. She had, he wrote, now reached a weight close to her target weight.

It was clear that Denise did not successfully block off her needs, but on the contrary, that she felt only too painfully aware of them and that she found it extremely difficult to tolerate the frustration of these needs. On one of the very rare occasions on which she was late, she eventually described how she had been stuck in the traffic. An ambulance had come and couldn't get by: she had got very wound up. She switched on the radio and it was much too loud and about all the things on the news which made her feel wound up (I presumed she was referring to tragedies and violence). She arrived twenty minutes late and thought . . . (she stopped). She didn't tell me what she thought, but I imagined it was that now she was here she couldn't see why she had felt so desperate about getting here or what it was she was coming for. I thought she was telling me about a part of herself that feels a tremendous urgency and emergency to get to me, and the murderous feelings and rage this leads to when she is frustrated and how her only way of dealing with this was to want nothing. She left the session saying 'now I have to face the bogeyman.' The situation she described also reminded me of an infant who gets so excited that she cannot feed. I thought it also described the way in which she stops herself from getting to the 'breast'. 'I want so much and I hate myself if I take,' she said one day. And on another occasion she could let me know how behind her wall of silence she felt intensely: 'I just have one basic feeling state which is a mixture of frustration and resentment and which is made up of hate, fear, horror, and makes me just want to crash about.'

One important way in which Denise dealt with her feelings of need was by perceiving me to be the demanding and needy one whom she could then frustrate and control. I would be hanging on to her every word, straining to hear her very soft voice, being left dangling when she stopped in mid-sentence, or when after half an hour's silence she would finally say three words but I couldn't grasp them or they didn't make sense, and she would never repeat or elaborate on what she had said, so I was left feeling that I had missed something which would have made everything clear! She controlled my 'feed' with great strictness so that I was constantly kept in a state of undernourishment but also in this way she could control my response to her, increasing my pleasure and excitement when she finally said something, after being deprived, just as she once told me how she can increase her own pleasure in eating by starving herself first.

I was also struck by how there was a sense in which she and I had to compete for resources. There was curious rhythm to the sessions: long silence ... I would say something fairly brief ... long silence ... she would say something fairly brief ... long silence ... I would speak again, etc. It was as if we had to take it in turns and it had to be equal shares. She wouldn't give me more than I had given her. There was a sort of rivalry as to which one of us was the more needy one or the more deserving of fulfilment. One day she was annoyed about her stomach rumbling and I took up that she didn't mention that my stomach had rumbled first (with hunger, I thought). She said: 'I thought to myself "I can beat you at that game".' On another occasion, when I pointed to the aspects of myself and of herself that she saw as never-satisfied infants, she replied, 'I wonder which greedy baby deserves to be fed.'

Denise also wanted to make out that talking was for my benefit only: 'what if I never talked? I think that you would tell me that I have to talk.' This was connected with the way, too, that Denise wanted to see me, as a voraciously demanding and never-satisfied parent. This was, of course, the sort of exacting internal parent inside her which really had the characteristics of a greedy never-satisfied baby. She told me once that she was doing an impossible wallpapering job for a woman, impossible because there wasn't enough paper, but the woman told her that she had to manage nevertheless. Meanwhile, this woman's mother was dying and Denise was filled with hate, fear and horror. I thought that she was describing how she feared she could not survive in the face of such a cruel, exacting part of herself, as she felt I, too, would not survive.

I also felt that Denise wanted me to experience something of a sense of hope which then becomes crushed (disappointment is a common experience, it seems, in those who deal with anorexic patients). I had a particularly acute experience along those lines one day. I was talking to her when suddenly I looked up and noticed that she had her hands on her head with her arms covering her ears, and I experienced a moment of acute panic and disorientation when I realized that I thought she had been listening but now found she was 'deaf' and my words had fallen in a void. I wondered to what extent she was communicating to me her own experience of sudden and utter aloneness when she expected contact, and how this would make her wish for self-sufficiency, or else wish to be one with a loved person. But even aloneness suggests the existence of another, and in that moment I felt that it was my identity as an analyst, or even my very existence, which had been threatened, and perhaps it is that very sense of identity and self which Denise is searching for through an anorexic solution.

Although Denise wanted me to understand her perfectly without having to explain anything, and wanted to be merged with me, she also felt extremely intruded upon when I did understand, and it was with great reluctance that she would let me know that I had got it right. Once when I commented on something she had said, she retorted: 'Oh! I just said it to create confusion,' I thought that Denise's great secretiveness was meant to humiliate me but also to protect her sense of separate identity. Denise could not find a way of taking in order to find her own sense of self. To take, for her, means to be taken over, and psychic annihilation.

The seeds of the second phase were sown gradually. Denise could begin to acknowledge her dependency on me as a separate person: 'I used to be able not to care, but now it doesn't work any more, that's what I meant yesterday when I said I wish people had left me alone.'

Rather than using the 'you' to refer to her own thoughts, Denise now used 'I' and addressed me more directly. This suggested to me at once greater differentiation between us and greater intimacy. She could now let me know how much she did want to come. The whole rhythm of the sessions changed. In a typical session she now started talking after a short silence. She said a few things before waiting for me to speak, and carried on if I remained silent. My countertransference changed too. I began to feel less concerned that Denise would break off treatment, even though she would occasionally threaten to, and it was still a very real possibility after holiday breaks. I no longer felt that I had a fragile baby on my hands whose survival depended on my perfect handling and tuning into. Simultaneously I noticed that I became less patient with her silences and less able (or willing) to tune in and read the non-verbal communications during these silences. I now expected more of her.

Denise never resumed her original studies and she many times repeated her anguished complaint that she didn't know what to do. (Years later she told me that during the early part of her analysis she had spent many hours every day exercising.) Then, about eighteen months after starting analysis, unbeknown to me, Denise applied and was accepted for a postgraduate degree, with the idea of becoming a French teacher. She only told me about this some months later when a clash with the times of her sessions was approaching. She told me with great difficulty, convinced as she was that I would laugh at her for thinking she was capable of it.

Denise started her course and this proved extremely difficult for her. She faced the same sorts of problems which presumably led her to interrupt her original studies. From the very first day she wanted to give up and to the end it was touch and go whether she would stick it out. I felt, much as I had felt before with the analysis, that the burden was on me to keep her from destroying it, and it felt like an enormously tiresome, discouraging, repetitive burden. I told her she was giving me the option of either being like a mother who would get exasperated and tell her to get on and do something and that would make her furious and she would want to stop doing anything, or like an over-indulgent mother who would say that it didn't matter if she didn't want to do anything, but then she would feel that I didn't care. This seemed to ease things temporarily.

Having managed to make it to the end of the course, the next problem was getting a job, or rather accepting a job, as Denise apparently had no problem being offered a job. She would say, with relief, that she didn't get the job, but on closer inspection it turned out that when she would be asked if she felt she could manage it, she would say no; or asked if she would accept the job if she was offered it, she would say no (and was then told she would have been offered it). Partly, of course, it was difficult for Denise to acknowledge that she wanted something, but also no job was the right one. For instance she didn't want to teach 'privileged' children because she wanted to make up for her own privileged education.

She did eventually accept a job and again this proved enormously difficult for her. Denise saw in the pupils her hatred of being taught and helped. 'I don't like teaching, at least if you're being taught you can kick the teacher. I don't want to teach people who don't want to be taught.' She found it excruciating to stand in front of a class, and felt watched and criticized. Denise also hated being a beginner, making mistakes, not being an experienced teacher straight away. She was convinced that it came easily to the other teachers, and she felt there was no way of getting help. She felt that she wasn't good enough for the work, but at the same time, that this sort of work wasn't 'good' enough (that is, worthy enough to make up for how bad she feels herself to be).

This was a familiar theme as we had often seen how Denise felt that only undoing the past would be tolerable and relieve her of her enormous guilt. She felt nothing was worth doing, because it could never be good enough to make up for her past spitefulness and recalcitrance, and also because there was no point doing something when she knew that she was bound to destroy it in the future.

Denise couldn't stand being defined as a teacher, or as anything, for that matter. She wanted to feel that all roads were open to her. She wanted to be different, special. I thought her secretiveness in the sessions had to do with this too. If she was clear and told me her thoughts, then she would be an 'ordinary' patient and I would know that her thoughts were ordinary.

Although Denise hated doing nothing, it became clear that now that she was 'doing something' both in her sessions with me and in her outside life, she felt herself to be in much more direct competition with me and with other people, and she found it intolerable not to be the best. She thought she did not have the authority and charisma she felt she needed to make the pupils listen and work, while she felt that I had that capacity to make her work. This is illustrated in the following episode.

In this session Denise spoke about the teachers having a meeting about safety. Everything is dangerous and she had felt in a panic. She spoke about how she doesn't like teaching (because it's 'dangerous', I thought) and then said she could only cope by telling herself that she's not going in the next day (until the last minute). I said that she was terrified by her wish to kill those children who were giving her such a hard time.

To my surprise she then told me a dream (the first in three years of analysis).

> There was this child who shrunk and I stepped on it and killed it. It was shouting and I trod on it. It was either shouting or it was dead. It was so hard when it was shouting and so easy to kill.

Later she replaced the idea of killing it by saying it turned into nothing. She went on to say:

> This morning I was teaching a first year, they were copying a text and I realized that there were still fifty minutes and I didn't know what to do. In those cases I start writing 'Hell, hell', back to front so others can't read it.

She thought that the pupils were laughing at her French accent. I thought that she was telling me about her hatred of the shouting child in her, and how easy it was for her to stifle it or put things in such a way that I can't 'read' her thoughts. She seemed also to be referring to a fear that in her maturation, that needy first-year child was shrinking and would be totally forgotten, especially as she felt she was either all screaming infant or else she had to completely squash that infant in order to function as an adult.

What I really want to bring out is the strength of her reaction to having told me a dream. She very nearly gave up her job (maybe her analysis) because she felt so exposed (in front of the pupils) – in fact, she did not go into work and was not sure she could ever go back again. After the weekend she came to her session in a rather manic mood and told me how she'd been doing a stunt race, wading through a river, and how she could really hold her own (in a group of men) even though she is small and that the only person in her group who had been faster was over six feet tall. She was nearly or totally silent for the next two sessions, and on the third she said, 'I wonder, if nobody can make me go into work, which they can't, what will happen.' It was only then that I saw more clearly that she wanted to prove to me that I couldn't make her work, and how taken by surprise she had been when she had found herself 'working', telling me a dream. I said she hated teaching and wanted to give it up when she felt that I could make her work while she felt she could not make her pupils work, that she'd felt elated with the stunt racing, not only because she'd done well, but also because she felt in that sphere she didn't have to compare herself with me.

She returned the next day saying that fortunately she had gone back to work today and it wasn't so bad. She then told me about classes she just could not control but that she hadn't told anyone. She said that she hadn't wanted just to dictate things to the pupils, but tried to use less conservative methods, but how some sixth formers had complained about this to the head teacher. I took up how she had wanted to be freer here with me, in particular in feeling able to tell me about a dream, but then how a part of herself had wanted to come and spoil this and reinstitute order and control. Maybe it was relevant that she spoke of the sixth formers, the most 'grown up', the side of herself most potentially in competition with me. After this she became able to tell me, with great shame, that she felt that in doing the job she was 'dressing up', and that she could only be a 'pretend teacher', and how it must be obvious that she is just like a child. I took up how she wanted to remain a child, and how she felt I would laugh at her for wanting to be like me. She said 'but that's it, how could that be possible, I'm miles away, it is laughable. . . . Anyway, I don't even want to be a teacher.'

I should mention here that she once let me know that she changed her clothes before coming to her sessions (even though she doesn't go home first) because she felt too ill at ease, that is, that she could not present herself to me as an adult woman. 'I feel intimidated by the girls at school who are blatantly sexual . . . but it does not mean I want to be like them', she could tell me, and now, for the first time, she told me that she was amenorrhoeic. For the first time she also told me that she had a boyfriend, a relationship she had been having for 'nearly as long as I've been coming here'. But still it was a great struggle for her to let me see a more grown up side of herself (the sixth formers want to be treated like children).

The destructive attack on her wish to be a grown woman, like her mother, and the concurrent scorn for her (and me, when I'm seen as the mother), because she feels she is 'miles away', made me think of my very strong countertransference feeling every time she cuts her hair from lovely reddish curls to a very short, hard, boyish cut, which I experience as a direct, almost physical, attack on myself.

It was only a couple of months after the episode. I just described that Denise one day told me that, in her words,

> something strange has been happening in the last month or so, without my even realizing it – I've put on more weight than I could have imagined possible, I don't know if you've noticed, and I wasn't even aware of it: when you're used to being preoccupied with it, it takes some getting used to. It's so different, I don't know how to take it.

She also told me that she can look forward to eating something, eat it and feel satisfied, that she can 'get it right'. She mentioned, too, how she had begun, for the first time, enjoying being with other people.

But still, Denise was struggling with her feelings of envy: 'the difference between us makes me inadequate,' she says. And she hates her job because she doesn't feel capable of being a teacher. It is very hard for Denise to accept that she might want to be an ordinary adult woman like me. 'I want to hang on to an unconventional idea of what matters,' she said, referring, I thought, to her wish for omnipotent self-sufficiency and scorn for the adult world.

> It still comes to me in a flash, I know it's not true, but it still comes to me in a flash that if I don't eat, everything will be alright and that if I do it will be worse . . . the worse thing is that I know it's going backwards.

I thought she was also referring to an idea that if she didn't take and learn from me, then she wouldn't have to need me and compare herself with me.

The third phase which I will describe was ushered in by Denise's increasing ability to tolerate intense feelings of need and dependency on me, in the fourth year of analysis. She told me quite cogently one day that in order not to be disappointed, a solution was not to want anything, but that the problem with that was that it also did away with the possibility of feeling good when she did get what she wanted, and this was worth the risk. Of course she did not always feel like this, and her anorexia was very graphically expressed when, on another occasion, she said 'what I can't swallow is the idea that all I want is to be looked after and give up all responsibility.' And yet Denise did make clear how much she wanted to be loved and nurtured, and I began to understand that her repeated statement that she could never do anything of value (in her working life) related to her fear that she could never be of value to me. This was another source of humiliation and envy in that she knew that I was of value to her.

Having been able to recognize how much she wanted from me, Denise could no longer avoid a new set of anxieties which were to form the main preoccupation of this third phase: 'What do you do if you want something but it's not there?' she asked. To begin with, this came out in the form of her thinking about how she could manage without coming to see me any more. She couldn't see the point of carrying on in the knowledge that, one day, she would have to stop coming. Weekends were different, she indicated, because then she could look forward to coming back. I say 'indicated' because still so much of the time it was up to me to decipher some fairly cryptic comments. However, very clearly, she said: 'When I'm not coming any more, one day, then the feelings I have for you and you for me will die.' Now we were coming nearer to what emerged as a very frightening concern that I could die, a concern that she was trying not to think about. When I put this into words for her, she said she spent the whole evening hating me for touching on a raw nerve and leaving her with it. Finally she said: 'If Jim wasn't there, I would die.'

I thought that she was telling me something of a sense that without me she would be left to starve, and I took up how I thought her anorexia was a way of being the one to control starving or not starving. (I thought that the aim was not death, but to escape death through a phantasy of omnipotent self-sufficiency.) In the next session, Denise told me that she can't cut herself off from her feelings as effectively as she used to, 'but how do you feel those things, the potential disaster and deprivation, and still carry on?' This was not just a rhetorical question, because Denise does want to know how I deal with such questions; whether I 'carry on' by denying the possibility of death.

One way in which Denise was still dealing with this question herself was by engaging in a highly dangerous sport. 'It's feeble to feel frightened,' she said to me, trying once again to prove that she is not limited by her bodily needs or characteristics. As with not eating, I think that Denise was wanting to prove in this way that she can transcend her body and hence prove her immortality.

Around this time, Denise was to miss a week and a half of sessions because of a long weekend away with her boyfriend, followed by a school trip. During this time I found a message on my answering machine one day saying that she would like to come to her session next day, and could I telephone her if this was not alright. When she came the next day she said that she had been certain that I would phone to tell her she could not come, but when I had not she became convinced that something must have happened to me. After this session she went on the school trip and a few sessions after her return she told me the following: her boyfriend, who had been out for the evening, did not return when she expected him. Throughout the night she kept dozing off and waking up to find that he still was not there. She got very worried knowing that he would telephone if he was not planning to come home. In the early hours of the morning she had the following dream:

> This little girl was having a medical examination and the woman doctor, I'm not sure if she was a doctor or what, was making a running commentary. She was pointing to a mole on her body and then she pointed to two bumps on her head; it soon became clear that the two were related, that they were malignant tumours, and there was this sense of tension and inevitability. But suddenly the woman said there was nothing wrong with her. The feeling of tension and of relief felt like too much.

Denise found out the next day that her boyfriend had tried to ring to explain that he would not be coming home, but she hadn't answered. I thought that in the dream Denise was depicting the malignant process which goes on inside her mind when she is not coming to her sessions, as when her boyfriend is away and she starts thinking that he has had a car crash, a process which cannot be interrupted by evidence of the contrary (my return, his phone call) and which is responsible for the extent of Denise's despair about the state of her internal objects and her feeling that nothing she can do is ever 'good' enough. The two bumps, I thought (but did not say) referred to her boyfriend and I, the two parents and the two breasts. The only way of retrieving such a hopeless situation in the dream is through a magical process where all is well after all. In fact, the dream had not been reassuring in spite of this conclusion. I thought that in the dream there was also reference to a feeling that I cross-examine her about what she has been up to in her mind during our time apart in an attempt to reveal her pervasive badness, her destructive thoughts. 'I wonder what it would be like not to have an imagination that gets carried away all the time,' she said a few sessions later, allowing me to know that behind her silence and the paucity of phantasmagorical elaborations, lies quite a different story.

It was becoming possible to talk with Denise about the difficulty in addressing directly the spoiling part of herself, a part of herself she, on the whole, is not conscious of. This is an area in which I had always had to tread very carefully, as her sense of worth was already so bruised and she was so sensitive to any remark on my part which she felt was distancing and critical.

Now that Denise was more able to stand feeling envious and did not need quite so much to scorn what she coveted, and now that she was markedly progressing in her analysis and in her external life, something else emerged which threw some light on her need to keep herself as a pre-pubertal child.

After the summer break, Denise had been feeling very negative about her job, saying that if people knew how it made her feel, surely they would not make her do it. She did not fit the job, she said, and she must do something about finding something else. For a while she almost managed to convince me about this, but eventually I took up that she was telling me that surely I could not know how humiliating she finds it coming here, how inadequate it makes her feel, because if I did I would not force her to face those feelings.

She came to the next session in quite a different mood, saying that she had been preparing herself quite well for starting work and felt happier about it. The following session was after her first day back at work. She was wearing a skirt and said that she had had enough of having to change her clothes before coming to her session. She also said that to her great surprise the day had gone well. She had been able to be firm with the pupils and set the tone for what she expected of them. She said it was necessary to make them feel that the work was important. For the next week, Denise said that it was so different, that it made all the difference not to feel totally inadequate. But then Denise began to develop the delusional belief that she had harmed me and that I was displeased with her, and she became anxious, pleading with me to tell her what she had done wrong and that it wasn't worth it if it was harmful to me.

It seems that Denise feels that she can only mature by quite concretely taking a part of me for herself, and this leads to persecutory anxieties and fears of loss of love. When, soon after this Denise started menstruating for the first time in very many years, she developed a gynaecological problem which required investigation and which she was convinced would require major surgery and the removal of an organ. It is as if only one of us can be an adult woman. In that sense, one can say that in stopping her physical maturation – in phantasy stopping time – she is protecting both her mother and herself from destruction and death.

In conclusion, I would say that anorexia nervosa is more than a disorder in the psychological meaning of body weight or a disorder in relation to food. It is an attempt to annihilate the very nature of human existence – inequality, progression through the life cycle, death. I suggested that one component of this state of affairs lies in a disturbance in the area of symbolization connected with a lack of a 'transitional space' with the primary object.

I described how Denise's pathology aims at avoiding comparisons – she attacks her own wish to be like the admired and idealized analyst as a feminine and sexual parent or as an awe-inspiring teacher – while the denial of emotional and bodily needs also is an attempt at mastery over death and a phantasy of immortality. She wants to be 'different', to avoid comparison, but more than this she wants to find an identity 'outside' the conditions of human existence. This leaves as yet, in this ongoing analysis, many unanswered questions regarding, in particular, the psychological and relational climate which necessitates such a massive transformation of reality.

SUMMARY

I have discussed anorexia nervosa, in this chapter, from the point of view of the anorexic's wish for and fear of fusion with her mother. I have described some of the feelings which are being defended against by this state of fusion, as well as some of the consequences, in particular the lack of a 'transitional space' and what this means for mental development. I illustrated this with the description of the first four years of the ongoing analysis of an anorexic patient, concluding that anorexia is an attempt to annihilate the very nature of human existence – inequality, progression through the life cycle, death.

REFERENCES

Bene, A. (1973) 'Transference patterns in a case of anorexia nervosa' (unpublished).

Berlin, I. N. *et al.* (1951) 'Adolescent alternation of anorexia and obesity', *Amer. J. Orthopsychiat.* 21: 387–419.

Boris, H. (1984) 'The problem of anorexia nervosa', *Int. J. psychoanal.* 65:315–322.

Bruch, H. (1974) *Eating Disorders, Obesity, Anorexia Nervosa and the Person Within*, London: Routledge and Kegan Paul.

Crisp, A. (1973) 'Primary anorexia nervosa or adolescent weight phobia' (unpublished).

Falstein, E. I., Feinstein, S. C. and Judas, I. (1956) 'Anorexia in the male child', *Amer. J. Orthopsychiat.* 26: 751–772.

Freud, S. (895) 'Extracts from the Fliess Papers: *Draft G*,' *S.E.* 1.

Glasser, M. (1979) 'Some aspects of the role of aggression in the perversions', in *Sexual Deviation*, ed. I. Rosen, Oxford: Oxford University Press, pp. 278–305.

Grunberger, B. (1964) 'Outline for a study of narcissism in female sexuality', in *Female Sexuality*, ed. J. Chasseguet-Smirgel, London: Virago, 1981, pp. 68–83.

Hughes, A., Furgiuele, P. and Bianco, M. (1985) 'Aspects of anorexia nervosa in the therapy of two adolescents', *J. Child Psychother.* 11 (1): 17–32.

Jessner, J. and Abse, D. W. (1960) 'Regressive forces in anorexia nervosa', *Brit. J. Med. Psychol.* 33: 301–312.

Kestemberg, E., Kestemberg, J. and Decobert, S. (1972) *La Faim et le Corps*, Paris: PUF.

Lacan, J. (1977) *Ecrits*, London: Tavistock.

Menzies-Lyth, I. Personal communication.

Minuchin, S., Rosman, B. and Baker, L. (1978) *Psychosomatic Families: Anorexia Nervosa in Context*, New York: Harvard University Press.

Palazzoli, S. (1978) *Self Starvation in the Treatment of Anorexia Nervosa*, New York: Jason Aronson.

Piaget, J. (1954) *The Construction of Reality in the Child*, New York: Basic Books.

Segal, H. (1957) 'Notes on symbol formation', in *The Work of Hanna Segal*, New York: Jason Aronson, 1981, pp. 49–65.

Sohn, L. (1985) 'Anorexic and bulimic states of mind in the psychoanalytic treatment of anorexic/bulimic patients and psychotic patients', *Psychoanal. Psychother.* 1: 49–56.

Sours, J. (1974) 'The anorexia nervosa syndrome', *Int. J. Psychoanal.* 55: 567–576.

Spillius, E. (1973) 'Anorexia in analysis' (unpublished).

Sprince, M. (1984) 'Early psychic disturbances in anorexic and bulimic patients as reflected in the psychoanalytical process', *J. Child Psychother.* 10: 199–215.

Tustin, F. (1984) 'Autistic shapes', Meeting of the Applied Section of the British Psycho-Analytical Society, 25 January 1984.

Weinreich, P., Harris, P. and Doherty, L. (1985) 'Empirical assessment of identity syndromes in anorexia and bulimia nervosa', *J. Psychiat. Res.* 19: 297–302.

Winnicott, D. W. (1971) *Playing and Reality*, London: Tavistock.

Part II

Reactivation of early representations in childbearing

Introduction to Part II

Joan Raphael-Leff

We have all begun our lives inside a maternal womb, but only a woman has the capacity to recreate her origins within the internal space of her own body. Inevitably, childbearing focalizes the inexorable human processes of gestation, birth, growth, entropy and death. A uniquely female experience, pregnancy thrusts a woman directly into a paradoxical experience – at one and the same time her own yet a repetition; primordial, eternal and universal yet intensely individual, subjective, timebound and culturally specific. In addition, for the woman living out in reality the very stuff of her inner life, carrying her baby as she herself and her siblings were carried within her mother's pregnant body, conception inevitably reactivates childhood pre-occupations with corporeal enigmas about the workings and content of the maternal body: procreative riddles about how babies are made and what they are made from; anxieties about her own capacity to contain, sustain, protect and nourish, and her entitlement to keep a baby. Aroused as well are issues of sexual difference and archaic clashes between creativity and destructive-ness, a revival of ancient feelings of mystification, awe, rage, envy and jealousies in relation to generational life forces and parental powers.

Melanie Klein (1928) identified worries about suffering internal damage as a result of the fertile mother's retaliation for envious attacks on her childbearing capacities as a specifically female anxiety. Clinical experience reveals that such anxieties are often reactivated when conception is problem-atic or a would-be parent is diagnosed to be subfertile. Judith Kestenberg (1956) too, focused attention on the body interior – the female 'inner genital' impulses which in toddlerhood are externalized in early maternal activities, and in adulthood are revitalized and reintegrated in the course of pregnancy.

I have suggested elsewhere (Raphael-Leff, 1991, 1993) that the impreg-nated womb may be likened to a seething cauldron, a receptacle for the parent's fantasies and projections, and unconscious transgenerational trans-missions, as the baby being created inside it is incorporated into the psychic world and imbued with numinous aspects of internal figures residing there. Thus each baby is born into a place within a constellation replete with fantasies and imbued by various family members with representations of their internal figures and projected aspects of themselves.

Pregnancy has been likened to a developmental phase (Benedek, 1959) entailing loosening of defences and possibilities for psychic reorganization and reintegration (Kestenberg, 1976), with hypercathexis of previously ignored inner-genital structures (Kestenberg, 1981). Psychoanalysts who have studied emotional aspects of childbearing have all emphasized both the reactivation of childhood wishes and activation of *new* growth enabling identification with, yet differentiation from, the archaic mother (Deutsch, 1944; Pines, 1990). Freud's view of the wish for a baby as originally oedipal and compensatory, derived from penis envy (Freud, 1933), is one strand of incestuous desires affecting some psychogenic difficulties in conception. Other disturbances relate to overidentification, indebtedness or competitive rivalry with the awesome fertile mother.

Psychoanalytically oriented researchers of pregnancy have found residues of unresolved conflicts relating to early relationships and conflicts over maternal identity. These manifest in regressive shifts, anxiety, oversensitivity, intensified defensiveness, magical thinking and increased dependency during pregnancy (Bibring *et al.*, 1961; Breen, 1974; Raphael-Leff, 1980). Revitalized issues flare up during pregnancy and at nodal points as the infant reaches the developmental level of the parent's own difficulties (Benedek, 1959) later to be unconsciously introjected by the child, and often reactivated in turn, during their own childbearing. Reliving bitter-sweet experiences of their infantile helplessness, parenting poses myriad opportunities to enact inner scenarios in concrete form and engage in interactions tinged with vicarious compensation or belated revenge as well as a chance for benign reparations. Where current interactions are overshadowed by these 'ghosts in the nursery' (Fraiberg *et al.*, 1975) therapeutic intervention helps people both to tease out what belongs to them and to make connections between their own early experiences and those encountered as parents.

I suggest that the puerperium is particularly stressful for the woman as the early months are dominated by sleepless exhaustion, hormonal fluctuations and inexorable day and night exposure to her baby's primitive emotions. She also has unremitting unmediated exposure to the smell, feel and touch of primal material. In their undisguised immediacy and interpenetrating self–other suffusion, discharged bodily substances – amniotic fluid, lochia, milk, faeces, urine, saliva, mucus, tears, blood, sweat – detonate latent sensory memories of the care-giver's own babyhood (Raphael-Leff, 1989).

In the context of total responsibility for a fragile needy other, at a time of personal vulnerability, the impact of reactivated emotions cannot be overestimated. Conversely, given the widespread prevalence and variability of postnatal disturbance in the West (up to 50 per cent of new mothers have been found to suffer some form of distress), I contend that it can neither be treated as a single entity nor attributed to one unitary cause. It seems helpful to delineate the many different reactive forms postnatal reactions may take (manic, symbiotic, depressive, delusional, obsessional, persecutory or bipolar), and to regard *a woman's puerperal state of mind as a function of many intersecting factors*, retriggered, current and/or recurrent, intrapsychic, interpersonal and socioeconomic, ubiquitous but unique to each woman with each birth. Furthermore, in my clinical experience vulnerability to postnatal distress is sensitized by a family history of perinatal complications, and precipitated postnatally by having to come to terms with discrepancies between each woman's unconscious representations of a fantasy baby coupled with her projected idealized or denigrated baby-self and maternal imago, and conscious expectations of mothering on the one hand, and the specific experiences of childbirth, motherhood and the real baby encountered, on the other (Raphael-Leff, 1985).

PSYCHOANALYTIC TREATMENT DURING THE PERINATAL PERIOD

Given greater accessibility of previous modes of being and uniquely permeable state of mind during childbearing, psychoanalytic therapy pre- and/or postnatally can be unusually fruitful. However, there are hazards. Increasingly, as the dyadic sanctity of the consulting room comes to encompass another live being, the analyst is unwittingly drawn into the powerful pull of psychic reality dramatized within the growing belly, or evident in interaction between mother and baby. She may be thrust into a situation of feeling contradictory responsibilities towards two clients – expectant mother and foetus – or caught between divided loyalties to two babies, teasing out confusion between her patient's baby-self and the baby visibly growing within the body or arms of the woman on the couch. Patients who become pregnant in the course of analysis often show remarkable changes, with vivid dreams, mood swings, magical thinking and greater accessibility of rich seams of unconscious material. Under impact of turbulent forces, an analyst may find herself dumbstruck by the pregnant patient's ego intactness in the face of flagrant presentation of such undisguised unconscious material, primitive fantasies and boundary disintegration. In fact, some therapists erroneously confuse these eruptions with catastrophic psychotic experiences and may become unnecessarily alarmed.

That said, unless the mother can extricate herself from her reactivated susceptibility, the infant's crude emotions are experienced as overwhelming threats to her adult psychic stability, revivifying facets of her own needy, greedy, weak or emotionally wild self. In the perinatal clinical situation, these inchoate experiences contribute in many female patients to loss of self- and bodily-cohesion, and temporary regression to an often agitated state of sensory dominated asymbolic impressions and psychosomatic manifestations which reverberate in the countertransference. During this time of resurgence, particularly powerful transferential 'implants' are projected by the expectant mother or one with a new baby, with intense inducement for the analyst to experience herself as idealized helpful, omnipotent or negative, helpless or dangerously powerful presence. Such emotional pressures necessitate careful self-scrutiny, as they may at times 'mesh' with existing countertransferential tendencies within the therapist rending it difficult to disentangle her patient's incitement from her own identifications (with grandmother, mother or baby), and her own inevitably reactivated enviousness or empathic impetus to gratify or protect the vulnerable woman and/or her foetus/baby.

Finally, as noted in the Prologue to this book, one experience unique to a female psychoanalyst is that of the occurrence of her own pregnancy in the course of her work with patients. One effect of the intrusion of that external reality into the consulting room is reactivation of each patient's most significant infantile conflicts with borderline patients noticing sooner, and reacting with greater intensity than neurotics (Lax, 1969). While it intensifies both transference and countertransference issues, most therapists regard their own pregnancy as an impetus towards growth in the patient with recall of repressed material, re-experiencing of separation fears, oedipal exclusion and death wishes to the baby (Penn, 1986). Other common manifestations are rage, envy of fecund woman or foetus, sexual curiosity, sibling rivalry, etc. (Raphael-Leff, 1980, 1993; Bassen, 1988; Lazar, 1990); identification with an all-powerful, magical mother (Mariotti, 1993); and countertransferential effects, such as fears of patient's attacks and guilt at interrupting the trajectory of treatment (Etchegoyen, 1993). Male and female patients have been found to react differently, with increased sexuality in the transferences of the former and sadness, envy and reactions of oedipal rivalry in women (Nadelson et al., 1974).

There has been virtually no literature on 'double' pregnancies, when the analyst's pregnancy coincides with that of her pregnant patient. In my clinical experience with individuals and groups of pregnant women, there are additional strains on the analyst's listening skills while she may be tempted to introspect herself, or wants to protect herself from the pregnant patient's anxieties or competitiveness, or to shield her foetus from raw emotions expressed in the session (Raphael-Leff, 1993).

Postnatal therapy might constitute a continuation of treatment begun during or before pregnancy. Nor a mother of a new baby may refer herself for therapy during this period of emotional turbulence as her own infantile issues are reactivated in the presence of her child. As the chapters in this book attest, perinatal psychoanalysis has a momentum all of its own as issues reverberate back and forth on several registers – between patient and analyst, patient and baby, patient and mother, analyst and baby.

THE CHAPTERS

Having set the scene, we begin Part II with a chapter by Dinora Pines, whose 'body' of work over the years has focused on women's unconscious use of their bodies in expression of their emotional preoccupations and ways in which primitive anxieties and conflicts, reactivated during pregnancy, find their expression in tendencies towards abortion or miscarriage (Pines, 1993). In Chapter 7 she explores the place of pregnancy as a developmental phase in a woman's 'lifelong task of separation-individuation' from her own mother. Exploring the dual identifications a pregnant woman experiences, both with her own life-giving mother and with the foetus growing inside her as she grew inside her own mother, Dinora also relates to the infantile wish to have a child, and the distinction between the wish to be pregnant and to be a mother. She has always stressed the *three-generational aspect of pregnancy*, a theme which is repeated implicitly by each of the contributors to this part, tracing the cumulative effects of three and sometimes four or more generations on interaction between parents and their offspring in the present, and reflected in various permutations in the transference.

In the next chapter, Paola Mariotti explores the defensive use of deeply rooted unconscious fantasies of procreation as a one-person event, and their effect not only on pregnancy and motherhood, but on a woman's relationships and identity as a thinking person. Having traced this idea in anthropological and historical myths which complement her clinical vignette, Paola Mariotti brings detailed material from a session with 'Mrs A' during her baby's tenth month to illustrate the effect of the one-parent fantasy on the mother–infant relationship. In addition, she discusses her own countertransference experience of transferential elements echoing the patient's mimetic identification with an idealized mother imago. This type of identification which stressing sameness allows only for repetition rather than a spontaneous authentic creative response, typifies both the original exclusive mother–daughter relationship described and the patient's current ongoing experience of mothering her own baby. Once difference is recognized, growth can begin to occur within the analytic relationship. As does Dinora Pines's patient, Mariotti's patient illustrates that the wish to be pregnant may be other than a desire for a baby, in this case a need to prove her parthenogenetic fertility. The chapter concludes with some thoughts on the way in which elimination of one parent reinforces omnipotent fantasies, thereby bypassing recognition of neediness and envy of phallic potency while denial of the two-parent relationship restricts one's own creative capacity.

Deborah Steiner develops the theme of revival of infantile longings in the mother and her susceptibility to enter into a *folie à deux* with her infant when adult reality testing capacities become submerged in maternal 'reverie'. Like Paola Mariotti's one-parent phantasy, the *folie à deux* is a delusional state.

It is one in which the mother becomes a willing collaborator in the infant's *illusion of an exclusive dyad*, arising when the mother uses her infant to gratify her own powerful erotic impulses, and to vicariously satisfy the needs of her own idealized baby-self. Through a clinical vignette, Deborah Steiner retraces the origins of the mother's denial of the baby's separateness and her yearning to provide her child with an experience of merger which she herself craves in relation to her analyst. Like Dinora Pines, and other contributors to this book, Deborah's case presentation explores the complex renegotiations that a mother undergoes during childbearing in relation to identifications with her own mother and her infantile self, and the difficulties that arise in distinguishing between her own reactivated infantile needs and longings and those of the child on her lap.

Chapter 10, by Maggie Mills, differs from many others in this book by bringing clinical material (brief therapy rather than analysis) from a sample of under-resourced mothers. Through outreach projects we get a rare glimpse into the lives of women who would not have the stamina or resources to seek analysis of their own accord. For this very reason we have included this chapter, and although the majority of these therapy clients have no prior knowledge of psychological theory, their stories confirm in graphic detail many of the same issues of transgenerational transmission of distress and ways in which the childbearing experience has catapulted the new mother back into her own infantile experiences of trauma.

The final chapter in this part, written by Alicia Etchegoyen, focuses on parental relationships to children who have been conceived or embraced to represent another child in the care-giver's mind. In some cases, manic avoidance of the reality of loss of a previous child, whether by death or adoption, or of another family member, is accomplished by concrete replacement – incorporation of a new baby who substitutes for the old. Given the complex family dynamics involved, a child suffers from growing up designated to be someone else, even, and perhaps especially, when this attribution is unacknowledged. Alicia brings detailed material from analytic treatment with a 9-year-old girl, illustrating the effect on Lucy's intellectual and emotional development of her unconscious identification with the secret birth and death of a previous handicapped child. This is followed by the case of Mrs A (there is an unexplained predilection of analysts for Mrs A!), illustrating the ill-effects of inhibition of mourning, and far-reaching consequences of denial not only on her foster children, but on the wider professional network involved with the family. Once again, as in Deborah Steiner's chapter, we glimpse how detrimental to the child's emotional and intellectual development parental projections can be.

In sum, we find that the clinical work of all these authors indicates that once a woman becomes a link on the female procreative chain, she draws on *multiple unconscious identifications and early experiences which underpin both the dangers and delights of entry into the illusory exclusivity of the mother–infant duo*. In recent years, with growing awareness of neonatal capacities to discriminate between care-givers and propensity to form distinct relationships with each, analysts have stressed the importance of expanding the concept of the primary dyad to encompass 'triadic' relationships – of the primary care-giver's mate and others. To my mind these must also include the often underacknowledged contribution of siblings, not only in terms of rivalry over parental resources but as a learning ground for reciprocal exchange, acceptance of turn-taking and the entitlement of others to their own share, rooted in connectedness and interdependence.

REFERENCES

Bassen, C.(1988) 'The impact of the analyst's pregnancy on the course of analysis', *Psychoanal. Inq.* 2:280–298.
Benedek, T.(1959) 'Parenthood as a developmental phase: a contribution to the libido theory', *J. Am. Psychoanal. Assoc.* 7:389–417.
Bibring, G.L., Dwyer, T.F., Huntington, D.S. and Valenstein, A.F. (1961) 'A study of the psychological processes in pregnancy and of the earliest mother–child relationship', *Psychoanal. Study Child*, 16:9–72.
Breen, D. (1974) *The Birth of a First Child*, London: Tavistock.
Deutsch, H. (1944) *The Psychology of Women*, New York: Grune & Stratton.
Etchegoyen, A. (1993) 'The analyst's pregancy and its consequences on her work', *Int. J. Psychoanal.* 74:141–150.
Fraiberg, S., Adelson, E. and Shapiro, V.(1975) 'Ghosts in the nursery: a psychoanalytic approach to the problems of impaired infant–mother relationships', *J. Am. Acad. Child Psychiat.* 14:387–421.
Freud, S. (1933) 'Femininity', *S.E.* 22:112–135.
Kestenberg, J.S. (1956) 'On the development of maternal feelings in early childhood', *Psychoanal. Study Child.* 11:257–291.
—— (1976) 'Regression and reintegration in pregnancy', *J. Am. Psychoanal. Assoc (suppl.)* 24:213–250.
—— (1981) 'Notes on parenthood as a developmental phase', in *Clinical Psychoanalysis*, vol.3, eds S. Orgel and B. Fine, New York: Jason Aronson, pp.199–234.
Klein, M. (1928) 'Early stages of the Oedipus conflict', *Int. J. Psychoanal.* 9:169–180.
—— (1932) 'The effects of early anxiety-situations on the sexual development of the girl', in *The Psycho-Analysis of Children*, London: Hogarth.
Lazar, S. (1990) 'Patients' responses to pregnancy and miscarriage in the analyst', in *Illness in the Analyst*, eds H. Schwartz and A. Silver, New York: International Universities Press.
Lax, R. (1969) 'Some considerations about transference and countertransference manifestations evoked by the analyst's pregnancy', *Int. J. Psychoanal.* 50:363–372.
Mariotti, P. (1993) 'The analyst's pregnancy: the patient, the analyst, and the space of the unknown', *Int. J. Psychoanal.* 74:151–164.
Nadelson, C., Notman, M., Arons, E. and Feldman, J. (1974) 'The pregnant therapist', *Amer. J. Psychiat.* 131:1107–1111.
Penn, L.(1986) 'The pregnant therapist: transference and countertransference issues', in *Psychoanalysis and Women: Contemporary Reappraisals*, ed. J. Alpert, Hilsdale: The Analytic Press, pp. 287–316.
Pines, D. (1990) 'Pregnancy, miscarriage and abortion', *Int. J. Psychoanal.* 71:301–307.

—— (1993) *A Woman's Unconscious Use of her Body*, London: Virago.

Raphael-Leff, J. (1980) 'Psychotherapy with pregnant women', in *Psychological Aspects of Pregnancy, Birthing and Bonding*, ed. B. Blum, New York: Human Sciences Press.

—— (1985) 'Facilitators and regulators: vulnerability to postnatal disturbance', *Journal of Psychosomatic Obstetrics and Gynaecology*, 1985a, vol. 4, pp.151–168.

—— (1986) 'Facilitators and regulators: conscious and unconscious processes in pregnancy and early motherhood', *British Journal of Medical Psychology* 59:43–55.

—— (1989) 'Where the wild things are', *Int. J. Pre & Perinatal Stud.* 1:78–89.

—— (1991) *Psychological Processes of Childbearing*, London:Chapman & Hall.

—— (1993) *Pregnancy: The Inside Story*, London: Sheldon Press (New York: Jason Aronson, 1996).

Chapter 7

The relevance of early psychic development to pregnancy and abortion

Dinora Pines

INTRODUCTION

Freud, a man of his time, believed that pregnancy and birth gratified every woman's basic wish. The gift of a child would partially compensate for the unfulfillable wish for a penis. My analytic experience does not confirm this view. It has led me to believe that there is a marked distinction between the wish to become pregnant and the wish to bring a live child into the world and become a mother. For primitive anxieties and conflicts arising from a woman's lifelong task of separation-individuation from her own mother may be unexpectedly revealed by the emotional experience of first pregnancy and motherhood.

In this chapter I shall focus on difficulties concerning a woman's identification with the internal representation of her own mother, an identification that is bodily reinforced when she becomes pregnant. I shall also discuss the revival in pregnancy of infantile fantasies about herself as the intra-uterine foetus in her mother's body which are activated by her narcissistic identification with the foetus now concretely inside her own body. The physically symbiotic state of pregnancy is paralleled by an emotional symbiotic state in the future mother where identifications with her own mother and with herself as the foetus may reactivate intense ambivalent feelings. Pregnancy therefore affords the future mother an opportunity to decide whether to let the foetus live or die. The analysis of a patient who repeatedly allowed herself to become pregnant but aborted the pregnancy each time will illustrate this theme. Transference–countertransference problems encountered in her analysis with a woman analyst reflected the difficult relationship to her own mother in which the infantile aspects had not been successfully resolved and integrated in her adult self.

FIRST PREGNANCY

Bibring *et al.* (1961) write: 'The special task that has to be solved by pregnancy and becoming a mother lies within the sphere of distribution and shifts between the cathexis of self representation and object representation.' For some women, pregnancy may be one of the most enriching stages of the life cycle, for when is one nearer to feeling like God than when creating a new life. In this way, for a young woman whose experience with her own mother has been 'good enough', the temporary regression to a primary identification with the omnipotent, fertile, life-giving mother, as well as with herself as if she were her own child, is a pleasurable developmental phase in which further maturation and growth of the self may be achieved. For other women, the inevitable regression occasioned by pregnancy and motherhood may be a painful and frightening experience. The infantile wish to merge with the mother and the opposing fear of it which occasioned a partial failure of self/object differentiation may be revived. In this way, fantasies about the primary unity of mother and baby cannot be successfully integrated with adult reality, where such differentiation is paramount.

THE INFANTILE WISH TO HAVE A CHILD

Childhood wishes to identify with a primary object, the powerful pre-oedipal mother, are foreshadowed in play and fantasy long before there is any possibility of parenthood (Deutsch, 1944; Benedek, 1959). Gender identity is established in early childhood, and sexual identity largely resolved by the end of adolescence. Physiological maturation of the body forces an important stage of emotional separation-individuation upon the adolescent. Genital sexuality drives the adolescent towards the first intercourse which confirms her right to own her body. There remains the later stage of parenthood to negotiate. First pregnancy affords a woman a further stage of identification rooted in a biological basis. She enters upon the final stage of being like her own mother, a physiologically mature woman, impregnated by her sexual partner – and in fantasy with mother's – powerful enough to create life herself. It follows that the physical changes of pregnancy facilitate a woman's bodily re-experience of primary unity with her mother, and at the same time afford an experience of differentiation from her mother's body which once contained her own. A further stage of separation-individuation is forced upon her.

Such bodily changes are inevitably accompanied by a re-enactment of infantile emotional development, with libidinal aggressive and narcissistic components of the relationship to the self and to the object, altered both in the inner and outer worlds. Uneasy conflicts relating to past developmental stages are revived during pregnancy and the young woman may become aware of primitive, previously repressed fantasies arising from childhood sexual theories about her own conception, intra-uterine life, and birth (Pines, 1972). It follows that positive and negative aspects of the self and of the object may be projected on to the unseen foetus as if it were an extension of them.

The unique combination of bodily and emotional feelings occasioned by first pregnancy affords a young woman an alternative means of resolving psychic conflict. The foetus may be physically retained, cocooned, and given life, or may be physically rejected as in miscarriage or abortion, when the mother may deny the foetus life and deny motherhood to herself. In this way, the body may again be used to express emotional states of mind as it was in earlier stages of infantile development. The little girl's fantasies of foetal survival concerning her siblings or herself may reinforce her feelings of omnipotence or helplessness. Such reactions are founded not only on early experiences of childhood and parenting but also on the family romance regarding the children's birth. If the little girl has been told of her mother's ambivalent feelings about her own conception it must, in my view, complicate her final identification, and make her ambivalent about pregnancy in her turn.

USE OF THE BODY AS AN ALTERNATIVE MEANS OF ACHIEVING SEPARATION-INDIVIDUATION

I shall now focus on the young woman's relationship to her body, to her self, to her own mother as an object, and to her experience of being physically and emotionally mothered. The mother is to her child both the symbol of the maturational environment and of motherliness itself. Her physical presence and emotional attitudes towards her child and its body are integrated with the child's experience and her conscious and unconscious fantasies. The representation of an internal mother created in this way is a lifelong model for her daughter to identify with and also to differentiate herself from.

It is generally agreed that the foundations of the self and the distinction between self and object are shaped by an integration of bodily experience with mental representation. It is only in early childhood that the little girl not only can begin to identify with her mother but also to introject a mutual feeling of bodily satisfaction between her mother and herself (Balint, 1973). I would add that if the little girl has not felt satisfied by her mother at the pre-oedipal stage, not felt that she herself has satisfied her, she can never make up for this basic loss of a primary stable sense of well-being in her body and with her body image unless she sacrifices her normal drive towards a positive oedipal outcome (Pines, 1980). Narcissistic injury, giving rise to narcissistic rage, envy of the mother and lack of self-esteem, may be painful and add to the difficulties of separation from her.

The child's separation-individuation is influenced by the mother's capacity to enjoy her own adult sexual body and her relationship to the father. If she is satisfied in her own life, the psychologically symbiotic stage of her infant's life is not unduly prolonged, and the atmosphere of mutual pleasure between the parents, the mother's own enjoyment of her body and of her self, offer the child not only a satisfying object to internalize and identify with but also give her hope of achieving such a destiny herself.

It follows that a mother who is not satisfied with herself as a woman and who cannot accept the father as a man, has difficulty in separating from the child in whom she hopes to find all that she herself has missed, and through whom she wants to live again. Fantasy and reality become blurred for the mother if the fusion and symbiosis of pregnancy are not psychologically severed. Fantasy and reality become blurred for the child if the mother's behaviour is not experienced as good enough adaptive mothering in which good and bad are integrated rather than split. This leads to difficulties of separation for mother and child alike. Does the child experience her body and later her thoughts and her fantasies as being clearly her own or are they still confused with her mother's, as her body was in the primitive, symbiotic stages preceding self and object differentiation?

Biological puberty necessitates a change of body image from that of a child to that of an adult woman capable of bearing a child herself. The girl's awareness of her developing adult body not only revives previous conflicts about her identification with her mother but also intensifies bodily feelings and stimulation. There is an upsurge of emotional regressive tendencies as well as a thrust towards maturation, and a compromise must be achieved between these two. A young woman's physiologically mature and sexually alive body establishes adult status but also enables her to split off and deny painful emotional states by substituting bodily sensations. In this way, feelings of love or hate towards the self or towards the object can be concretely expressed, depression avoided and self-esteem raised. It follows that a sexual act which, to the outside world, appears to be an act of adult, genital sexuality, may unconsciously become a means of satisfying un-fulfilled pre-genital longings for the mother and for being mothered. In my experience, adolescent girls who precociously embark on heterosexual rela-tionships are using their bodies to re-experience the most primitive contact between mother and child. Foreplay is satisfying but they are usually frigid on penetration. In this way, they attempt to establish an object relationship which will compensate for an earlier lack of internalization of a satisfied and satisfactory mother–child relationship, an attempt that is doomed to failure since physical penetration or emotional involvement with a sexual partner reactivates the primitive anxieties of merging or annihilation of the self which the mother–infant relationship originally evoked. What has not been achieved in these girls is growth towards a more mature identification with the mother's adult alive and sexual body, capable of sexual response to penetration by the father and of being impregnated by him. Nor are they able to value their sexual partners or other objects as real people with emotional needs since all they seek is a return to the infantile omnipotence of the baby. Physical maturation, well-trained intelligence, and worldly success may not affect or influence the regressive fixation of this aspect of emotional growth to an infantile stage. Mature object love in which the needs of self and object are mutually understood and fulfilled, cannot be achieved and the birth of a real baby might be a calamity.

CLINICAL MATERIAL

Mrs X was a 36-year-old white teacher who sought help for a severe depression. She had a broken marriage and numerous affairs with coloured partners behind her. She had longed to be a writer but had become intellectually blocked during her university training and so had become a teacher and professional literary critic instead. She had always been interested in dreams and dreaming. In the first few sessions of the analysis, it became clear that her depression had begun nine months after she had had her last abortion, resulting from her relationship with her current coloured lover. She had consciously planned it, with no hesitation or apparent guilt since she came from a country where sexual relations between people of different races were forbidden. A coloured child would not have been tolerated by anyone, especially her own mother. After this event, Mrs X left her current job and came to this country with her lover who had cared for her and treated her very tenderly after the abortion, as if she were the lost baby herself. Mrs X enjoyed the dependence upon him as if she were the baby and he the parent, until the moment when her baby would have been born and she would have had to assume the maternal role herself.

Mrs X was the elder of two intelligent and attractive daughters. Her father, a passive and retiring man, had died of carcinoma of the penis after a long hospitalization when she was 15 years old. Her mother was a vigorous, attractive woman who had married her lover immediately after her husband's death. Before he died, Mrs X's father told her that he had left her some money to go to college and she had been guiltily aware of her wish that her father should die sooner than he did, since his prolonged suffering was distressing for the whole family. After his death, Mrs X's mother told her that no money was available for her education, but it was quite obvious that Mrs X's mother had money for other expenses she considered more essential, such as clothes and make-up to enhance her daughter's physical appearance, just as she used her money to enhance her own. This was but one incident in a lifelong situation in which Mrs X's separate emotional needs and ambitions had not been acknowledged by her mother, although she had always cared for her body. Mrs X had always felt that her attractive body and appearance had never satisfied her mother but had been used by her as an extension of her own in order to attract men. Mrs X's mother frequently told her that she had never been sexually satisfied by her father, and Mrs X felt that it had followed that she had never satisfied her mother either. She was aware of her mother's secret assignations with lovers despite the father's illness, and was angered by his passive acceptance of this situation and of his impending death. The anger was never verbalized and she remained the good child but began to fail academically since she felt confused and unable to think. Adolescence enabled her to find an alternative way of dealing with her painful situation. By using her body she could bypass the painful affects of mourning his loss and the narcissistic rage that her mother's involvement with her lover evoked in her. Her body also enabled her to regain the regressive, primitive satisfaction of the mother–baby relationship in which she sought comfort since her mother could not comfort her in any way. Mrs X's mother was angry at her daughter's attempts to separate from her and made her guilty in return. Eventually, the situation became so intolerable that Mrs X made an abortive suicide attempt. The policeman who saved her and took her back to her mother severely reprimanded her and told her that she was her mother's property until she was 18 and had no right to kill herself. This confirmed her conviction that her body was her mother's and not her own.

A dream and its associations later in the analysis helped us to understand her dilemma. In the dream, Mrs X was crying and turned to her lover for comfort. In response, he came towards her and removed a false white front and offered her his black breast to suck. But the male breast gave no milk and Mrs X was left hungry and desperate. Following the working through of the dream, and the material that followed, Mrs X recognized that in every man she was looking for her mother and that even in someone who was physically so different, the relationship was basically a repetition of the emotionally uncomfortable one she had had with her own mother in which she felt she was clinging on to someone who could deny her life and food, as in the dream, at any minute. The dream marked a moment of insight in which she had to recognize that she longed for the maternal breast which she could never find again.

Mrs X's relationship with her mother had been uneven; symbiotic and mutually safisfying in the beginning but stormy as soon as Mrs X, as a child, tried to move away and become emotionally separate. At any move she made, her mother was enraged, demanding and authoritarian. She told Mrs X repeatedly what a bad child she was, and angrily told her that even in the womb she had defied her and that she had, in fact, tried to abort her during pregnancy. Mrs X was never openly angry with her mother although she was provocative, but was left with an image of herself as a bad child and a representation of her mother as a potentially murderous figure. Mrs X's relationships with men followed a similar pattern. They had always been stormy, and she provoked the men to violent anger although she herself showed none and remained the victim. The relationships were always brought to an end, mainly by Mrs X herself. In this way, she was in fantasy not only the baby who has to cling on to keep alive but also the mother who had to abort the foetus in her turn. The fantasy of clinging to life in spite of her powerful mother's attempts to abort her had been the basis of a narcissistic, omnipotent fantasy which she acted out by making decisions of life and death for the foetus.

After this dream, Mrs X disclosed that she had had three planned abortions during her adult life, each time becoming pregnant with a man whom she seduced into the relationship. None of the men wanted children. Shortly after aborting the foetus she aborted the relationship with the man, just as she had had two previous attempts at therapy which each time she had also aborted. What also emerged during her analysis was that emotional closeness in which she sought and regained the earliest pleasure of the symbiotic, mutually satisfying relationship with her mother also revived primitive fears of merging since the mother could not recognize her as an emotionally separate being with needs of her own or let her separate in her turn. Pregnancy was therefore, for Mrs X, a concrete proof that she owned her own body and that she was a woman in her own right; but emotional separation from her mother was not achieved. If the foetus grew and became a baby who would be fed at her breast, she could never emotionally be a baby again and this she could not give up. The infant's omnipotence and merging with the mother was what she longed to return to. Once her sexual identity and separateness from her mother's body had been concretely established by pregnancy she could abort the foetus as if it were a meaningless part of herself. Yet Mrs X remembered the dates at which these babies might have been born and how old they would have been.

What became meaningful in the course of her analysis was Mrs X's use of her body to seek revenge on her dominating mother. Her sexuality was enjoyed with men her mother disapproved of and she gave her no grandchild to replace herself with. We understood that in this way, by aborting the foetus, her relationships and her previous attempts at analysis, Mrs X had felt herself to be even more grandiose and omnipotent than the bad and murderous aggressor-mother with whom she was identified. The foetus also represented herself as the unwanted, difficult child her mother had said she was and the murderous aggressor-mother. There was no viable alternative to identification with a bad mother and a bad child.

This was subtly reflected in the transference. Mrs X had been referred to me by a colleague in her own country. When I first saw her I did not have a vacancy and wanted to refer her to a colleague. As soon as I had told her this, Mrs X, despite her distress, insisted that she could only work with me and would wait. Shortly, I had an unexpected vacancy and we began to work together. What Mrs X had undoubtedly understood in the first interview was my interest in the narrative of her first pregnancy and abortion, since pregnancy had been a special area for my analytic interest. My difficulty in finding her a vacancy and her persistence in waiting for me had been a transference manifestation of her basic omnipotent fantasy of clinging to an ambivalent mother and seducing her into giving her life. Mrs X attempted from the first to establish an ambivalent countertransference in which we would re-enact a sado-masochistic relationship. Payments of fees were frequently in arrears and holiday breaks were never adhered to by her. This was her attempt to make me into a greedy, demanding, angry figure who would make her guilty at having a separate existence. Mrs X could not lie on the couch but brought many dreams which at this stage were prolific and colourful. She wrote them all in a notebook which she brought to each session, but what was striking was the little-girl affectless voice in which she read them to me. She also interpreted the dreams very cleverly, leaving me no room for my own creativity as an analyst. My role was to be the admiring spectator of her cleverness and her ability to control the whole situation by being both analyst and patient. This was a re-enactment of her family romance. She had been the admired first child and grandchild. Her mother had often told her that she had considered her, as a baby, cleverer than herself. In this way, the childhood situation of omnipotence and helplessness was repeated. The cleverness of the baby was used to disguise the feelings of anxiety at the beginning of analysis. The dreams were good and fruitful products but she could not risk my interpretations lest they prove to be critical attacks which would fragment her precarious sense of self. Once she had tested my capacity to be patient, to contain and tolerate this situation, without becoming the destructive and controlling parental figure that she wanted me to be and yet hoped I would not be, Mrs X could lie on the couch and allow herself to regress in the analytic situation.

Numerous instances of her lover's controlling and often sadistic behaviour were related to me in an affectless voice while I silently experienced feelings of outrage and pity for her as the helpless victim of his cruelty and wondered how she could survive. It was as if we were together repeating a primitive psychological symbiotic stage of the mother–infant relationship in which the baby's non-verbal experiences are mediated not only by the mother's response to that infant, but also by her own past history and current life. In this way, my countertransference, based on my response to my patient but also on my own life, was to be the most subtle tool available for Mrs X's analysis.

Following our understanding of the analytic situation, much of the work that followed was centred upon Mrs X's need to remain in a state of emotional fusion with her mother despite her opposing wish to be separate and free. Since childhood she had related all her probems with her parents to friends and acted according to their reactions of indignation on her behalf since she had no way of judging for herself. She said, 'I feel as if the central core of my self is missing.' We understood that the inability to remain pregnant was a symptom of deeper feelings of the need to remain empty and dead. As the therapeutic alliance developed, Mrs X began to be more in touch with her own feelings. She was now frightened of her own dreams since she now allowed me to interpret them in order to be helped; but the loss of control and infantile omnipotence were difficult to bear, as was our deepening closeness. Her depression and sadness, not only about the loss of her position as the clever baby both in the analysis and with her lover, but also about the loss of her professional identity as the clever critic, her mother, was verbalized and enabled her to be sad also about the loss of the last pregnancy. But it was curious that she expressed no guilt about it. Nevertheless, every session in which we understood each other and insight was deepened was immediately followed by a negative therapeutic reaction or by the intensification of the sado-masochistic aspects of her relationship with her lover. It was as if the establishment of a satisfying and satisfactory relationship between us was both too pleasurable and too threatening.

Interpretations that showed understanding aroused Mrs X's fears of fusion with me and she again used her body in order to separate us by having intercourse with her lover before every analytic hour. In this way, the excitement of good emotional closeness with me and the fear of merging was diffused by a physical experience of orgiastic fusion with a man. We now understood that on a deeper level every man was provoked by Mrs X's tales into hating her mother and separating them. Her sexual affairs with coloured men were to use her body as if it were an extension of her mother's and subtly to humiliate her in this way. Mrs X's mother frequently criticized her and reproached her, saying, 'How can your body which was once in mine feel anything for a man I cannot tolerate!' In this way, we could see that Mrs X's mother shared her daughter's fantasy of owning her body and of fusion with her. Mrs X's fears of her mother's envy of her were also avoided by her choice of a man she could not envy. This was a re-enactment of her intense childhood envy of her attractive mother, repeated in her adolescence, and seen in the transference in her envious attacks upon our work together. We were not to be mutually satisfied and excited by the creation of a living experience together but to conceive a child which Mrs X would then abort. This was reflected in Mrs X's own creativity, where she could create exciting and lively ideas for her students to execute but could not sustain them herself. In this way, her inability to produce a live baby was complemented by her inability to write since she projected her destructive wishes on to the outside world in which every reader was the critical, sadistic mother with whom she felt fused.

Our analytic work now was focused upon the projection of sadistic impulses on to her mother in the first instance and on to her analyst in the transference. Mrs X could now begin to accept her own sadism. She said, 'I do what my mother only wanted to do.' Later she wept, saying 'I murdered those babies.' Interpretation of Mrs X's inability to accept the good mother either in her analyst, her mother or herself led to reveal a fantasy which had secretly predominated her childhood and had never been repressed. In the fantasy there had never been a time when she had not existed. She had always been an egg hiding in her mother's womb waiting to be fertilized by her father's sperm. By means of this fantasy she had been part of the parental intercourse at her own conception. It followed that in fantasy she had not only caused the cancer of the penis from which her father died by biting his penis when he penetrated – mouth and vagina being indistinguishable – but the primary fusion of mother and child was maintained in which it was not clear whether she was her own mother or herself. Any pregnancy of her own was thus in danger of fulfilling the oedipal wish which had not been repressed. The fertilized egg, the foetus that was inside her, could be concretely expelled without guilt since it represented both the dangerous cancer that had killed her father and the sadistic aspects of herself fused with those that she had projected into her mother. We could now see the calamity that faced her if she felt better in analysis. If she could accept her parents as good and capable of satisfying each other, just as she would have to accept her analyst and herself as being good and capable of a satisfying relationship, then she would have to face an overwhelming sense of guilt at having in an omnipotent fantasy destroyed their marriage; and it followed that in her omnipotent fantasy she also destroyed her own analysis. The price she paid for this sadistic fantasy which was never suppressed was heavy in her life. She could struggle for the fulfilment of her conscious wish to achieve an adult relationship, a mature biological feminine identity, an academic success, but would deny herself fulfilment of these aims. She could survive, but not grant herself a licence to live, since she felt her mother had never done so.

It became clear that the unrepressed incestuous sexual fantasy of the earlier pre-oedipal phase and of the oedipal phase had dominated Mrs X's life. The sadistic pleasure contained in this powerful fantasy, and in her pleasure at having defeated her mother in the womb and given her pain, not only drove her to choose coloured sexual partners, physically unlike her father, but also those who did not want children. In this way, she solved her ambivalent wishes by relying on their views. Thus she could abort the unborn child who also represented the hidden oedipal partner, the dead cancerous father whom she could destroy again. A dream, and its associations following analysis of this material, revealed another aspect of her dilemma. Following our mutual decision to terminate the analysis in a year's time, since Mrs X had to return to her own country, she dreamed that she had decided to have an abortion. It had been noteworthy that she had neither wished to become pregnant nor wished to have an abortion now except in her dream. In the dream, after the abortion the doctor showed her the foetus and gave her some of his own blood for the paternity test. It looked painful, but the doctor did it to help her. In her associations it emerged that the foetus was a cancer, a representation of the father inside her whom she could not mourn and let go. No sexual partner could replace him since emotional separation from him would confirm his destruction, just as separation from her mother was unconsciously equated with her death. The foetus that could be destroyed by abortion and replaced by a new pregnancy was a concrete bodily representation of both parents whom she both loved and hated. In thinking about her father's death, from this point in her analysis, Mrs X realized that she had thought he had never separated from his own mother and that in her fantasy his death was equated with a return to the womb. In this way, death and intra-uterine life before birth were unconsciously equated.

Analysis has allowed Mrs X to mourn for her dead father. Previously repressed memories of the good times between her parents and herself have emerged. She is beginning to write again and was helped to do this by recalling the memory of her dead father as a loving parent who cared for her, and it was as if she were writing for him again. She has achieved a more mature relationship with her mother and has been able to say to her, 'If my father had lived my life would have been different', and her mother has for the first time also allowed herself to cry for her first husband. They have since shared grief and mourning for the death of the mother's second husband. Mrs X dreams of pregnancy and abortion but no longer has to act it out. She is wondering whether to continue with her unsatisfying relationship with her lover or whether to separate from him and fulfil herself in her own right. She has met a white man with whom she feels she could have a more suitable relationship. The acceptance of her own sadistic wishes as well as those of her loving feelings and the mourning for her father has offered her a choice of living or surviving.

CONCLUSION

The conclusions that form the final part of this chapter are not only drawn from the analysis of Mrs X but also from my clinical experience with other women patients. First pregnancy is an important developmental phase in a woman's lifelong task of separation-individuation from her own mother. To be pregnant offers a woman a further stage of emotional identification with the pre-oedipal mother, based on a biological foundation. The experience of a child inside her own body also enables a woman to differentiate her body from that of her mother, from whence she herself came. The concrete physical experience of symbiosis between the mother and the foetus now inside her adult body is paralleled by an emotional symbiosis. Mother and child at this stage are felt to be a self-object. A woman, pregnant for the first time, has to achieve a new adaptive position both within her inner world and the outer object world. The internal identifications with her own mother as the object and the narcissistic identification with the foetus as if it were herself are heightened by the normal regression experienced in pregnancy. Maternal pre-conceptive ambivalence, if known to the little girl, may distort the outcome of a young woman's first pregnancy since the biological basis for identi-fication with her own mother is now achieved for the first time. The foetus inside her body now represents good and bad aspects of the self and of the object and the mother may not give it licence to live if she herself feels that she has never been granted one by her own mother. The pregnant mother's ambivalance towards her unborn child may reflect earlier intense ambivalent feelings towards her own mother, resulting in a difficulty in self-object differentiation and further difficulty in separation-individuation. A weak relationship with an undemonstrative father does not help the child to separate from the mother nor to view herself as a child loved and wanted by both parents and endowed with a life of her own. A pervasive sense of guilt at being alive despite the mother's preconceptive ambivalence may give rise to problems in living to the full, since the child may feel she has a licence only to survive. Pride in survival despite the powerful, murderous aggressor-mother may also be a source of omnipotent fantasies for the child and a justification for sadistic fantasies re-enacted in wider object relationships. Separation is unconsciously equated with death of the self or the object. Difficulties in accepting the mother as a good mother may lead to a woman's difficulties in accepting the creative and life-giving aspects of herself.

SUMMARY

The developmental phase of pregnancy and motherhood have been described and discussed, with particular emphasis on a woman's lifelong task of separation-individuation from her mother. A little girl's wish to have a child in identification with her mother was described. The emotional development and fate of this wish affects and is affected by the vicissitudes of physiological maturation.

First pregnancy affords a young woman two further stages of emotional identification: with the omnipotent life-giving pre-oedipal mother, now based on a biological foundation, and also with the foetus, as if she were her own child. Where the mother has been 'good enough', this is a pleasurable developmental phase, in which further maturation and growh of the self may be achieved.

For other woman the inevitable regression occasioned by pregnancy and motherhood may be a frightening experience, if the body has been used to avoid split-off and painful states of mind. Primitive anxieties and conflicts based on the experience of being mothered may be reactivated. A distinction has been drawn between the wish to become pregnant and the wish to become mother to a live child.

The analysis of a patient who repeatedly allowed herself to become pregnant but aborted the pregnancy each time has illustrated this theme. Transference–countertransference problems encountered in her analysis with a woman analyst reflected the difficult relationship to her own mother, in which the infantile aspects had not been successfully resolved and integrated in her adult self.

REFERENCES

Balint, E. (1973) 'Technical problems found in the analysis of women by a woman analyst', *Int. J. Psychoanal.* 54: 195–201

Benedek, T. (1959) 'Parenthood as a developmental phase', *J. Amer. Psychoanal. Assoc.* 7: 389–417.

Bibring, G., Dwyer, T. F., Huntington, D. S. and Valenstein, A. F. (1961) 'A study of the psychological processes in pregnancy', *Psychoanal. Study Child* 16: 9–72.

Deutsch, H. (1944) *The Psychology of Woman*, New York: Grune & Stratton.

Pines, D. (1972) 'Pregnancy and motherhood: interaction between fantasy and reality', *Brit. J. Med. Psychol.* 45: 333–343.

—— (1980) 'Skin communication: early skin disorders and their effect on transference and countertransference', *Int. J. Psychoanal.* 61: 315–323.

Chapter 8

Creativity and fertility

The one-parent phantasy

Paola Mariotti

Mr and Mrs A were a subfertile couple. Their only son was born after three miscarriages, and was the result of countless attempts to conceive in every possible way: naturally, with artificial insemination (AI) with Mr A's sperm and with the help of more invasive techniques, such as in vitro fertilization (IVF), which at the time Mrs A was in analysis with me was still a new procedure. After their son was born, the result of AI, they tried to conceive again but without success. On the surface Mrs A was bearing well under the strain of her 'medical procedures' as she called the IVF treatments and AI.

Their difficulties seemed to lie with Mr A, as his sperm count tended to be low and with low motility. In spite of this, his wife had conceived following intercourse although the pregnancies resulted in multiple miscarriages, and Mrs A sometimes said that she felt she was responsible for their difficulty to carry through a successful pregnancy. Indeed, although she used to complain about her husband on many many counts, for a long time she did not show any sign of anger, or even irritation, at him being at least a contributing factor to their problems. When I pointed out to her the remarkable absence of negative feelings in this specific area, she said it was not his fault after all. She often came up with these kinds of 'reasonable' comments, which were not as reasonable and as logically consistent as they seemed: they often had the flavour of clichés, whose function was to put a stop to a line of enquiry rather than to develop it.

However, Mrs A did not feel angry at her husband, who in fact was hardly getting a mention in her tales of doctors, clinics, other women in a similar situation, statistical results of various types of procedures, her own hormonal levels, etc. In particular Mrs A would discuss at length with me, with her obstetrician, and, last but certainly not least, with her mother, what were the right things to do to become pregnant: the right food, the right vitamins, the right exercise. Could she drive, could she entertain, could she fly or go on holiday after an IVF, or would she endanger a possible pregnancy? It could be argued that she was a very considerate woman who desperately wanted to become a mother; yet, as one listened to her, the question arose of what she thought would actually make her pregnant. She would give to this question an apparently rational answer, and say that she hoped a 'medical procedure' would be successful, but in fact her confidence that perhaps this month she would conceive, or her fear that she would not, depended on her physical, and to a lesser extent mental, state. Excitedly, she reports that she has been completing her course of vitamins, she has been resting, she has not been too emotional in analysis, and therefore she 'feels' she will become pregnant. She predicts her hypothetical pregnancy with totally unrealistic almost touching, optimism, which will be painfully shattered when a few weeks later, disappointed and disbelieving, she would have to realize that she was not pregnant. Her husband's sperm count was hardly ever mentioned as a factor affecting the likelihood of conceiving.

I am proposing that a suitable model to describe the undertow affecting Mrs A's beliefs and behaviour is represented by the hypothesis that she held a deeply rooted and unconscious phantasy of procreation as a one-parent event. To be more precise, in this model the mother was essential and the father superfluous. This was not of course a rationally held belief: what I call the one-parent phantasy could be described as a mental arrangement, a structure which gave order to my patient's experiences. Her feelings about conception seemed to suggest that one person 'had' the product of conception, to which no contribution was required from an Other, so that her own origin was related to her mother only, and her child's only to her. The link between parent and offspring was not only of exclusivity but also involved being identical, since no external influence contributed to the offspring's conception. The reproductive process seemed to imply repetition rather than procreation. Within this framework there was no possibility of development, as the product of conception could not grow and be enriched: instead it was bound to be evacuated, an outcome which my patient sometimes feared and sometimes wished for. As I hope to show in this chapter, this phantasy underpinned my patient's attempt to be effortlessly creative both physically and mentally: she expected ideas and thoughts to be delivered to her, by me or by others, in a finished form, to which she had nothing to add. Analogously, the baby was to be produced by her without the creative participation of her husband, or implanted inside her, without her own active involvement.

This particular phantasy fulfilled various functions in Mrs A's inner world. As a defence, it helped her to short-circuit her oedipal conflicts, her rivalry with father for mother's affection, and also her intense competitiveness and envy of him, and of men in general. In this chapter, however, I will focus on how this phantasy affected her relationships, her experience of procreation, and her identity as a woman and as a thinking person.

It should be noted that an unconscious phantasy is not a rational opinion. Of course Mrs A knew perfectly well how babies are conceived. I am using the notion of unconscious phantasy (Isaacs, 1948) to describe a very early pre-verbal and in any case non-verbal attempt to make sense of experiences affecting the infant in relation to her external and internal world. Unconscious phantasies may find bodily expression and they underpin not only much of one's behaviour in a specific area, but also constitute the impenetrable bedrock to which feelings, opinions and beliefs owe their ultimate justification. They do not lend themselves easily to being verbalized: during the analytic process they are approached many times and in many different ways so that the affective and intellectual connections established by the patient are alive and capable of developing. An unconscious phantasy does not represent the external reality as such, as it is structured along the lines of the understanding that a very young child has of the events taking place around her.

In order to avoid misunderstandings, I would like to make clear at the outset that what I call the phantasy of the single parent is to be understood within an intra-personal context, not as a social phenomenon: it does not refer to those women or men who because of choice or circumstances are raising their children alone. People who live together in a stable relationship may nevertheless hold a more or less unconscious conviction that their spouse is not an essential partner in the generation of their children. On the other hand a lone parent, even in the complete physical absence of her partner, may have him firmly established in her mind, loved or hated, respected or reviled, as the father of her children.

It could be argued that a woman can become pregnant without knowing her partner at all, who may be a chance acquaintance with whom no other contact but casual intercourse was ever established. In fact no matter how uninvolved and short-lived the relationship between the two partners was, the man's participation was absolutely essential to the child's conception. If the mother can acknowledge the irreplaceable quality of the father's contribution and is not inclined to mistake the father's quick disappearance for his non-existence, she does not fall into the phantasy that she is the only parent – even though she may well be the only responsible and loving parent.

However, the argument that the father does not count as a parent if he disappears immediately after conception has another important implication. The question of where babies come from, a question to which many, including Freud, attribute great importance for the development of the human mind, becomes either meaningless or answerable in ultimately relativistic terms, if the father is a contingent factor, to be regarded as relevant to the child's existence only if he complies to certain socially determined criteria, such as maintaining an ongoing relationship with the child. The same argument should apply to the mother. If social standards determine whether or not a couple are the child's parents, the relation between generations becomes in its essence a variable, conditional to the circumstances, and can be shifted in accordance to evolving mores. To dismiss the level of biological reality as meaningless would seem to consign the issue of the intergenerational relationship to contingent arguments.

In this chapter I will briefly discuss how the one-parent phantasy is discernible in diverse contexts, namely social anthropology and history. In those areas one can see that such phantasy can be used to develop the enquiry about humankind's origin but also contains the potential to warp or freeze that enquiry. I shall then turn to clinical material from Mrs A's analysis to discuss and illustrate my hypothesis that the one-parent phantasy underpinned the patient's own sense of her mental activities and of procreation which in some respects were experienced as identical: first in terms of the importance, or otherwise, of an external agency to foster conception, growth and development; second in the manner of dealing with the potential or actual product of conception, be this a foetus or an idea.

This was recognizable in the analytic transference to me, in her description of her relationship with her son and, very importantly, with her mother. She experienced her failure to conceive as monthly repeated miscarriages, or anal expulsions, of an embryo which she could not creatively feed, and she experienced in the same way her 'loss' of the analytic work. Finally, I will briefly discuss the concept of the parental couple and some consequences of its disavowal.

ONE PARENT, ONE SEX: ANTHROPOLOGICAL AND HISTORICAL CONSIDERATIONS

The question of the origin of humankind and the parallel question of individual procreation has been addressed at a historical and ethnographic level in many different ways. Beliefs about the issue of human origin as expressed in creation myths and other religious manifestations can be a distinguishing characteristic of social and cultural groups. Particularly significant for the topic of this chapter are the myths and beliefs about one-parent procreation.

In relation to the origins of humankind it is possible to find a considerable number of myths revolving around an original ancestral figure from which men and women derive (Perelberg, 1995). The primal parent has frequently, but by no means always, female connotations. For instance, the Paleolithic 'Venus' statuettes, whose precise significance is still impossible to ascertain, have been compared to present-day tribal representations of a female mythical ancestress from which the tribe descends (Eliade, 1978). It has been pointed out that even though the female figurines have been found in a wide area ranging from Siberia to France and Italy, no satisfactory male equivalent has been discovered (Young, 1993). Or, in the Sumerian Tablets one finds that the goddess Nammu, whose pictograph is the same as the one for the primordial sea is the 'ancestress who brought forth all the gods'. According to Eliade (1978, p.58), 'the watery mass is identified with the original Mother, who, by parthenogenesis, gave birth to the first couple, the Sky (An) and the Earth (Ki), incarnating the male and the female principles.'

The issue of the one parent has been widely debated also in terms of individual procreation. In 1903 the anthropologist W. E. Roth reported that an aboriginal Australian North Queensland tribe did not seem to recognize the connection between sexual intercourse and pregnancy, and that they were unaware of the part played by the father in the process of conception. Later, Malinowski (1929) provided a well-known example of a culture which seemed to totally ignore the role of the father in the procreative process; indeed, he saw this as a distinctive element of the Trobrianders he studied. Controversy raged for years: some anthropologists felt that those tribes were simply ignorant of the facts of life, but others disagreed, and in 1966 E. Leach vigorously stated that '[d]octrines about the possibility of conception taking place without male insemination do not stem from innocence & ignorance: on the contrary they are consistent with theological argument of the greatest subtlety' (p. 85–86). He went on to suggest that such beliefs are a species of dogma having a social significance and he compared them to the idea of the virgin birth familiar to the Christian world, to which I shall return later.

Social anthropological enquiry is also relevant when applied to Western cultural icons, such as the Oedipus myth. According to Lévi-Strauss (1977) the Oedipus myth

> has to do with the inability, for a culture which holds the belief that mankind is autochthonous (. . .) to find a satisfactory transition between this theory and the knowledge that human beings are actually born from the union of a man and a woman. . . . The Oedipus myth provides a kind of logical tool which relates the original problem – born from one or born from two? – to the derivative problem: born from different or born from same? (p. 216)

Lévi-Strauss presents his somewhat idiosyncratic structural analysis of the myth's 'constituent units'. In my personal understanding of his interpretation, Oedipus, with his swollen foot, struggles to stand up and succeeds in slaying the Sphinx, the autochthonous 'monster unwilling to permit men to live'. He walks away alive, but he is doomed by his incapacity to face his two parents together: the tension in the myth develops between the 'overrated relationship' (with his mother) and the 'underrated relationship (with his father)'. The tension between excessive parental bonds is in counterpoint to Oedipus' barely standing up and killing the Sphinx.

I would not like to suggest a facile usage of psychoanalytical concepts to extrapolate the meaning of mythological accounts. I have presented a few, very succinct anthropological examples in order to point out that the question of procreation does not bear a simple answer. Even Malinowski is at times doubtful that his 'savages' are really as ignorant as they appear to be, and Lévi-Strauss's structural analysis of the relationships between various elements in the Oedipus myth seems to point towards understanding the myth as an expression of the complex tensions between different ways of addressing the issue of human origin, ways which are expressed in the myth's different 'constituent units'.

Later in this chapter I shall describe how the one-parent phantasy is connected, in my patient, with an inability to be creative. I would like to stress that this cannot be simplistically applied to mythological, religious or social beliefs current in another culture or in another era.

I shall return now to the myth of single parenthood provided in Western culture by the belief in the birth of the godhead from a virgin woman, which maintains that a special child, a god-like son, can be generated in the absence of sexual intercourse between the parents. Religious beliefs can be used to rationalize personal unconscious beliefs, as it was the case with Mrs A, who was a devout Catholic and lived in a Catholic country. She surrounded herself with religious people exhalting the value and importance of motherhood while by and large ignoring the connection between motherhood and sex, or at least avoiding an open acknowledgement that the experience of becoming a mother is inevitably linked to a sexual act. Medical procedures such as artificial insemination or, even more, IVF, GIFT, etc., bypass the human sexual relationship, and may foster a belief in a nearly parthenogenetic birth, while the man's contribution, which is after all essential, is brushed aside. The woman's contribution is also reduced to the sum of her medical examinations, and the real protagonist is the doctor with his, or her, medical apparatus, whose unstinting attention is given not to a woman or to a would-be mother, but to a patient. This was certainly true for Mrs A, who was one of the very first patients treated with IVF in her country and therefore, to her satisfaction, the object of great medical excitement.

The primitive Trobrianders and Aborigines, and my unhappy patient, are not alone in wrestling with the issue of the number of people, and the degree of difference, required to make a baby. A long list of distinguished thinkers, philosophers and doctors seem to have adhered to the belief that if two people are necessary, then only one sex is involved. In the reproductive process the other parent assumes a somewhat accessory status. The historian Laqueur (1990) has described what he calls the one-sex model, which, he argues, was prevalent in the Western world's cultural development until the eighteenth century. In his book he quotes extensively from a large number of thinkers who 'discovered' great similarities between male and female sexual organs, reaching in many cases the conclusion that the female sex was a 'less perfect' variety of the male one.

Laqueur argues that 'believing is seeing'. As the foundations were laid of a science which stated it was based on facts and empirical observations and whose conclusions rested their authority on their claim to being objective, the observations were selected as proof and confirmation of what the observer had already in mind, namely the one-sex model. In the context of such a model, he proposes that the difference between men and women for centuries was that of a gender difference, culturally and politically determined. In other words, the sexual characteristics relevant to the assignment of gender were connected to ideological presuppositions and power relationships, not to the (vaguely perceived) anatomical differences. The body's sexual differences recognized as relevant are a consequence of social requirements, not a cause. Laqueur supports with a wealth of historical material the statement that 'until the mid-nineteenth century, when it was discovered that the union of two different germ cells, egg and sperm, constituted conception, it was perfectly possible to hold that fathers mattered very little at all' (p. 57). Laqueur suggests that 'the one-sex model can be read . . . as an exercise in preserving the Father, he who stands not only for order but for the very existence of civilisation itself' (p. 58). If historically the one-sex model had indeed postulated, often explicitly, men's superiority, this is not inherent in the model. On the contrary, as Laqueur points out, 'the real question in the classical model is not . . . – why woman? – but the more troublesome question – why man?' (p. 20). A woman is obviously necessary for the process of procreation to take place but the risk for men was, as sometimes happened, to be thought necessary merely to 'ignite' the process of conception.

I will discuss later how in order to maintain the one-parent phantasy it is necessary to disavow the experience of the creative parental couple. Thinking of the one-sex model in this context I would argue that the difference that matters is not which sex is deemed to be the only term of references or even whether there are objective differences between females and males – at an early embryological stage there are not recognizable anatomical distinctions, and as for the chromosomic difference, it does not address the question of the way the difference between women and men is perceived and experienced – the question is whether it makes sense to think of one sex in any other way but in, explicit or implicit, relation to the other. The tension for definition of each sex aims to the somewhat reciprocal proximity of the other, as can be seen especially in the cultural elements manifested in gendering, where the qualities historically defining one sex acquire significance in references to the other sex, either by contrast or by similarity. Gender, with its cultural and political connotations, has been a determinant element in the definition and in the understanding of sexual differences and processes. It is in relation to gender that the unconscious phantasy of the one parent is operational – the gender distinction that matters in this case is that one sex is intrinsically creative and the other is in a somewhat subordinate position, servicing the creative act rather than participating in it.

This brief review of mythological and historical accounts of procreation and sexuality has shown that creation myths as much as medical research can be seen as attempts to come to terms with and develop further some of the central questions that have interested the human mind. It is possible to think of individual psychopathological manifestations as personal last-ditch solutions to those same dilemmas, solutions though which to a greater or lesser extent have been made necessary by the presence of problematic factors preventing the harmonious development towards a more realistic conclusion.

It has been my intention to illustrate the complexity of the apparently simple issue of procreation. Now I shall attempt to describe how one person, Mrs A, has been wrestling with this question, and the difficulties she has encountered, as they can be understood within the context of a psychoanalytic treatment.

MRS A AND THE ONE-PARENT PHANTASY: CLINICAL VIGNETTE

I discussed earlier the proposition that unconscious phantasies constitute a sometimes disguised basis for thoughts and behaviour. I will return now to my patient, Mrs A, in order to illustrate this proposition with some clinical material. I will try to describe the work of interpretation required to read in the clinical material the relatively coherent phantasy of one-parent procreation. I will discuss (a) how in my patient's relationship with me I thought I could recognize transferential elements reflecting that phantasy; and (b) how similar and other elements could be found in her reported relationship to her son and to her mother. Finally, I will suggest that the one-parent phantasy may interfere with mental creativity.

A few words about Mrs A's background: her parents seemed to have had a stable marriage. She spoke rarely and dismissively about her father; often and very admiringly about her mother. She had a younger sibling, born when the patient was 1½ years old. She reported that mother's second pregnancy had been difficult and there had been unspecified medical complications.

A powerful source of information about the patient's inner world is provided by the transference to the 'here-and-now' of the analytic sessions. For a long time an ideal relationship of a kind seemed to happen in the consulting room: my patient sooner or later would end up agreeing with what I said, even though often my comments seemed to make not the slightest bit of difference to her way of thinking. For many years in analysis she responded compliantly to interpretations, tended to explain away her feelings with tired clichés and gave few signs of spontaneity, originality or creativity. In her sessions, she seemed to behave in a similar way to what she reported was her school performance, when she felt that her work was diligently done, but lacking in creativity. She appeared to be a 'good patient', co-operative in taking up whatever I said. Sometimes she was tearful, but very rarely openly angry, and she was wary of expressing feelings in an unguarded way. She told me that she did not have feelings for, or against, me, because of our relationship being 'professional', which meant impersonal and somewhat distant. Gradually she became able to recognize that under the surface she experienced me, sometimes, in a very intensely negative way. She also used to feel that it was bitterly unfair that I set the dates for holiday breaks, and that, if she decided different dates for her holidays or if she had to cancel appointments because of her fertility treatments at the hospital, she was charged for the missed sessions. Once, after one year of analysis and before her successful pregnancy, I suggested to her that she felt that by charging her I meant that she should come to her sessions, even though this may jeopardize her treatment. She replied in a sad, resigned voice that of course I was right to expect her to come to analysis at all costs and that she just did not understand well enough that she should not miss sessions. She did not comment about the cruel unsympathetic aspect of what she felt were my rigid expectations that analysis should be more important than her fertility treatment.

A few sessions after this exchange she came with a dream. This was the first session after I had moved my consulting room to a new location, an office where other psychoanalysts also worked. Mrs A started by saying how nice the new place was, she had met other people in the waiting room; then she told me her dream. She was having a medical procedure. Perhaps she was already pregnant, but she needed to have a transfusion. She asked a woman doctor to do it, but the doctor said no, she was busy, she had lots of things to do. Mrs A pleaded: this pregnancy was so important. The doctor said that someone else could do the transfusion, but there was nobody around. The patient then went on talking to me of her next IVF, saying that the present month did not seem right, she was busy organizing a holiday, but she felt that in two or three months the procedure would work. I suggested she was talking about the analysis as well – I had moved to a new place, she thought I would be busy and she was afraid that her analysis would not work well for a while. She agreed, adding that she would not be able to give attention to anything else if she had just moved. She then said that she wanted to be important, and she felt she was not.

The material I have presented I think sums up the mixture of feelings Mrs A often conveyed to me: despair and hopeless needs – rarely represented so directly, her dependency on an indifferent and ultimately very cruel object, quite transparently myself, the object who was indeed supposed to be the very person who should have best been able to help her in her predicament. Also she was attempting to placate me by praising the new consulting suite without mentioning irritation or anger at the thought that I might not be able to concentrate on her in the usual way, and her need to 'make things all right', for instance talking about her holiday.

However, the communication which is most directly relevant to my present argument concerns her experience of my feelings and reactions which she expresses with certainty as being the same as her own. She implied in her dream and she verbalized in her associations that of course I shall not be able to give her adequate attention; indeed it will be impossible for me to carry through the analysis, just as she could not start a pregnancy then, with the preoccupation of her holidays in mind. My understanding of her communication is that she was not wondering whether I would react as she would, but that she was sure that I did feel like her. Her certainty about my feelings in this and other material suggests that Mrs A believed her and my mental functioning to be not so much similar as identical. This is a significant distinction. If she had been wondering, perhaps fearing, whether my state of mind might be like hers, there would have been space in her mind for a painful but imaginative questioning: her expectation of my state of mind could have been enriched with memories, reflexions, feelings, integration of opposites leading gradually to further development. As it was, the situation for her was already laid out, cast in stone one could say, and there was no need, and no room, to develop thoughts or feelings.

About a year later Mrs A became pregnant. This followed her realization in analysis of her disappointment that the well-known elderly professor who had been treating her for infertility had delegated some of the work to his assistant, a woman doctor. The patient was able to experience feeling abandoned, and being jealous of other patients who were still looked after by him. Moreover, around the time she actually became pregnant she casually remarked that the woman doctor who was now treating her seemed to be pregnant. A few weeks later it became apparent that this was the case.

I shall now report the résumé of a session that took place about ten months after the patient had had her baby, from which it is possible to gain an impression of the complicated relationship between herself and her son and how the husband was seen in this family picture. This session took place approximately two years after the dream described above.

Mrs A started by saying that there were a few things she wanted to tell me. She always started like this . . . yesterday's session seemed so far away. (She did indeed very often usher in her sessions with some similar comment, which gave the impression that the work of the previous session had somewhat vanished from her mind and also that that work might have to be repeated, but that she could do nothing about it.)

She then went on with complaints about her husband who according to her was more devoted to his parents than to her. In particular she seemed to resent the time he gave to his mother, who was lost and lonely when her own husband was away for work. She also made it clear that she did not trust her mother-in-law to look after the baby properly. (I thought to myself that she was piling up criticisms of her husband and his family who came across as inadequate and uncaring, and of no use to her and her child.) I reminded her of the previous day when she had somehow contrasted her irritation with her husband with her own good relationship with her baby. She dismissed it, but said that she did want to talk about her son.

Yesterday they had gone to a playgroup with other mothers and babies. The babies were younger than her son, yet some were bigger than him, and they were drinking juice from a cup, but with her son, who is now 10 months, 'it is a battle to get 4 oz of juices in him in the whole day.' (The patient seemed quite anxious about the child's intake of fluids, and I felt unsure as to whether he was still being breast-fed.) I said that as far I knew he was still being breast-fed. Yes, she said, the doctor said she should stop, but he has no comforter, does not suck his finger, his only comforter is the breast. I pointed out that the baby seemed to be getting on fine, yet she kept herself busy with him measuring and worrying about the juice. (Looking back at my comment I think that I felt alarmed about a situation where the feeding mother with her contented baby were ignored and my patient was becoming a mechanical ounce-counting juice provider, supported by the convenient opinion of a doctor. She seemed intent to deprive herself and her child of a satisfactory feeding situation – not surprisingly, a battle had already been engaged with the child. However, Mrs A's anxiety had a highly intrusive quality and seemed to be centred, in this and other cases, on the comparison between her baby and other children.)

She agreed that she had not thought about him getting milk. (I think that Mrs A was truthful in saying that she had not thought about the milk: the breastfeeding relationship with her son, intimate and life-giving as it was, was now inevitably coming to an end and separation was literally unthinkable for her. At this point our discussion about feeding stopped: it was not my impression that she felt strengthened or reassured about her child's health, or her capacity to look after him. She opened the next sentence, after a brief pause, with a characteristic 'Anyway –' which meant that the subject had been dismissed and dropped from her mind.)

Anyway, what happened yesterday was that at first all was fine but soon her baby began to cry and they had to leave. She did not mind as she was not enjoying herself. As they walked out of the door, her son stopped crying, and she saw in the corner of her eye that he gave a little smile, so she said 'You are a little monkey', but she felt quite pleased that he wanted to be only with her. The boy gave a huge smile, after which he had a sleep and then he was in a very good mood. I asked her whether she was thinking that her son expressed the same feeling she had, namely that other people, like her husband or the other mothers, were tiresome, and they were better off being by themselves, mother and son. She agreed and said that with some exceptions she does not even like her son to be with his father. Sometimes she sets up little tests, to see if her husband is adequate (to look after the little boy), but he always proves what she expects him to prove, namely that he is inadequate. I commented that her husband was therefore excluded from the ideal relationship between herself and her baby: he was unnecessary and perhaps today some of her resentment against her mother-in-law was due to the old lady missing her own husband so much. Mrs A agreed that her mother-in-law represented a very different point of view from hers in relation to men, and produced examples of it, but concluded the session with an oft-repeated, and very clichèd, wish that her husband were different and more close to her.

I have chosen this session to illustrate how intensely Mrs A wished to exclude everyone else from her relationship with her son, cost what it would in terms of his development and of her enjoyment. Her husband in particular was clearly regarded as untrustworthy and unnecessary. She intrusively manipulated the baby's contact with the external world, counting the ounces of juices the boy was supposed to drink, while at the same time denying the mutually creative feeding experience, which had been quite successful but was coming to an end. My comments about breastfeeding were abandoned after she said that she had not thought about it.

Further evidence of Mrs A's exclusive bond with her son and of its implications could be found in her descriptions of a great closeness between them, that she was trying to maintain at the expense of his developing independence. Sometimes she seemed to be worried about it, but often she would say with a satisfied smile in her voice that she thought it was very nice the way he behaved, polite and shy, not boisterous at all. She would point out that he was not like other boys, but rather behaved as she, the patient, used to behave as a child. She saw no similarity between her husband's relationship with his mother, and her son's with her. She insisted that the little boy had taken after her, and that they were as close as she had been to her mother whom, at the beginning of her analysis, she regarded as perfect: 'she could not have been a better mother.'

The tight bond between Mrs A and her mother was illustrated in many ways, and especially at the beginning of the analysis it seemed to the patient to be totally unproblematic. Mother had to be consulted for every decision including, literally, the colour of the wallpaper in her own house. But this was all right because mother 'really knew better'. With me she was compliant and agreeable, yet, as the dream shows, she experienced me, the doctor, as very cruel and indifferent, ready to withdraw from her what she wanted most: the transfusion which would confirm her pregnancy.

During her attempts to become pregnant she sometimes dreamt of a child, who was her child but was not with her because it had been kidnapped or stolen from her. When she was pregnant she was constantly worried that something bad could happen to her and she talked of her 'superstitious fear of the evil eye' which could somehow harm her baby.

Rejection was always round the corner. If she felt she was being treated badly, even cruelly, like in her dream, by someone important, such as myself or her husband, she would accept it and try to justify her aggressor. All her complaints about her husband were carefully engineered so that nothing would change, as she felt, and she said that change could only be for the worse and her husband would abandon her. With her placating attitude she conveyed a fear that, unless she obeyed some strict unspoken rules, she would be thrown out by me. One such rule seemed to require her to be dependent on me. Once she brought me some material indicating that she thought that analysis was yet another demand in her busy life, which she would have happily done without. I interpreted her feeling of not needing me. The following session she was very distressed. She was sure I intended to terminate her analysis because she had conveyed her feeling of not needing me and I must be angry with her for not appreciating me. She tried to reassure me that indeed she needed me and she knew it. We came to understand this as a repetition in the transference of her experience of her mother as someone who could mercilessly sever any emotional contact with her daughter unless she (the daughter) was utterly dependent. She thought for a long time that such an attitude in her mother was perfectly justified.

MOTHER AND DAUGHTER: CREATION OR REPETITION?

I propose to conceptualize this woman's very close relationships with her mother and with her son, from which father and husband were absent, and her difficulty in accepting the difference in our positions within the analytic relationship, with a model where the creative process, in its essence the result of the conjunction of different elements leading to a new conclusion, is replaced by the repetition of the same. In the latter case there is no need of an Other to bring about the wished-for result, no need of entering into a relationship with an external reality which may be frustrating as well as fulfilling, nor is there a challenge to one's own very identity inevitable in the presence of a new analytic insight as there is when a new baby claims his relationship with his new parents.

In this context it seems significant that she conceived just a few weeks after the doctor treating her had become pregnant, although Mrs A was never able to discuss her feelings in regard to the doctor with whom she insisted the relationship was purely professional.

However, Mrs A often noticed similarities between herself and her mother, which as the analysis progressed she found more and more disquieting, especially when they regarded their ways of being mothers. My hypothesis is that Mrs A had an (unconscious) phantasy which dated from her early infancy based on a fundamental 'sameness' beween mother and daughter, which led her to expect to make a baby just like, and when, she experienced her mother having babies. If the father could be eliminated as essential other parent, one crucial difference between herself and her mother would also vanish. Outside the oedipal couple mother's adult sexuality had become an empty signifier. Pregnancy was eventually the result not of a process of procreation but of a corporeal transfusion. With the elimination of father the transmission of a preformed baby from mother inevitably implied a lack of creativity in her own body. The concreteness of the conception had a parallel in the paucity of her mental creativity. Failed separation from mother and avoidance of the father prevented her access, to use the Lacanian expression, to the symbolic register.

Mrs A was fused with an image of mother, which held her in an idealized embrace where she could only mould herself to mother, rather than being herself. Breaking free of that embrace meant on the one hand losing a fantasized position with mother, analogous to her own child's in relation to her, as part of a mother–child couple from which the husband/father was excluded and deemed unworthy. On the other hand she did not seem to have in her inner world an image of a dynamically developing sense of separation: the mother (or analyst) supposedly so skilled and caring, was ready to cast her off and abandon her if she failed to conform to expectations. One of her manoevres to stave off this catastrophe was to comply and submit: in analysis this meant accepting my interpretations and repeating what I had said like a good little girl. In this way she was giving up her capacity to be creative and could only have mother's, or the analyst's, ideas. Because of the fundamental, all-pervading placatory nature of the process, the ideas so conceived could not be modified and enriched by herself or by anyone else. What she was taking in from me were particular, definite and lifeless products, called ideas, which were not supposed to develop inside her and had a limited lifespan. On a different occasion, on a different day she needed different ideas, just as in her dream she needed a transfusion to be pregnant, or to maintain and support her pregnancy. She lacked a capacity to nourish and think her own ideas, a capacity which in this case I equate to the mothering function.

The concept of identification with mother is complex and potentially confusing. Mrs A was stuck in her identification with a rigid idealized image of her mother, which she 'pinned on' her external mother, whose advice she used to require very often, and which she experienced as a rigid internal object when for instance she attempted to guess what in a given situation would be the 'right' thing to do. She had not internalized the creative mothering function which for a mother ranges in a continuum from conception of the embryo to her capacity to respond authentically, and appropriately, to her child's emotional communications.

A successful internalization of the mothering function would seem to require that the child be capable of distinguishing between her mother and herself as a daughter, and of recognizing that mother is involved in a relationship with father to which the child has no access. In other words, in order to internalize the mothering function a little girl has to accept that she has not got it – yet.

I have used the concept of function because of its non-concrete connotation: it is equally meaningful if it refers to the psychological or to the physical domain. It implies the development of one's own capacity to be a mother, a capacity which my patient had, to an extent, replaced with imitation or repetition of what she perceived to have been her mother's behaviour. It is possible that when her doctor had become pregnant Mrs A's tendency to repeat facilitated her own pregnancy. Mrs A, however, denied any connection.

The abstract element present if one thinks of mothering as a function allows for a space which in each specific situation is to be saturated by the particular experience – a saturation which depends on the situation and cannot be fixed in advance, nor can it be repetition of a previous behaviour. The mothering function cannot be fulfilled by a fixed specific gesture and requires constant live creativity. In contrast to this, my patient did not have access to the abstract level and she was stuck with the particular example. Her mothering creativity, which was not absent and developed further in analysis, was, however, at times very limited, replaced by her attempts to do the right thing in mother's eyes. She needed a baby to prove her creativity: but the 'proof' could work only so long as the baby was a baby, then further proof was needed, and a further one, and so on.

The disappointment in her adult subfertility resonated with the bitterness and stubbornness of a young child's omnipotent wish. When talking about her wish for a baby she would refuse to consider her husband's difficulties and would say to me: 'It is true that I do not want to think about it. I do not really believe it matters [it being her husband's subfertility]. What's wrong with not wanting to think about it? If I do, it makes me feel depressed.' She certainly made it very clear that wishful thinking was much more attractive than having to accept a depressing reality: in a similar way, in her own mind she had not given up the phantasy of a special, and especially beautiful, relationship with her mother. The mourning process for a second pregnancy was difficult because in her early childhood she did not have the opportunity to accept that she was not like mother, in that mother's creativity was due to her ability to join with father and make another baby. I believe that she had not internalized from childhood the difference between herself as a child and her sexual mother, and as an adult she could not find help in the sexual woman within herself, but was trapped in an infant's system of beliefs, stamping her foot with the utter despair and frustration of a young child who is unable to comprehend why her wish is not becoming reality.

The importance of recognizing and coming to terms in an appropriate way with aggressive feelings, directed especially against the mother in childhood and later, has been observed and discussed by many authors. Dinora Pines (1993) has described the complex intrapsychic relationship with their own mother experienced by women who have difficulties conceiving or maintaining a pregnancy. Negative feelings, such as fear, anger and rage, if excessive, make it difficult for a woman to identify with a good, helpful and creative image of mothering. In some cases this may mean repeated terminations of pregnancies, while in others a woman may not find within herself a comforting figure who would help her to mourn her hopes for a baby and would provide her with the capacity to be creative in other areas, if motherhood proves to be impossible.

Melanie Klein (1957) linked a particular type of aggression to creative difficulties when she wrote:

> envy of creativeness is a fundamental element in the disturbance of the creative process. . . . The super-ego figure on which strong envy has been projected becomes particularly persecutory and interferes with thought processes and with every productive activity, ultimately with creativeness. (p. 202)

One may feel somewhat hesitant to attribute definite feelings of envy to an infant and I think that in the case of my patient one could end up oversimplifying her predicament. However, some traits in her personality suggested problems in dealing with envious feelings: in her marriage for instance she tended to compete with her husband as she did with men in general. Her fear of the evil eye also indicates a deep, primitive fear of an envious object. Moreover, the comparison between herself and mother left her drained of self-esteem, as her (idealized) mother was felt to need continuous praise and support, which the patient provided by presenting herself as inferior and in need of advice and help.

I would like to add some considerations on the absence of the father in my patient's history, both in terms of her own father and of her child's. Elsewhere (1993) I have discussed the importance of the acknowledgement of the father as a person, separate from infant and mother and relating to mother in a relationship from which the child is excluded. Such acknowledgement is preceded by, and signficantly linked to, the infant's capacity to allow for things unknown to exist, in his/her mind or in the external world. The father who, as a person in his own right, cannot be conceptualized by the infant, is gradually recognized as occupying a place in mother's life to which the child has no access. In this theoretical model, the child's capacity to conceive of an unknown space, inhabited by relationships not dependent on herself, can be regarded as a precursor of her capacity to allow her thoughts to develop in her mind in a new, unpredictable and creative way.

The interpretative model I have been discussing above focuses on the primitive unconscious phantasy of the single parent. However, the same clinical events which underpin this approach can be understood in different ways; indeed they are interpreted at different levels in different stages of the analytic treatment. In particular, one thinks of the directly defensive function fulfilled by eliminating one parent, which enables the patient to sidestep the oedipal conflicts. As if this were not enough, in the case of Mrs A, she was uncomfortably aware of her rivalry with men professionally, and with her husband, and while she was very dismissive of the notion of penis-envy, which, she said, not by coincidence has been invented by a man, she could not deny her resentment of men's phallic potency, and deep annoyance for needing a man's penis in order to have a baby. Doing away with one parent allows the child to deny need, while supporting the identification with one omnipotent parent. Limentani (1991) describes how it is possible for the analyst, let alone for the patient, to be drawn into a denial of father's importance. He points out that an absent father is in fact very much present in his withdrawal. Nobody knows that better than the analyst when his/her patient can maintain his oedipal triumph only by reducing the analyst to the position of an impotent father.

THINKING AND THE PARENTAL COUPLE

The concept of 'parental couple' is a way of describing the internal image of the process leading to a creative act. It is an image rooted in the recognition of one's parents as people who outside one's control have joined together with (some) love to make a new life. The notion of a couple underlines the presence of two people relating to each other to bring about a creative outcome. In the more recent developments of psychoanalytic theory the creative parental couple when it is successfully internalized is seen as opening the way to the creative thinking process where different thoughts are allowed to join and new thoughts are allowed to develop as a consequence. In a collection of Kleinian papers on the oedipal complex, Britton links the capacity to observe and learn to the experience of being in the 'third position' within the oedipal triangle:

> If the link between the parents perceived in love and hate can be tolerated in the child's mind, it provides for him a prototype for an object relationship of a third kind in which he is a witness and not a participant. (Britton *et al.*, 1989, p. 87)

The development of the mental structure alluded to with the term 'parental couple' is complex and beset with difficulties. It requires the acknowledge-ment of both parents as separate and independent from oneself, capable of creative activity from which the child is by definition excluded; the gender difference between the parents is a reminder of one's limitations and need of the other.

The denial of differences is crucial, according to the French psychoanalyst Chasseguet-Smirgel, for the development of a perverse solution which annihilates differences in gender or generation. The perverse solution denies the difference between adult sexuality, which takes place between the parents, and the child's sexual activity, between pre-genital sexuality and genitality. Britton *et al.* (1989) does not refer specifically to perverse patients when he suggests the expression 'oedipal illusions' to describe a phantasy which evades the acknowledgement of the essential difference between parental relationship and the parent–child relationship (p. 94).

Chasseguet-Smirgel (1985) proposes that in the anal stage of development there is a tendency to experience everything as being the same, and the anal stage precedes pre-genitality. The perverse solution denies the difference.

Ultimately, however, 'to try and replace genitality by the stage that normally procedes it is to defy reality. It is an attempt to substitute a world of sham and pretence for reality' (pp. 127–128). She links perversion to a failure to internalize the paternal function of 'barrier against incest' (p. 121). The father and his adult genital sexuality is devalued in favour of pre-genital merging with mother. The capacity to appreciate reality and to think are jettisoned in the process. In order to counterbalance the emergence of awareness of the infantile nature of one's perverse attachment, its idealization is established and fostered: indeed, Chesseguet-Smirgel describes it as a 'compulsion to idealize' (p. 91).

My patient, Mrs A, did not suffer from any form of clinical perversion, but it would seem that some of the elements which may lead to perversion played a part in her psychopathology. Her compliance to me and to her idealized mother reflected a deep difficulty in creatively thinking her own thoughts. 'Thinking: that is the enemy', writes Chesseguet-Smirgel, describing the attack perpetrated against recognizing differences, and therefore reality; and she could be writing for Mrs A.

The compulsion to idealize the exclusive relationship with mother, which leaves no space in the patient's mind for the creative sexual relationship between the parents, is one powerful factor that prevents the patient from developing her own creativity. Her need to protect herself from the traumatic awareness of her predicament by not thinking is yet another step away from creativity.

CONCLUSION

In this chapter I have described a phantasy which I believe represents an attempt to address the question of where babies come from. I have presented some historical and social anthropological material suggesting that the question of why two parents and not one, has a long and distinguished history. In my patient's life the phantasy of the one parent represented a powerful limitation to her creativity. It tried to compensate for, and cover up, the despairing feelings experienced when the patient was unable to be in touch with an alive and genuinely creative mothering figure. I have also discussed how this unconscious phantasy may be seen as underpinning disturbances in her experience of her thinking process as well as of procreation.

REFERENCES

Britton, R., Feldman, M. and O'Shaughnessy, E. (eds) (1989) *The Oedipus Complex Today: Clinical Implications*, London: Karnac Books.

Chasseguet-Smirgel, J. (1985) *Creativity and Perversion*, London: Free Association Books.

Eliade, M. (1978) *A History of Religious Ideas*, Chicago: The University of Chicago Press.

Isaacs, S. (1948) 'The nature and function of phantasy', *Int. J. Psychoanal.* 29: 73–97.

Klein, M. (1957) 'Envy and gratitude', in *Envy and Gratitude and Other Works*, London: Hogarth and the Institute of Psycho-Analysis.

Laqueur, T. (1990) *Making Sex: Body and Gender from the Greeks to Freud*, Cambridge, Mass.: Harvard University Press.

Leach, E. (1966) 'Virgin birth', *Proceedings of the Royal Anthropological Institute* 33–39.

Lévi-Strauss, C. (1977) *Structural Anthropology*, London and New York: Allan Lane.

Limentani, A. (1991) 'Neglected fathers in the aetiology and treatment of sexual deviations', *Int. J. Psychoanal.* 72: 573–584.

Malinowski, B. (1929) *The Sexual Lives of Savages in North-Western Melanesia*, London: Kegan Paul.

Mariotti, P. (1993) 'The analyst's pregnancy: the patient, the analyst and the space of the unknown', *Int. J. Psychoanal.* 74: 151–163.

Perelberg, R.J. (1995) 'The psychoanalytic understanding and treatment of violence: a review of the literature and some new formulations. Pre-circulated paper to the 16th International Colloqium at the Anna Freud Centre', *Bulletin of the Anna Freud Centre* 18: 89–122.

Pines, D. (1993) *A woman's Unconscious Use of her Body*, London: Virago Press.

Young, G. (1993) *The Dying Goddess*, Pittsburgh: Dorrance Publishing Co.

Chapter 9

Mutual admiration between mother and baby

A *folie à deux*?

Deborah Steiner

Blest the babe . . . who, when his soul
Claims manifest kindred with an earthly soul,
Doth gather passion from his mother's eye . . .
(Wordsworth, 'Prelude 2', 1805)

These lines from Wordsworth's 'Prelude' capture vividly a certain quality in the contact between a mother and her new baby; a mutual searching intensity at moments oblivious to the outside world, which evokes very mixed emotions in an outsider or onlooker. They also suggest that the mother's passionate admiration for her baby and vice versa is a desirable ingredient for the baby's good beginning in life.

I would like in this chapter to explore elements of the very early mother/infant relationship which give it the peculiar and exclusive intensity that many mothers find both disturbing and gratifying. I will try to illustrate, using material from a patient who had her first baby while in analysis, how the close involvement between the mother and the baby which is essential at this stage if the relationship is to flourish, also contains the seeds of conflict and difficulty, which most mothers encounter, both at this stage and later with weaning, in allowing the baby to be separate. I want to look at the primal relationship in terms of a love affair, a *folie à deux*, in which both parties, mother and baby, eagerly and willingly engage, and in which the exclusion of the immediate oedipal rival, the father who also represents external reality, is a potent factor.

Freud in his paper on Leonardo da Vinci, underlined the erotic nature of the primary attachment between the mother and baby when he wrote:

A mother's love for the infant she suckles and cares for is something far more profound than her later affection for the growing child. It is in the nature of a completely satisfying love-relation, which not only fulfils every mental wish but also every physical need; and if it represents one of the forms of attainable human happiness, that is in not little measure due to the possibility it offers of satisfying, without reproach, wishful impulses which have long been repressed and which must be called perverse.

(1910, p. 117)

Freud is implying that gratification of unconscious sexual needs in the mother is as potent a force in the primal relationship as the conscious wish to satisfy the emotional and physical needs of the infant. He suggests too that this 'love affair' ends, or changes, as the child grows.

The phase that I am concerned with is more or less that in which Winnicott describes the mother as being in a state of 'primary maternal preoccupation' (1958). This he sees as a 'heightened sensitivity ... especially towards the end of the pregnancy ... [which] lasts for a few weeks after the birth of the child' (p. 302). Winnicott's 'preoccupation' invites the question with what or whom is the mother preoccupied and this is a question I would like to address. However, when Winnicott goes on to say: 'Only if a mother is sensitized in the way I am describing can she feel herself into her infant's place, and so meet his needs' (p. 304), this to me evokes a potentially dangerous situation where the conscious, adult capacities of the mother might become unavailable to both.

Another question which arises in connection with this situation is whether the moments of intense mutual admiration between an ordinary mother and her infant have an important function in the infant's development. Can one envisage an infant thriving well who never had moments of feeling absolutely the most important person in the world to the mother (or other consistent carer) at this very early stage in life?

Such intense moments involve idealization, both of the object and of the self. At such moments a state of mutual projective identification exists in which undesirable or dangerous aspects of both baby and mother are split off and felt to reside elsewhere, maybe in the father, the mother's parents or other siblings. In this way the feeling of closeness is enhanced, and feelings of separateness and loneliness kept at bay. For the new-born baby, such close involvement physically and mentally by the mother means the difference between life and death. What does it mean for the mother? With a new-born infant the mother, one might speculate, is having both to mourn the loss of the baby in her womb, and to that extent the baby of her fantasy, while at the same time establishing a relationship with the real baby whom she must make a conscious effort to nurture.

Melanie Klein wrote in her paper 'On the sense of loneliness':

Integration ... means losing some of the idealization – both of the object and of a part of the self – which has from the beginning coloured the relation to the good object. The realization that the good object can never approximate to the perfection expected from the ideal one brings about de-idealization: and even more painful is the realization that no really ideal part of the self exists. ... the need for idealization is never fully given up, even though in normal development the facing of internal and external reality tends to diminish it.

(1963, p. 305)

She goes on to quote a patient who felt 'the glamour had gone' when the idealization of the self and of the object had diminished, giving relief but also leading to a sense of loneliness.

Freud referred many times to the element of seduction in the early mother/infant relationship. In the paper on Leonardo da Vinci he seems to suggest that the Mona Lisa smile, at once seductive and cold, may be an expression by the artist of his childhood experience of a mother who had a tender and passionate attachment to him in the absence of his father, yet who handed him over to another woman to be cared for. And in his later paper on 'Femininity' (1933, p. 124) Freud speaks of 'the slights, the disappointments in love, the jealousy, the seduction followed by prohibition' all inherent in this first relationship, giving it the tone of an intense love affair.

J. Laplanche in his book *New Foundations for Psychoanalysis* (1989) took further the notion of primal seduction – that is the mother's seduction of the baby with her tenderness and physical care – making the point that the 'deviant adult', i.e. the seductive mother, is so because:

given that the child lives on in the adult, an adult faced with a child is particularly likely to be deviant and inclined to perform bungled or even symbolic actions because he is involved in a relationship with his other self, with the other he once was.

I would say that this refers to the mother's involvement with aspects of her own infantile self projected into the baby and admired and loved, and that this is an inevitable process in the development of the relationship. However, the infant's development as a separate individual also depends on the mother's capacity to be in touch with an integrated self, both loving and hating and therefore not idealized.

Laplanche proceeds to ask the question:

Can analytic theory afford to go on ignoring the extent to which women unconsciously and sexually cathect the breast, which appears to be a natural organ for lactation? It is inconceivable that the infant does not notice this sexual cathexis. . . . it is impossible to imagine that the infant does not suspect that this cathexis is the source of a nagging question: what does the breast want from me, apart from wanting to suckle me, and come to that why does it want to suckle me?

The use of words such as 'perverse' and 'deviant' seem disturbing in this context because they challenge our tendency to idealize the mother/infant duo and keep it untainted with feelings of aggression and sexuality. And while not wanting to press the analogy too far, the questions are similar to a patient asking of an analyst: 'why are you doing this; why are you so interested in me; what do you want of me; what are you getting out of it?', questions that the analyst needs constantly to be asking him/herself. The elements of perverseness or deviancy lie to some degree, it seems to me, in the inequality in the relationship and in the ever-present wish for gratification, through power or idealization. If such wishes to be admired and idealized remain persistently unconscious and unacknowledged inwardly in the analyst, the analytic relationship would be in danger of becoming a kind of *folie à deux* in which more disturbing aspects of the patient's emotional life would remain untouched.

In an interesting paper called 'A psychoanalyst looks at a hypnotist: a study of *folie à deux*' (1994), A.A. Mason goes further and suggests the mutuality of the seduction. He maintains that a successful hypnotic trance is an intense transference fantasy of powerful projective identification:

> The most dramatic and powerful effects of this fantasy are produced when it exists in its most primitive,i.e. magical or omnipotent form in a patient and when the patient meets a therapist in whom this fantasy is also powerfully present. Then, 'I wish to possess' and the corollary and mirror image of this wish i.e. 'I can be possessed' has found a practitioner who also wishes and believes he or she can possess another human being. A duet such as this is what I believe to be the basis of the hypnotic state.

He goes on to liken this to the highly charged duet of mother and infant. The infant projects into the mother as the container unmanageable feelings of fragmentation and death an I t·us rids himself of unbearable pain and fear. Part of this process is the omnipotent fantasy that he possesses and controls the breast. The mother not only contains and manages the baby's feelings but also 'fosters' the fantasy of control in the early weeks and months through her responsiveness to his needs. The infant omnipotently fantasizes that he possesses the breast and the mother willingly allows that this is so. 'His majesty the baby' commands and mother obeys; in this situation the baby captivates the mother by his exclusive need for her and her alone and she responds by being seduced. With her total commitment to the physical care and feeding of the infant she seduces him with the belief that he is the only one for her. Mason argues that as in a hypnotic trance this could be seen as a delusional state in which the mother is a willing collaborator. Thus the baby's limited view of the external world being the breast finds resonance in the mother as she nurses and cares for him.

In development the longing for such a *folie à deux* arrangement is never totally given up but is repressed and remains as unconscious wishes and fantasies in adult life. In a family an expression of this might be the persistent coupling of a parent and child in which the other parent is feared or looked down on as a dangerous intruder. In the analytic situation, unconscious wishes in the patient for a special, exclusive relationship may often dovetail, as it were, with unconscious needs of the analyst and give rise to a kind of mutual admiration society, which is actually inimical to further understanding and insight.

All patients, including those whom one would not regard as very ill, have ideas and fantasies about their analyst which they regard as facts and which are maintained as such alongside more rational or critical thoughts that might contradict these ideas. The notion of being the analyst's 'favourite' or simply the 'only' patient is a very common one and may subtly gratify the analyst's need to be admired and idealized. It would be folly to assume that analysts are free of such wishes and fantasies. It is indeed striking how universal the desire is to realize this fantasized relationship and how powerfully any evidence to the contrary can be disavowed, ignored or dismissed. The patient may try in all sorts of subtle ways to find confirmation of the mutuality of the duet and I will give a brief vignette to illustrate what I mean. The material comes from the first year of an analysis, at the end of the week preceding a Bank Holiday weekend. It also follows my telling the patient that I would be taking a week's break a short time after this.

The patient, a woman in her early thirties, had been complaining about her husband, accusing him of neglecting their 3-year-old daughter when she wanted to play with him. The general tone was that men were creatures from whom children had to be protected. The next day she brought a dream in which she was in a group trying to solve a crisis of some sort. Two women in the group were widows, one of whom was a senior colleague who she feels is a warm and human person, the other a friend from university whom she now hates as a false, insensitive person. Her daughter and her mother were also in the group and there was a terrible sense of depression and passivity. She associated the dream to the recent death of her maternal grandfather and said that her grandmother had expressed a wish to kill herself after this loss. Her mother, with whom the patient has an extremely close relationship, was depressed after the loss of her father. The overall feeling was of depression and inertia in the absence of male figures which seemed also to be linked to her anger with her husband the previous day. The patient then reported another row with her husband who had refused to agree to go with her and their daughter to a theme park because he did not like such places. The patient was furious and became sarcastic and cruel with him. In telling me this she seemed to become closely identified with and allied to her daughter in attacking her husband. It felt to me also that she wanted to draw me into this and at one point I commented that she seemed to want her own determination and strong views to be admired by me as strengths while presenting her husband as cruel and mean. There was a long pause; she then said in an irritable voice that she felt quite childish; she wanted me to know that her husband is just as bad as she is. I said to her that I thought she had wanted to be together with me like a mother and daughter agreeing that father should be dismissed but that she now felt that I had abandoned her and was being mean and cruel and siding with her husband. The next day she began the session by saying that she had nothing on her mind and that she was looking forward to the Bank Holiday weekend. After a pause she said she was going to the GP – which she was reluctant about because it wasn't her own GP as he had retired. She felt there wasn't much point in going because he had been the one whom she really liked and trusted. She then spoke about a senior colleague whom she had forgotten to consult on an important matter which had been wrong but she didn't really care because she didn't value this colleague's opinion anyway. I thought she had come back to the session feeling disappointed and angry with her analyst whom she experienced as the faithless and disappointing doctor, rejecting her overtures to be of the same mind as her (the two widows in the dream) in dismissing the men. This shed more light on the two figures in the dream, the idealized 'warm and human' figure, the totally attentive, feeding mother, and the false, withholding mother who is feared and hated. In reality the latter seems to have been attributed to her husband against whom she expressed rage and contempt. In the transference the hated figure was experienced as me deserting her, repudiating her attempts to seduce me, and making her feel small.

I think the patient was relating to me from an unconcious baseline that she and I were engaged in an analytical *folie à deux*. A crisis looms, the long weekend and week's break with the implications of my external life, which threatens to arouse painful oedipal conflicts. The dream suggests that she feels I have betrayed her and become the faithless doctor or false friend who having entered into a seductive alliance with her was now abandoning her. The dream and the subsequent interaction with me seems to be an attempt to restore a situation in which we were together but on the basis of there being no men on the scene – the two widows. This gratified her wish to be in a close and exclusive duet with me but also gave rise to fears of passivity and stasis where nothing could come alive.

There are many individuals in whom this kind of mechanism enters into their attempts to form relationships. A friendship may be quickly embarked upon with a passion and intensity that turns to hatred and contempt when the partner turns away to another relationship of any kind because it is immediately felt to be an unforgivable betrayal of a longed for relationship which would serve to exclude the real world.

While being a willing participant in the *folie à deux* with her new baby, the mother has to be able to keep external reality within hailing distance so to speak. For example, when the baby becomes increasingly aware of the parents as a couple and experiences oedipal rivalry the mother has to bear not only the disturbance in the baby but also being the hated, faithless mother not the adored good mother. From birth onwards, and particularly at weaning, the mother is constantly having to relinquish, with considerable pain and loss, not only the special relationship with the baby but also idealized aspects of herself as the perfect all-giving mother. As the baby matures and makes his first bids for freedom and independence, many women experience feelings of depression and abandonment. The wish to avoid such painful feelings contributes to difficulties in 'letting go' of the primal relationship. Allowing the baby to become separate means giving up the gratification of being the exclusively needed figure and resisting powerful impulses to seduce the child to remain close. The capacity in the mother to identify not only with a loving mother but also with a father figure who can facilitate the separation process then becomes necessary for the baby's development

It is the quasi-delusional primary relationship between a mother and her new-born infant, with its passionate sexual undertones and implicit meaning that 'you are all the world to me and I to you', that I want to explore in describing a patient, Ms L, as she struggled with her task of looking after her new-born infant. I suggest that in the initial impact of the birth of her baby, she returned to primitive processes of splitting and projection as a defence against violent negative feelings which threatened the idealized relationship with the baby, and contributed to a need to exclude the baby's father, and her own mother, who were felt to contain rage, envy and hatred of the new baby and its possession of the mother. This appeared in the analysis in relation to her analyst and gave rise to conflict about whether she could continue in analysis.

I will first look at the very early stages of her relationship with the baby and the difficulties she later encountered in separating from him, particularly in weaning, through the shifts and movements in the transference. While she was struggling to identify herself as a mother with the baby, she was faced in the analysis with being in touch with areas of her personality which I think she feared were inimical to her relationship with the baby.

Ms L was the eldest of three children. Her sister was born when she was 17 months old. Her recollections of her childhood suggest that she managed intense feelings of rivalry and jealousy of her sister by being a good child and helpful to her mother. However, she describes with considerable uneasiness a relationship with her mother in which she seemed to be secretly in control and was treated rather like a 'confidante'. The impression is of a withdrawn and compliant child, unlike her sister, who was more vociferous and demanding. The family situation seems to have been one in which the parents barely coped with the demands of three small children, but have in fact remained together though with considerable difficulties. Her father is remembered by Ms L as strict and sometimes harsh with the children in trying to stop them upsetting their mother and making her ill. In the course of the analysis this picture has somewhat changed and her mother has emerged at times as more robust and more able to face reality than her father.

Ms L discovered she was pregnant for the first time when she had been in analysis for six years. In that time she had established a stable relationship with the father and although she and her partner wanted children she spoke of the prospect with some trepidation. She had a good job, a lot of freedom and was anxious about the changes a baby would necessitate. On the day, a

Saturday, which she learned for certain that she was pregnant she had felt a secret pride at being the only one in the world who knew of it. On the following Monday she brought a dream about her analyst of which she could only remember a scrap which was that the patient was wearing a red silk jacket. This was a combination of a jacket I had worn at a Saturday event that she had attended and in which I was taking an active part, and a red silk shirt of hers of which one of her clients had been envious. She also associated it to the jacket of a close friend of hers who was trying in vain to have a child. Ms L told me about the pregnancy but expressed reluctance to tell her mother because she would 'get drawn into something' with her.

The dream seemed to suggest that Ms L, with her pregnancy, had become confused with her analyst. In telling me about the pregnancy but not her mother she seemed to be treating me as her 'confidante' as her mother had treated her.

The 'secret pride' had a quality of excitement about stirring up envy in other people at her success in the conception, for example in the friend who could not conceive. What seemed clear was that the presence of a new baby was for Ms L already fraught with conflict and anxiety in relation to her actual mother and her internal objects.

The baby was born just before a break and so she did not return to the analysis until after the holiday. Her partner let me know when the baby had been delivered and I sent her a card congratulating her. Soon afterwards she rang to thank me for the card. She sounded excited and delighted with her baby son and rang me a second time as she had forgotten to tell me the name they had chosen. It was quite unlike the subdued and rather depressed pregnant patient on the couch. Although sending the card was an ordinary response to make I think it was also taken by Ms L as me 'getting into something' with her which she felt excited about. On her return she then felt disappointed and let down when I did not continue to congratulate her nor agree that she no longer needed analysis. When Ms L returned to the analysis anxieties of a persecutory kind came to the fore. These focused at first on dangers threatening the baby from the childminder. She was worried that the minder was not looking after him properly and perhaps did not like him and that the smoke from her cigarettes was harming him. She had thoughts of installing a tape recorder to hear what went on when she wasn't there. She felt her husband was not intervening enough to stop the childminder doing things that would harm the baby, i.e. smoking. While this was her primary concern she also believed that I was harming the baby by 'insisting' she came to the analysis. She became preoccupied with thoughts of leaving the analysis altogether or cutting down her sessions and there was enormous pressure on me to agree to this, filling me with anxieties and doubts about whether I was being helpful to her in maintaining the analysis or actually threatening the relationship she was trying to establish with the new baby. In the transference I was felt to be the source of these bad experiences because my 'demand' that she come to analysis every day sprang from a jealous wish to separate her from her baby. She believed that I could not tolerate the disruption to the analytic relationship that the baby inevitably brought. At this point I was constantly struck by how unaware she seemed to be of any ambivalent feelings she might have about the baby. She seemed to need to present her relationship to the baby as ideally good. Negative feelings were located externally, in the childminder and in the analyst. It seemed also significant that there was during this period almost no reference to her partner, the father of the baby. I think that her own feelings of anger or rivalry towards the baby (perhaps as the hated sibling who was getting all the attention) were projected into her husband and her analyst enabling her to maintain an idealized relationship with the baby. Any attempt at this stage to interpret such feelings *in her* were immediately felt to be envious attacks on my part devised to interfere with her good relationship with the baby and were therefore useless. I think this was an attempt, using primitive processes of splitting and projection, to rid herself of destructive and needy aspects of herself in her struggle to establish herself as a good mother.

This presented an immediate threat to the continuation of the analysis as the offer of daily analysis was for Ms L at this stage an expression of the analyst's jealousy of her closeness to the baby. The following dream, which she had when the baby was 5 weeks old, illustrates the internal predicament she felt herself to be in.

She was having twins, but one had not yet been born; she was then in a large crowded place where there were a lot of floors. She was in danger from a man who wanted to do something to her against her will; she was running away and fighting him at the same time; there were no proper rooms. Eventually she got away and went to her mother; but she was lying very ill in the road but it seemed to be in a railway station.

The crowded place with many floors seems to be indicative of the impact the birth of the baby had had on Ms L's state of mind and the different levels of identification and conflict she is exposed to. One of the conflicts evidently concerned the sexual demands of her partner. The dream in fact occurred at a time when Ms L was finding it difficult to put the baby in his own room and thus make room for her partner. I think the twins represent herself and the baby, scarcely differentiated. The baby who was not yet born may represent a third figure who cannot be allowed to come between her and her ideal baby – her partner with his sexuality, or her analyst with her greedy demands. The unborn child may also represent aspects of herself that cannot come out into the open for fear they would interfere with the perfect primal relationship. The last part of the dream seemed to suggest that Ms L was terrified of becoming ill, perhaps depressed, or not able to think properly (no proper room). Given her fears of my hostile jealousy, the analysis represented at some level an intrusion likely to harm rather than help her. Although the patient was in reality managing competently her dream suggests that at this stage this depended on massive projection of very difficult feelings – a process that left her depleted and exposed to persecutory anxieties. In the dream she tries to get help from her mother who is, however, ill and abandoned and so unable to help her. This seemed to throw more light on her fears of being 'drawn into something', i.e. identified with, a mother who is felt to be in a very bad way – either depressed and ill or envious of her daughter's youth and sexuality. The dream was helpful in gaining some understanding of why she felt doubtful about getting help from me – there was confusion about whose needs the analysis was actually serving at this point.

For my patient fears of this nature took the form of a preoccupation at this point about whether she should stay in the analysis. However, despite her fears that our relationship was detrimental to her relationship with the baby there was also an adult side of her that could recognize her need for the analysis and she continued to come regularly. Her impulse to stop the analysis immediately gradually gave way to an expressed wish that she and I could think about a 'proper' ending as she called it. At this point, however, she was sure the only options were either a sudden separation with no feelings about it at all, either in her or in me, or an endless analysis. The fact that some of this could be understood and talked about seemed to be in itself 'proper room' which gave her some relief.

The following session and a dream illustrate Ms L's conflicts about coming to analysis which predominated at this time. The baby was 6 weeks old and breastfeeding was established. Ms L arrived on a Monday morning and began the session by saying that she felt very tired; the baby had put on weight; she had felt heavy all over the weekend. She thought that her friend's baby would be born prematurely. She then reported a dream as follows:

> There was a mix-up over a baby, mine was being carried by another woman and I was looking after someone else's baby. The baby looked like a sea-horse; I felt very torn; there was a metal nozzle attached to the baby's mouth and the nipple; I pulled it off and the nipple came off too.

She made the following associations: the nozzle looked like a bicycle pump connection and seemed to be screwed in so that when she pulled it off there was no blood or anything. Although it wasn't her baby in the dream, she loved it because she was used to it. She had also been very struck by the contrast between warm flesh and cold metal. The sea-horse reminded her of a programme she had seen – the male sea-horse incubates and gives birth to the young who are exact replicas of the parents and immediately independent of them. Ms L went on to talk of walking around with the baby all the time because he screamed if she put him down. She also mentioned her dislike of the baby sucking F's (her partner's) finger.

The dream seems to come at a time when the baby is thriving –

breastfeeding and putting on weight. This, however, seems to fill Ms L with depression and tiredness and in the dream with feelings of alienation – someone else's baby and the metal nozzle between her and the baby. This is surely about a baby who is developing and therefore becoming more separate while at the same time 'attached' to the breast. There is a singular lack of 'passion' in the dream – she loved the baby because she was 'used to it'. But she does feel 'torn' suggesting an emotional tussle between warm passionate feelings and cold detachment. There is in her associations a suggestion that this now is father's baby – the sea-horse and the nozzle reminiscent of her partner's finger that the baby sucks on – with whom she cannot identify in the same way. I think the ideal baby who is hers alone is the *'folie à deux'* baby who is felt to be now abandoning her and destroying this ideal couple. The dream seems to be a dramatic response to the baby's increasing separateness and awareness of his father and I think indicates Ms L's difficulty in adjusting to this advance. It is the baby then who is threatening to disrupt the primal duo and Ms L's reluctance to put him down may have sprung from her unconscious wish to regain it and her guilt about hating him for this disruption. The dream seemed to express very vividly a fear of losing her nipple – a symbol of her power and control over the baby

I thought Ms L felt very torn about coming back to the analysis after the weekend in the sense that she was uncertain about which of us needed her to come – the mix-up over the baby. Over the weekend she had become detached from her infantile self which was split off and felt to be mine. She then felt tired at the thought of having to return on Monday and 'pick me up' like a screaming demanding baby. The real baby sucking on her partner's finger reminds her of this aspect of herself for which she feels distaste.

Ms L's need to deny any negative feelings towards the baby was, as I described earlier, I believe a return to primitive processes of splitting and projection. The dream seemed to indicate the breaking down of this defensive structure, enabling her fears to come more into the open in the analysis. Ms L continued to deny such feelings though with less conviction. In other words there seemed to be a less rigid split between her unconscious mind which is acknowledging conflicting feelings of closeness *and* detachment from the baby, and her conscious mind that denies any ambivalent feelings towards him. There seems to be a longing for a painless separation and a belief that if this cannot be then there can be no separation. Hence her difficulty in actually putting C down. The problem springs from her fear of being the object of the baby's hatred and rage when he is denied gratification which I think is mixed up with her own unconscious infantile anger and resentment towards the other baby, her sister, who came between her and her mother.

For the new mother a complex renegotiation is taking place regarding her actual identification with her own mother and with her infantile self. She has to give up her destructive rivalry towards her mother in order to identify with her in motherhood, and her grievance against her father and wish to triumph over him by achieving what he failed to give her in the oedipal situation. In the past Ms L managed to maintain a 'special' relationship with her mother by projecting troublesome feelings into her sister who was felt to be a demanding and fractious baby. To some extent her mother seems to have fostered this though it is hard to know to what extent it is Ms L's fantasy and what was reality.

The exclusion of the father sexually is a common problem following the birth of a baby. If the new mother's relationship with her own mother was based on a perverse collusion which diminished and excluded father, her identification with such a weakened figure impairs not only her capacity to 'return' to her husband or partner sexually following the birth of a baby, but also weakens the mother's internal resources which would help her to establish boundaries and bring a sense of reality into the *folie à deux* situation with her infant. Being able to include the father would also depend on the mother having worked through the loss of the ideal relationship to her own mother, which I think Ms L had not been able to do.

Ms L breast-fed her son until well into his second year. As the baby grew older, she spoke not of the pleasure of breastfeeding but rather of her increasing discomfort as he seemed more and more demanding for the breast. She found it difficult to deny him it when he became persistent and angry and would frequently give in because she believed not to do so was being cruel. I think the discomfort arose from unconscious feelings of guilt about the gratification the baby's greedy needs afforded her while leaving her partner feeling frustrated and impotent. In the course of the analysis much work had been done on Ms L's anxieties about her greed, and her wish that I would be 'tough' and 'keep her on the straight and narrow' so that she would not be allowed to take advantage of me. So any ordinary demand, like a change of time, was almost impossible for her to make, and any concession by me gave rise to enormous anxieties about my internal state and whether she had forced me into something. This was very reminiscent of my dilemma about whether to 'give in' to her demands that she give up the analysis or reduce the sessions and whether I was being harsh and cruel not to do so.

Ms L's baby was at this time a very poor sleeper and was often brought into the parental bed ostensibly so that they could get some peace. In effect they could not as the child would not in this situation 'leave her alone'. She described him as 'climbing all over her' or 'tearing at her tee-shirt' which evoked an impression of a sexual assault. In bringing him into bed, about which she was desperately uncertain, it seemed to me that she was responding to unconscious wishes of her own for some sexual gratification. Her son's passionate attachment to the breast at this stage discomfited Ms L precisely because it stirred passionate and desirous wishes in herself and her wish to regain the primal *folie à deux* relationship that had been such a source of gratification to her. This led to perverse behaviour in which she would take the baby into their bed when he cried but withhold the breast, stimulating further excitement and desperation in him when he would 'climb all over her'. She would then 'give in' resulting in feelings of anger and resentment that he was manipulating her. It seemed as if she was seducing the child – raising his hopes and then dashing them, so that again the question of whose need was being satisfied became unclear. It seemed to me that Ms L's repeatedly bringing the child into the parental bed could be seen as an instance of Laplanche's 'bungled actions' in which unconscious processes were operating in a way that impeded her ability to help the baby separate from her. It seemed to me probable that the child's restlessness and sleeping problems at this time were caused not only by his anger and grief at losing the breast but also by confusion and anxiety about 'what the breast wanted of him'.

Difficulties arise for the mother and the baby when the illusion contained in the *folie à deux* is dispelled, either from moment to moment as the baby develops or more dramatically and finally with weaning. Both mother and baby then experience feelings of betrayal and disappointment. The mother's ability to make the painful withdrawal from this seductive state and thus enable the baby to begin to separate will be influenced by her internal identification with firm and robust parental figures. When the mother's and baby's needs become confused and indistinguishable the delusion is maintained and may become detrimental to the child's emotional and intellectual development.

The passionate love affair between a mother and baby which in my view augurs well for the relationship, needs the gradual intervention of external reality, from the actual father but also from paternal qualities in the mother, if the child's emotional and intellectual life is to develop optimally. The *folie à deux* that I have described may promote the infant's sense of value and worth but it also contains the seeds of confusion and stasis. For if such a situation is prolonged the narcissistic wound suffered by the child when he has to face reality is all the more acute and later oedipal conflicts cannot be worked through. The process of separation from the mother is of necessity destructive of the idealized dyad and is inevitably resisted to some extent by both mother and baby. If the child's bids for freedom from the primal intense relationship with mother are felt to be too threatening and are inhibited, this may result later in impairment of emotional and intellectual progress.

REFERENCES

Freud, S. (1910) 'Leonardo Da Vinci', *S.E.* 11: 117.
—— (1933) 'On femininity', *S.E.* 22: 112–135.
Klein, M. (1963) 'On the sense of loneliness', in *Envy and Gratitude*, London: Hogarth.
Laplanche, J. (1989) *New Foundations for Psychoanalysis*, trans. D. Macey, Oxford: Blackwell.
Mason, A.A. (1994) 'A psychoanalyst looks at a hypnotist: a study of *folie à deux*', *Psycho-analytical Quarterly* 63: 641–679.

Winnicott, D. (1958) *Primary Maternal Preoccupation: Through Paediatrics to Psychoanalysis*, London: Karnac Books.

Wordsworth, W. (1805) 'Prelude 2', Norton Critical Editions, eds J. Wordsworth, M.H. Abrams and S. Gill.

Chapter 10

'The waters under the earth'
Understanding maternal depression

Maggie Mills

Up the sides of this depression grew sheaves of the common rush, and here and there a peculiar species of flag, the blades of which glistened in the emerging sun like scythes. But the general aspect of the swamp was malignant. From its moist and poisonous coat seemed to be exhaled the essences of evil things in the earth, and in the waters under the earth.
Thomas Hardy, *Far from the Madding Crowd* (1874)

The psychic state we call depression can be construed as both an entirely appropriate sensitivity to the effects of systemic stress in a given social structure, and paradoxically, a psychodynamic defence – with the actual numbing and cocooning characteristics of depressive symptoms preventing the sufferer from getting to grips with the painful emotions awakened, and working them through. The paradox is that in *depression* people are in touch with their feelings in a thoughtful, intensely preoccupying way, but while present these feelings are somehow also rendered blankly inaccessible to intervention so that the sufferer is left stricken in a kind of despairing limbo. There comes then the sudden realization that they are well and truly trapped in a hopelessness that has no way forward.

This is exactly what happens psychically when women whose basic human obligations were not met in their family of origin get put back in touch with their own childhood experience as they take up their own mothering role in giving birth to and bringing up their own children. There are features quite unique to young mothers' depressive experience which have to do with the fantasy they have created about their own mothers and their own experience of being mothered where there has been no effective break in the continuity of the relationship and no prolonged separation, or loss through early maternal death (Bowlby, 1980).

The clinical research and practice in this chapter draws on a population who rarely come to the attention of the psychoanalytic community. It comes entirely from the existence and experience of under-resourced mothers in urban settings in Britain who are the main carers of their babies and young children whether or not they have the presence and active participation of the father and/or partner. About five hundred women, most usually clinically depressed (according to DSM III criteria) have taken part in four different projects[1] with which the author has been involved over the last fifteen years.

These women have managed to hang on to some sense of psychological well-being by constructing for themselves a fictional, idealized, wonderful mother. In our most recent project – an intensive intervention with families having severe problems with their children – women are asked to create a personal grid (Billinge, 1992). This incorporates their own spontaneous attitudes to their own mothers, descriptions of other good and bad models of parenting, an assessment of their own parenting performance, and the 'perfect mother'. This ideal mother is easily mobilized inside them and turns out to be in dire contrast to the reported characteristics and remembered failings of the actual mother. The early infantile split of the good/bad mother is still lurking in these women's psyches ready to be activated.

Of course, this perfect mother withers in the face of reality – a young mother actually having to care in every way, for a baby of her own. This intimate contact is a potent influence in unlocking memories of the real happenings in her own childhood whether she likes it or not. Back come emotions in memory, feelings and specific images repressed and denied – many of which do not accord with the idyllic and satisfying treatment that was fantasized as part of a lifelong defence against disillusion and object-loss.

An illustration of this phenomenon is the experience of different women who attended the Shanti project for brief psychotherapy and talked, two years after termination (Reader, 1993; Mills, 1996) of the use they had made of therapy to explore how they were parented – often in the light of being parents themselves.

> I thought I had a wonderful childhood and this *perfect* parent. We looked realistically (in the therapy) . . . and just seeing it hadn't been this wonderful thing, except in my imagination And then at nineteen I'd had this nervous breakdown.

> I was able for the first time to explore negative feelings I had towards my mother. I'd *pretended* that I had this wonderful relationship with my mum. . . . but I didn't.

> I talked a lot about my childhood . . . some things I never realised I thought or knew. I'd *blocked* them out. It's very *confusing*. I don't know where it's all come from.

There is evidence here for the existence of an illusion of the ideal mother in the face of problematic early handling, which for these women can be reconstructed in the transference neurosis and brought safely to consciousness and explored in a containing therapy. But, as Main *et al.* (1985) found, in many parents there is often confusion, an absence of anger (integral to the drama of the 'idealized' lost object) and a general absence of processing relating to the events of childhood. In everyday life, the idealized mother is no longer of use in the service of denial and painful childhood material gets unblocked in the context of a hefty dose of intimate daily contact with one's own children. These childhood memories impede an identification with a mother's own mother that would help and support her in a woman's own maternal role (Stern, 1995).

This loss of a tie to the mother that becoming a mother herself involves, and an unreconstructed, or incompletely worked through tie at that, can certainly be understood as precipitating a pathological process of mourning. Freud (1917) in 'Mourning and melancholia', recognized the link between depression and the loss of idealized aspects of the self or an important other. Depression becomes manifest where a false perfect mother both has to be given up and is not available as a psychic support and identification to facilitate the mothering of the next generation. As Raphael-Leff (1991) suggests: 'If a mother has defensively glorified her internal experience of her neglectful mother, she herself will become over-anxious and a non-ideal mother by comparison' (p. 484). But there may also be an identification with the fantasy of a: 'dissatisfied and depressed mother who has to be kept appeased by the daughter giving up or inhibiting her own potential satisfaction and enjoyment of having produced her own child' (Laufer, 1993, p. 74).

Certainly the story we heard time and time again in researching maternal depression (Cox *et al.*, 1987) was that women's distress and dissatisfaction with their own early home life had led them to make an early escape from an unsatisfactory parental tie through a pattern which included truanting, a lack of decent employment prospects, early sexual partnership and a resulting pregnancy with 61 per cent of depressed mothers in the study being under 21 at the birth of their first child.

But the promise of a fresh start with a first baby, 'something of my own to love and be loved by', fails to materialize. Instead, the fantasized idyll of the 'cosy nest', the myth that in giving their offspring the good care they had not received themselves they could repair the loss of the idealized mother, is dispelled. Disillusion sets in, for under-resourced and under-supported as many mothers are today in our inner cities, the reality is that it is extremely difficult to be a satisfied and successful parent, and mothers find they are starting to fail in their mothering role, intolerably, just as they suspect, their mothers failed them.

External and internal reality coincide for such mothers. Half the women living with a partner who attended Newpin (Cox *et al.*, 1991) described a discordant relationship, while 80 per cent had been left by a partner during

a pregnancy or in the first six months after the birth of a child. No sign here
of Winnicott's (1965) facilitating environment. He also suggests a manifest
connection between mother and child in the context of pathological depression.

> analysis of depression involves an understanding of the mental mechan-
> isms of introjection, and the theory of an inner psychic reality localised in
> the patient's fantasy – in the belly or the head or in some other way within
> the self. The lost object is taken into this inside place and there subjected
> to hate; till hate is expended and recovery from depression or mourning
> takes place . . . often spontaneously. (p. 231)

The concrete location of this symbolized loss is often the body of the young
child itself which, until quite recently, was in the mother's 'belly' anyway –
a part of her, and not yet fully individuated from her. There is a kind of poetic
justice that it is the existence of this offspring that instigates, through
unlocking childhood memories, all the psychic trouble with the status of the
idealized mother that leads to depression. This offspring now becomes its
symbolic abode and subject to maternal rage and hate. How else can we
explain the universal research finding (Radke-Yarrow *et al.*, 1985; Mills and
Puckering, 1985; Hammen, 1991; Patterson, 1990; Stevenson, 1982) that it
is maternal affective negativity, hostility denigration and criticism that so
strongly, and damagingly, characterize observed interaction in the homes of
depressed mothers with young children.

Maternal depression usually develops in the early months after a baby is
born (Cox, 1988; Murray, 1991; Kumar *et al.*, 1986). Onset depends on some
coincidence occurring between the actual caretaking routines and involvement with a young child and the feelings this contact evokes in the mother,
which in turn lead to the opening up of denied aspects of the mother's own
handling during childhood. I illustrate with a case from our ongoing, Mellow
Parenting, intervention project (Puckering, 1994):

> A young, very depressed mother could not bear having to cope with her
> fifteen month old daughter or come near her at all when she was upset and
> crying. She would let the child get on with it, absenting herself, and in the
> creche could often be seen talking determinedly to a female friend and
> deliberately ignoring her daughter's distress. At home she said it sent her
> mad. Several weeks into treatment (the group met weekly for a whole day's
> structured programme) and after sustained efforts by the project leader, to
> no avail, to effect some rapprochement between mother and child, the
> mother broke down and started to cry herself – all the while rubbing her
> back and saying it hurt. The story that transpired was heartbreaking. She
> had always believed she had a wonderful mother while knowing she feared
> and mistrusted her step-father. With the persistent crying of her own child
> there awoke in her a memory of herself lying on her back on a pebbly track

in front of her mother's car crying, and beseeching her mother to take her with her for the once weekly shopping trip. She never did and her daughter was sexually assaulted regularly in her absence.

In this case a child crying (her own) brought back unbearable memories of a child crying (herself) which brought back not only this early trauma but also the reality of an unprotective and absent mother in contrast to the fantasy of a supportive mother she always thought she had. The same material that had been so agonizing to disclose both precipitated her depression and put a barrier – insurmountable I am sure, without treatment – between herself and her child. That crying child was herself.

Crying, in fact, and high rates of distress were *the* distinguishing features of children's behaviour observed at home when their mothers were depressed and had been for much of their young lives (Puckering and Mills, 1986). In addition, when three, largely comparable samples of inner-city, 'at risk' families are examined (Puckering *et al.*, 1995), it is the young children of depressed mothers who show the most crying – three times as much in fact.

Depressive illness impairs mothers' responsiveness in meeting the needs of their offspring and it certainly makes sense that women coping with their own psychic pain will have particular difficulty assuaging the distress of a dependent child. Green (1986) sums up their predicament by supposing that there is:

an imago which has been constituted in the child's mind, following maternal depression, brutally transforming a living object, which was a source of vitality for the child, into a distant figure, toneless, practically inanimate. . . . Thus, the dead mother, contrary to what one might think, is a mother who remains alive but who is, so to speak, psychically dead in the eyes of the young child in her care. (p. 142)

As he says, 'Her heart is not in it.' Caretaking is mechanical and characterized for us by a research code called 'floating' where mothers stared into space over the tea mug – child unnoticed. It is an unenlivened environment, living with an unavailable depressed mother who cannot contain or 'mop up' distress. Young children repress and deny their misery only to discover in themselves as adults an underground pool of tears: Hardy's metaphoric 'waters under the earth' from which this chapter takes its title.

I should like now to talk about a young mother called Colette. Since it was a brief therapy of just sixteen weeks I cannot demonstrate in fine detail some of the profound changes in her attitudes towards herself and her objects that other writers in this volume have been able to report. She came to terms, however, with major inter- and intrapsychic problems during the therapy and subsequently. Two years on, she wrote her view of the therapy (intended for an article on Shanti and included here with her permission) and I shall conclude this chapter with her account.

Colette had come to Shanti feeling increasingly lonely and miserable since her closest friend went abroad eighteen months previously. Her compensatory and compulsive over-eating also distressed her and she was asking for help in handling her little girl, a spirited 2 year old, whose challenging behaviour was fast wearing her down as a single parent, and making her feel resentful. She was scared of hurting her child and said their battles reminded her of struggles she'd had with her own mother, 'a power-crazed, flirtatious, mean and sentimental woman' whom she had no wish to resemble but felt increasingly, in her tussles with her own daughter, that she did.

In her assessment interview she was diagnosed as clinically depressed with severe functional impairment and a psychiatric disturbance of more than two years' duration. She described herself as a white, working class, Irish woman born in Britain and a lesbian in her mid-twenties living on her own with her daughter who is mixed race – having a Nigerian father. She stressed how important it was to her to have a working class therapist and accepted the standard contract of sixteen once-weekly sessions, assessed as well motivated to change her relationship with her child which was the current focus of her internal turmoil.

From the moment therapy started, Colette was torn between compliance and antagonism. For instance, the window in the therapy room had to be open. This would be her escape route in case the therapist proved intolerably controlling and dominated her cruelly as her mother had done. When I interpreted this to her, she told me that she was capable of taking her emotions and spirit out of her body – out the window literally – leaving behind just her overweight shell; protective fat acquired so she couldn't be got at. As a little girl she tried shutting herself up in a cupboard to avoid her mother's own depressed gloom and her irritable intrusiveness, but mother's obsessive need to win their battles 'wore her down'. (This was the expression she had used about her own child in the first session.)

I left her the freedom to get away if she so wished. She was able to connect this with her early behaviour and tell me that in an attempt to hold on to her pride and some semblance of herself she would go blank and freeze and never ever let her mother see how much she minded being hurt. Mother called her an unfeeling lump of stone; but the small child inside was on fire! I could interpret for her the contrast between her mother who demanded a false self response from her at all times, and the therapy where I could both contain her and acknowledge her rage.

Moreover, this artificial freezing, a lifelong mechanism for survival, afforded no relief for the expression of her violent feelings, particularly anger, which now felt so overwhelming she dared not let them out. If I was a middle class woman, there was no way in which I could understand how she had felt. She told me that she'd only ever hit her mother once, in her teens, in retaliation for being walloped with the frying pan. In the first session she recalled how a kid in infant school kept flicking dirt on her drawing. She got angrier and angrier, finally biting the kid's finger who wound up in hospital while Colette felt awful and guilty. She felt she could not share her sorrow and remorse with someone like me, who would be likely to preach at her and not understand anything of the despair which had led her to act in this way, since words of course would be useless as a method of communication between us.

Later it transpired that as part of a teenage gang she had gone around beating men up. There were no potent helpful men in her life. Her father was described as a gentle giant, but no use in the war against mother, except the night she left home at 16 when he held her mother back from using a knife on her because she thought her daughter had been chatting up their lodger. I tried to show her how men had had to be marginalized and denigrated so that she had great difficulty in using the creative masculine aspects of me and my relationships to help her come to terms with some of the difficulties of her situation, but she never really appreciated my thinking in this area.

Colette's mother could not allow her daughter to develop her own sexuality. Indeed, on the traumatic night when Colette had to leave home she was in effect being punished for the content of her mother's own fantasy that she was sexually active and attractive. After the therapy I reflected on Colette's choice of a lesbian lifestyle as a way of solving this conflict but I do not think I could have found a way of putting this to her during our work together.

As it turned out, her mother's worst fear and expectation was that she would bring home a black lover. Colette both fulfilled these fears and found a covert way to express her own hostility to her mother by becoming pregnant with a mixed-race granddaughter whom predictably her parents had never seen nor wished to see. She was terribly torn between elation at having triumphed over her mother in this way – and put a safely irrevocable distance between them – and the longing to be accepted and admired by her mother as a mother herself. When I interpreted this to her, it came as a real surprise that what to Colette had seemed a casual sexual encounter, which had been in no way important to her, had had such a momentous significance in her inner world. It seems to me that this new understanding did a great deal to reinforce the positive transference that had quietly been emerging during our early sessions.

Nowadays, she wished she could stand under bridges and scream as trains passed to exorcize the violent feelings. Not surprisingly, she feared exploding at her daughter and could now trust me enough to be honest about her very real fears of not being able to control her own aggression. Nevertheless, she could be touchy, secretive and suspicious.

Seven sessions into the therapy, it shook her to realize that at the exact time of a session cancelled by the therapist's illness she had totally lost her temper with a friend she worked for in a row over a missing pair of scissors. Colette could appreciate that her rage and even the scissors were destined really for me as the friend whom she felt had cut her adrift and not been there for her.

My interpretation of this neglect put her in touch with the neglect in her childhood which she had never let herself examine heretofore. She remembered sitting for hours on some stairs minding her younger brother after her mother had enjoined her not to move. When her mother finally returned home, she felt quite numb which we could link to the feelings of inner emptiness which she still felt inside herself.

Her response to this interpretation was to tell me of memories that milk bottles at home were marked and the fridge was like Fort Knox – just like her mother inside. This mother kept a lush box of chocs on the table in the front room which was for herself; not as one might expect sweets for the kids, who were forbidden to touch. Once Colette stole one and spent days in apprehension waiting to be found out, whereupon she got belted. I tried to show her that she feared that if she took anything of value from the therapy I would be bound to treat it as a theft and punish her accordingly, either by physical threats or desertion.

Her neediness often had me in a dilemma. Her eating, her weight (she was at this time some stones overweight) and her body image were highly sensitive areas for Colette. If I talked about this issue directly it would seem as if I became like her mother having prescriptive rights over her body and this would be likely to trigger more self-destructive behaviour. Addressing the emptiness inside her was really the therapeutic task. Her neediness would often manifest itself as a kind of compliance, and a longing to be accepted in the therapy for the extremely intelligent young woman she was. I had to avoid (and wasn't always successful) a collusive tutorial relationship which might have prevented her experience of real anguish. On the other hand it was important that the therapist whom she saw as a strong professional woman, but also envied, would validate her, not only her feelings but her worth as a person of talent who could achieve things.

I felt the best way to do this was by not avoiding the painful feelings with which she was struggling. On the whole, it was not hard to foster her self-confidence in this regard but in other ways her self-esteem was fragile with contempt for herself always ready to surface in reaction to the internalized maternal denigration. Punishing herself was what seemed to keep her alive. Since she was well aware of this mental mechanism, I avoided interpreting it, and I think that she appreciated what she felt as my tact in this regard.

When any account of a therapy is given, it inevitably sounds as if the therapist always knew exactly what was happening and what they were doing. This therapist often did not. I sometimes felt quite frightened of Colette; sometimes getting into a persecuting position and having to wait and wait until a way out could emerge from Colette's stuck emotional and angry freeze. On reflection, I realize that all I could do for her was to try and be a container, in Bion's (1959) sense of the term, which often meant apparently doing nothing. However, once she had used me in this way, my capacity to try and understand the meaning of what was going on and to interpret it in a non-punitive and sometimes helpful way was clearly different for her from her own mother's inability to hold her in a loving and reflective way and something that she could contemplate in terms of her own child.

A way out from this cycle did emerge in the therapy when Colette once again mentioned the loss of a 'friend' which turned out to be her daughter's pushchair – an important, indeed vital part of her very restricted life, that had finally come to bits. She felt helpless and alone without it and associated these feelings with the imaginary friends she had as a child and the presence of an unseen friend, a kind of guardian angel, whom she felt accompanied and protected her as an adult.

This was the role I felt I might be occupying when, in a painfully embarrassed penultimate session – a full squirming twenty-five minutes of silence – there emerged an episode of sexual abuse that Colette reported experiencing during a summer holiday in Ireland at the hands of a male family friend whom she had trusted. Colette had brought a screen memory – which I had not understood – to a previous session. She told me about her embarrassment when her trousers had fallen down as she stood on a chair to change a light bulb and the family around her had laughed. But it was her brother's holiday snapshots that actually brought back the memory – she was wearing the same trousers that had been pulled down during the abusive incident, which she felt she would never be able to disclose to anyone if she didn't manage to do it with me during the therapy.

I had been silently willing Colette throughout this session to reveal what was so troubling to her and what by now I rather expected might be the content of the disclosure. I had tried to be receptive and attentive and certainly felt Colette's embarrassed impotence. But in terms of the psychotherapeutic strategy of both containing her and not avoiding painful feelings, I felt that it was crucial for Colette herself to voice the experience in order for her to feel she rather than me, or her mother, now had control and autonomy over her body.

Perhaps sharing this shame together with the difficulties of ending always inherent in brief therapy combined to cause Colette to miss her last session. I wrote pointing this out to her and another time was arranged, and the painful feelings of separation and loss were negotiated between therapist and client – perhaps for Colette for the first time, and not without difficulty for me.

When Colette described her emotions in a follow-up session six months later, they now *felt* different; anger differentiated from loss, sadness separate from misery, rather than an intense mass of confused, undifferentiated, unvoiceable pain. Her daughter she still found taxing and difficult but she said she felt able to contain her own and her daughter's feelings more of the time. Anger of course is to be expected if a mother has symbolically invested her child with the significance of her lost, idealized object and locates it in the child for then they will bear the brunt of this rage and blame. I certainly hoped our work together might obviate the necessity for her to continue to project her own anger and distress on to her little girl, thus preventing the continuation of a depressive intergenerational cycle of distress – uncontained and unexpressed. For Colette, the drawback to brief therapy was that it had made her feel so 'emotionally open' and vulnerable. I had felt disquiet on terminating, since, not surprisingly, there was an urgency and intensity to the unresolved feelings still inside Colette.

With nearly half of inner-city, under-resourced mothers at home with young children suffering from clinical depression (Cox, 1988), this brief history tells us something of the young mothers we can expect to find in primary NHS care and more often still uncared for in the community. The women we see have substituted an idealized internal mother (based not on real experience but on phantasy) for their actual depressed and rejecting mothers and their desire to have a child often in their teens or early twenties is linked to their wish to please and mollify their internal objects. The child they produce is of course nothing like the ideal child whom they would like to offer to their internal mothers as a gift and thus is often rejected. They then have to come to terms not only with this rejection but also with the recrudescence of the whole early scenario which is reactivated through their own children and the demands that they make upon the mothers.

I think that it is at this point where they have to accept both the losses of their early lives and come in contact through the ordinary distress of young children with their own primitive distress and helplessness that they fall into the same states of lethargy and depression from which their idealizing defences have protected them for so long. This is obviously a key point in their mature adult development: in cases like Colette, it offers the chance to come for therapy.

She got in touch with 'the waters under the earth', finally undammed the distress and, as she says later, grieved for her childhood. At the time, however, her frozen stuckness in the transference, literally a deadening pain, put me in mind of Winnicott's (1965) discourse about 'aliveness or liveliness' in the communication between mother and child (or analyst and patient for that matter). He talks of depressive or depressed mothers whose: 'central internal object is dead at a critical time in her child's early infancy and her mood is one of depression. Here the child has to fit in with the role of a *dead object*' (p. 191).

The mother's unconscious preoccupation is with the idea of the child's deadness who has to counteract the 'anti-life factor' derived from the mother's depression with a forced and false liveliness that interferes with the natural maturing of the emergent ego. I think it likely that these mothers do often treat their offspring as if they were dead and feel much the same way themselves (suicide attempts and ideation were not uncommon with these mothers and sometimes only having a dependent child stopped them).

Women who are depressed cannot, unlike well mothers, link into their child's world and their communicative reciprocity is much impaired. Nothing lively happens between them. The practice of intersubjectivity presupposes someone sentient there to communicate with, but these are 'minimalist' mothers, not deliberately neglectful, but what is the point of sustained and interesting chat if in fantasy your child cannot be experienced as lively or alive? In turn the child, to use Green's (1986) beautiful evocation of an analytic experience, is faced with:

> a mother who was absorbed either with herself or with something else, unreachable without echo, but always sad. A silent mother, even if talkative. When she was present she remained indifferent, even when she was plying the child with her reproaches. (p. 154)

The depressive demeanour of the 'dead' mother finally switches young children off. What seems to happen is that a maladaptive pattern of interaction gets set up: deadening covert distress is succeeded by unmanageable overt anger, the relationship is stuck in cement, and there are high rates of psychiatric disorder in the children (Cox, 1988; Stevenson, 1982; Weissman, 1974) with relationship difficulties persisting after the depression spontaneously remits (Stein *et al.*, 1991; Hammen 1991). Indeed, it often felt in writing this chapter as if I was describing a set of Russian, babushka, painted dolls; symbolic mothers stacked inside each other. That idealized, lost mother may well herself have been depressed, as was her daughter, and round again goes the cycle to future generations of children of depressed mothers.

So what is to be done? We know that individual, psychodynamic psychotherapy can provide 'a fresh start' (Brown, 1993) for under-privileged, under-resourced women who by reason of their gross childhood deprivation and/or cultural and ethnic backgrounds would not normally be accepted for treatment and indeed might also be very unlikely to seek it. Women who choose to come of their own accord appreciate an unbureaucratic (Shanti occupies a maisonette on a Brixton estate), non-medical and medication-free approach. As one woman in her research interview said, 'Having a safe, friendly, anonymous place to come, made difficult and painful disclosures possible.'

Psychotherapy is offered just for women and all staff are female too. In several hundred clients, I never once had one who complained that men were excluded . . . or asked why. What I think would surprise our client group is Winnicott's (1957) assertion that 'in unconscious fantasy, the woman figure has no limits to her existence or power.' That is not how they experience the phallocentric discourses of their everyday world where they exist without much access to economic independence, with only limited outlets for their creative talents and with little experience of an unmenaced physical autonomy.

We may have created for clients at a structural level something like Winnicott's transitional space. What I am saying is that women implicitly think that somehow they have a natural affinity with each other, and of course much mutual identification goes on. But we know that as the clinical work progresses, it becomes apparent that this is an illusion and that the pre-oedipal situation with mother can present pitfalls of many kinds and undetected technical problems specific to woman to woman working. For example, there is Enid Balint's (1993) discussion in her classic paper, 'What does a woman want?' (Chapter 1 in this volume) and Klein's (1932) early paper dealing with a woman's fantasy of an unconscious attack on the contents of the mother's body. Nevertheless, this supposed affinity, this romantic readiness for hope in a shared female world gets women in the door for help. As one woman said in her follow-up research interview (Mills, 1993): 'It gave me a lot of comfort and confidence seeing all those women at Shanti. . . . different sizes, races, shapes, voices, working there and able to be happy. I never belonged in my family.'

We share a lot more as women than the experience of oppression. Certainly the universal hassles of combining childcare and a job unite us. There is fertile territory in gender, sexuality and femininity, but I want to concentrate on the female body and its history which may be 'steeped in imagination' as Cohen (1994) points out, but is highly problematic for the status of women. Consider the extent to which cultural, medical and social assumptions gave us the floating wombs and nasal passages of Freud's hysterics or our modern-day madness involving the concretization of the body in the (usually female) anorexic.

What draws women together is the knowledge that discourses about their bodies are one way of confirming dominant social values (Cohen, 1994). There are deep-rooted cultural prejudices about women – often sadly internalized by women themselves – and women learn to experience their bodies as negative. The contents of the womb itself, such as menstrual blood, were perceived as unclean in many religions and childbirth required a Churching ceremony to return a mother to the human race. As Ussher (1991) says:

> Women's reproductive cycle and sexuality are socially constructed as unnatural, polluted . . . as a liability rather than a strength. . . . We are taught that our bodies are weak: that they make us distressed and mad. Is it any wonder then that we turn to our bodies and reproduction as a source of attribution when we *feel* mad? (p. 253)

Women's common experience can, however, be construed and used constructively. We have inhabited and we each have a womb. Our first introjections after all are with other women – our mothers. Women have in common an intimate contact with the female body which experiences the same rhythms and rituals as it develops and changes across the life cycle. But what defines them to each other is the potential for babies inside; the capacity to form and nourish the astonishing intricacy of another human being. Some women may experience the womb – if woman to woman therapy at Shanti can be so construed – as something that harbours and nurtures them as in a pregnancy and pushes them out into the world when their time-limited sessions are over. These fantasies should be especially congruent for the women described in this chapter who are struggling with depression in the context of their own childbearing and childcaring.

Of course, as psychodynamic approaches acknowledge, each woman's experience is still unique to her. We find that genuine change is possible without it being necessary to create a complete transference neurosis and work it through (Hildebrand, 1986). Freud after all was convinced that it was possible to help people understand something of their psychic problems in a very brief time (his early patients got brief psychotherapies) and through that insight initiate major changes in their lives. We get much important information in the first session but as Freud pointed out, what takes the time is understanding its meaning. Brief work does require an ability to think and act quickly; perhaps a considered use of textural analysis, intuition and empathy to pick up from the fleeting clues offered something of the transferential organization, and working often in the 'here and now', provide a holding and containing relationship in which benign partial regressions can take place. In this way affect, always to be followed, can be expressed and elucidated without engaging in a 'head on' effort to remove defences.

Memories and fantasies are elicited and released but interpretations are usually couched in terms of the woman's adaptive modes of managing feelings and impulses in her object relationships rather more than in terms of primitive unconscious phantasy. Potential transference implications and links need clear and active reflection back since there is no time to consign material to the 'shelf' and browse later or wait for a sure conviction of the 'rightness' of an interpretation. One must concentrate on a set of dynamics thought to be important for the focus of the therapeutic work and pick up material in the service of elucidating these. It can be vital to confront and in the context of a positive therapeutic alliance one can achieve more in brief work. Few women we see have ever successfully negotiated separation from anyone important in their lives, which have often been full of painful losses, so the issue of termination is kept in mind and worked on from the beginning. Unlike analysis, there is not the redemptive certainty of tomorrow's session. There is, however, if desired, a follow-up session some months later which can help the working through.

It may be wondered what this kind of work has in common with the practice of psychoanalysis. Of course sixteen weeks is scant time for patient and therapist to get used to each other and scant time to ascertain and validate 'clinical facts'. Of course brief work can be seen as rough and ready 'first aid'. But psychoanalysis is not only a technique, as Haynal (1988) says, 'it is much more a relation between two people'. What is offered in analysis and in brief work is the framework of a two-person relationship.

It is certainly true that too much of the working through must be left to the patient alone to accomplish – although I think when things go well in brief work, something of an 'observing ego' emerges and something of the therapeutic process gets internalized so a woman is enabled to get on with things by herself with the internalized relationship as the catalyst for change. But we are surely all doing what Enid Balint (1993) describes as important:

> Sometimes to remove obstacles which are blocking the patient's ability to get in touch with a thought or a dream, or an impulse holding them up. The analyst sometimes must point out such obstacles, which prevent the patient finding what they are looking for but which have been put there by the patient themselves so as to avoid having to undertake a painful task. (p. 122)

What is radically different of course is the technique in brief work and analysis; *how* this knowledge can be shared, and at what level, in a way that will be therapeutic, especially given that in brief work the patient may not be so ready and able to understand what is going on in their internal world and tolerate insights about their unconscious projections. It is often confusing for those engaged in brief work that nearly all the accounts of process to be found in the literature are derived from clinical experience in the conduct of a full analysis which can obviously be misleading if taken as a model for brief work.

What is to be resisted, however, is the damning idea (Ussher, 1991) that under-resourced, under-privileged women are too taken up with the myriad stresses of their external reality to be capable of using the 'luxury' of exploring their psyche. On the contrary, we know from evaluative research that studied a hundred consecutive, brief, focused therapies carried out at Shanti (Reader, 1993) that the achievement in therapy of insight, self-affirmation and self-perception that was reality based was the best predictor of women's psychological well-being two years after therapy ended. Success with this client group, however, does certainly require an ability to bear in mind how their external and internal worlds coincide and interact.

Brief, psychodynamic psychotherapy can help such women free them-selves from all manner of psychic predicaments, and particularly their vulnerability to depression in the context of motherhood and childcare – as Colette's own account now illustrates.

'When I look back I now realize that I had been suffering from bouts of serious depression for most of my life. Up until the birth of my daughter I had dealt with (or escaped from) my depression by abusing myself with alcohol, drugs and later compulsive eating. Even though the birth of my child was a joyous and momentous occasion in my life, I found the day-to-day struggles of raising a child on my own with very little money and practical support, overwhelming.

When she was 2 years old, I found her demands and tantrums unbearable and often felt jealous that she was able to express her anger and frustrations and I wasn't "allowed to". One day it was too much and I realized that if I didn't try to sort myself out I would never be a decent mother or a happy, content and fulfilled woman. I'd always resisted the idea of therapy – partly because I thought I could handle my problems myself, and partly because I felt it was a middle class thing for middle class women who could afford it.

Starting the process of therapy was very difficult for me. I felt extremely uncomfortable with my middle class therapist who I assumed would never have any understanding of my working class Irish, Catholic culture. I was overwhelmed at the thought of having someone all to myself for one hour each week who was there to listen to me. I had always been very secretive and inhibited about expressing my feelings, and it seemed almost impossible to know where to begin or what to talk about.

My pain was so intense and consuming, I didn't know words that could articulate what I felt. Often in the session I would be silent, but choking with anger and pain; and also anger at my inability to express myself with words which always seemed to be inadequate. I found it very helpful when the therapist suggested that my pain went back to a time in my life when I didn't know any words and this gave me a perspective I hadn't had before.

Sometimes I regret that I didn't make more use of my sessions. I held a lot of stuff back for various reasons. Sometimes because I felt ashamed, or maybe because I thought the therapist wouldn't understand and sometimes it was plain resistance. "Not wanting the therapist knowing too much about me." That time in my life feels like a blur. I was just about functioning, coping with the basics of living but there seemed to be no end to the tears and anger and feelings of rejection and loneliness. I thought I'd feel like that forever.

I gradually began to trust the therapist, not completely, but enough to feel safe to open the lid on my feelings, just a crack. All through my therapy, despite my insistence on labelling my therapist as middle class and myself as working class – with all the prejudice and limitations inherent in these labels – I increasingly felt treated as an equal. The therapist was always honest and straightforward and obviously respected and valued me for who I was, something which always surprised me.

But sometimes, more importantly, when breakthroughs or connections were made, she helped me to see that it was *me* who had made the connections. I always wanted to give her all the credit because I thought so little of myself and I think this was probably the most valuable thing I learnt – that I did have power and control with my life – that I wasn't completely powerless in just letting things happen to me, people taking advantage and abusing me, my daughter walking all over me, my body getting fatter and fatter and not feeling I had the power to do anything about it.

After leaving therapy it seemed as if nothing had changed, other than that I was crying a lot which I had never done before. Now three years later I can see so clearly that the process of my development only began *after* I finished therapy, that something was sparked off – perhaps the therapist enabling me to take back my self or my power – whatever.

I needed to grieve over my childhood which I did for a long time. I still ate compulsively, allowed people to take advantage of me – even more so than before the therapy – but somehow the ball had started rolling and I was too much wanting to change to stop. The grieving and anger took about eighteen months to deal with, and it will never really go away but now I can have flashes of anger and sadness that I wasn't loved and cared for as a child the way I needed to be, and then let them go again without letting those feelings almost disable and cripple me.

Slowly changes have taken place. I have more confidence in myself, I am not afraid to ask for what I need emotionally in my relationships. I have a better understanding of my feelings and how I fall back into my old patterns of behaviour. But my relationships with friends are easier and more fulfilling because the more I can accept myself warts and all, the more I can accept my friends just as they are.

I no longer have an emotional need to hang on to my weight to protect myself and have let go of my "excess baggage". The understanding I have of my development and the pain I experienced as a child and adult woman also gives me an understanding and wish to support other women going through similar experiences and I now do some voluntary work as a Befriender in a genuine way rather than when I had a need to rescue and help people. Because now I've rescued and looked after myself. I know it will be a long and slow process before I feel that I have reached my potential and feel fulfilled, happy and creative. (I can also accept that I may never be those things completely.) But I feel strongly that I've come too far down the road to go back.

It feels absolutely wonderful not to have that unbearable, indescribable burden of pain, and I just don't get depressed the way I used to. Of course, I still get fed up and feel "down" but it rarely lasts very long and I now have a clearer understanding about *why* I feel the way I do (when fed up) and the confidence to know *how* I can change it and enough respect and liking for myself to *want* to change whatever it is that is making me unhappy.'

ACKNOWLEDGEMENTS

I am grateful to the mothers and children whose experiences I have shared. I acknowledge Colette's contribution and thank her for it. My thanks also to

Christine Puckering, and to Anne-Marie Sandler whose perceptions were helpful to me in the writing of this chapter.

NOTES

1 (a) SLUFP, the South London Under Fives Project – research on the impact of maternal depression on young children.
(b) Newpin, a network of therapeutic communities supporting parents in a psychodynamic way.
(c) Shanti, an NHS service (West Lambeth Health-care Trust) which offers brief psychodynamic psychotherapy to women, often from ethnic minorities.
(d) Mellow Parenting, a project located in a child psychiatric day unit and many social services family centres in Scotland with a DHS-funded research evaluation currently in progress (Puckering *et al.*, 1994).

REFERENCES

Balint, E. (1993) *Before I was I: Psychoanalysis and the Imagination*, London: Free Association Books.

Billinge, M. (1992) 'Assessing families where there is "grave concern"', *Child Abuse Review* 5 (3): 6–11.

Bion, W. (1959) 'Attacks on linking', *Int. J. Psychoanal.* 40: 308–315.

Bowlby, J. (1980) 'Loss, sadness and depression', in *Attachment and Loss*, vol. 3, London: Hogarth.

Brown, G. (1993) 'The role of life events in the aetiology of depressive and anxiety disorder', in *Stress: An Integrated Approach*, eds C. Stanford and P. Salmon, Chichester: Wiley.

Cohen, E. (1994) 'The body as a historical concept', in *The Good Body*, eds M. Winkler and L. Cole, New Haven: Yale University Press.

Cox, A. (1988) 'Maternal depression and impact on children's development', *Archives of Disease in Childhood* 63: 90–103.

Cox, A., Mills, M. and Pound, A. (1991) 'Evaluation of a home-visiting and befriending scheme for young mothers', *J. of the Royal Society of Medicine* 84: 217–223.

Cox, A., Puckering, C., Pound, A. and Mills, M. (1987) 'The impact of maternal depression on young children', *J. Child Psychology and Psychiatry* 28: 917–930.

Freud, S. (1917) 'Mourning and melancholia', *S.E.* 14: 245.

Green, A. (1986) *On Private Madness*, ch. 7, London: Hogarth.

Hammen, C. (1991) *Depression Runs in Families: The Social Context of Risk and Resilience*, London: Springer-Verlag.

Hardy, T. (1874) *Far From The Madding Crowd*.

Haynal, A. (1988) *The Technique at Issue*, London: Karnac Books.

Hildebrand, P. (1986) 'Issues in brief psychotherapy', *Psychoanalytic Psychotherapy* 3(1): 1–14.

Klein, M. (1932) *The Psychoanalysis of Children*, London: Hogarth.

Kumar, C., Cogill, S., Caplan, H., Alexandra, H. and Robson, K. (1986) 'Impact of postnatal depression on the cognitive development of young children', *Brit. Medical Journal* 292: 1165–1167.

Laufer, E. (1993) 'The female Oedipus complex and the relationship to the body', in *The Gender Conundrum*, ed. D. Breen, London: Routledge.

Main, M., Kaplan, N. and Cassidy, J. (1985) 'Security in infancy, childhood and adulthood: a move to the level of representation', in *Growing Points in Attachment*, eds I. Bretherton and E. Waters, Monographs of the Society for Research in Child Development 50, serial no. 209, nos 1–2, Chicago: University of Chicago Press.

Mills, M. (1993) 'Psychotherapy for women', *J. of Mental Health* 2: 89–92.

—— (1996) 'Psychotherapy for women from ethnic minorities in the inner city', in *Planning Community Mental Health Services for Women: A Multiprofessional Handbook*, ed. S. Jackson, London: Routledge.

Mills, M. and Puckering, C. (1985) 'What is it about depressed mothers that influences their child's functioning?' in *Recent Research in Developmental Psychopathology*, ed. J. Stevenson, London: Pergamon.

Murray, L. (1991) 'The impact of postnatal depression on infant development', *J. of Child Psychology and Psychiatry* 49: 1–39.

Patterson, G. (1990) *Depression and Aggression in Family Interaction*, New Jersey: Lawrence Erlbaum.

Pound, A. and Mills, M. (1985) 'A pilot evaluation on Newpin', *Assoc. Child Psychology and Psychiatry Newsletter* 7: 13–19.

Puckering, C. (1994) Personal communication.

Puckering, C. and Mills, M. (1986) 'A comparison of children's emotional distress in three "at risk" family groups', Paper presented to 3rd International Child Psychology and Psychiatry Conference, Paris.

Puckering, C., Cox, A. and Mills, M. (1993) 'A long-term evaluation of Newpin', *Research Report to the Department of Health.*

Puckering, C., Mills, M. and Cox A. (1995) 'The effects of family background, marriage and maternal depression on children's emotional modulation', in *Childhood Depression*, ed. G. Forrest, ACCP Occasional Papers no.11: 53–66.

Puckering, C., Mills, M., Rogers, J. and Cox, A. (1994) 'Mellow mothering: process and evaluation of group intervention for distressed families,' *Child Abuse Review* 3: 299–309.

Radke-Yarrow, M., Cummings, M., Kuczynski, J. and Chapman, H. (1985) 'Patterns of attachment in normal families and families with parental depression', *Child Development* 56: 884–

Raphael-Leff, J. (1991) *Psychological Processes of Childbearing*, London: Chapman & Hall.

Reader, L. (1993) 'Evaluation of a psychotherapy service for women in the community', *SHANTI: Final Report to the King's Fund.*

Stein, A., Gath, D., Bucher, J., Bond, A., Day, A. and Cooper, P. (1991) 'The relationship between postnatal depression and mother–child interaction', *Brit. J. of Psychiatry* 139: 39–57.

Stern, D. (1995) *The Motherhood Constellation*, New York: Basic Books.

Stevenson, J. (1982) *Preschool to School: A Behavioural Study*, London: Academic Press.

Ussher, J. (1991) *Women's Madness: Misogyny or Mental Illness*, Hemel Hempstead: Harvester Wheatsheaf.

Weissman, M. (1974) *The Depressed Woman: A Study of Social Relationships*, Chicago: University of Chicago Press.

Winnicott, D. (1957) *The Child and the Family*, London: Tavistock.

—— (1965) *The Maturational Processes and the Facilitating Environment*, chs 17 and 21, London: Hogarth.

Chapter 11

Inhibition of mourning and the replacement child syndrome

Alicia Etchegoyen

INTRODUCTION

In this chapter I wish to refer to a syndrome seldom discussed in the literature, that of the 'replacement child'. It was first described by Cain and Cain (1964) as the conscious decision by one or both parents to conceive in order to replace a child who had died a short time earlier. Poznanski (1972) considers that the syndrome refers to a child who is deliberately conceived to replace a sibling who has died or to an existing sibling who is assigned the role within the family. She believes the syndrome occurs more frequently than has been reported. This may be the result of lack of recognition by physicians and the family's reluctance to report it. Her paper thus expands the concept of the 'replacement child' and points to a possible higher incidence of the problem.

More recent studies support this view, suggesting an association between perinatal loss, unresolved bereavement and an increased incidence of conception, the majority of which occurs within a year of the previous child's death.

Rowe *et al.* (1978) conducted a retrospective study on twenty-six families who had suffered a perinatal death. Out of the twenty-six mothers, six experienced a prolonged grief reaction (12–20 months). The authors found that the only predictor of morbid grief reaction was the presence of a new baby in the home, closely following the death of the index child, e.g. mothers with a surviving twin baby or a subsequent pregnancy within five months of the loss were significantly more likely to present signs of morbid grief than those without subsequent pregnancy or one more than six months later.

Rubin and Ferencz (1985) compared pregnancy rates for mothers of infants with congenital heart disease and mothers of healthy infants, as controls, over a three-year period. Mothers of infants who died of heart disease had a significantly higher pregnancy rate than the control group.

Rosen (1982) comments that it is not uncommon for parents to conceive a child soon after the death of one of their children. He argues that the concept of replacement child should be extended to include those parents who wish to conceive shortly after the diagnosis of handicap in an existing child. In other words, the loss of a child by death or the loss of the anticipated 'ideal child' by defect, may both lead to a replacement.

I concur with the view that the 'replacement child' syndrome occurs more commonly than is reported. The wish to replace may be 'open' or 'hidden' by repression, denial, or secrecy. I believe that this 'hidden replacement syndrome' often goes unrecognized, in some cases of miscarriage, still-birth and adoption. Following Rosen (1982) a wider definition of the syndrome is suggested to include all cases in which there is a conscious or hidden wish to replace a dead or handicapped child or a child who has been given away to adoption.

To my knowledge, the cases described in the literature correspond to the 'open' category. The incidence of 'hidden' replacement cases is to be determined. I suggest that the distinction between 'open' and 'hidden' replacement may be clinically useful. I have found in my clinical experience that the 'hidden' cases often present a diagnostic and therapeutic challenge and that they may easily be missed if the clinician is not alert to the possibility of their existence.

I shall now follow with a theoretical appraisal of the origins of the syndrome and its effects on the functioning of the replacement child, the family, and the professional network. Two clinical examples, that of an 'open' and that of a 'hidden' replacement, will be presented to illustrate in detail some of the theoretical points. I shall conclude with some thoughts on the therapeutic approaches and management of the condition.

THEORETICAL APPRAISAL

There is general agreement that the origins of the syndrome stem from the parental incapacity to mourn and work through the loss of the child. Mourning is replaced by pregnancy or adoption. Bowlby (1980) describes four stages of normal mourning:

1 A phase of numbness from a few hours to a week.
2 A phase of yearning and searching for the lost figure lasting some months to years, in some cases.
3 A phase of disorganization and despair.
4 A phase of greater or less degree of reorganization.

In his seminal paper 'Mourning and melancholia' (1917) Freud proposed that the work of mourning consisted of painful acceptance of the reality of the loss of the loved object. He thought that initially the loss is denied by an identification with the object: 'the shadow of the object shall fall upon the ego.' (p. 244) This is followed by libidinal detachment when 'reality testing has shown that the loved object no longer exists and it proceeds to demand that all libido shall be withdrawn from its attachments to that object' (p. 244).

In her paper 'Mourning and its relations to manic depressive states' (1940),

Klein makes a fundamental connection between mourning and the infantile depressive position. She postulates that the loss of a good external object reactivates unconscious depressive anxieties about damage and loss of the good internal object in childhood. The work of mourning therefore involves the working through of both an external and an internal loss. It means that the mourner is faced with a more extensive and painful task than had been anticipated. Klein considers that the capacity to mourn in later life and to recover is dependent on the resolution of the depressive position in childhood.

Following Klein, Steiner (1993) describes in more detail the nature of the anxieties and psychic pain involved in the work of mourning. In the early stages of mourning the reality of the loss is denied. By way of projective identification (a fantasy of omnipotent control) the subject attempts to possess and preserve the object. This inner process of identification with the object commonly gives rise to symptoms of heaviness, deadness, malaise and hypochondria, and may contribute to psychosomatic illness. For the work of mourning to proceed the subject has to let the object go, to let it 'die', facing intense anxiety about the object's loss and his own survival without it.

Relinquishing omnipotent control over the object means that the subject's inability to protect and restore the object has to be acknowledged, in psychic reality. It involves as well the reawakening of the infantile situation of conflict between aggressive and reparative wishes towards the object. The experience of these situations evokes intense guilt, desolation and pain. This corresponds to Bowlby's phase of disorganization and despair.

For mourning to reach a satisfactory conclusion the reality of the loss has to be accepted. It entails a process of psychological separation and dif-ferentiation from the objects, which is achieved through the painful task of sorting out what belongs to the self and what belongs to the object. The end result is that the object is perceived more realistically and disowned parts of the self are gradually taken back into the ego. The outcome of this process is that of enrichment and strengthening of the ego. This corresponds to Bowlby's phase of reorganization.

Clearly, the working through of mourning is a difficult process and disturbances may occur at any stage. Covering the extensive literature on abnormal and pathological mourning is beyond the scope of this chapter. I shall focus on the inhibition of mourning and pregnancy.

Lewis (1979) suggests that a bereavement during pregnancy is difficult to mourn. He assumes it is emotionally incompatible for the mother to be both intensely involved with the live baby and simultaneously with thoughts and feelings about the dead person, as happens during mourning. In most cases the mourning process is inhibited or it is only incompletely carried out.

Bereavement as an outcome of pregnancy, following a still-birth or perinatal loss, also presents specific difficulties. The fusion of two opposite realities, birth and death, confronts the mourner with intense feelings of unreality and confusion. Several factors may contribute to the inhibition of mourning by replacement following perinatal loss: professional, social attitudes, underlying parental and family dynamics.

It is only recently that awareness of the impact of perinatal loss has taken place. This is evident in the published literature. The professional interest in the subject has led to considerable change in the management of still-birth and perinatal death (Condon, 1986, 1987; Lewis, 1979, 1983). Nevertheless, it has to be recognized that responding appropriately to perinatal loss places considerable emotional demands not only on the grieving family but also upon the health care team. Raphael-Leff (1991) suggests that the life promoting health professionals are often themselves shocked by the death and may avoid talking to the bereaved parents lest it stirs up their own feelings of disappointment, frustration and guilt. A conspiracy of silence (Bourne, 1968) about the event or inappropriate reassurance, such as encouraging the mother to have another baby soon, are not altogether uncommon.

Menzies Lyth (1975) refers to society's difficulties in facing the meaning and significance of death. She argues that death has now replaced sex as a taboo subject. 'Mention of death is sometimes treated as an obscenity' (p. 208). She thinks that such attitudes inhibit the process of mourning as do the relative lack of public mourning rituals and of private support from relatives and friends in contemporary society.

What are the underlying psychodynamic processes connected with child replacement? In a very inte.es ing paper Alby (1974) writes about the unconscious motivations, conflicts, and fantasies occurring in a number of replacement pregnancies conceived during another child's fatal illness, often at the time of a final relapse. She suggests that the mother's deep need to replace the dying child is motivated by unconscious ideas of abandonment and betrayal towards the ill child and by feelings of ambivalence and guilt. The pregnancy is also used as a manic defence to repair the mother's narcissistic wound of having a 'damaged' child. She believes that in some cases the impending loss is experienced as a catastrophic narcissistic trauma. The pregnancy thus represents a desperate attempt to ward off primitive anxieties of psychic disintegration and overwhelming depression in the mother.

Alby's observation that in some cases the replacement is used as a defence against primitive anxieties, in the face of the mother's narcissistic vulnerability, resonate with my own clinical practice. The experience of the loss as a catastrophic psychological trauma has therapeutic implications that will be discussed later.

Cain and Cain (1964) suggest that the parents' intense narcissistic investment in the dead child and the mother's psychological vulnerability are major factors in the decision to replace.

Bowlby (1980) described a disposition towards compulsive care-giving and a tendency to assert independence of affectional ties connected to narcissistic functioning.

Losses also have a profound effect on the family and its relationships. Lieberman and Black (1987) refer to dysfunctional family patterns of avoidance, idealization and prolonged grief in reaction to loss. The authors comment on the well-known fact that losses in the family are often quickly followed by gains through marriage, conception or birth. Substitution or replacement of those who have died may be the reason for the changes.

Disturbed grief may also be expressed in angry patterns of relationships within the family, sometimes leading to the destruction of the family unit. Lewis (1983) refers to family feuds, depressive anniversary reactions and in some cases provocation of a replacement pregnancy over the next generation. Guyotot (1982) writes about the coincidence of birth and death, usually the death of a parent or grandparent, in and around pregnancy, which dislocates fundamental preconceptions of cause and effect, of time and sequence. Confusion of names, personal attributes, dates, are frequently encountered in family members, which suggests an impairment of symbolization and introjection of the loss.

Finally, how is the replacement child affected by the unmourned loss? The impact of the unresolved bereavement in the early mother–child relationship is well documented. Lewis (1978, 1979) refers to the profound disturbance of mothering following perinatal death, ranging from the mother's inability to care for the baby to confusion with the dead child, rejection, neglect, and in some cases, physical abuse of the replacement child.

Drotar and Irvin (1979) suggest that an infant's death can have a deep and long term influence on the mother's capacity to relate and adapt to subsequent children. Cain and Cain (1964) found that the replacement children had been brought up by overprotective parents, in homes dominated by images of the idealized dead child. They were found to have a shaky sense of identity, low self-esteem, and general immaturity.

In a paper on psychotherapy with a 6-year-old child, Reid (1992) describes the mother having perceived the baby as 'a problem' from the beginning and being unable to develop a positive relationship with the child throughout the years.

Legg and Sherick (1976) view the replacement child syndrome as a developmental interference which may adversely impinge on the child by making demands that the immature ego cannot respond to. The parent of a replacement child is inevitably in conflict because of emotional over-investment in a child who is also a constant reminder of the dead sibling. The authors stress the replacement child's lifelong problem of achieving a 'loving and liveable' sense of identity.

Overall, replacement children face significant problems in the areas of psychological identity, separation and survivor's guilt. A replacement child is, by definition, ascribed the identity of another child, who is usually idealized. The substitute child has an impossible task; to make up for the parent's loss he has to become the ideal. The inevitable failure results in a pervasive inner feeling of inadequacy and handicap. Identification with the dead, lost or damaged sibling contributes to feelings of unreality and confusion at the core of his being and sometimes may lead to severe depression with suicidal ideas.

Unconscious survivor's guilt may have a crippling effect on the child's development. There is often a feeling that the replacement child has no right to develop and succeed by his own resources. Intellectual inhibition, lack of healthy assertiveness, general passivity and emotional immaturity are common. The parents' unconscious hostility to the child's efforts to achieve a separate identity may also militate against growth.

Some of the long term psychological effects on the 'replacement child' have been described in detail. Sabbadini (1988) reports on the analysis of a woman in her early thirties, a replacement for a nine months older sister. The patient came to treatment with a fragile sense of identity, inability to make lasting relationships, and depression.

Porot and Portelli (1993) published a self account of a 42-year-old man, a replacement child for a baby brother, suffering from lifelong relationship problems and an inability to be a good father to his son.

More research is needed on the effect that being a replacement child may have on his or her own attitudes towards sexuality and parenthood. The significance of the parent's wish to produce a substitute of a particular gender has yet to be ascertained.

CLINICAL EXAMPLES

Case 1

I will now describe the psychoanalysis of a 9-year-old girl, a replacement child for a Down's syndrome baby, to illustrate in detail the psychological effects of the substitution and the family dynamics.

Lucy, as I call her, was referred to the local clinic at the age of 9 years and 3 months, because of her school's concern about her over a considerable period of time. Her teacher was in despair about getting through to her. She seemed to daydream and produced very little work. She was very isolated and unable to initiate anything. She spent a lot of time on her own, playing at running a restaurant or a school. She was bullied and perceived as odd by other children. An in-depth assessment of Lucy and her parents was carried out at the clinic over a term.

The relevant background history was that Lucy was born abroad when mother was 44 and father in his early fifties. She had 16-year-old twin brothers, apparently doing well. Mother described no problems during pregnancy or birth. Lucy was a 'quiet, beautiful baby'. Mother was unable to breastfeed. One of her breasts got 'blocked' and the baby did not suck. Lucy took to the bottle hungrily and kept it up to five years. She did not like solids and was generally slow at milestones. Lucy started to attend a playgroup when she was just 2, did not settle and refused to go back. The family had to return to England suddenly a few weeks later, due to political upheaval. When in England she attended a playgroup for two terms and enjoyed it. On transferring to nursery school, aged 3, Lucy did not settle and did not make friends. From then on, her school difficulties persisted. Psychiatric/psychodynamic assessment of Lucy indicated profound intellectual inhibition, severe emotional detachment and tenuous contact with reality at times.

Lucy's mother came across as rather fragile and brittle. Discussion about Lucy's difficulties sent her into panics of explosive anxiety which did not respond to professional support. The clinic team felt concerned about the mother's desperate need to avoid painful or upsetting feelings.

A series of family meetings involving the twins was suggested as part of the assessment. The parents declined as they thought their sons' involvement was neither relevant nor appropriate. A full analysis (five times a week) for Lucy and weekly meetings for parental guidance and support was recommended. This recommendation was based on the clinic's knowledge of the parents and the nature of Lucy's difficulties. It was felt that the severity and extent of Lucy's problems, which affected not only her learning but her overall functioning, needed intensive psychotherapy.

Although indicated, there was no question of mother having help in her own right. She clearly indicated that she equated having psychological difficulties with a mental breakdown.

On my first meeting with the parents, mother conveyed her great expectations about Lucy's abilities. As father put it, mother wanted Lucy to be a 'world beater'. Mother found it extremely difficult to accept that her daughter had severe emotional problems and was of average ability. Psychological testing at the age of 9.2 years gave her a full IQ of 116, a reading age of 9.3 years and a spelling age of 8.4 years. Mother was terrified that having analysis would label Lucy as a psychiatric or handicapped case. Mother described Lucy in idealized terms: a beautiful, artistically gifted child of special sensitivity. I learnt that great allowances were made at home to avoid upsetting Lucy. Father acknowledged that Lucy was not developing well and that she needed help.

When they were about to leave, mother told me that Lucy was a planned baby following a miscarriage a year earlier. On the second interview I learned that mother had an unplanned pregnancy when she was 43. A Down's syndrome baby was born at eight months. Father said the baby died shortly after birth. Mother was surprised as she thought that the baby had been still-born. Following this event, mother decided to have another baby as she 'needed to succeed' with a well baby. Mother had no doubts that she would have a beautiful baby who would be all right.

The birth of the Down's syndrome baby was a family secret. It was interesting to learn that Lucy's spontaneous comment about having treatment was that 'she was not handicapped to need help'.

Analysis started with father's support and mother's reservations, which included attendance to regular meetings at the clinic, to discuss their worries about Lucy and feelings around the death of the previous child. I was aware that parental support may become an issue for the success of the treatment.

On careful discussion with the clinic team we decided to proceed in the face of Lucy's great need of treatment. It was hoped that regular contact with the clinic would allay some of the parents' anxieties and perhaps enable mother to get some help for herself.

I think Lucy's history and presentation illustrate some of the features of the replacement child syndrome. The mother conveys profound denial of the reality of the birth of a handicapped baby ('it was still-born'), and like-wise her feelings about it. There has been no recovery from the trau-matic experience. It has been turned into a 'non-event' (Bourne, 1968) by encapsulation and avoidance (the family secret). This pathological way of operating is colluded with to some extent by father. The solution is a planned pregnancy to preserve mother's precarious sense of psychological functioning.

Lucy's identity as a separate person with problems in her own right is not recognized. There is evidence to suggest idealization and overprotection by both parents. Mother's literal equation of psychological difficulties with handicap suggests a confusion of Lucy's identity with that of the dead baby.

Mother's vulnerability is evident in her denial of any anxiety or depressive feelings, during pregnancy or after the birth. This is not in keeping with the anecdotal and research findings (Phipps, 1985). My overall impression was that mother seemed to lack words to express her feelings and had an impaired capacity to reflect and think about her worries. The powerful, underlying emotions, I believe, were nevertheless perceived by the child, reflected in her fear of being seen as handicapped.

I thought that the father was more in contact with both the reality of the loss of the handicapped baby and Lucy's crippling difficulties. His need to protect mother from anxiety and pain was, however, paramount, and at times overrode his genuine concern and empathy for his daughter's problems and need for help.

The analysis was conducted following the technique of child analysis described by Klein (1932), and further described by I. Pick and H. Segal (1978). Klein considered the child's play in the unstructured situation of the session as the equivalent of free association in the analysis of adults. Theoretically she suggested that there are object relationships from birth, with a rudimentary ego capable of experiencing anxiety and of reacting to it defensively. She thought therefore that the analysis of children could be carried out with the same rigour as adult analysis by interpretation of the early transference and careful attention to the countertransference. Interpretation of the child's unconscious conflicts is based on data gathered by close observation of patterns of the child's verbal and non-verbal behaviour and play.

The issue as to whether the sex of the analyst affects the transference and countertransference has been increasingly discussed in the literature in recent years (Pearson, 1983; Chasseguet-Smirgel, 1984; McDougall, 1988; Lasky, 1989; Lester, 1990). I follow the view that the sex of the analyst, though significant, is not in the long run a predominant factor. The cornerstone of the psychoanalytic method is that patients will transfer aspects of relationships with their significant figures from the past on to the present.

Following Klein (1952), Joseph (1985) has developed the concept of transference (and by implication countertransference) as representing 'total situations'. She suggests that the analyst's task, regardless of sex or other real characteristics, is to investigate and interpret the meaning of the 'total situation' which comprises the emotional relationship with the analyst in the 'here and now' and its connections with the historical past.

First Session – 19 November
Lucy was wearing smart clothes, in a rather Victorian way: a hooded coat with a fur trim on it, with toggle buttons, a blue skirt and an immaculate white jumper. I noticed her pretty features and long blonde hair. There was a general quality of lifelessness, stillness and oddity about her which was shown by sudden grimacing or facial twitches. She was very quiet. Eventually, she drew a lamb and told me she liked sweets. She ended by doing some sums as if she was coming for extra tuition. At the time, and for a considerable period, she insisted that school was wonderful and the work extremely easy.

I thought this first session portrayed Lucy's profound intellectual and emotional inhibition. Her quietness conveyed that she felt empty of thought, unable to express herself and interact. Her drawing of a lamb and her wish for sweets represented, in a condensed and overdetermined way, important areas of her psychopathology. As we later came to understand, the lamb was her passive, immature and idealized self. Her wish for sweets represented her expectations, which were reinforced by her family's functioning, that hard realities should be made 'sweet' by avoidance, reassurance and over-protectiveness. Lucy's use of denial, which mirrored mother's, is thus evident from the very beginning.

Analytic work in the first year centred around Lucy's unconscious conviction that she did not need to take in from anybody. For months, feelings of profound inadequacy and despair were evoked in the countertransference by Lucy's detachment and lack of interest in what I had to offer, as a teacher or mother in the transference. We gradually came to examine her picture of self-idealization and self-sufficiency and its consequences: the profound inhibition of intellectual curiosity and of healthy self-assertiveness.

Lucy found it upsetting to give up her picture of herself as a 'sweet little lamb' together with her demands in the transference that I should be a protective, overconcerned parent taking away her every worry.

I started to talk, in the maternal transference, of her possible fear that I would not like or could not manage any messy, painful emotions or feelings of inadequacy from her. I will now present a session which illustrated clearly some of the factors responsible for her learning inhibition.

Session 19 October, eleven months into the analysis
Lucy came in a cheerful, chirpy mood, looked at me, looked at her box of toys, got out some sweets and started to suck them noisily. She went to the couch and began to try to lift the mattress and stand it against the wall, failing in her attempts. She tried several times. I commented that she was trying to do something quite difficult. Still chewing her sweets, she said brightly 'I'm going to try and try.' She continued for several minutes and looked quite tired. I told her that I thought she was showing me how she felt inside: that she feels all the time she is trying very hard and doesn't quite manage. This may be what happens at school. She slowed down. I went on to say that I thought she was showing me how she felt driven by something inside her, like a nagging voice saying 'try harder', 'do better', which must make her feel very tired. She stopped the activity and the sucking of the sweets. She came close to me and said in a very low and strained voice, 'I try, but my work is never good enough . . . I am never good enough.' There was a poignant silence. I said that she was conveying to me how hurtful it feels not to be good enough. She looked up, quickly went to the table and produced a drawing, full of crossed brown messy lines (quite unlike her usual pictures of pretty flowers), and a very small red spot in the middle. She said to me, 'This is how I feel. When it is not good enough, I feel like this, lost', pointing to the dot. She looked at me anxiously and then looked away. I said that when she feels little, no good, it stirs up the fear that I may not like to know about it. I went on after a short silence about her possible worry that I would be the sort of mummy who only wanted children who do well. She drew some lines across another page and told me where she stood at school (in the bottom stream). She seemed withdrawn, sucked some sweets and drew some pretty flowers. I commented that she found it quite difficult to hold on to the painful feelings stirred up when she felt little and lost with fears that I couldn't stand it. Perhaps she was now trying to have a 'sweet session', keeping herself and me happy.

This session, in my mind, represented a turning point in the analysis. Lucy was able to acknowledge for the first time her deep-seated feelings of inadequacy and depression. She could not sustain emotional contact with the analyst for long, due to her fear about the object's state of mind. Her withdrawal illustrated, I thought, the fundamental problem in the early relationship with the mother, experienced as unable to contain anxiety and distress, internalized as fragile and very demanding at the same time: 'you must do better.' Initially, I understood that Lucy's withdrawal was anxiety driven. Later on I came to appreciate more fully the extent of Lucy's passive wish to move away into an idealized world of 'sweet, lovely pictures'.

Working through some of these issues produced marked symptomatic improvement academically and socially. Lucy's improved capacity to take in and learn from the analyst and the teachers also faced her with the terrifying task of having to learn about her damaged self. She told me spontaneously that she had always felt abnormal and handicapped. I understood this as her unconscious identification with the Down's syndrome baby and the very cut-off mother of her early years. This was her 'core of depression' and it brought intense and poignant feelings in the analysis, which panicked mother, as shown in her letter to me in May, sixteen months into the analysis.

> I was greatly disturbed yesterday when I collected Lucy. She was in a terrible state and was crying all the way back. I am not normal, I am mad, I am handicapped. She was trying to explain to me that she had somebody inside her that was uncontrolled. I didn't recognize her words. They were not hers. I never wanted her to know that you were a doctor, this experience is going to stay with her for life and what I want is for her to forget it as soon as possible.

Around that time Lucy learnt that she had been offered a place at a senior school of her mother's choice. Naturally the academic success reinforced mother's and Lucy's ambivalence about the analysis. It was possible, however, to enlist father's support for the analysis to continue for another year. He had come to realize that Lucy needed support to face and work through her deep-seated feelings of unhappiness. A session in June, seventeen months into the analysis, conveys Lucy's feelings of suicidal depression and depersonalization.

> She told me she had a secret which I did not understand. God had made her special, different to other people . . . she was angry I had not guessed her secret. I said she found it upsetting if I did not understand her instantly and perfectly. I thought she was trying to tell me that sometimes she felt out of touch with herself and with other people. . . . She was very agitated and shouted 'you do not understand' several times. I tried to describe the baby's feelings of being burdened with something she could not grasp (the maternal depression and the dead baby) and her feeling

nobody could help her. She calmed down . . . she told me that on her 8th birthday she was given a doll. She had feelings inside, she felt strange, like crying. She felt it again at 9, 9½ and every day at 10. I commented that she was telling me that she had felt, and still feels, very unhappy inside. She was tearful. She said she wanted to go to God, she felt terrible . . . coming to see me made her feel terrible . . .

Material about the dead baby started to come out very slowly. I learnt that the parents had told her of it at the beginning of the analysis. Initially, I took up Lucy's facial twitches and grimacing as her way of communicating that something was wrong, out of sync. The symptoms improved over some weeks and the material changed. I learnt about a world of secret stories and imaginings. Some had to do with images of love, volcanoes, death. These were somewhat balanced by imaginings about God. She told me the following fantasy:

> She belonged to a special clan and could be in three places: in the galaxy, with God and nowhere. Nowhere, she explained, was the Earth. In Heaven she did not need to talk, there was no atmosphere, no air. There was instead something like steam or mist. Heaven was like a box and letters were carved in the misty air, they looked silky. She sounded very excited. I commented on it but also in the possibly frightening feelings like being nowhere or in a box, like a dead person.

As the material unfolded Lucy's deep feelings of suicidal depression and identity confusion together with her wish to withdraw into a world of exciting stories and idealized picture of Heaven became apparent. She told me that she could hear or talk to God in the quiet.

> Perhaps she is alive . . . perhaps she is dead . . . perhaps being here in the session, the world, the trees, the chair is unreal . . . she thought she was not really here (on Earth). God had sent her mind to Earth, she is really in Heaven, she is invisible.

Naturally, Lucy found talking about these feelings frightening and often retreated into her secret world of imaginings, where I could not reach her. Alternatively, she would become physically aggressive, trying to push me away.

I was acutely aware at the time of the tenuous parental support towards the analysis. The parents had not engaged in regular meetings at the clinic. Mother had made it clear all along that Lucy was having treatment to help her to learn at school. Exploration of mother's personal issues or the family functioning were not welcomed by her. The father did not dispute mother's views.

I tried to talk about Lucy's impossible dilemma. On the one hand there was her own fear to face the 'dead-like', 'unreal' confused feelings the analysis was uncovering and her realistic anxiety (closely replicated in the transference) that her mother could not tolerate them. On the other hand it was clear that she would only become 'alive' if she could disentangle herself from the dead baby.

In mid-October I had to stop two sessions because of Lucy's aggressive and dangerous behaviour. She had been playing with a rope 'jokingly', trying to pull it around her neck. She had attacked me when I had stopped her. A few days later she told me that both her mother and herself thought she was ready to stop; I was keeping her in prison. I was not surprised to receive a telephone call from her father shortly after. His wife was very upset about Lucy continuing with treatment. He had decided that 'for the sake of his wife's mental health' Lucy should stop at Christmas.

Lucy had mixed feelings about ending: she felt freer in herself but more muddled and upset than when she started. She wished to forget that she ever had problems. Mother told me, at our last meeting, that forgetting and ·withdrawing were not necessarily a bad thing. She had decided to ignore the fact that her handicapped baby had died, she had held to this fantasy for a month. She had felt no pain or anxiety. I indicated to the parents that unresolved mourning over the handicapped baby was still a significant problem for Lucy and the family. I suggested that help for the family as a whole or for mother should be considered. I suggested a reassessment at Easter. The parents did not get in touch.

I think the development of the analysis and the premature interruption at two years clearly illustrate the pathogenic effects of inhibited mourning. The dead baby, denied existence and meaning in the mother's mind, could not be mourned. Paradoxically it was kept alive as a debilitating influence in Lucy's development. It is an interesting question why the handicapped baby could not be mourned.

Although I had no first hand knowledge of the mother's internal world and early history, it seemed to me that her way of functioning was based on self-idealization, that is a picture of herself as 'successful mother of beautiful children'. The birth of the damaged baby was experienced as a psychological catastrophe. Mother's fragile sense of identity had to be reinstated by another successful pregnancy. There is also some evidence to suggest an unfavourable combination between Lucy's constitution and mother's conviction that forgetting is a good thing. I am referring to Lucy's tendency to withdraw passively into an imaginary world in which there was no pain and frustration, as she probably did as a baby not working hard at the breast. Lucy's weak sense of identity turned her into a recipient for mother's projections (her depression and terror of the dead, damaged baby).

I believe that the uncovering of the problem in Lucy's analysis was experienced concretely as a threat to mother's mental health. The father again colluded with mother's avoidance by stopping the analysis.

Case 2

Powerful emotional undercurrents are particularly complex in the 'hidden replacement' cases. Unless careful diagnosis of the situation takes place, the professional network may get caught up in the family's defensive system. This is illustrated with the following example.

I will now describe the case of Mrs A, the adoptive mother of an 11-year-old girl I shall call Margaret and her 8-year-old brother Damian. The children had been placed for adoption with a couple thought to be 'eminently suitable' by an experienced professional team. I will discuss how the professional network painfully came to discover fourteen months after the children had been placed that the fundamental underlying motive in the wish to adopt was mother's secret and compulsive guilt-ridden need to replace a lost baby.

Margaret and Damian had had a disturbed and unsettled life. Their father was known to be violent and left when Damian was born. Mother was a heroin addict, had a chaotic lifestyle and a succession of boyfriends. There was some evidence to suggest that the children had been exposed to pornographic videos and that Margaret may have been sexually abused. The children were taken into care by Social Services aged 9 and 6, on grounds of neglect and emotional abuse. It was decided that contact with mother would cease and that the children would be put for adoption together. At the time of being received into care both children showed symptoms of emotional and behavioural disturbance. Margaret suffered from day and night time enuresis. Antisocial behaviour included stealing and physical and verbal abuse of figures in authority. She was unable to make peer relationships and to learn at school. Damian's behaviour was immature and at times odd. He related by a constant stream of talk consisting of silly jokes and disjointed comments about what was going on in his head. He seemed to live in a fantasy world populated by cruel and violent figures. Although of good intelligence he was functioning at school at educationally sub-normal level. Damian was fascinated by violence and spent most of his free time looking at horror movies or magazines.

The children were placed in a Home, awaiting adoption. A year later, a couple seriously considered taking them but withdrew at the last moment, to the children's (then aged 10 and 7) bitter disappointment. The couple were put off by the problems envisaged adopting such a disturbed pair of children.

Mrs A had married at 23, wanting to have a large family, a wish that had been pervasive since adolescence. Over the next four years she had seven miscarriages, followed by an ectopic pregnancy, and the following year, at age 28, a failed IVF. Recurrent gynaecological problems ended in hysterectomy at the age of 33. Mrs A had considerable work experience with mentally handicapped, disturbed adolescents. The couple approached a reputable adoption agency two years later. Mrs A indicated that she would be prepared to adopt an older child who had suffered abuse. After a six-month period of extensive assessment it was the general opinion that the couple had worked through their sad losses and they were recommended for adoption 'wholeheartedly'.

The children, then aged 11 and 8 years, moved in January, with the plan to adopt later in the year. The adoption agency offered regular meetings with the prospective parents for support and discussion of management issues and regular family meetings. The family was referred to the Department in September. There was concern about mother's level of anxiety over and above that of a realistic response to the children's emotional and behavioural disturbance, which was on the increase. Mrs A seemed unable to take in any professional advice. She was becoming increasingly demanding of the agency's and of the GP's help out of hours, which she seemed unable to use. On the initial interview I was struck by father's benevolent detachment and by mother's overwhelming anxiety. We learnt that the parents' sexual relationship had ceased when the children had moved in. The parents denied that there were marital tensions.

Individual assessment of each child revealed that they were both highly traumatized by their disturbed and violent past. It was clear that they had developed a strong attachment to the couple in spite of their obvious difficulties and that they were motivated to be helped. The team decided that individual psychotherapy for each child was indicated to help them work through some of their past experiences so as to be 'free' to relate to their new parents.

It was agreed that community support for the parents and the family would continue with clear boundaries, on agreed regular times, and that therapeutic input to the parents' anxieties and marital difficulties would come from the Department. Regular reviews with the network were to take place once a term. Treatment of the children started in January.

Just before the first review, at the beginning of May, I learnt from the adoption agency that new information about Mrs A's background had come to light. Dr B, the couple's GP, had expressed his concern about the stress Mrs A was experiencing and had conveyed his strong reservations about the couple's suitability for adoption. It was then discovered that Mrs A had had several psychiatric admissions for depression and overdoses during the early years of her marriage.

Unknown to Mr A, Mrs A had had a poor relationship with her mother, a difficult childhood and adolescence, with a query of sexual abuse by father, and indeed had had a son at 17 who was adopted at 6 months by her own mother. The pregnancy was apparently the outcome of a rape by a stranger at a party. Mrs A's son had been brought up believing Mrs A to be his older sister.

I would postulate that the parent's denial and concealment of the truth somewhat affected the network (conflict by proxy). What was denied within the network was the seriousness of Mrs A's difficulties and her unbearable guilt. Mrs A's compulsion to have a baby to replace her son became enacted by the network. It started by the first GP's failure to disclose. It continued when the team assessing the parents as prospective adopters failed to diagnose that the wish to adopt did not represent a psychological move forward, the outcome of successful mourning, but a massive avoidance of depression and loss.

In spite of their obvious shock and distress at the disclosures, the adoption agency courageously decided to bring the information into the open and to continue to support the placement. The parent's initial reaction was on the whole positive. Mrs A was enormously relieved that her 'guilty secret' was out, and her husband, though understandably upset, became closer and more supportive of her as a mother.

Over the next few months, Mrs A's anxiety noticeably decreased and her management of the children improved. The couple were, however, extremely reluctant, almost antagonistic, to look at Mrs A's depression and at the significance of Mrs A's natural child in their relationship. Mr A felt that his wife's psychiatric disturbance was to be forgotten, it had happened long ago. Mrs A thought her natural son was a 'closed chapter' and should remain so.

Several questions remained unanswered, such as whether the natural son was the outcome of an incestuous relationship, or to what extent Mr A had been totally ignorant of his wife's 'guilty secret', or had unconsciously been aware and colluded with her compulsion.

Our area of work was therefore constrained to supporting and guiding parental management. This work, together with the psychotherapy of the children, was successful enough for the adoptions to take place two years later, when the children were 13 and 10½ years old. Mrs A's guilt, however, remained unresolved. She was unable to give herself much credit for any improvement in the children and felt unable to return to part-time work which she had enjoyed in the past. The couple's sexual relationship did not return. A series of psychosomatic complaints and a major accident occurred (Mrs A seriously burnt her foot by dropping a tin of hot oil), before the adoption seemed to indicate an unconscious self-punishing wish.

We had agreed to keep in some contact after the adoption, the children having finished their treatment, but we did not hear from them. A few months later we learnt from the GP that Mrs A had had a depressive breakdown and had been admitted to a nursing home.

In trying to understand how this state of affairs came about one is struck by the couple's extensive use of denial to deal with painful issues. Mr A denied the significance of his wife's overdoses, psychiatric hospitalizations and marital tensions. Mrs A kept the existence of her baby a secret, not only to others but to herself. The loss of the baby was denied and disavowed. Pain and guilt were avoided by replacing the adopted son with Margaret and Damian. We came to understand that for Mrs A, Damian unconsciously represented her replacement baby. Margaret was closely identified with Mrs

A's damaged self she wished to dissociate from and to repair by manic omnipotence.

It seems to me that the couple's powerful denial and omnipotence affected the network. It was not possible to ascertain why the first GP did not disclose the information to the agency. Mrs A indicated that confidentiality was not an issue. She had assumed her GP would inform the agency about her background. We may speculate that he may have 'forgotten', which may have been aided by the couple's failure to disclose or remind him of the relevant facts.

With the benefit of hindsight, it would appear that the professional network had failed to be alerted by the number of miscarriages within a very short period to explore the possibility that the pregnancies were driven by a compulsion to repeat rather than by resolution of bereavement and loss. Omnipotence may have 'infiltrated' the team, stirred by Mrs A's obvious search for a baby. It is possible that Mrs A unconsciously affected the team by conveying, in a subtle and intense way, a strong appeal that she should be looked after and rescued from her sad circumstances of repeated bereavement. The professional team responded in a way by enacting her wish; by allowing her to adopt. It is clear that if the adopting agency had had all the relevant information about the couple, there would have been strong concerns about their suitability as adoptive parents.

THERAPEUTIC CONSIDERATIONS

The clinical examples illustrate the pathological and far-reaching consequences arising from the inhibition of mourning. Therapeutic intervention rests on the fundamental concept that the work of mourning can only begin when the reality of the loss has been experienced.

I would suggest that the more intense the denial of the loss, the more likely the damaging effects on the replacement, the family and the network. I believe the two cases described represent the most severe end of a spectrum, and merit some detailed discussion. In both instances the internal and external reality of the loss were disavowed and the intolerable feelings were split off and projected. Lucy's mother thought that her baby had been born dead. Mrs A turned it into a 'closed chapter'. Lucy's mother projected her unbearable feelings of failure and pain of having a damaged baby on to Lucy, together with her unconscious demand that her daughter should become a 'success' to restore her mother's fragile self-esteem. Lucy's passivity and her tendency to avoid frustration by withdrawal into a fantasy world possibly contributed to a 'pathological fit' in which she became the recipient of her mother's unwanted feelings. Mrs A projected her intolerable feelings of guilt and her own omnipotent wish to be 'rescued' into the professional network. An omnipotent response (Mrs A was given two children) got enacted by the team.

The appropriate professional response of realistic diagnoses of Mrs A's unresolved mourning did not take place.

Both fathers went along with the denial of the significance of the loss and of the mothers' emotional fragility. These families were remarkable in their reluctance to accept psychological help to work through the loss and for breaking off treatment. The powerful defences used (projection, disavowal, manic omnipotence) to ward off psychological awareness may indicate that for these mothers the loss of their babies represented a catastrophic trauma.

Freud (1920) wrote about trauma and its effects: 'We describe as traumatic any excitations from outside which are powerful enough to break through the protective shield' of the ego (p. 29).

Garland (1991), interviewing victims of natural disasters, describes 'the very inarticulacy created by the scale of the breach in the protective shield' (p. 510). She refers to the victim's overwhelming sense of helplessness and disintegration, experienced as a state of psychological breakdown.

Hyatt Williams (1981) mentions the intrapsychic state of affairs that occurs when a traumatic experience is not worked through psychologically. A state of 'psychic indigestion' ensues. The unmetabolized experience remains, like a foreign body, in a sort of emotional limbo. The intrapsychic constellation, however, continues to be active underground and may erupt in times of emotional stress.

I agree with Garland (1991) and others that the noxious effect of the traumatic event is due to the breaking down of the person's capacity for symbolic thinking about the experience. Without it, feelings about loss, destructiveness and death cannot be worked through. No containment, as described by Bion (1962), is possible. In the clinical examples, mourning was avoided, short-circuited. What happened was a concrete substitution of a lost baby for a new one.

I believe that in these cases the replacement syndrome represented a desperate attempt to regain a sense of psychological balance. The attempt was bound to fail because of the very nature of the unmetabolized experience, confined to the non-symbolic realm. I would suggest that, for these mothers, the traumatic experience was concretely equated with a mental breakdown. I believe the 'fear of breakdown', as described by Winnicott (1963), explained their resistance to psychological interventions.

Lucy's analysis had to be interrupted for the sake of mother's mental health with the father's collusion. In the case of Mrs A, the emotional undercurrents of the hidden replacement syndrome were particularly complex and affected the network. There was literally a breakdown in communication between agencies and possibly an unconscious collusion in the network which prevented a careful appraisal of the situation. Mrs A's breakdown was temporarily kept at bay by her attempts to adopt. She remained, however, barely coping, in a state of chronic depression, fundamentally affected by the closed unmourned chapter of her adolescent pregnancy.

It is important to be aware that in these severe cases psychological intervention, though badly needed, may not be forthcoming. Appropriate diagnosis should alert the network to the potential pitfalls and help plan realistic intervention. Limited therapeutic aims, such as symptomatic improvement of the replaced child, may be achieved.

In the less severe cases the research evidence (Leon, 1990; Raphael-Leff, 1993 and others) indicates that psychological intervention in the form of short term therapy, counselling and/or self-support groups may help to get the mourning process started. It is important to recognize, however, that the resolution of mourning takes longer than we originally anticipated and is sometimes measured in years (Bowlby, 1980; De Frain et al., 1991). Its course may not be that of progressive resolution but may be marked by both forward and backward moves.

Nevertheless, if the process can begin so that the dead baby 'can be picked up and brought back to death' (Lewis, 1978) a new space for creativity and growth will become available.

REFERENCES

Alby, N. (1974) 'L'enfant de replacement', *Evolution Psychitrique* 39 (3): 557–566.

Bion, W. (1962) *Learning from Experience*, London: Heinemann.

Bourne, S. (1968) 'The psychological effects of stillbirths on women and their doctors', *Journal of the Royal College of General Practitioners* 16: 103–112.

Bowlby, J. (1980) *Loss*, London: Hogarth and the Institute of Psycho-Analysis.

Cain, A.C. and Cain, B.S. (1964) 'On replacing a child', *J. Am. Acad. Child Psychiatry* 3: 443–445.

Chasseguet-Smirgel, J. (1984) 'The femininity of the analyst in professional practice', *Int. J. Psychoanal.* 65: 169–178.

Condon, J.T. (1986) 'Management of established pathological grief reaction after stillbirth', *American Journal of Psychiatry* 143 (8): 987–992.

—— (1987) 'Predisposition to psychological complications after still birth: a case report', *Obstetrics and Gynaecology* 70 (3): 495–497.

De Frain, J. *et al.* (1991) *Sudden Infant Death: Enduring the Loss*, Lexington Books.

Drotar, D. and Irvin, N. (1979) 'Disturbed maternal bereavement following infant death', *Child: Care, Health Development* 5 (4): 239–247.

Freud, S. (1917) 'Mourning and melancholia', *S.E.* 14: 243–258.

—— (1920) 'Beyond the pleasure principle', *S.E.* 18: 7–64.

Garland, C. (1991) 'External disasters and the internal world: an approach to psychotherapeutic understanding of survivors', in *Textbook of Psychotherapy in Psychiatric Practice*, ed. J. Holmes, Churchill Livingstone: 507–532.

Guyotat, J. (1982) 'Recherches psychopathologiques sur la coincidence mort–naissance', *Psychoanalyse a l'Université* 7 (27): 463–476.

Joseph, B. (1985) 'Transference: the total situation', in *Psychic Equilibrium and Psychic Change*, eds E. Bott Spillius and M. Feldman, London: Tavistock/ Routledge, 1989, 156–167.

Klein, M. (1932) 'The psychological foundations of child analysis', in *The Writings of M. Klein*, vol. 2, London: Hogarth and the Institute of Psycho-Analysis, 1981: 22–39.

—— (1940) 'Mourning and its relation to manic depressive states', in *The Writings of M. Klein*, vol. 1, London: Hogarth and the Institute of Psycho-Analysis, 1981: 344–69.

—— (1952) 'Some theoretical conclusions regarding the emotional life of the infant', in *The Writings of M. Klein*, vol. 3, London: Hogarth and the Institute of Psycho-Analysis, 1981.

Lasky, R. (1989) 'Some determinants of the male analyst's capacity to identify with female patients', *Int. J. Psychoanal.* 70: 405–418.

Legg, C. and Sherick, I. (1976) *Child Psychiatry and Human Development* 7 (2): 113–136.

Leon, G.I. (1990) *When a Baby Dies*, Yale University Press.

Lester, E. (1990) 'Gender and identity issues in the analytic process', *Int. J. Psychoanal.* 71: 435–444.

Lewis, E. (1978) 'Help for parents after stillbirth', *British Medical Journal*, Feb. 18: 439–440.

—— (1979a) 'Inhibition of mourning by pregnancy: psychopathology and management', *British Medical Journal*, 2 July 7: 27–28.

—— (1979b) 'Mourning by the family after a stillbirth or neonatal death', *Archives of Disease in Childhood* 54 (4): 303–306.

—— (1983) 'Stillbirth: psychological consequences and strategies of management', in *Advances in Perinatal Medicine*, eds A. Milunsky *et al.*, vol. 3, New York: Plenum: 205–245.

Lewis, E. and Page, A. (1978) 'Failure to mourn and stillbirth: an overlooked catastrophe', *Br. J. Med. Psychol.* 51: 237–241.

Lieberman, S. and Black, D. (1987) 'Loss, mourning and grief', in *Family Therapy: Complementary Frameworks of Theory and Practice*, eds A. Bentovim *et al.* Academic Press: 251–265.

McDougall, J. (1988) 'Interview', in *Women Analyze Women*, eds E. Hoffaman Baruch and L.J. Serrano, New York: New York University Press: 63–84.

Menzies Lyth, J. (1975) 'Thoughts on the maternal role in contemporary society', in *Containing Anxiety in Institutions*, vol. 1, London: Free Association Books, 1988: 208–221.

Person, E. (1983) 'Women in therapy: therapist gender as a variable', *Int. Rev. Psychoanal.* 10: 193–204.

Phipps, S. (1985) 'The subsequent pregnancy after stillbirth: anticipatory parenthood in the face of uncertainty', *Int. J. Psychiatry Med.* 15: 243–264.

Pick, I. and Segal, H. (1978) 'Melanie Klein's contribution to child analysis: theory and technique', in *Child Analysis and Therapy*, ed. J. Glenn, Jason Aronson: 427–449.

Porot, M. and Portelli, C. (1993) 'Jean-Pierre, enfant de replacement ou la suspicion illegitime', *Annales Medico Psychologiques* 151 (2): 142–143.

Poznanski, E.O. (1972) 'The "replacement child": a saga of unresolved parental grief', *J. Paediatr.* 8: 1190–1193.

Raphael-Leff, J. (1991) *Psychological Processes of Childbearing*, London: Chapman and Hall.

Reid, M. (1992) 'Joshua: life after death. The replacement child', *Journal of Child Psychotherapy* 18 (2): 109–138.

Rosen, G. (1982) 'Replacement child: expanding the concept', *Developmental and Behavioural Paediatrics* 3 (4): 239–240.

Rowe, J. *et al.* (1978) 'Follow-up of families who experience a perinatal death', *Paediatrics* 62: 166–170.

Rubin, J.D. and Ferencz, C. (1985) 'Subsequent pregnancy in mothers of infants with congenital heart disease', *Paediatrics* 76: 371–374.

Sabbadini, J. (1993) 'The replacement child', *Contemporary Psychoanalysis* 24 (4): 528–547.

Steiner, J. (1993) *Psychic Retreats*, London: Routledge.

Williams, A. Hyatt (1981) 'The indigestible idea of death', unpublished paper.

Winnicott, D. (1963) 'Fear of breakdown', in *Psychoanalytic Explorations*, eds C. Winnicott *et al.*, London: Karnac Books: 87–95.

Part III

Female experience in the psychoanalytic process

Introduction to Part III

Rosine Jozef Perelberg

From a very early stage, psychoanalysis maintained that the psychic reality of sex had to be distinguished from the anatomical reality. In his 'Three essays' (1905), Freud suggested that there is no one-to-one correlation between biology and psychology. Men and women are not physically or socially 'made' as male or female but become such.

Initially, however, Freud assumed a symmetry in the development of what he called the Oedipus complex. Boys love their mothers and feel rivalry for their fathers; girls desire their fathers and are jealous of their mothers. Freud was still a 'vulgar empiricist' at that point (Laplanche, 1980, p. 81). In an essay written in 1925, Freud distinguished between the psychosexual history of boys and girls. Until then the boy had been the model for his theory but now Freud recognized the importance of the pre-oedipal phase in which boys and girls have both feminine and masculine attributes. Both infants in this phase love the mother, and both have to relinquish her in favour of the father. The girl has to transfer her love from her mother to her father, whereas the boy gives up his mother with the understanding that he will later have a woman of his own. In this model, boys identify with their fathers as their masculine identity is established. The little boy learns his role as his father's heir. The little girl, on the other hand, has to continue to identify with her mother while at the same time abandoning her as a love object and turning to her father instead. For Freud this turning away from the mother is based on frustration and the disappointment that she cannot satisfy her mother, and is accompanied by hostility.

During this initial stage bisexuality is characteristic of both sexes. What is it, then, that is repressed in the oedipal phase? In the main body of his work Freud oscillated between two hypotheses. According to the first, what is repressed and constitutes the nucleus of the unconscious in each human being is the side that belongs to the opposite sex. According to the second hypothesis, both sexes 'repudiate femininity' (Freud, 1919, 1937), a fact which is an essential element of the asymmetry between the sexes. This repudiation, Freud suggests, is the bedrock of psychoanalysis and part of the great riddle of sex (1937, p. 252). It is part of the domain of what is unanalysable for Freud.

In his debate with Ernest Jones, Freud indicated that Jones profoundly misunderstood the fundamental nature of sexuality and that Jones had returned to a biological reductionism. To quote Freud:

> Your work fits into that of authors such as Horney, Jones, Rado, etc. who do not come to grips with the bisexuality of women and who, in particular, object to the phallic phase . . . I object to all of you to the extent that you do not distinguish more clearly between what is psychic and what is biological, that you try to establish a neat parallelism between the two. . . . we must keep psychoanalysis separate from biology just as we have kept it separate from anatomy and physiology. (Freud, 1935, pp. 328–329)

Freud's fundamental thinking throughout his work on sexuality was that the opposition between masculinity and femininity is not presented as a *fait accompli* to the child. The individual is not born but is constituted through sexual differentiation (Freud, 1933). There is also a fluidity between the two:

> psychoanalysis cannot elucidate the intrinsic nature of what in conventional or in biological phraseology is termed 'masculine' and 'feminine': it simply takes over these two concepts and makes them the foundation of its work. When we attempt to reduce them further, we find masculinity vanishing into activity and femininity into passivity, and that does not tell us enough. (Freud, 1920, p. 171)

Minski (1996) pointed out that Freud sees 'identity as always divided, unstable and made precarious by a potentially subversive unconscious' (p. 2). This author suggests that object relations theory sees identity as 'capable of becoming unified, stable and authentic'.

The distinction between penis and phallus is fundamental to Freud's differentiation between biological and psychic reality. Penis designates the anatomical and physiological reality (Laplanche, 1980, p. 56). Phallus, on the other hand, exists *outside anatomical reality*. Lacan suggests that it is the signifier of the mother's desire. The central question of the Oedipus complex thus becomes to be or not to be the phallus, i.e. to be or not to be the object of mother's desire (D'Or, 1985, p. 102). The role of the father also becomes symbolic – he represents the impossibility of being the object of mother's desire. The triangularity of the oedipal structure refers to the structure of alliance between mother, father and child and contrasts with a dual perspective with its emphasis on narcissistic mirroring and the exchangeability of self and other.

Chasseguet-Smirgel distinguished between the image of the mother as *herself* possessor of a penis from the imago of the mother as *holder* of the paternal penis. In the former, a woman identifies herself with an autonomous phallus. In the latter there is an identification with the 'paternal penis woman'

(1964, p. 124). More recently Birksted-Breen has suggested the distinction between phallus and 'penis-as-link' (1996). Whilst the former is 'representative of omnipotence and completion' (p. 651), of narcissistic organisation, the latter represents the 'mental function of linking and structuring' and the internalisation of the parental relationship.

Whilst Breen is making an important distinction between two different types of object choice, her use of the *penis* to signify the linking function risks a return to a biological 'penis-centred' (see also Steiner, R. 1996) emphasis on the male organ. This is indeed what Freud attempted to distance himself from (see the quotation above, 1935, pp. 328–9). As discussed above the phallus, in contrast, cannot be reduced to the anatomical reality of the male organ. The phallus is not possessed by anyone and represents an unconscious phantasy about the object of the mother's desire (see Mitchell, 1974; Mitchell and Rose, 1982; Perelberg, 1990; Kohon, 1996). What there is in contrast with the phallus is a lack, an impossibility, an absence, a gap – everything that is not there and is not possible, a fundamental renunciation which is at the basis of the human order. I think that the notion of the 'paternal penis woman' (Chasseguet-Smirgel) and 'penis-as-link' (Birksted-Breen) represent attempts to put something in the place of the phallus. Both masculinity and femininity, however, contrast with the phallus, both expressing a lack. Femininity, however, takes the position of representing this lack whereas with masculinity one can harbour the illusion that the penis *is* the phallus.

Chasseguet-Smirgel herself stresses that both sexes experience themselves as 'painfully incomplete' because of the primary incompleteness in relation to the mother (1964, p. 112). She suggests that ultimately women do not wish to become like men 'but want to detach themselves from the mother and become complete, autonomous *women*' (p. 118). For her there is a defensive function of the theory of phallic monism, the result of the repression of an earlier piece of knowledge. Thus psychoanalysis can comfortably postulate a disjunction between knowledge and phantasy. The knowledge of the existence of the female organ is not in contradiction with the phantasy of a phallic monism as representing a wish for 'completeness'.

There is another dimension of this discussion which I do not think has been acknowledged in the literature, which is that Freud defined patriarchy as the law of the *dead* father. In Totem and Taboo he described the primal patricide committed by the original horde, who killed and devoured their father. This was followed by remorse and guilt (as they both hated and loved their father) and the dead father became more powerful than he had been while alive. The dead father is thus the possessor of the phallus. As a social anthropologist I find it is very interesting to link this myth present in Freud's work with a notion present in so many traditional societies which is that the individual only becomes a full person when dead and constituted into a (phallic) ancestor (Perelberg, 1996). See, for instance, the Tallensi in Fortes, 1949). In my reading of the anthropological literature I have also noticed the way in which the phallus appears as an important symbol in many funerary rituals.[1]

What does it represent in these contexts? Why should the phallus be an important symbol in funerary rites? Bachofen has suggested that the funeral rite 'glorifies nature as a whole, with its twofold life and death giving principle. . . . That is why the symbols of life are so frequent in the tomb' (1967, p. 39). This is then what also accounts for the fact that the theme of sexuality and fertility dominates the symbolism of funerals (e.g. amongst the Lugbara of Uganda, in Middleton, 1960; the Trobriands, in Malinowski, 1948; and the Kashi, in Parry, 1981). I would suggest that what is being emphasized in the contexts of these rites is both separation and integration, part and whole, masculinity and femininity and life and death. I would further suggest that it is the finite, limited quality of the facts of culture that are ultimately denied in the symbol of the phallus. From this perspective the phallus is not only signifier of a power structure but of universal fears, beliefs, and wished for states of completeness and plenitude.

Thus the phallus, unlike the penis, is possessed by nobody (male or female) and it represents the combination of both sexes, where neither is given up. The confusion between penis and phallus implies the reduction of the Law of the Father to the rule of the actual living male. This is Freud's myth of the beginnings of society. In the beginning, there is an infantile phantasy of phallic monism, which is a phantasmatic structure organizer of sexual development. Gallop has pointed out that if this myth is internalized, then the living male has no better chance of achieving the sovereign position than does the living female (Gallop, 1982, p. 14).

Freud suggested that the catastrophe of the Oedipus complex represents the victory of the human order over the individual. His writings are therefore about the creation of this order and how it becomes separate from biology (see also Mitchell, 1974). Through the Oedipus complex, the individual enters the symbolic order by establishing the differences between the sexes and the generations. The child is forever excluded from the primal scene between the parents.

I have indicated elsewhere (Perelberg, 1995a, 1995b) that there are 104 references to violence in Freud's complete works and that the majority of these concern the primal scene and the Oedipus complex. In most of these examples, violence is related to a founding myth about the beginnings of man's history, and the Oedipus complex. It is a creation myth of mankind which, for Freud, is repeated in the history of each individual and which includes the phantasies of murder and robbery. Ingredients of this story include children's beliefs that the sexual act is an act of violence; the idea that if left to themselves, sons would kill their fathers and sleep with their mothers; the notion that the prohibition of incest is related to the founding of civilization. It is a profound and violent renunciation that is instituted in the human order. The idea that parental intercourse is an act of violence in the phantasy of the child also figures in the writings of Klein (1945) and post-Kleinian writers (see Britton et al., 1989).

In psychoanalytic terms, the acceptance of an order based on the differentiation between the genders and the generations and on the incest taboo introduces the individual to an experience of renunciation and mourning (Cosnier, 1990). This is the source of identifications and thus of the foundation of psychic reality (Freud, 1917). As Lévi-Strauss has suggested, together with the incest taboo, and as corollary of it, it is the differentiation between the sexes and the generations that inserts the person into an exogamous system of exchange (1947).[2]

THE CHAPTERS

The authors adopt different positions in relation to the above debate.

As a representative of the papers on female sexuality written by the women analysts of her time (see Raphael-Leff's Prologue) we have selected Riviere's paper where she suggests that women 'may put on a mask of womanliness to avert anxiety and retribution feared from men' (p. 228 below) and present themselves in a seductive or flirtatious way. Riviere further suggests that there is no difference between genuine womanliness and the masquerade and gives several examples of women patients who cannot take themselves seriously on an equal footing with men. Riviere follows on from Klein's views of the early oral sadistic impulses of the little girl towards both parents and the wish to penetrate the mother's body and devour its contents which include the father's penis, her faeces and children (p. 233). These early sadistic phantasies, according to Riviere, raise enormous anxiety in the little girl. She attempts to placate her mother and identifies with the father but puts the masculinity she thus obtains 'at the service of the mother' (p. 234). At the same time, however, she experiences resentment towards the father and her womanliness is an attempt to placate him. Her fear of him, however, is never so great as her fear of her mother.

Butler has discussed Riviere's idea of masquerade in an important way. Does the term imply a feminine desire that must be negated, or is it a construction of femininity itself? She quotes Irigaray: 'the masquerade . . . is what women do . . . in order to participate in man's desire, but at the cost of giving up their own' (in 1990, p. 46). Femininity becomes thus something taken on by women who wish for masculinity but fear retribution from their fathers. This debate around the term 'masquerade' contains the central issues that have been discussed in this book, in terms of whether femininity is defined as a lack, a negative term, as a desire to be repressed or whether it has a positive definition of its own.

Jane Temperley suggests that the loss or castration of infantile omnipotence involved in the acceptance by the child of her/his place in the oedipal triangle needs to bring no specific handicap or marginalization to daughters. Temperley takes Jerry Aline Flieger's characterization of feminists into three groups ('father's daughters', 'mother's daughters' and 'prodigal daughters') as the starting point for her discussion. She suggests that the first two categories indicate a preoccupation with power and ownership. The phallus of Lacan's symbolic order is concerned with mastery and power. The emphasis in the Oedipus complex is on the child's sexual wishes and prohibitions by the father. She contrasts that with the procreative male genital which, according to her, Klein describes as restoring the mother and giving her babies. (See also Breen's notion of penis as link, as discussed above.) Contrasting and comparing Klein and Lacan, Temperley suggests that contemporary Kleinian thinking emphasizes that it is the acceptance of a parental couple that marks the painful birth into psychic reality and symbolic order.

This seems to me to be compatible with Freud's original ideas on the primal scene and the Oedipus complex, as discussed above. Freud described what he believed is a central fact of the human condition, which is that a renunciation takes place within the nuclear biological family. This, for him, constitutes the foundation of human order. The hypothesis is that human order requires a fundamental and violent rupture with the 'natural order'. Freud's work emphasizes the phantasy of a violent sexuality of the primal scene and that each human being has to lose and renounce their mother in order to enter the symbolic domain. I think that if Temperley' s chapter plays down the catastrophe implied in the process on the one hand, on the other hand she is pointing to what it is that is achieved in the process: symbolic order, depressive position and participation in humankind.

Perhaps one could also suggest that when Freud discusses the Oedipus complex he is aiming at building a theory that is clinical but also provides an interpretation of human nature and culture whereas Klein seems to focus on individual clinical work and the outcomes expressed in individual pathways.

The notion of mourning and renunciation is also present in Joan Raphael-Leff's concept of 'generative identity'. This is a construction of the self as a creatively generating entity which has its origins in the recognition of male/female reproductive differences. Raphael-Leff points out her understanding that each person comprises a 'fluid configuration of multilayered coexisting feminine and masculine identification . . . albeit inscribed on anatomically differentiated male and female bodies'. 'Generative identity' arises out of the recognition of sexual difference and from early identifications with and sublimation beyond the procreative capacity of the parents/begetters. Raphael-Leff is able to maintain the link between the bodily bases of one's perception of sexual identity ('For however free the spirit, we are none of us disembodied') and its relationship with an experience of the mental space necessary for creative freedom. In her clinical discussion Raphael-Leff presents the analysis of a woman who presents a dramatic struggle between masculine and feminine elements.

In Chapter 15 Valerie Sinason discusses issues of body representation, sexuality and procreation in psychoanalytic psychotherapy with abused and learning disabled girls. They bring to therapy their phantasies of either a damaging act of parental intercourse or of their own violence in the womb. Their extra dependency on their mother makes movement towards separation and individuation extremely difficult and painful. They have to face the fear of the murderous mother, a phantasy which may have a basis in reality, as well as having to be able to identify with the mother's body in their effort to individuate and develop their feminine identity. Sinason indicates how in the transference the female analyst becomes both the pre-oedipal mother who wishes to destroy her damaged baby and a handicapped baby herself. With great sensitivity she discusses several examples indicating that the issues of sexuality and gender are present with equal force and significance in women struggling with problems of disability.

NOTES

1 An example of a phallic symbol which is linked to funerary rituals amongst the Asmat can be found in the Metropolitan Museum of New York. The Asmat celebrated death with feasts and rituals that both commemorated the dead and incited the living to avenge them. The Mbis had the shape of a canoe with an exaggerated prow that incorporated ancestral figures and a phallic symbol. My hypothesis is that phallic symbols are present in funerary rituals because at those occasions there is an attempt to re-create a social order that is 'complete' and contains a promise of eternity. Steiner, R. (1996) has also pointed out the link between the phallus and death rituals, although he offers a different interpretation from the one I am attempting here. Leach (1961) has suggested the way in which religious ideology uses the promise of rebirth in order to negate the finality of death. This idea stresses the way in which 'irreversibility' is disguised as 'repetition'. One can understand it in terms of the way in which the limited nature of the facts of culture – the fact that culture has to 'select' rules that are acceptable or not acceptable – needs to be denied in death. Thus in myths of origins in different societies social rules are non-existent, broken up or inverted, perhaps in an attempt to reincorporate aspects which had to be 'given up' in the constitution of the society itself. (The very idea of the paradise lost might be an illustration of that.) Thus it is common for one to have incest and murder in rites of origins, acts which have to be given up in the foundation of society itself and the construction of its social rules.

2 What is inaugurated is very well expressed in Lévi-Strauss's words: 'To this very day mankind has always dreamed of seizing and fixing that fleeting moment when it was permissible to believe that the law of exchange could be evaded, that one could gain without losing, enjoy without sharing. At either end of the earth and at both extremes of time, the Sumerian myth of the golden age and the Andaman myth of the future life correspond, the former placing the end of primitive happiness at a time when the confusion of languages made words into common property, the latter describing the bliss of the hereafter as a heaven where women will no longer be exchanged, i.e. removing to an equally unattainable past or future the joys, eternally denied to social man, a world in which one might *keep to oneself*' (1947, pp. 496–497).

REFERENCES

Bachofen, J.J. (1967) *Myth, Religion and Mother Right*, London: Routledge & Kegan Paul.

Birksted-Breen, D. (1996) 'Phallus, penis and mental space', *Int. J. Psychoanal.* 77 (4): 649–657.

Britton, R., Feldman, M. and O'Shaughnessy, E. (eds) (1989) *The Oedipus Complex Today*, London: Karnal Books.

Butler, J. (1990) *Gender Trouble*, London: Routledge.

Chasseguet-Smirgel, J. (1964) 'Feminine guilt and the Oedipus Complex', in *Female Sexuality*, ed. J. Chasseguet-Smirgel, London: Maresfield Library, 1985.

—— (1986) *Sexuality and Mind*, New York and London: New York University Press.

Cosnier, J. (1990) 'Les Vicissitudes de l'identité', in *Devenir 'Adulte'*? eds A.-M. Alléon, O. Morran and S. Lebovici, Paris: PUF.

D'Or, J. (1985) *Introduction à la Lecture de Lacan*, Paris: Denoel.

Fortes, M. (1949) *The Web of Kinship among the Tallensi*, London: Oxford University Press.

Freud, S. (1905) 'Three essays on the theory of sexuality', *S.E.* 7: 125–243.

—— (1913[1912–1913]) 'Totem and taboo', *S.E.* 13: 1–162.

—— (1917) 'Mourning and melancholia', *S.E.* 14: 237–258.

—— (1919) 'A child is being beaten', *S.E.* 17: 179–204.

—— (1920) 'The psychogenesis of a case of homosexuality in a woman', *S.E.* 18: 146–172.

—— (1925) 'Some psychical consequences of the anatomical distinction between the sexes', *S.E.* 19: 243–258.

—— (1933) 'Femininity', *S.E.* 22: 112–135.

—— (1935) 'Freud and female sexuality: a previously unpublished letter', *Psychiatry*, 1971, pp. 328–329.

—— (1937) 'Analysis terminable and interminable', *S.E.* 23: 209–253.

Gallop, J. (1982) *Feminism and Psychoanalysis: The Daughter's Seduction*, London: Macmillan.

Klein, M. (1945) 'The Oedipus complex in the light of early anxieties', in *Love, Guilt and Reparation*, London: Hogarth, 1983.

Kohon, G. (1987) 'Fetishism revisited', *Int. J. Psychoanal.* 68: 213–229.

—— (1996) Contribution to the discussion of Dana Birksted-Breen's paper 'Phallus, penis and mental space' at the British Psycho-Analytical Society, unpublished.

Laplanche, J. (1980) *Castration Symbolisations Problematiques II*, Paris: PUF.

Laplanche, J. and Pontalis, J.-B. (1985) *The Language of Psychoanalysis*, London: Hogarth and the Institute of Psycho-Analysis.

Leach, E. (1961) 'Two essays concerning the symbolic representation of time', in *Rethinking Anthropology*, London: The Athlone Press.

Lévi-Strauss, C. ((1947) *The Elementary Structures of Kinship and Marriage*, Boston: Beacon Press, 1969.

Malinowski, B. (1948) 'Baloma: the spirits of dead', in *Magic Science and Religion*, London: Faber & West.

Middleton, J. (1960) *Lugbara Religion*, London: Oxford University Press.

Minski, R (ed.) (1996) *Psychoanalysis and Gender*, London: Routledge.

Mitchell, J. (1974) *Psychoanalysis and Feminism*, Harmondsworth: Penguin.

Mitchell, J. and Rose, J. (eds) (1982) *Feminine Sexuality*, London: Macmillan.

Parry, J.P. (1981) 'Death and cosmogony in Kashi', *Contributions to Indian Sociology* 15: 337–365.

Perelberg, R.J.(1990) 'Equality, asymmetry and diversity: on conceptualisations of gender', in *Gender and Power in Families*, eds R.J. Perelberg and A. Miller, London: Routledge.

—— (1995a) 'Violence in children and young adults: a review of the literature and some new formulations', *Bulletin of the Anna Freud Centre* 18 (2): 89–122.

—— (1995b) 'A core phantasy in violence', *Int. J. Psychoanal.* 76 (6): 1215–1232.
—— (1996) Contribution to the discussion of Dana Birksted-Breen' s paper 'Phallus, penis and mental space' at the British Psycho-Analytical Society, Bulletin.

Chapter 12

Womanliness as a masquerade

Joan Riviere

Every direction in which psychoanalytic research has pointed seems in its turn to have attracted the interest of Ernest Jones, and now that of recent years investigation has slowly spread to the development of the sexual life of women, we find as a matter of course one by him among the most important contributions to the subject. As always, he throws great light on his material, with his peculiar gift both clarifying the knowledge we had already and also adding to it fresh observations of his own.

In his paper on 'The early development of female sexuality'[1] he sketches out a rough scheme of types of female development, which he first divides into heterosexual and homosexual, subsequently sub-dividing the latter homosexual group into two types. He acknowledges the roughly schematic nature of his classification and postulates a number of intermediate types. It is with one of these intermediate types that I am today concerned. In daily life types of men and women are constantly met with who, while mainly heterosexual in their development, plainly display strong features of the other sex. This has been judged to be an expression of the bisexuality inherent in us all; and analysis has shown that what appears as homosexual or hetero-sexual character traits, or sexual manifestations, is the end-result of the interplay of conflicts and not necessarily evidence of a radical or fundamental tendency. The difference between homosexual and heterosexual development results from differences in the degree of anxiety, with the corresponding effect this has on development. Ferenczi pointed out a similar reaction in behaviour,[2] namely, that homosexual men exaggerate their heterosexuality as a 'defence' against their homosexuality. I shall attempt to show that women who wish for masculinity may put on a mask of womanliness to avert anxiety and the retribution feared from men.

It is with a particular type of intellectual woman that I have to deal. Not long ago intellectual pursuits for women were associated almost exclusively with an overtly masculine type of woman, who in pronounced cases made no secret of her wish or claim to be a man. This has now changed. Of all the women engaged in professional work today, it would be hard to say whether the greater number are more feminine than masculine in their mode of life and character. In university life, in scientific professions and in business, one constantly meets women who seem to fulfil every criterion of complete feminine development. They are excellent wives and mothers, capable housewives; they maintain social life and assist culture; they have no lack of feminine interests, e.g. in their personal appearance, and when called upon they can still find time to play the part of devoted and disinterested mother-substitutes among a wide circle of relatives and friends. At the same time they fulfil the duties of their profession at least as well as the average man. It is really a puzzle to know how to classify this type psychologically.

Some time ago, in the course of an analysis of a woman of this kind, I came upon some interesting discoveries. She conformed in almost every particular to the description just given; her excellent relations with her husband included a very intimate affectionate attachment between them and full and frequent sexual enjoyment; she prided herself on her proficiency as a housewife. She had followed her profession with marked success all her life. She had a high degree of adaptation to reality, and managed to sustain good and appropriate relations with almost everyone with whom she came in contact.

Certain reactions in her life showed, however, that her stability was not as flawless as it appeared; one of these will illustrate my theme. She was an American woman engaged in work of a propagandist nature, which consisted principally in speaking and writing. All her life a certain degree of anxiety, sometimes very severe, was experienced after every public performance, such as speaking to an audience. In spite of her unquestionable success and ability, both intellectual and practical, and her capacity for managing an audience and dealing with discussions, etc., she would be excited and apprehensive all night after, with misgivings whether she had done anything inappropriate, and obsessed by a need for reassurance. This need for reassurance led her compulsively on any such occasion to seek some attention or complimentary notice from a man or men at the close of the proceedings in which she had taken part or been the principal figure; and it soon became evident that the men chosen for the purpose were always unmistakable father figures, although often not persons whose judgement on her performance would in reality carry much weight. There were clearly two types of reassurance sought from these father figures: first, direct reassurance of the nature of compliments about her performance; second, and more important, indirect reassurance of the nature of sexual attentions from these men. To speak broadly, analysis of her behaviour after her performance showed that she was attempting to obtain sexual advances from the particular type of men by means of flirting and coquetting with them in a more or less veiled manner. The extraordinary incongruity of this attitude with her highly impersonal and objective attitude during her intellectual performance, which it succeeded so rapidly in time, was a problem.

Analysis showed that the Oedipus situation of rivalry with the mother was extremely acute and had never been satisfactorily solved. I shall come back to this later. But beside the conflict in regard to the mother, the rivalry with the father was also very great. Her intellectual work, which took the form of speaking and writing, was based on an evident identification with her father, who had first been a literary man and later had taken to political life; her adolescence had been characterized by conscious revolt against him, with rivalry and contempt of him. Dreams and phantasies of this nature, castrating the husband, were frequently uncovered by analysis. She had quite conscious feelings of rivalry and claims to superiority over many of the 'father figures' whose favour she would then woo after her own performances! She bitterly resented any assumption that she was not equal to them, and (in private) would reject the idea of being subject to their judgement or criticism. In this she corresponded clearly to one type Ernest Jones has sketched: his first group of homosexual women who, while taking no interest in other women, wish for 'recognition' of their masculinity from men and claim to be the equals of men, or in other words, to be men themselves. Her resentment, however, was not openly expressed; publicly she acknowledged her condition of womanhood.

Analysis then revealed that the explanation of her compulsive ogling and coquetting – which actually she was herself hardly aware of till analysis made it manifest – was as follows: it was an unconscious attempt to ward off the anxiety which would ensue on account of the reprisals she anticipated from the father figures after her intellectual performance. The exhibition in public of her intellectual proficiency, which was in itself carried through success-fully, signified an exhibition of herself in possession of the father's penis, having castrated him. The display once over, she was seized by horrible dread of the retribution the father would then exact. Obviously it was a step towards propitiating the avenger to endeavour to offer herself to him sexually. This phantasy, it then appeared, had been very common in her childhood and youth, which had been spent in the Southern States of America; if a negro came to attack her, she planned to defend herself by making him kiss her and make love to her (ultimately so that she could then deliver him over to justice). But there was a further determinant of the obsessive behaviour. In a dream which had a rather similar content to this childhood phantasy, she was in terror alone in the house; then a negro came in and found her washing clothes, with her sleeves rolled up and arms exposed. She resisted him, with the secret intention of attracting him sexually, and he began to admire her arms and to caress them and her breasts. The meaning was that she had killed father and mother and obtained everything for herself (alone in the house), became terrified of their retribution (expected shots through the window), and defended herself by taking on a menial role (washing clothes) and by *washing of* dirt and sweat, guilt and blood, everything she had obtained by the deed, and 'disguising herself' as merely a castrated woman. In that guise the man found no stolen property on her which he need attack her to recover and, further, found her attractive as an object of love. Thus the aim of the compulsion was not merely to secure reassurance by evoking friendly feelings towards her in the man; it was chiefly to make sure of safety by masquerading as guiltless and innocent. It was a compulsive reversal of her intellectual performance; and the two together formed the 'double-action' of an obsessive act, just as her life as a whole consisted alternately of masculine and feminine activities.

Before this dream she had had dreams of people putting masks on their faces in order to avert disaster. One of these dreams was of a high tower on a hill being pushed over and falling down on the inhabitants of a village below, but the people put on masks and escaped injury!

Womanliness therefore could be assumed and worn as a mask, both to hide the possession of masculinity and to avert the reprisals expected if she was found to possess it – much as a thief will turn out his pockets and ask to be searched to prove that he has not the stolen goods. The reader may now ask how I define womanliness or where I draw the line between genuine womanliness and the 'masquerade'. My suggestion is not, however, that there is any such difference; whether radical or superficial, they are the same thing. The capacity for womanliness was there in this woman – and one might even say it exists in the most completely homosexual women – but owing to her conflicts it did not represent her main development, and was used far more as a device for avoiding anxiety than as a primary mode of sexual enjoyment.

I will give some brief particulars to illustrate this. She had married late, at 29; she had had great anxiety about defloration, and had had the hymen stretched or slit before the wedding by a woman doctor. Her attitude to sexual intercourse before marriage was a set determination to obtain and experience the enjoyment and pleasure which she knew some women have in it, and the orgasm. She was afraid of impotence in exactly the same way as a man. This was partly a determination to surpass certain mother figures who were frigid, but on deeper levels it was a determination not to be beaten by the man.[3] In effect, sexual enjoyment was full and frequent, with complete orgasm; but the fact emerged that the gratification it brought was of the nature of a reassurance and restitution of something lost, and not ultimately pure enjoyment. The man's love gave her back her self-esteem. During analysis, while the hostile castrating impulses towards the husband were in process of coming to light, the desire for intercourse very much abated, and she became for periods relatively frigid. The mask of womanliness was being peeled away, and she was revealed either as castrated (lifeless, incapable of pleasure), or as wishing to castrate (therefore afraid to receive the penis or welcome it by gratification). Once, while for a period her husband had had a love affair with another woman, she had detected a very intense identification with him in regard to the rival woman. It is striking that she had had no homosexual experiences (since before puberty with a younger sister); but it appeared during analysis that this lack was compensated for by frequent homosexual dreams with intense orgasm.

In everyday life one may observe the mask of femininity taking curious forms. One capable housewife of my acquaintance is a woman of great ability, and can herself attend to typically masculine matters. But when, e.g., any builder or upholsterer is called in, she has a compulsion to hide all her technical knowledge from him and show deference to the workman, making her suggestions in an innocent and artless manner, as if they were 'lucky guesses'. She has confessed to me that even with the butcher and baker, whom she rules in reality with a rod of iron, she cannot openly take up a firm straightforward stand; she feels herself as it were 'acting a part', she puts on the semblance of a rather uneducated, foolish and bewildered woman, yet in the end always making her point. In all other relations in life this woman is a gracious, cultured lady, competent and well informed, and can manage her affairs by sensible rational behaviour without any subterfuges. This woman is now aged 50, but she tells me that as a young woman she had great anxiety in dealings with men such as porters, waiters, cabmen, tradesmen or any other potentially hostile father figures, such as doctors, builders and lawyers; moreover, she often quarrelled with such men and had altercations with them, accusing them of defrauding her and so forth.

Another case from everyday observation is that of a clever woman, wife and mother, a university lecturer in an abstruse subject which seldom attracts women. When lecturing, not to students but to colleagues, she chooses particularly feminine clothes. Her behaviour on these occasions is also marked by an inappropriate feature: she becomes flippant and joking, so much so that it has caused comment and rebuke. She has to treat the situation of displaying her masculinity to men as a 'game', as something *not real*, as a 'joke'. She cannot treat herself and her subject seriously, cannot seriously contemplate herself as on equal terms with men; moreover, the flippant attitude enables some of her sadism to escape, hence the offence it causes.

Many other instances could be quoted, and I have met with a similar mechanism in the analysis of manifest homosexual men. In one such man with severe inhibition and anxiety, homosexual activities really took second place, the source of greatest sexual gratification being actually masturbation under special conditions, namely, while looking at himself in a mirror dressed in a particular way. The excitation was produced by the sight of himself with hair parted in the centre, wearing a bow tie. These extraordinary 'fetishes' turned out to represent a *disguise of himself* as his sister; the hair and bow were taken from her. His conscious attitude was a desire to *be* a woman, but his manifest relations with men had never been stable. Unconsciously the homosexual relation proved to be entirely sadistic and based on masculine rivalry. Phantasies of sadism and '*possession of a penis*' could be indulged only while reassurance against anxiety was being obtained from the mirror that he was safely 'disguised as a woman'.

To return to the case I first described. Underneath her apparently satisfactory heterosexuality it is clear that this women displayed well-known manifestations of the castration complex. Horney was the first among others to point out the sources of that complex in the Oedipus situation; my belief is that the fact that womanliness may be assumed as a mask may contribute further in this direction to the analysis of female development. With that in view I will now sketch the early libido development in this case.

But before this I must give some account of her relations with women. She was conscious of rivalry of almost any woman who had either good looks or intellectual pretensions. She was conscious of flashes of hatred against almost any woman with whom she had much to do, but where permanent or close relations with women were concerned she was none the less able to establish a very satisfactory footing. Unconsciously she did this almost entirely by means of feeling herself superior in some way to them (her relations with her inferiors were uniformly excellent). Her proficiency as a housewife largely had its root in this. By it she surpassed her mother, won her approval and proved her superiority among rival 'feminine' women. Her intellectual attainments undoubtedly had in part the same object. They too proved her superiority to her mother; it seemed probable that since she reached womanhood her rivalry with women had been more acute in regard to intellectual things than in regard to beauty, since she could usually take refuge in her superior brains where beauty was concerned.

The analysis showed that the origin of all these reactions, both to men and to women, lay in the reaction to the parents during the oral-biting sadistic phase. These reactions took the form of the phantasies sketched by Melanie Klein in her Congress paper, 1927.[4] In consequence of disappointment or frustration during sucking or weaning, coupled with experiences during the primal scene which is interpreted in oral terms, extremely intense sadism develops towards both parents.[5] The desire to bite off the nipple shifts, and desires to destroy, penetrate and disembowel the mother and devour her and the contents of her body succeed it. These contents include the father's penis, her faeces and her children – all her possessions and love-objects, imagined as within her body.[6] The desire to bite off the nipple is also shifted, as we know, on to the desire to castrate the father by biting off his penis. Both parents are rivals in this stage, both possess desired objects; the sadism is directed against both and the revenge of both is feared. But, as always with girls, the mother is the more hated, and consequently the more feared. She will execute the punishment that fits the crime – destroy the girl's body, her beauty, her children, her capacity for having children, mutilate her, devour her, torture her and kill her. In this appalling predicament the girl's only safety lies in placating the mother and atoning for her crime. She must retire from rivalry with the mother, and if she can, endeavour to restore to her what she has stolen. As we know, she identifies herself with the father; and then she uses the masculinity she thus obtains by *putting it at the service of the* mother. She becomes the father, and takes his place; so she can 'restore' him to the mother. This position was very clear in many typical situations in my patient's life. She delighted in using her great practical ability to aid or assist weaker and more helpless women, and could maintain this attitude successfully so long as rivalry did not emerge too strongly. But this restitution could be made on one condition only; it must procure her a lavish return in the form of gratitude and 'recognition'. The recognition desired was supposed by her to be owing for her self-sacrifices; more unconsciously what she claimed was recognition of her *supremacy* in *having* the penis to give back. If her supremacy were not acknowledged, then rivalry became at once acute; if gratitude and recognition were withheld, her sadism broke out in full force and she would be subject (in private) to paroxysms of oral-sadistic fury, exactly like a raging infant.

In regard to the father, resentment against him arose in two ways: (I) during the primal scene he took from the mother the milk, etc., which the child missed; (2) at the same time he gave to the mother the penis or children instead of to her. Therefore all that he had or took should be taken from him by her; he was castrated and reduced to nothingness, like the mother. Fear of him, though never so acute as of the mother, remained; partly, too, because his vengeance for the death and destruction of the mother was expected. So he too must be placated and appeased. This was done by masquerading in a feminine guise for him, thus showing him her 'love' and guiltlessness towards him. It is significant that this woman's mask, though transparent to other women, was successful with men, and served its purpose very well. Many men were attracted in this way, and gave her reassurance by showing her favour. Closer examination showed that these men were of the type who themselves fear the ultra-womanly woman. They prefer a woman who herself has male attributes, for to them her claims on them are less.

At the primal scene the talisman which both parents possess and which she lacks is the father's penis; hence her rage, also her dread and helplessness.[7] By depriving the father of it and possessing it herself she obtains the talisman – the invincible sword, the 'organ of sadism'; he becomes powerless and helpless (her gentle husband), but she still guards herself from attack by wearing towards him the mask of womanly subservience, and under that screen, performing many of his masculine functions herself – 'for him' – (her practical ability and management). Likewise with the mother: having robbed her of the penis, destroyed her and reduced her to pitiful inferiority, she triumphs over her, but again secretly; outwardly she acknowledges and admires the virtues of 'feminine' women. But the task of guarding herself against the woman's retribution is harder than with the man; her efforts to placate and make reparation by restoring and using the penis in the mother's service were never enough; this device was worked to death, and sometimes it almost worked her to death.

It appeared, therefore, that this woman had saved herself from the intolerable anxiety resulting from her sadistic fury against both parents by creating in phantasy a situation in which she became supreme and no harm could be done to her. The essence of the phantasy was her *supremacy* over the parent-objects; by it her sadism was gratified, she triumphed over them. By this same supremacy she also succeeded in averting their revenges; the means she adopted for this were reaction-formations and concealment of her hostility. Thus she could gratify her id-impulses, her narcissistic ego and her superego at one and the same time. The phantasy was the mainspring of her whole life and character, and she came within a narrow margin of carrying it through to complete perfection. But its weak point was the megalomanic character, under all the disguises, of the necessity for supremacy. When this supremacy was seriously disturbed during analysis, she fell into an abyss of anxiety, rage and abject depression; before the analysis, into illness.

I should like to say a word about Ernest Jones's type of homosexual woman whose aim is to obtain 'recognition' of her masculinity from men. The question arises whether the need for recognition in this type is connected with the mechanism of the same need, operating differently (recognition for services performed), in the case I have described. In my case direct recognition of the possession of the penis was not claimed openly; it was claimed for the reaction-formations, though only the possession of the penis made them possible. Indirectly, therefore, recognition was none the less claimed for the penis. This indirectness was due to apprehension lest her possession of a penis *should be* 'recognized', in other words 'found out'. One can see that with less anxiety my patient too would have openly claimed recognition from men for her possession of a penis, and in private she did in fact, like Ernest Jones's cases, bitterly resent any lack of this direct recognition. It is clear that in his cases the primary sadism obtains more gratification; the father has been castrated, and shall even acknowledge his defeat. But how then is the anxiety averted by these women? In regard to the mother, this is done of course by denying her existence. To judge from indications in analyses I have carried out, I conclude that, first, as Jones implies, this claim is simply a displacement of the original sadistic claim that the desired object, nipple, milk, penis, should be instantly surrendered; secondarily, the need for recognition is largely a need for absolution. Now the mother has been relegated to limbo; no relations with her are possible. Her existence appears to be denied; though in truth it is only too much feared. So the guilt of having triumphed over both can only be absolved by the father; if he sanctions her possession of the penis by acknowledging it, she is safe. By *giving* her recognition, he *gives* her the penis and to her instead of to the mother; then she has it, and she may have it, and all is well. 'Recognition' is always in part reassurance, sanction, love; further, it renders her supreme again. Little as he may know it, to her the man has admitted his defeat. Thus in its content such a woman's phantasy-relation to the father is similar to the normal Oedipus one; the difference is that it rests on a basis of sadism. The mother she has indeed killed, but she is thereby excluded from enjoying much that the mother had, and what she does obtain from the father she has still in great measure to extort and extract.

These conclusions compel one once more to face the question: what is the essential nature of fully developed femininity? What is *das ewig Weibliche?* The conception of womanliness as a mask, behind which man suspects some hidden danger, throws a little light on the enigma. Fully developed hetero-sexual womanhood is founded, as Helene Deutsch and Ernest Jones have stated, on the oral-sucking stage. The sole gratification of a primary order in it is that of receiving the (nipple, milk) penis, semen, child from the father. For the rest it depends upon reaction-formations. The acceptance of 'castra-tion', the humility, the admiration of men, come partly from the over-estimation of the object on the oral-sucking plane; but chiefly from the renunciation (lesser intensity) of sadistic castration-wishes deriving from the later oral-biting level. 'I must not take, I must not even ask; it must be *given* me.' The capacity for self-sacrifice, devotion, self-abnegation expresses efforts to restore and make good, whether to mother or to father figures, what has been taken from them. It is also what Radó has called a 'narcissistic insurance' of the highest value.

It becomes clear how the attainment of full heterosexuality coincides with that of genitality. And once more we see, as Abraham first stated, that genitality implies attainment of a *post-ambivalent* state. Both the 'normal' woman and the homosexual desire the father's penis and rebel against frustration (or castration); but one of the differences between them lies in the difference in the degree of sadism and of the power of dealing both with it and with the anxiety it gives rise to in the two types of women.

NOTES

1 *Int. J. Psychoanal.* 8 (1927).
2 'The nosology of male homosexuality', *Contributions to Psycho-Analysis* (1916).
3 I have found this attitude in several women analysands and the self-ordained defloration in nearly all of them (five cases). In the light of Freud's 'Taboo of virginity', this latter symptomatic act is instructive.
4 'Early stages of the Oedipus conflict', *Int. J. Psychoanal.* 9 (1928).
5 Ernest Jones, 'The early development of female sexuality', p. 469, regards an intensification of the oral-sadistic stage as the central feature of homosexual development in women.
6 As it was not essential to my argument, I have omitted all reference to the further development of the relation to children.
7 Cf. M. N. Searl, 'Danger situations of the immature ego', Oxford Congress, 1929.

Chapter 13

'The casket and the key'

Thoughts on creativity, gender and generative identity

Joan Raphael-Leff [1]

> For Spirits when they please,
> Can either Sex assume, or both; so soft
> And uncompounded is their Essence pure,
> Not ti'd or manacl'd with joint or limb,
> Nor founded on the brittle strength of bones,
> Like cumbrous flesh; but in what shape they choose
> Can execute their aery purposes,
> And works of love or enemity fulfil.
> (Milton, *Paradise Lost* I:425–431)

It was one of Freud's earliest cornerstones that in the Unconscious, un-shackled from our bodies, we are psychically bisexual and (like Milton's spirits) in our minds can 'either Sex assume, or both'. Through identification we each personify characteristics ascribed to the other sex and more importantly, internalize attributes, traits and qualities of our closest intimates, irrespective of their gender and our own. In this chapter I would like to focus on difficulties that arise when gendered aspects of the self are self-denigratory and/or in conflict with each other, linking this with a disturbance in what I call 'Generative Identity'. Furthermore I suggest that in these cases, the sex of the analyst becomes markedly important in the analytic process.

GENDER IDENTITY

'My whole body feels liquid', says Gardenia, a high-powered executive, on my couch in the penultimate year of a long analysis.

> As if I'm leaking. *How can I talk about it?* . . . afraid of being all sweaty and dripping out in a puddle. Feels very shameful, as if my body is melting and people will laugh at my desperation and incontinence. On the weekend, I felt quite mad thinking James watches and scornfully witholds what I want. Murderous, wanted to kill him but full of self-loathing, felt like jumping under a bus. Didn't know who was who, afraid I'd lost myself then suddenly realised it *was* me being taken over inside by a deadly brutal

self. *A ruthless male part of me that mocks me for having desires.* Something hard in me ridicules anything feminine and sensitive in me, vulnerability, openness – laughs at it and stamps all over it. I feel so intimidated by it, so needy and desperate, unable to pretend to be a proper woman . . . Growing up, the idea of having sexual wishes felt dirty and perverse. My father always expected instant gratification, hated needing anything. My mother's frumpy, completely asexual. Treated me like a traitor for wanting anyone but her. As a teenager, with each new boyfriend, I'd become violently possessive, following him around everywhere. He'd seem to have the *key* to me. It consumed my life, everything else was swamped by it. Any idea of my own capacities, interests and achievements. I'd begin to hate myself, seeing him as a cruel person keeping me on a leash, witholding the key. He had everything I wanted to be and wouldn't give me what I needed.

A thoughtful new perspective arises out of this breakthrough moment of recognition that the deadly battle is in fact a scripted internal drama between different aspects of herself. Her introspective words reveal awareness of the conflictual nature of her desires as an intricate mixture of erotic and addictive, accepted and denigrated and the complex nature of her identifications and counteractions. *Questioning* how to talk about her feelings relates to shame and transferential anxiety that I'll respond like either or both her parents. A mixture of excitement and embarrassment accompany resurfacing of a memory of her father laughing as he watched her masturbate, aged 3–4. She's concerned I'll disapprove; regard her feelings as forbidden, treacherous, 'not nice'. *Thinking* about her feelings, she becomes 'a woman with a body *and* a mind'. *Telling me* relates to my female sex.

The following weeks reverberate as Gardenia asks herself 'terrifying questions – *who am I, what do I want and how much do I invent everybody around me?*'

Despite what I've made of myself, my encounters with men have been ridiculous, all or nothing, no build up to a relationship, just all sex bypassing getting to know a man. Looking back I've always chosen fantasy men to plunge in with. Odd merger with no intimacy. . . . Not a meeting of two separate people but (I'm still embarrassed to say this) wanting to be raped, all prodding and poking and getting inside each other. Like a secret addiction to excitement – out of control, not integrated with other parts of life . . . wanting some *special thing* from them that would animate me. *Semen, seeds* . . . Even with longstanding partners it was a sham, not a relationship at all but just a body with sensations alleviating emptiness and using the man to fill myself magically. Every time I sold myself out. . . . So desperate to be desired I didn't let an exchange

run its course. . . . Just wanting to control a man; to have an effect;
to worm my way in and make him give me what I wanted which was his
baby but more than that, *some key to me* seemed only a man's admiration
could give me. As if some man being attracted to me would suddenly make
everything clear; something would declare itself. No, it would clarify *me*.
My feminine identity would come into focus, I would know who I am. I've
kept such sharp division between the sexes. Tried to be a boy-surrogate for
my parents and renounced female pleasures in the broadest sense, comfort,
softness, understanding; then flipped with boys into the opposite, a liquid
poured into his fantasy vessel.

In adulthood, her intense craving for an intimate interpenetrative relationship has resulted in several impassioned 'dark' involvements (at times
impetuously embarked upon in analytic breaks) marked by that all-pervading
desire for the 'key'. Immediate metamorphosis thwarted, she would submit
to enslavement to the man's escalating demands for unremitting, un-
conditional 'placental'-type nurture in return for which she expected he'd
wave his 'magic wand' and change her.

Since adolescence she had adamantly abhorred the idea of ever having a
baby, rationalizing childlessness as a means of demarcating difference from
her mother. In her late twenties, some years after coming into analysis, she
became aware of a sense of childish incapacity, lacking the wherewithal to bear
a child, followed by impotent feminine rivalry, physical repulsion and horror,
murderous anxieties about being pregnant with a greedy/needy baby (brother)
competitive with her own infantile needs. ('Dreamed beating off disgusting
kittens crawling all over me [?] overrun by uncontrollable baby feelings.')

In time, projection and physical enactment lessened with discovery and
possession of an 'inner space' and depression ensued with rock bottom painful-
ness of 'the inconceivable truth' she 'ought never been conceived', feeling
herself a 'poisonous (prenatal) little slug-thing with no right to be alive', an
unbearable 'screaming baby' with 'monstrous' needs, a deficient 'not-boy'
at odds with mother's preconceptions, later to become her compliant 'doll'.
Gaining a personal perspective, painful truths were now faced – unwanted-
ness, separateness, helplessness, exploitation ('I was her waste basket').
Sexual difference and childish limitations, idealization of males and favourit-
ism ('no wonder had to live in dream world – to block out impotent rage
watching my brother in the Garden of Eden. I felt cast out but I'd never even
been taken in'), and finally, exclusion from the parental pair. It was some
years before she experienced a subjective view of the world rather than
mother's eyes looking through Gardenia's eyeholes.

Offering neither instruction nor mould, the self-reflective analytic space
posed great difficulties to this woman who had spent so much of her life
operating from a false-self defined by, and finely tuned to, others' ex-

pectations. Being on 'a journey' with another woman who could hold her in mind, be present, take in, recognize, hear and respond to a range of dimly felt voices, acknowledge infantile and adult, mad and sane, 'masculine', 'feminine' and ungendered selves, without preconceived ideas of outcome or destination, was a new experience. Process took precedence over content. Eventually, as Gardenia gradually established some sense of integrated selves and temporal/spatial continuity within herself, two seemingly incompatible but complementary vectors operated simultaneously: her own budding striving to be creative, and a regressive gravitational pull back into timeless, desireless oblivion of the *generating gestating womb*, with ultimate hope of 'rebirth'. Gripped by this 'dream world' at various times during the course of the analysis, she nestled in the blanket, silent but for occasional yawns and grunts, seemingly unable to think or formulate words, feeling she was not on my lap but *in* it, concretely held inside my female body, gestating in the darkness of my womb. At these times, I felt no impetus to interpret.

In her mid-thirties, biological clock ticking away, desire erupted, not for pregnancy, but to be 'given' a baby. This wish became all-consuming at times, masked at first by preoccupation with meeting The Man who would transform her life, evolving into desperate rage at dependence on an as yet unknown male to fill her so she could 'find' the key to herself and 'grow up'.

Finally, in her eighth year of analysis, after extricating herself from a disastrously denigrating relationship which replicated the childhood pattern of 'trying harder' to meet impossible demands at the expense of her own needs, she spent some years without a partner, during which she fruitfully explored the unconscious dynamics of previous choices and her own malign contribution. Gradually, with ownership of identifications, Generative Identity consolidated.

The sobering realization of years lost while 'waiting for a rescuer' underlined distress at her aloneness despite readiness for a loving relationship. 'It's been a struggle to hold on to what's real', yawns Gardenia after a recent phase of intense regressive engrossment in the analysis.

A desperate struggle to stay awake. Kept drifting off into an internal dream world, not valuing real friendships. Like an addiction . . . dreams of being special, indulged; making no effort at all just being looked after in secrecy . . . merging . . . [You seem to be wanting to drift off here too] Yes. All too transparent . . . being *an eternal baby* . . . done it vicariously – looking after these big baby boyfriends and ending up wanting to murder them. . . . enormous confusion . . . [silent sobbing] It's this very desire *to be* a baby that's made me so desperate to *have* a baby to indulge. So sad. So much wasted energy. Those exciting men I believed would fill me, give me the key, just tantalizing stereotypes of my brothers and father. Pretend games they played which became part of me and I remained in love with it . . . an idealized picture of people who never were. Acting out some very vain, superior, unengaged macho part of myself – seemed glamorous but actually callous and cold . . . mocking, denied my wanting. While waiting to be rescued I haven't lived. [long pause] If only could make friends with the aggressive male part of me I would be stronger, more powerful. . . . Appalled by this trap, this prison I've lived in, the depth and power of it and how far I've had to come to discover what's stopped me living my own life.

I shall return to Gardenia later.

GENERATIVE IDENTITY

From the outset I want to stress my position. Far from neat binary categories of masculine or feminine identities, I have found that psychoanalytic treatments reveal rich plurality not only across patients, but within each person – a fluid configuration of multilayered coexisting feminine, masculine *and* non-gendered identifications (conscious, preconscious and unconscious; primary, secondary; introjective, projective; pre- and post-genital/oedipal; cognitive, ideational, sensorimotor; realistic, depreciative or idealized) – albeit inscribed on *anatomically* differentiated male and female bodies. For however free the spirit, we are none of us disembodied. This medley, I further suggest, undergoes sea changes at crucial transitional phases throughout the life cycle (particularly in relation to childbearing/rearing), with temporalized intensification of some identifications and rigidification of others, causing internal realignments and recurrent reinterpretations of symbolic meanings of various representations of sex, gender, sexuality, eroticism, fertility, generativity and maternity/paternity.

Before inviting Gardenia to speak again for herself, I shall unfurl some of my own thinking about these issues, against the background of gender research which has gradually demarcated various components of gender identity: core gender identity (Stoller, 1976, 1985; Money and Ehrhart, 1972), gender role acquisition (Tyson and Tyson, 1990) and sexual partner orientation (see O'Connor and Ryan, 1993). My own contribution is to tease out a further component I propose to call 'generative identity'.

On the basis of work with over 150 patients (one to five times per week), over twenty years' specialization in a psychoanalytic practice devoted to reproductive issues (and twenty-three longitudinal mother/baby observations in a community playgroup setting), I suggest that beyond mental representation of one's core identity as male or female, and in addition to acquisition of feminine or masculine psychosocial roles (possibly as conjoint 'interactive representations', [Sandler and Sandler, 1978]), and elaboration of hetero/homosexual desires and choices, there is a psychic construction of the self as a *generating entity* rooted in recognition of male/female reproductive differences. Its acquisition constitutes a quantum leap in self-appraisal.

I propose that generative identity is marked by acknowledgement of basic facts of life:

1 Sexual dimorphism (either female or male).
2 Union of difference (fertilization between female-derived ovum and male-derived sperm).
3 Functional limitations (child is prepotent; male/female restriction to impregnation *or* gestation).

Observers (Mahler *et al.*, 1975; Galenson and Roiphe, 1976) have noted depressive effects following discovery of sexual differences on the toddler's 'love affair with the world'. In my view, factors relating to sex fixity and finiteness lead to depressive repercussions. Becoming foreclosed at this divisive point (however shakily) are differences and limitations, not only of *core gender* (I am only female or male, not the other sex or both) but of *generativity* (females carry/suckle babies, males impregnate) and of *generation* (adults have babies; children cannot). Whereas the first two are bounded by restrictions of irreversible anatomical facts, the latter implies postponement. Generative identity is therefore postulated as a specific aspect of gender identity constituted around recognition of finite reproductive realities. It does not instigate sexual differentiation but arises out of recognition of sexual difference, and to achieve sublimation, must rise above it (Raphael-Leff, 1995).

Through the work of mourning, gender envy, generational jealousy, omnipotent losses and realistic limitations of generative identity can be absorbed.[2] Nevertheless, acceptance does not necessarily indicate isomorphic correspondence between anatomy and representation, and for both sexes, restrictions are repeatedly disavowed, reversed and residually held throughout life on parallel tracks. However, denial of limitation leads to magical resolutions (such as narcissistic phallic idealization or the fantasy of immaculate conception) by which necessary painful reorganization is avoided. Likewise denial of difference. Virtual non-acceptance of the reality of anatomical markers and reproductive restrictions is psychotic. 'I myself could never say (knowing myself to be a man) "I am a girl". I am *not mad* that way,' says Winnicott's patient in a paper that focuses on split-off other-sex parts of the personality (Winnicott,1966) (my emphasis).

To sum up the argument so far, I propose generative identity as a pivotal aspect of gender identity predicated on awareness of difference and demarcation of one's own generative potentialities, based on early identification with procreative capacities of parents/begetters.[3] As such it is related to (but by no means synonymous with) the Oedipus complex. It entails acknowledgement of bedrock gender limitations: being only one sex; prepotent and only half of future procreative coupling. Paradoxically, once generative identity is achieved, sublimation entails psychic suspension of these restrictions, through application of multiple non-gendered creative attributes and abstraction of joint capacities of both sexes (of which unselfconscious masturbation is a precursor). With generative identity a momentous conceptual

shift occurs from being someone else's creature/creation to being a *creator.*
Creativity is achieved by a person making the imaginative leap of meta-
phorically repossessing all capacities, including those of progenitors (i.e.
mental 'intercourse' creates a mental 'baby' of the mind).[4]

In other words, I contend that once generative identity is acquired, in order
to bring her or his own originality to fruition, a child of either sex must
psychically *free creativity from procreativity* – liberating it from the corporeal confines and age restrictions of his or her somatic gendered body, through
mental assumption of simultaneous generative stances of both sexes.

However, and this is the crux of my argument, I suggest that under
circumstances non-conducive to healthy self-realization, generative identity
may become distorted in two ways. First, *denial* of any one/various combinations of these restrictions. Magical or omnipotent solutions predominate,
marked by refusal of difference or suspension of mourning. I shall not deal
with these here. Or else, entrenched humiliation at masturbation and/or
internalized inflated/incongruous/oppressive gender representations leads to
inner strife, curtailing creative freedom and its prerequisite mental 'space',
(as my clinical fragments showed).

In my clinical experience, this latter distortion is manifested in four
overlapping ways:

1 *Polarization* of unintegrated, incompatible, split off or mutually exclusive
embattled gendered aspects of the self and their concretized enactments.
2 *Conflation of procreative and creative capacities.* Confined to bodily
functions, either sex feels incomplete and at the mercy of the other sex: a
woman unable to function effectively without 'seminal' male input, or a
man lost without the nurturing 'womb/placenta' of a woman. Ascribing to
male power the 'key' to her 'locked' internal treasure 'casket', a girl feels
unable to develop her own talents, feeling shut out of her creative
powerhouse until granted access by a penis/male permission (as Gardenia
illustrated).[5]
3 *Conflation of the reproductive interior and inner space.* When, in addition,
the locus of creativity is unconsciously assigned to the procreative womb,
a little girl's generative identity remains physically tethered. Her mental
space and capacity to think are curtailed by the concrete sense of containing
within her body a primal cavity such as that from which she herself
originated, which must remain inoperative not only until puberty, but until
such time as it is *impregnated and inhabited by another.* (A boy may
harbour delusions of possessing a womb or as in (2) desperately pursue
one.)
4 When generative identity is not achieved, the person remains a 'child' –
creation or extension of the parent(s) – overawed by magical omnipotence
attributed to the self-sufficient potent phallus, the parthenogenic fecund
womb or the idealized originary progenitive intercourse. When, through
enmeshment with her mother, the girl is in thrall to the original matrix (the

imagined numinous intra-uterine space I have elsewhere designated as the 'chora' (Raphael-Leff, in preparation)) and archaic maternal rights, her creativity is stymied not only by self-disenfranchisement, postponement and subjugation to male input as above ('sleepwalking through life'), but by awesome fear of the mother's rivalrous wrath coupled with poignant yearning to return to a state of prelapsarian fusion, often manifest in female to female psychoanalytic treatment in profound regression on the couch.

CLINICAL MATERIAL

My opening vignette touched on representational shifts occurring through the analytic process in unconscious symbolic meanings of sexuality, eroticism, sexual difference, fertility and generativity. To illustrate the four points specified above, I bring a series of extractions from an earlier stretch of the same patient's analysis. (Needless to say, these are by no means the only themes she is pursuing at any one time.)

'Helen is like I was,' says Gardenia in the third year of her analysis.

a princess waiting for the world to arrive and wake her up to reality. No initiative and no depth, like a doll in a box. I want to break her to pieces! Her red eyes, red not from tears but rotten, dead. Decomposition oozing out of her eyes. Makes me want to abort her, as if she's inside me, like a parasite, rotten and poisonous! My mother said I was born blue . . . used to think it meant not cold and bad circulation but poison; a criticism: should be born robust and independent. Hate her!! Could murder her–me, seductive-child part of me, wheedling and whining, inching its way into twosomes, waiting to be wanted and pitied and praised.

Gardenia's hatred comes in the aftermath of impulsively (and, she feels, inexplicably) spending Saturday night in a sexual threesome with Helen (a casual acquaintance) and her boyfriend. Unable to move beyond the child/adult divide, she is still 'wheedling and whiningly' engaged in oedipal issues, unfree to express both aspects of the parental coupling in psychic terms. Desperate to break out of the sterile internal impasse but unable to abstract it, Gardenia is driven to *concrete* enactment of a polymorphous triangle. She conveys awareness of her own curtailed agency and rage at this 'sleeping beauty'-like aspect of herself, but is incapable of releasing it, can only conceive of aborting her 'friend' from her 'box' (as she feels her mother wished to physically abort her and mentally did). Archaic intra-uterine/neonatal 'grudges' hinted at here are recurrent themes that emerge full blown ten years later.

During the weeks following the triadic sexual encounter, Gardenia begins to formulate her sense of deficient (generative) mental 'space', connecting this both with early maternal emotional absence/intrusions and the disillusioning birth of her brother. Casting this space within the *maternal* body, she disavows separateness. And (as the sequence of sessions increasingly illustrates), by locating it within the reproductive body interior she designates its activation to a catalyst penis/man rather than her own capacities.

> no inner space to digest 'cos it's all full of secrets and other people's deposits. My mother dumped her feelings about Jim [younger brother] on me. *My* feelings never seemed valid. It's incredible the way I'm seen to be filled in with her stuff. Mum took away my meagre space by having him. Winkled out anything that was mine, thoughts, friends, poems, even my room. She literally gave my brother my space. Now . . . battleground. If got nothing else I'll fight for my bit of space to not have it invaded. Strange. I have a fantasy of a wonderful man knocking on the door – just appearing and moving in to take possession . . . opposite of what I'd like to happen in real life. Logically I'd want him to respect my space, not inhabit it without a word of negotiation. Don't understand this strange idea.

Gardenia seems vaguely aware of having introjected a transgenerational world beyond her ken, which very much later, when she was able to conceive of her mother's subjectivity as separate from her own, emerged as misogynistic legacy of self-devaluation of females-defined-by-males in her maternal grandmother's family of origin. Deprived of maternal 'reverie', she neither internalized a 'containing'/processing function (Bion, 1962) nor cultivated mental space that would enable her to metabolize her own thoughts. Gardenia's concrete symbolic equation (Segal, 1957) of room=womb mother==self prevents her from 'digesting'/processing her feelings beyond the incorporative 'battle' and incomprehensible craving for a male inhabitant.

Eleven days later the concept of psychic space (albeit, still conflated with reproductive space) and the idea of 'taking charge' creatively within it, have begun to materialize through internalization of our interactive work:

> taught myself to misperceive, to see me from the outside. . . . Feel I've had to break down into lots of elements to unarrange them . . . playing with the pieces, taking charge of them in a creative way . . . making space where there was a hole, an area of non-being, no space, feelings of disappearing. . . . Mum didn't see me and my needs and couldn't reflect it or hold me . . . double hole, her disappearance too. . . . She thinks I am only there to reflect her! Realized part of what I had to reflect for her is to *be* her by having a baby. Was determined never to have one; not to be like her! Later I was desperate to have a baby, to fill the gap, hole. . . . Now beginning to feel space. Doesn't need filling. Reclaiming bits of myself. Funny, thought I'd feel more lonely if separate. When I tried to be part of boyfriends, felt fused but lonely. Here, we're together.

Gardenia's long analysis had a distinctly cyclical 'layered' pattern to it. Each phase lasted many months, with issues worked–reworked in relation to different events at later stages. With decreasing intensity, each subsequent phase began with acute panic states and florid emotions, including disturbingly vivid dreams, psychosomatic manifestations, kinesthetic experiences on the couch and strong, idealized, denigratory or paranoid transferential feelings which once worked through, gradually subsided, followed by a plateau of steady consolidation before the explosive eruption of another phase, dealing with ever more primitive content or the same transferential concerns in a more complex form.

The depressive nadir of each phase was experienced as entrapment in a dark narrow underground 'man hole' from which it felt virtually impossible to climb out. Overdetermined symbolic meanings of this recurring imagery included confinement in a mental 'hole' of 'nothingness' and insubstantiality which defied expression; imprisonment in a timeless secret 'bolt-hole' into which she'd escaped to 'hibernate' (I'm invisible, a naked colourless slum spider crawling around inside a drain'); captivation in the birth canal, craving foetal oblivion in intra-uterine womb-space; a perilous shaft to a deep area of 'unspeakable awfulness of not being taken seriously'; nebulous sensations of 'incestuous manipulation, being poisoned, drugged, not really alive'; a shameful gaping internal 'female hole' of emptiness with 'something vital missing', yearning to be filled by an illusion/man/baby; a genital hole to be plugged by a penis; an anal connection ('smelly belowground sewer') to the controlling mother all enacted in 'dark' 'sleazy' claustrophobic relationships ('secret life with James. Wanted him to climb inside whole, fill me up . . . great desire to get inside him, into his bottom, wished I had a penis').

Seeking analysis in her late twenties, Gardenia felt aware of unfulfilled potential, feeling she was 'not all there'; had no voice, no vote. In a very early dream a strange little male creature burst through the garden door, and rushing in, crammed himself down her throat silencing her. This aphonia came to signify the marked internal battle between split 'macho' and 'feminine' aspects of herself and very gradually we came to recognize oscillations of *mutually exclusive feminine/masculine identifications* as a dominant feature of her life. On the couch the tone, timbre and quality of her voice often varied from robust to a strangulated whisper, accompanied by violent throat-clearing. Enacted stereotypical experiences of *being* her father/ brothers (arrogant, exciting, sadistic, indulged), or her mother (omniscient, vilified, despicable, masochistic) and/or fulfilling the counter-role they ascribed her (voiceless neuter; invisible family-maintenance-skivvy) eventually were replaced by thoughtful exploration of her own emotional *experience* (yearning, rage, denigration, exploitation) as her father's daughter, mother's daughter or brother's sister. Ultimately she experienced herself as a 'multi-voiced' person in her own right rather than a conglomerate of incongruous ventriloquous implants dominated by internal 'voices' speaking critically about her.

Over the years, in narrative and transference, her parents alternated as pitied victim and hated bully until eventually their (collusive) *relationship* was recognized. Similarly, her rosified childhood came to be described as a 'living death' in which all creative outlets (including singing) were blocked. Achievements were desperate attempts to please her parents in vain hope of gaining their approval. Looking back she depicted having spent her childhood yearning for adulthood, the magical 'one day' when she would 'come to life', with the aid of a Prince-Charming-husband. In time she came to acknowledge unconscious complicity in inertia, naming some deeply ingrained underpinnings: 'so strong in me these beliefs that my desires are atrocious; that children have no rights; you can't be adult unless you're a parent; not a Woman without a baby; without a Man you're dead; not really a person on your own.'

My femaleness played a crucial role in this analysis. In her inner, as in her external world, 'female' was synonymous with 'unentitled'. Introjected family ethos dictated she could become nothing unless possessed by an idealized man (penis). Alternatives meant remaining a powerless little girl lacking assertive initiative; finding a powerful man or *becoming* one by eradicating the weak feminine in herself and appropriating an omnipotently unquestioning 'masculine' position. Given this self-denigration, awareness of me as a bold woman able to listen, empathize and explore, combining family and professional life, steadfastly served the therapeutic alliance whatever the positive or negative, maternal, paternal or other transference.

To prepare herself for a career, Gardenia had broken out of her cloistered traditional family, successfully operating in Business School from what she called a rigidly 'male stance'. However, this brittle self-sufficent 'macho' front collapsed into female submissiveness in a sado-masochistic sexual relationship, the break-up of which led to suicidal depression, a serious breakdown featuring derealization and depersonalization. Nevertheless, having recovered, she used her considerable intellectual capacities to obtain academic qualifications (albeit saying her thesis was tame and derivative rather than original), eventually gaining an eminent professional position, although her parents remained, as ever, more impressed by the lesser achievements of her younger brother.

During the early years of analysis, panic stricken Gardenia complained of non-existence, 'vanishing' between sessions. As a child she had experienced school phobia and in adulthood, fears of travelling or spending nights away from home. 'Disappearing' continued to occur during all breaks with accompanying bouts of helpless despair, anorexia and agoraphobia.

Gradually, painfully, as Gardenia began to gain substantiality and a sense of herself as a distinct person (rather than 'not there', her parents' 'thing' or a chameleon-like reptilian creature), she also began to examine and define various facets of herself through recognition of them in others (as with Helen), initially through projective identification, feeling at times possessed by another, disowned or taken over by polarized internal aspects (which dictated oscillating extreme patterns of behaviour from manic activity to total inactivity, alcoholic binges, smoking, compulsive eating or severe restriction of intake). Eventually, processes became less somatic and concretized; the mood-swing pendulum decelerated, then mostly abated.

Contemplating the nebulous emptiness to be stuffed with food, 'busyness' or baby, led to recognition of painful, gaping self/other absence, which mourning converted to a potential space for exploration and increasing trust in her capacity to activate and sustain herself. Trusting her place in my mind and discovering the means of self-replenishment, solitude became less terrifying, and eventually even enjoyable.

My own interpretations decreased as, solidifying a fluid yet continuous experience of integrity rather than previous discrete warring selves (voiceless woman, exploited 'neuter', greedy boychild, ruthless businessman, ancient lizard or deprived helpless little girl), Gardenia became more adept at listening to her own insights. Belief in a real, reciprocal relationship resulted in relinquishing the 'master plan', enabling her to take realistic steps towards meeting a partner. Instead of passively awaiting rescue/release through an indiscriminately coveted/stolen *key* (idealized penis or magical baby), she'd gained access to her own '*casket*', utilizing her reflective talents in poetry writing ('living out in rich everydayness, inner treasures unburied') singing and pop song composition ('I am who I am and want to be, I can only do what I do in my way').

A sequence of pre-summer break sessions give some idea of these progressions. Some months after the sexual threesome a new sense of her bodily self as *potentially gestative* emerged. Developing backache, Gardenia complained of various physical pains, nausea and vomiting, eventually linking these to (maternal) emotional gestation:

> Feel pregnant with myself like my mother . . . wanting to do it differently yet find I'm doing the same as Mum. . . . My Dad confuses me with Mum; she confuses me with herself; I don't exist in my own right. Only my brother Dan exists but not as himself. Battle to differentiate myself. I'm either part of them or non-existent. . . . that's the hole! the hole is confusion. Waiting to be rescued. Breakdown is going into the hole. No conscious choice.

Four days later for the very first time she arrives ten minutes late:

> Psychoanalysis lags behind life. Hay-fever eyes, nose running. Moisture pouring out of me. Must feed myself something vital or I'll break into little pieces. Brittle, dry. Summer. Descending into deepest layer . . . core. Not trapped inside, can make forays out when I want to. But I'm not down to essence; feeling as though sessions until now been based on another register. Summer defreezing – something's going on I can't tell about 'till after. [Some process is happening that needs nourishment to keep going. Womdering if you can nurture yourself during the break.]

Moisture's revealing sickly tired fragile egg-like me, very sensitive to changes heat/cold . . . needs wrapping in cotton-wool. . . . strong enough to go out and meet people but wants to be pampered at home for a bit. Old difficulties of bringing baby-like parts here. Felt humiliating. Breaks were like being dropped; abandoned. Starved myself in advance. Being determined enabled me to survive. Sounds mad. 'Doll in the box' feeling: when you're not there I'm stuffed behind glass. [I'm wondering whether coming late is a way of expressing that although you feel fragile and anxious about the break you also feel stronger, wanting to seek answers in yourself, to find out how to be *You* in your own way?] mmmm . . . I've always arrived on the dot. Always aware when time to finish. But I'm feeling anchored by something deep inside more than clocks. Breaking the mould. Less compliant. So much so that sometimes I lose sight of what others would like of me at all. Now feel defiance, desperate overreaction, impatience with psychoanalysis: 'I'll get there by myself!' Paradoxical, 'cos know could never have got here without you. Tendency to feel the answers are in somebody else; now less and less. As if on some level I'm taking for granted your trust I *can* but don't dare grow up. This summer a lot of 'oughts' and what I 'should' be like have evaporated, been suspended. . . . Feel freer to delve inside and be me. Major shift: less things *have* to be done or can do them in my way.

Yet so great is her trepidation at assuming her own agency, that a week later, fearful of my disapproval and envy, Gardenia hints at having holiday plans that must remain 'private and secret', saying she'd feel 'more exposed' telling me about them than talking about sex.

To illustrate the cyclical nature of her concerns and spiral of consolidation I bring material from sessions two years later. In the fifth year of her analysis Gardenia describes a dream:

a man . . . woman . . . I was both, either. Whole of woman's body was searched internally for evidence of intimacy. I went to great lengths to hide it. A world like 1984. Overwhelming feeling that any sign of love had to be hidden, would be caught out and punished. Drab world, no colour, warmth, liveliness, comfort – just grim survival. I woke, whole body tense. Such familiar territory. But when I thought about it I told myself it was *my own dream*. I could decide to stop it and 'plant' some optimism. So I started work on my windowbox, digging up weeds and scattering seeds.

For the first time she conceives of a capacity to cultivate her own 'seeds' rather than waiting for a man's. Later, the bare allotment she transformed into a flourishing flower and vegetable garden became a metaphor for internal burgeoning, as was her compost heap, a 'magnificent, self-generating system' of processed matter that served to fertilize and encourage growth.

It is a few days after the next summer break. Gardenia, bronzed and pleased to be back, has a new boyfriend, Robert:

In a dream last night – me in my body, in my stomach, all curled up in pink, soft, warm stuff. . . . Connected to feeling I want to get *pregnant*. Used to think I could never grow a baby. Something wouldn't allow me to, like childhood dreams of barbed wire . . . felt choking and full of dust. Insides all ripped to bits by barbed wire, bloody mess, as if since I was born, somebody (my mother?) said: 'you're not good enough. Can't even be trusted to care for anybody or feed anything or look after your baby brother properly.' Feels as if I was sterilized as a girl when Dad forced Mum to have an abortion. Terrible thing for her, sad after she came out of hospital. Then, I didn't understand why. No one to help her and he'd cut down her jasmine. I still shared a room with my brother. Hated it! Chaotic and messy, shabby, horrible room full of junk. Every morning I was terrified to go to school, forced out of the house crying, every morning so cold. . . . Only felt safe in granny's garden, everything fitted there, had a place. I was the only child there. I missed her so much when she moved away.

Aware of her unusual compassion towards her mother's enforced abortion and vandalized garden (despite herself feeling 'forced out of the house' into the 'cold', then and now) I acknowledge the hierarchy of female 'gardens' and Gardenia's missing my help over the break as her mother missed *her* mother's. Interpreting her sadness at her inner mess and longstanding aborted creativity I validate the newfound hope in her dream of finding a safe, fertile 'garden'/womb-space here and inside her, which, as old 'junk' is sorted, she may trust herself to nurture and expand.

Leaning on my being female and permitting her to be fertile, old scenarios are unconsciously fought and enacted. Dreams convey confusion coupled with new determination to fulfil 'forbidden feminine desires':

Life rushing by, crammed in like sewing machine stitches. House with locked and bolted door; don't know if front or back door. As if I was trying to break into something where I had no right to be. My sister-in-law was inside and lots of women in pairs with little bundles of towels. Looking for safe place to leave my stuff. I was hammering at the door wanting to get in. . . . I think my dream's about reproduction time. Urgency at opening up the closed door to get my 'bundle'=baby before it's too late.

And further polarized confusion in the next day's conflicted tirade:

Know the meaning of period pains! Cheated! Furious! My babies stolen! Feel like ripping out diaphragm and getting pregnant. Afraid of my incapacity to have something good and not spoil it. It's so wonderful sometimes and feel I don't deserve it, must make it rotten, throw it away. I've been waiting so long. Feel quite savage about it! But feel very hard, like a wall. Not going to let him in! He was so tantalizing. Seduced me with talk about living together and having babies, then he said he's unsure. Degraded me! Just a body! *Thing*! Could spirit me away when he didn't want me like my father would just make us all disappear into thin air. Wish I hadn't taken so much . . . get knife and rip into him! . . . Something very evil about him, way he gets into me like a creature, like the male creature in that old dream. Yesterday got into me through the phone, almost tangible how he gets inside . . . now very difficult to get him out. Sick and tormenting me inside! Something much worse and awful twisting under anger, really distorted, deforming. Takes away what's human in me. Scratching and blaming, hideous stuff; trying to claw out more and more from me. Making me feel there wasn't enough or if there was anything it's suspect and bad. I tolerate constant questioning of my loyalties and feelings as if using and exploiting him, sucking me out as if I was cruel and didn't have any right to ask or talk. He says I made him feel like a thief in the night but he wants to get as much as possible for as little as possible! Gets away with it . . . devious. You bastard make up your mind!! Made me aware I want babies, then took them back. I need space too! He's taken all mine, then took himself away; left no smell of him, nothing to sniff at. . . . He's got it all, like fat baby passively being fed and looked after [pause] . . . I bloody hate my brother and feel furious with my parents. Ridiculous sickness they have treating me as unreasonable but expecting me to sympathize with Jim; to them he's their baby and I'm not. I feel so repulsive and unwanted as if Robert sees me as a fat unwanted slob. Get lost! I don't want you! As if I'm trying to steal from him and he'll be tough minded and stop me. As if I was having a tantrum, forcing him like a devouring bitch. . . . I said incoherent things, blamed him for making me want things, babies and everything . . . I'm not a monster for wanting it all!

After a week of explosive raging she has moved on again:

Liberated by anger, not paralysed by my fears. Furious with Mum. Always taking me for granted, ignoring me. Tried to be a good daughter, took no pleasure, only bare necessities, enough for survival. Realize my parents are frightened of Jim's tantrums. Believe if he doesn't get enough he'll fall to pieces. Shocking for me to be so angry! Poison's coming out. . . . Not just skin but inside of body. Feel very little, wrapped up inside – well insulated like a boiler, but then bits of me do disappearing act, inside feels shitty, devouring, empty . . . little monster gets inside me and turns it bad. Feel infertile . . . made to feel as if words were actions. Unveiling of beast, seen as attacking, castrating . . . afraid to open my mouth . . . must appease and be nice. Robert's like an ungrateful squirming difficult baby who won't be held, making me feel like a bad mother who can't satisfy it. I woke from dream trying to shoot a gun that wouldn't shoot. I told Robert: 'wish I was you.' He comforted me and I felt safe but when he does his 'women are dangerous' routine, 'must keep you in your place', I get upset . . . made to feel monstrous for wanting babies.

Over the next weeks, and much work within the maternal transference, binary enmity (male-instigated pregnancy/male-induced abortion) and sibling rivalry give way to ideas of gender co-operation rather than opposition, and a notion of creative existence outside as well as within strict sexual division:

I want real collaboration – partnership, where it feels possible to create something together even if ultimately not a baby because I'm too old; have something *together* rather than always wresting something from each other. Relationship is so superficial. Scared he'll disintegrate before my very eyes. Not a drama between us but between each and own self. I'm striving, not for a *thing*, but for something inside: friendly, loving, accepting of myself . . .

At the end of the day I'm dependent on a man to have babies but not to live and write poetry. Quite puzzled by this feminist bit of me digging its heels, blind and relentless and desperately protective of my own needs. Feel unable to move out of that state as if I'd be destroyed and annihilated; blasted apart and left with nothing. I'd like the courage to stand up for myself but make token gestures rather than a real bid for freedom. No real independence yet . . .

I saw my powerhouse as male. Kept nothing feminine back for myself, relinquished it all . . . lost bit by bit. Ambition, career plans. That male aspect takes over my whole life and every minute of the working day. Must hang on to my creativity, fight for it . . . not safe yet, still being born; if bring it out it'll be endangered. To-ing and fro-ing . . . spirited away. Discontinuous growth impedes it, but inkling of feeling free. . . . All the time there's more around but quite a struggle. Afraid it'll slip back.

Years later, towards the end of her analysis Gardenia has a dream:

I was in the garden of my parents' house. No longer dark, dreadful place. They were gone but I'd taken it over and made it thrive. Such a variety! Profusion of colourful flowers although it was autumn, late in the year. Not neat, a bit higgledy-piggledy and full of happy accidents and surprises – seeds I'd planted at various times, others I'd carefully brought together. I woke feeling happy . . .
[What do you think your dream is about?] Oh, my internal garden. . . . Accepting who I am and where I've come from. No longer railing angrily against my parents. I'm not their creature any more. I was their produce but I'm *Me*. Created this lovely garden and it's mine to enjoy!

DISCUSSION: CREATIVITY, GENDER AND GENERATIVITY

A world of made

is not a world of born – pity poor flesh
and trees, poor stars and stones, but never this
fine specimen of hypermagical
ultraomnipotence
(e.e. cummings, from 'Pity this busy monster, manunkind')

In this chapter I put forward the suggestion that creativity is predicated on belief in one's own entitlement to generate. Proposing a further component of gender identity constituted around recognition of finite reproductive realities, I posited as the basis of 'generative identity' acceptance of the male/female adult/child divide in relation to reproduction.

Although related to the Oedipus complex, generative identity is by no means synonymous with it. It does not instigate sexual division but arises out of it and to achieve creative sublimation, must rise above it. Furthermore, changing family structures (increasing prevalence of single parent families including primary care-giving fathers; same-sexed co-parenting; self-insemination and medically assisted conception; far-reaching reproductive technologies including gamete donation; posthumous impregnation with frozen sperm; or use of ova from aborted foetuses) impel us to inquire what implications these have for oedipal transactions. Conversely, introduction of the fantastic as commonplace in the lived experience of many children forces us to re-examine classical concepts, and even to raise heretical questions, such as whether the 'primal scene' is inevitably heterosexual.

Answers necessitate delineating various components of the oedipal situation, namely, the triangulatory aspect, its excluding nature, the sexual relationship, gendered (sexual differences), generational (adult/child) and generative (biological-mother/father) aspects, relating these to specific family constellations of origins and care-givers. Of these six components, only two necessarily apply to heterosexuality, one of which (especially in cases of IVF, surrogacy, sperm donation) may be representationally structured at a fundamental level of gamete-combination rather than male/female (mother/father) sexual interaction. Similarly, within primal phantasies, we can draw distinctions between erotic scenarios (of whatever sexual combinations) and ontogenic phantasies pertaining to dual-sex origins.

Nevertheless whether primal myths encompass sexual union or not and whatever the family pattern, acquisition of generative identity denotes awareness of originating from the union of two *different* elements (ovum and sperm), gestation in, and birth of, a female body, and having a part capacity to reproduce (either impregnate or be pregnant). (That said, from cross-cultural observations, I am aware of the contextual overlay of bodily representations of conception, gestation, male contribution, etc.) Finally, regarding creativity, I hold that once acquired, generative identity must be suspended in order to achieve desexualized sublimation through assumption of joint generative capacities of both sexes and co-operative integration of internal 'feminine/masculine' multiple identifications and capacities.

This chapter began with Freud's early notion of a psychically bisexual disposition (1899). Despite his psychoanalytic quest after 'how a woman develops from a child with a bisexual disposition' (1932, p.116), psychic androgeneity became superseded by reification of antithetical tendencies and post-oedipal consolidation of unitary masculine *or* feminine identifications (repression of qualities of the opposite sex). As noted in my Prologue to this book, polarization arose within the context of controversies between Freudian theories of gender formation locating initiation of sexual difference in phallic monism, and opposed asumptions (Jones, Klein, Horney, etc.) around ignorance or innate knowledge of the existence of vagina/womb, and primary femininity for one or both sexes. My argument in this chapter implies it is not merely recognition of 'existence' but representation of *function* that defines gender. (Gardenia's notion of herself as empty passive container awaiting man's seminal input echoes Aristotelian ideas of female earth/oven/womb gestating the ready-made homunculus, and post-Platonic conceptions of female as flawed male, views upon which narrow psychoanalytic definitions of gender rest (for historicization of gender metaphors see duBois, 1988; Laqueur, 1990).)

Thus, over the generations, for many psychoanalysts successful gender acquisition has come to mean linear acquisition of (innate or acquired) unitary (same-sex) identifications and coherence of sex, gender and desire. Likewise exegetically streamlined developmental assumptions that from the moment of knowing oneself to be a boy or girl, experience comes to be (re)categorized according to normative, socially prescribed, sex-appropriate terms. Gender uniformity figures even in formulations that posit gradual emergence of sexual division out of an early undifferentiated state in which toddlers of both sexes at first indiscriminately ascribe sexual characteristics to themselves and others. Once focally aware of anatomical difference both little girl and boy are required not to relinquish being 'unlimited' but to develop gender identity under the hegemony of one sex by abandoning 'incongruent' self-representations (Fast, 1978, 1979). One effect of the tendency in psychoanalytic theory to pathologize *conflicts* of cross-sex identifications, has been to obscure the inevitable impoverishment of either sex by inability to *integrate* cross-gender identifications (Maguire, 1995; Derrida, 1982).[6] Furthermore, many theoreticians commonly blur the distinction between gender identity as self-definition and gender identity as 'masculine' or 'feminine' wishes or behaviour (May, 1986).

Although some Independent British psychoanalysts continued to emphasize the mixture of 'male and female elements' of the personality (Payne, 1935; Brierley, 1932, 1936; Winnicott, 1966), it is only more recently, mainly among American psychoanalysts, that normal gender identity is being acknowledged as a less than coherent entity: a subjectively defined artifact defending against chaotic flux (May, 1986), a retroactively transformed complex construction (Ritvo, 1989) composed of multiple shifting identifications (Benjamin, 1988), dialectically contextualized (Sweetnam, 1996) and performatively constituted and legitimated (Butler, 1990, 1993) rather than the stable endpoint achievement of an internally consistent identity.

What underpins this chapter then, is my own view of gender identity as a dynamic, multifarious representation composed of a mix of various and varying components psychohistorically set to blend or conflict. A fluid relational construct acquired both through interpersonal exchange and osmotically transmitted attributions. I see the mechanism of acquisition of generative identity as similar to acquiring a 'theory of mind' through a process of intersubjective exchange, i.e. approaching subjective mental representations of one's own beliefs and desires by understanding the minds of others (see Trevarthen, 1987; Cavell, 1991; Fonagy and Target, 1996). (By 'osmotic' transmission I mean introjection of shifting configurations, gestated long before the child's birth in unconscious images of self, other and fantasy-baby in the parent's mind coupled with a melding of complementary or clashing expectations, desires and sedimentation of generational residues carried over from the ancestral pool of each partner (Raphael-Leff, 1991)). In Gardenia's case, despite overt conflict, both parents idealize sons representing ego-ideals and devalue females. Mother's collusive refusal of female sexuality deflected desires into self-sacrificial devotion to furthering visions of male grandiosity. Although she may never have a baby, ultimately by grasping her own generativity and reconciling antagonistic identifications Gardenia has grown from alternating stereotyped monovocality to integration of multifaceted identity: 'masculine', 'feminine', non-gender-labelled, imaginative and realistic inner voices, including a new 'raucous, forthright' one, expressed in everyday speech, poetry, script and song.

Representations of gender and generativity also reside preformed in the mind of each clinician, and like all preconceptualizations, inevitably colour our dialogue with patients. I hold that in female cases of disturbances in generative identity, the female analyst's sex is of central importance in facilitating a woman's belief in entitlement to self-generated access to her own inner 'casket' of riches. It is my belief that suspension of normative injunctions and awareness of the complexity of our own gender configurations and countertransferential vicissitudes may in time facilitate something hitherto unheard in this 'speaking-space' between women.

NOTES

1 These ideas were first presented to the '52 Club in 1990. I'm grateful to Michael Dorfman for critical comments on a previous draft.

2 The degree to which generative identity becomes an integral part of gender identity is revealed in the existential upheaval when in adulthood, a would-be parent is diagnosed infertile.

3 The *process* of acquisition of generative identity seems indistinguishable for both sexes, but the *path* by which it is reached may differ, and there may be differential identification with the intra-uterine 'chora' (Raphael-Leff, in preparation).

4 While the wish for a baby and dollplay have been noted in boys as well as girls

(Jacobson, 1950, 1968) by some these are regarded as manifestations of introjected socially defined feminine and masculine mores, i.e. gender-role identification (Abelin, 1980; Tyson and Tyson, 1990); by others as inborn gender characteristics (Parens *et al.*, 1976) or expression of maternal 'instinct' (Kestenberg, 1956, 1968). I draw a crucial distinction between the (socially ingrained) wish to *care* for a baby and a desire/belief in a capacity to *create* (initially, a baby), recategorizing the latter within a fourth dimension of gender identity – that of 'generative identity'.

5   Penis envy in this context may be reframed as 'key envy' – craving neither organ, social power nor illusion of phallic self-sufficiency, but the desire to possess the key to her own 'casket'.

6   'No monological discourse – and by that I mean here mono-sexual discourse – can dominate with a single voice, a single tone, the space of this half-light, even if the "proffered discourse" is then signed by a sexually marked patronymic,' says a contemporary philosopher. 'I would like to believe in the multiplicity of sexually marked voices. I would like to believe in the masses, this indeterminable number of blended voices, this mobile of unidentified sexual marks whose choreography can carry, divide, multiply the body of each "individual" whether he be classified as "man" or "woman" according to the criteria of usage' (Derrida, 1982, pp.183–184).

REFERENCES

Abelin, E. (1980) 'Triangulation, the role of the father and the origins of core gender identity during the rapprochement subphase', in *Rapprochement*, eds R. Lax, S. Bach and A. Burland, New York: Jason Aronson, pp.151–179.

Benjamin, J. (1988) *The Bonds of Love: Psychoanalysis, Feminism and the Problem of Domination*, New York: Pantheon Books.

Bion, W.R. (1962) *Learning from Experience*, London: Maresfield Reprints.

Brierley, M. (1932) 'Problems of integration in women', *Int. J. Psychoanal.* 13:433–448.

—— (1936) 'Specific determinants in feminine development', *Int. J. Psychoanal.* 17:163–180.

Butler, J. (1990) *Gender Trouble: Feminism and the Subversion of Identity*, London: Routledge.

—— (1993) *Bodies that Matter: On the Discursive Limits of 'Sex'*, London: Routledge.

Cavell, M. (1991) 'The subject of mind', *Int. J. Psychoanal.* 72:131–140.

Derrida, J. (1982) 'Choreographies', in *The Ear of the Other*, London: University of Nebraska Press, 1984.

duBois, P. (1988) *Sowing the Body: Psychoanalysis and Ancient Representations of Women*, Chicago: University of Chicago Press.

Fast, I. (1978) 'Developments in gender identity: the original matrix', *Int. Rev. Psychoanal.* 5: 265–274.

—— (1979) 'Developments in gender identity: gender differentiation in girls', *Int. J. Psychoanal.* 60:443–454.

Fonagy, P. and Target, M. (1996) 'Playing with reality', *Int. J. Psychoanal.* 77: 217–234.

Freud, S. (1899) *The Complete Letters of Sigmund Freud to Wilhelm Fliess 1887–1904*, ed. J.M. Masson, Cambridge, Mass.: Harvard University Press, 1985.

—— (1932) 'Femininity', in *New Introductory Lectures on Psychoanalysis*, S.E. 22: 112–135.

Galenson, E. and Roiphe, H. (1976) 'Some suggested revisions concerning early female development', *J. Amer. Psychoanal. Assoc.* 24: 29–57 (supplement – female psychology).

Jacobson, E. (1950) 'Development of the wish for a child in boys', *Psychoanal. Study Child* 5:139–148.

—— (1968) 'On the development of the girl's wish for a child', *Psychoanalytic Quarterly* 37:523–558.

Kestenberg, J.S. (1956) 'Vicissitudes of female sexuality', *J. Amer. Psychoanal. Assoc.* 4:453–476.

—— (1968) 'Outside and inside, male and female', *J. Amer. Psychoanal. Assoc.* 16: 457–520.

Laqueur, T. (1990) *Making Sex: Body and Gender from the Greeks to Freud*, Cambridge, Mass.: Harvard University Press

Maguire, M. (1995) *Men, Women, Passion and Power: Gender Issues in Psychotherapy*, London: Routledge.

Mahler, M., Pine, F. and Bergman, A. (1975) *The Psychological Birth of the Human Infant*, London: Hutchinson.

May, R. (1986) 'Concerning a psychoanalytic view of maleness', *Psychoanal. Rev.* 73: 579–597.

Money, J. and Ehrhart, A. (1972) *Man and Woman, Boy and Girl*, Baltimore: Johns Hopkins University Press.

O'Connor, N. and Ryan, J. (1993) *Wild Desires and Mistaken Identities: Lesbianism and Psychoanalysis*, London:Virago.

Parens, H., Pollock, L., Stern, J. and Kramer, S. (1976) 'On the girl's entry into the Oedipus complex', *J. Amer. Psychoanal. Assoc.* 24:79–107.

Payne, S.A. (1935) 'A conception of femininity', *Brit. J. Med. Psychol.*15:18–33.

Raphael-Leff, J. (1991) *Psychological Processes of Childbearing*, London: Chapman & Hall.

—— (1995) 'Imaginative bodies of childbearing: visions and revisions', in *The Imaginative Body: Psychodynamic Therapy in Health Care*, eds A. Erskine and D. Judd, London: Whurr.

—— (in preparation) 'Maternal "chora" as gestational space'.

Ritvo, S. (1989) 'Panel: current concepts of the development of sexuality (reported by S.Vogel)', *J. Amer. Psychoanal. Assoc.* 37:787–802.

Sandler, J. and Sandler, A.-M. (1978) 'On the development of object relationships and affects', *Int. J. Psychoanal.* 59:285–296.

Segal, H. (1957) 'Notes on symbol formation', *Int. J. Psychoanal.* 38:391–397.

Stoller, R.J. (1976) 'Primary femininity', *J. Amer. Psychoanal. Assoc.* 24:59–78 (supplement – female psychology).

—— (1985) *Presentations of Gender*, New Haven: Yale University Press.

Sweetnam, A. (1996) 'The changing contexts of gender between fixed and fluid experience', *Psychoanal. Dialog.* 6:437–459.

Trevarthen, C. (1979) 'Communication and cooperation in early infancy: a description of primary intersubjectivity', in *Before Speech: The Beginning of Interpersonal Communication*, ed. M.M. Bullowa, New York: Cambridge University Press.

—— (1987) 'Sharing makes sense: intersubjectivity and the making of an infant's meaning', in *Language Topics: Essays in Honor of Michael Halliday*, eds R. Steele and T. Treagold, Philadelphia: John Benjamins.

Tyson, P. and Tyson, R.L. (1990) *Psychoanalytic Theories of Development: An Integration*, New Haven: Yale University Press.

Winnicott, D.W. (1966) 'The split-off male and female elements to be found clinically in men and women: theoretical inferences', in *Playing and Reality*, London: Tavistock, 1971.

Chapter 14

Is the Oedipus complex bad news for women?

Jane Temperley

There has been a lengthy dialogue between psychoanalysis and feminism. In its more recent phase, during the last twenty or thirty years, Freud was at first often seen as the bastion and exemplar of prejudice against women. Then, largely via Lacan, the very theories of the castration complex and phallic monism, which had caused such objection among feminists, were seen instead to illuminate the position of women in a society that is structured by patriarchy in its language, thought and sense of individual identity. Classical psychoanalytic ideas about the castration complex were seen as providing an explanation of why at levels far removed from conscious rationality women are perceived, not as inferior, but as disadvantaged and marginalized. Psychoanalysis was turned to for help in explaining the depth and intractability of the attitudes that disadvantaged and often disparaged women.

What particularly intrigued me when I first came upon this dialogue was the prominence in it of Freud's classical views about castration carried forward by Lacan's theory that, for the achievement of a sense of sexual identity and differentiation, for the use of language and logic, for sanity, the phallus must become the signifier and this means that women are particularly hampered in achieving a sense of their own agency in a world of male signification.

I realized anew that, though I had been taught Freud's classical theories about the psychology of women, those are not the theories that underpin the psychoanalytic practice of most British analysts. Ernest Jones disagreed with Freud about the phallic phase of development which Freud promulgated in 1923 and which is basic to his mature and final views on the psychology of women. He challenged Freud's assertion that children know of only one genital – in Jones's opinion the phallic phase is a defence against the disturbance aroused in the child by his/her awareness of sexual difference and parental intercourse. His views were shared and elaborated by Melanie Klein and it became and remained a distinctive aspect of the British psychoanalytic tradition that it differed from Freud on the development of female sexuality. What surprised me was that Freud's views, which do see women as disadvantaged, are well represented in the feminist dialogue with psychoanalysis while the mainstream British tradition about the psychology of women has often gone unmentioned.

Freud's own views on female psychic development were not finally crystallized until the 1920s. In the only analysis of a child in which he participated, that of 5-year-old Little Hans, he himself interpreted the child's phantasies of breaking and entering into a forbidden space as indicating an unconscious awareness of the vagina. As late as 1919, in the paper 'A child is being beaten', where he puts the Oedipus complex in its final supreme place as the nucleus of the neuroses, he makes no mention of the castration complex or of penis envy and sees the girl's sexual wishes towards her father as springing from innate feminine desire. Throughout the 1920s and 1930s controversy over the question of female sexuality and whether or not the castration complex was basic to it or peripheral was one of the most prominent issues in psychoanalysis.

I want to draw attention to a detail in one of Freud's last papers on the subject, 'Female sexuality', published in 1931. In this paper he mentions Mrs Klein's early dating of the Oedipus complex – so he clearly had her theories in mind. It is in this paper alone that he suggests that the daughter's tendency to feel antagonism to her mother might not be accountable for solely in terms of resentment at not having a penis. He suggests instead – and it has quite a Kleinian ring to it – that both sons and daughters will feel a peculiarly archaic ambivalence towards their mothers because she is the first object. Sons deal with this antagonism by diverting some of it on to their oedipal rival, the father.

In an earlier paper, 'Our own worst enemies' (1984) for *Free Associations*, I suggested that this unconscious ambivalence towards our mothers could lead women to champion an equality with men which was actually a betrayal and denigration of what is specifically feminine, motherhood. I was influenced by Chasseguet-Smirgel (1976) who points out that our extreme dependence on our mothers in infancy and the inequality of power and vulnerability in that relationship can lead both sons and daughters to redress this original imbalance by overvaluing the penis, what the woman does not have.

Since I wrote that article this bias in feminists' aspirations has altered. The aim of equal opportunities in a male world has to some extent been replaced by the defence of motherhood and female values in the face of that male world.

Jerry Aline Flieger (1990), in a paper called 'The female subject: (what) does woman want?', categorizes feminists using a psychoanalytic perspective into three groups: 'Father's Daughters', 'Mother's Daughters' and 'Prodigal Daughters'. I propose to use her first two categories and to offer an alternative to her third category.

Father's Daughters, as I understand Flieger, are those feminists who accept Freud's and Lacan's views about the psychological position of women. They see Freud's and Lacan's position as clarifying the situation with which feminists have then to contend. They do not challenge the basic validity of their phallocentric theory.

According to Freud, children know of only one genital, the penis. At first they assume everyone has one or, in the case of girls, will develop one. When, at the time of the Oedipus complex, they realize that this is not the case, both boys and girls regard females as castrates. Girls are in fact psychologically little boys who have to reconcile themselves to their deficiency by seeking an indirect substitute for the penis by turning to men in the hope that they will get from them a child, preferably male. I don't think it has been sufficiently stressed not only what a limiting view of female sexuality this is but how it reduces what is sexually desirable about men in women's eyes to their capacity to give them babies. For Freud 'It is not until development has reached its completion at puberty that the sexual polarity coincides with male and female' and then 'maleness combines the factors of subject, activity and possession of the penis: femaleness takes over those of object and passivity' (1923, p. 145).

Lacan, basing himself on Freud, describes how the possibility of order, of language, of sanity and of gender depends upon the establishment of the Law of the Father. In his reading of Freud the essence of the Oedipus stage is that the father interposes his authority to put an end to the illusion of unity between mother and child. This is necessary for the establishment of the Symbolic Order which is basic to our capacity to use language, to think and to live in an ordered society. It means, however, that the phallus, the symbol of the male organ, becomes the signifier. Women, as in the passage of Freud quoted above, become elusive objects, sought for and enquired after by men but with questionable capacity to speak or think in their own right as active subjects. They are profoundly marginalized. Jane Gallop (1990) describes how in the social reality behind the Oedipus complex men exchange women for heterosexual purposes but the real intercourse is that exchanged between men.

Some of the Mother's Daughters also accept Lacan's account. If the Symbolic Order is so inevitably phallic, they suggest that women should repudiate it, elevating what is pre-oedipal and not constrained by logic in its place. Flieger points out that this group is in danger of reinforcing the most reactionary of prejudices against women, by retreating from logical thinking as an area fit only for men. They also conflate the pre-oedipal, Lacan's *Imaginaire*, with the maternal, subscribing to a notion that because the child's relation to the mother is at first pre-oedipal that is where the mother herself belongs.

There are also non-Lacanian Mother's Daughters. I am taking Nancy Chodorow (1989) as an example. She turns to British Object Relations theory to vindicate the importance of the mother in infantile psychosexual development. She emphasizes identification with the primary object, thereby postulating that both boys and girls start from a feminine position. This theory is the opposite of Freud's, who postulates that prior to the Oedipus complex children of both sexes take their mothers as objects and believe themselves to be little men. In Freud's theory it is little girls who have painfully to readjust their whole view of themselves and whose subsequent sexual identity is problematic. In Chodorow's theory girls have a security in their sexual identification with their mothers and it is boys who have to differentiate themselves and whose masculine confidence is always vulnerable.

The theories of the Father's Daughters and the Mother's Daughters, to my mind, share two characteristics. The first is an undue preoccupation with power and ownership. Freud postulated that after the oral phase we pass through the anal and phallic phases before reaching the phase of genital primacy and the Oedipus complex. The importance of these psychosexual phases has been overlaid in later psychoanalytic theory by the increasing stress on the nature of the object relations the child is experiencing.

Nevertheless the anal phase is usefully linked with object relations which emphasize control and ownership of the object – 'mother (if she is the object) belongs to me and should do as I wish.' Freud's phallic stage lays particular emphasis on display and performance – the object is to be impressed or made to feel inferior. The genital phase, with the arrival of the Oedipus complex, according to classical theory, meant the transcending of these controlling, dominance-minded attitudes and the establishment of the capacity to love the object, to feel concern for the object and to recognize the object's separate autonomy.

Lacan's account of the Oedipus complex and the Symbolic Order seems to me to import into it an excess of those elements of control, dominance and ownership that ought, according to the classical theory described in the previous paragraph, to have been largely superseded with the passing of anal and phallic phases. It certainly corresponds with such practices as the wife's assumption of her husband's surname and with the attitudes reflected in the Christian marriage service: 'Who giveth this woman?', addressed to a male member of her original family. That there are these essentially anal elements in our present culture doesn't mean they are integral and necessary elements of the Symbolic Order. Ruth Salvaggio (1990) suggests that in fact Lacan was struggling to find a way for readers to relate to the study of texts and for men to relate to women which subverted the idea that they were to be 'mastered'. The phallus of Lacan's Symbolic Order is that of the phallic phase and is concerned with mastery. It should be differentiated from the procreative male genital which Klein described children regarding as the organ that gratifies and restores the mother and gives her babies.

Too much of debate between the Father's Daughters and the Mother's Daughters seems to be conducted in terms of genital rivalry. 'My genitals are the really significant ones – yours don't exist or, though important at a later stage, have only belated and precarious recognition.' This is the attitude of the phallic phase. Sexual difference seems to be about establishing for one sex *vis-à-vis* the other that it has the genitals that are really important. Lacan and Freud marginalize women. Chodorow reverses the Freudian imbalance with its excessive stress on the penis, but in the process marginalizes men.

The second characteristic the Father's Daughters and Mother's Daughters share is a tendency to overlook the sexuality of the mother. The Mother's Daughters celebrate the strong confident identification that the girl makes with her mother, but they do not explore the specifically sexual implications of this happy identification. To identify with a mother is inevitably to confront the reality that to be a mother involves being a man's (originally father's) sexual partner. This produces a double sense of rivalry. To acknowledge that a sexual relation with father is intrinsic to being a mother faces the girl immediately with a realization that mother has an order of relationship from which the child is excluded. The daughter feels excluded and rivalrous with the father but also, insofar as she identifies with her mother, she becomes *her* rival. To want to be like mother – whatever mother's present relation with father – puts the girl in sexual competition with her mother. Recognition of mother's sexuality causes further ambivalence – if she has a sexual relation with father to produce one baby, they can produce more and this stirs multiple rivalries, with the parents for being able to do this, and apprehension of the advent of baby rivals. Much of the disparagement of women comes not from men but from daughters who have never been able to forgive their mother's sexuality and who consciously or unconsciously subscribe to the marginalization of such contemptible creatures.

Flieger's third category was Prodigal Daughters – feminists who escaped from the constraints of the old discourse and brought in a new and altering perspective. What Flieger didn't consider was the possibility of a feminist who was the daughter of a mother *and* father, of a parental couple – a strange and telling omission. The sexes in so many feminist accounts vie with each other for dominance and power. They rarely come together in sexual intercourse, to please themselves and each other and to produce babies. Do we have here an enactment, among theorists of sexual development, of our universal resistance to the significance of parental sexuality?

Freud's account of the Oedipus complex emphasizes the child's sexual rivalry with the parent, particularly the parent of the same sex. The father's prohibition of the boy's incestuous wishes is experienced by the boy as the threat of castration and he relinquishes these wishes, accepting oedipal reality and internalizing the father's prohibition. The emphasis in this account and in Lacan is on the child's sexual wishes and their prohibition by the father.

Kleinian analysts have put a different emphasis on the nature of the Oedipus complex. What the child has to accept is not primarily the prohibition of his incestuous wishes but the reality of his position in relation to the sexual relation of his parents. Chasseguet-Smirgel conceptualized it as accepting the difference between the sexes and between the generations.

Ronald Britton, in his paper 'The missing link: parental sexuality in the Oedipus complex' (1989), described how the child needs to relinquish the omnipotent control of the object (through projective identification) to mourn the loss of this controlling relationship and to accept that his parents have a relationship with each other that excludes him. If he can make this transition he can internalize a capacity to think, based on his separateness from, but relation to, a creative parental couple. Kleinians stress the link between the depressive position and the Oedipus complex. The mechanisms of the paranoid position, in particular the use of projective identification in order to control the object and to deny separateness, have to be relinquished and the separateness of the object, including mother's relation to father, to be accepted.

Hanna Segal, in her paper on symbol formation (1957), highlights the way in which projective identification interferes with symbolic thought. Symbolic thought, she suggests, requires the autonomy of the three agents involved – the symbolizer, the object to be symbolized and the symbol. Where there is projective identification the autonomy and separateness of these categories is infiltrated and the result is concrete thinking, the confusion of symbol and symbolized that characterizes psychosis. The child must accept the separateness and independent intercourse of his parents in order to avail himself of his own capacity to think, a triangular activity, and of his own sexual potential. The symbol user has to allow the autonomous creative marriage of symbol and symbolized in order to think. Similarly the child has to allow the autonomous creative intercourse of the parents in order to internalize and avail himself of such a capacity in his own sexual life.

Klein and Lacan are in agreement about the importance of the Symbolic Order and also that the father and his penis are experienced as interposing a limit between mother and child. Often this is enacted over the parental bed. The child would like to stay in the parental bed, preventing and denying parental intercourse and the possibility of new babies. The father is often experienced as the one who intervenes to put the child in a separate room and to assert the separateness and reality of the parents' intercourse. What is experienced by the child as an intolerable exclusion and loss offers him the possibility of a room, a mind and a sexuality that is his own. The father, as third term in the triangle, challenges the projective system that can entangle mother and child. In Kleinian theory he does this, not to establish his authority but to defend the possibility of a creative relationship between woman and man that should be as free of mutual control and dominance as all three terms in Hanna Segal's delineation of symbol formation. The Oedipus complex is not bad news for women but the possibility both of autonomy and of a sexual relation to men that respects and avails itself creatively of the difference.

Kleinians and Lacanians share the view that the Oedipus complex is a nodal psychic transaction and that how we each negotiate or fail to negotiate it has the most profound effect upon our sexuality. It also has the most profound effect on the use we are able to make of our minds, on our ability to think and to use symbols including words. Kleinians and Lacanians would also argue that this transition involves at some level a tremendous sense of loss, a caesura, a transition which is necessary in order to participate in the world of speech and symbolic expression but which makes the subject feel shorn and incomplete in a new and sometimes terrible way. For Kleinians this transition involves the relinquishment of phantasies of omnipotent control of the object through projective identification with and the acceptance of separateness. Separateness in turn involves the pain of exclusion from the object's other relations, particularly the primal scene. It is the loss of this illusion of omnipotent control via projective identification that is the true 'realization of castration'.

I will illustrate such phantasies in a patient who sought to maintain an idealized identification with her analyst, transferring on to her the way in which she had lived in projective identification with her father's penis or her mother's body. This idealized identification involved, however, an extremely rigid control of the analyst and an intolerance of any unanticipated, even minor, divergence in the analyst's physical conduct of the session. The analyst was invasively tyrannized by the patient but the patient's mind was in turn taken over and tyrannized by ruminations about the analyst. She had little mental latitude for anything but her analyst and the concreteness of her need to control the analyst was always liable to make symbolic understanding meaningless. In the external world builders had been called in to do repairs on her house but her need to control the house and the builders threatened her literally with insanity. The house represented the mother's body in which the patient lived by projective identification and the arrival of the builders prompted her realization that, for the house to be of use to her, she had to allow an intercourse between the parents that she did not control. Psychically she had to distinguish between the house, as a building which needed repair, and her concrete equation of it with the maternal body within which she held sway. When she relinquished her omnipotent phantasies of being inside and in control of her idealized analyst she was faced with a deep sense of desolation which led her to bewail that her analyst was now no more than her analyst. The possibility of using the house as a home which needed builders or the analyst as someone whose thoughts, though not under her control, might help her (i.e. as her analyst) seemed at this stage a very dubious compensation.

This is a Kleinian account of a patient struggling with the sense of lack intrinsic in the transition to oedipal reality and the Symbolic Order. The recognition of the father's relation to mother, that the builders must have access to the house, is central to this caesura. (To call it a caesura is to refer to the violence of the obstetrician father's intervention to pluck the child from within the mother and so save both of them.) Where the Kleinians differ from the Lacanians is about whether this transition, brought about by the limits the father's role puts upon infantile omnipotence, involves a lasting disadvantage to women, rendering them 'objects' in a world of male signification. The Kleinian view is that it is not primarily the limiting power of the father that has to be accepted but the reality of our separateness, our dependence on objects we do not control and of our relation to parents whose independent intercourse has to be acknowledged. Freud wrote of the internalization of the parents, as the nucleus of the superego, following the Oedipus complex. Kleinians would stress the nature of the relationship between those internal parents, the degree to which, as man and woman, they are allowed to enjoy each other. It is the acceptance or the restoration of a parental couple, not just the father's authority, that marks the painful birth into psychic reality and the Symbolic Order. There is no intrinsic reason why parental intercourse need confer the man with the qualities of subject and the woman with those of object unless the child is still, in her or his unseparateness, projectively identified with the phallus and seeking thereby still to control the mother.

REFERENCES

Britton, R. (1989) 'The missing link: parental sexuality in the Oedipus complex', in *The Oedipus Complex Today*, London: Karnac Books.

Chasseguet-Smirgel, J. (1976) 'Freud and female sexuality', *Int. J. Psychoanal.* 57: 275–286.

Chodorow, N.J. (1989) *Feminism and Psycho-Analytic Theory*, London: Polity Press.

Flieger, J.A. (1990) 'The female subject: (what) does women want?', in *Psycho-Analysis and . . .*, eds R. Feldstein and H. Sussman, London: Routledge.

Freud, S. (1919) 'A child is being beaten', *S.E.* 17: 179–204.

—— (1923) 'The infantile genital organisation: an interpolation into the theory of sexuality', *S.E.* 19: 141–148.

—— (1931) 'Female sexuality', *S.E.* 21: 225–243.

Gallop, J. (1990) 'Why does Freud giggle when the women leave the room?' in *Psycho-Analysis and . . .*, eds R. Feldstein and H. Sussman, London: Routledge.

Klein, M. (1928) 'Early stage of the Oedipal complex', in *The Writings of Melanie Klein*, vol. 1, London: Hogarth, 1976.

—— (1945) 'The Oedipus complex in the light of early anxieties', in *The Writings of Melanie Klein*, vol. 1, London: Hogarth, 1975.

Salvaggio, R. (1990) 'Psychoanalysis and deconstruction and women', in *Psycho-Analysis and . . .*, eds R. Feldstein and H. Sussman, London: Routledge.

Segal, H. (1957) 'Notes on symbol formations', *Int. J. Psychoanal.* 38: 390–395.

Temperley, J. (1984) 'Our own worst enemies: unconscious factors in female disadvantage', pilot edition of *Free Associations*, pp. 23–38.

Chapter 15

Gender-linked issues in psychotherapy with abused and learning disabled female patients

Valerie Sinason

'Then she said: I bet you're going with somebody else, just because she's got legs!'
(From 'The Blue Mermaid' by Debbie Russell, in *Stories by Unknown Women*, Islington Elfrida Rathbone Project for Women with Learning Difficulties, eds Jenny Sprince and Barbara Stepha, 1987)

This chapter examines the key gender issues in psychoanalytic psychotherapy with a female therapist and a female learning disabled patient. First of all, the creation myths and symbolic representations of the vagina and womb that aid or hamper psychosexual development are explored through work with a normal girl in order to highlight the extra developmental task that the learning disabled[1] female undertakes. Through individual and group psychotherapy with girls and women the themes of genital representation, masturbation, concept of intercourse, pregnancy and childbirth are explored.

INTRODUCTION

Individual and group psychoanalytic psychotherapy with learning disabled children and adults has only become established as a treatment in the last ten years in the UK (Sinason, 1993b). Initially, it was considered that such treatment required a high intellectual and verbal ability. However, at the Tavistock Clinic and St Georges Hospital Medical School in London it was found that emotional intelligence and a wish to understand were the pre-requisites for such treatment. Perhaps unsurprisingly the main pioneers have been child-trained psychoanalytical psychotherapists and psychiatrists used to understanding non-verbal communications. The key issues in such therapy are separating out the consequences of the irrevocable organic handicap from what I have called (Sinason, 1993b) secondary handicap, the debilitating defensive way deficits are exaggerated in order to defend against the shame of difference. Whilst session lengths and psychoanalytic attitude are the same as for any other patients there are certain shared themes that emerge in such treatments including the pain, shame and loss involved in having a disability, envy and hatred for normality (including the parents who created them) and extra dependency needs.

In this chapter I will describe psychoanalytic psychotherapy with abused and learning disabled (handicapped) girls and women and the issues that have proved particularly gender-linked, such as body representation, sexuality and procreation. First of all I will delineate the painful sexual predicament that all organically disabled patients are in. In phantasy and in reality they see themselves as products of a damaging intercourse and this affects their oedipal strivings. Then I will focus on specific bodily issues that emerge in female patients.

HANDICAPPED CREATION

In his poem 'The Hunchback in the Park' Dylan Thomas movingly imagines a mocked hunchback trying to daydream a physically normal woman as a partner for himself in compensation for his predicament. Literature is full of abandoned yet hopeful figures searching, via a sexual other who does not have the same difficulties, for wholeness and healing. Innate biological and attachment needs are implicit in this. Finding a partner with similar emotional and biological deficits or impediments would have an effect on future offspring. However, whilst the male fashions the longed-for female out of his rib or his art and is the creator of her it is rarer to find a female Pygmalion. Whilst the fairy godmother, a good relatively non-envious mother, can give Cinderella permission to have a sexual life (but only up until midnight) and a King and Queen can tell the pre-genital Prince he must have a sexual life, a ball, it is the Prince who takes executive phallic action, having the 'balls' to find his own choice.

Princesses, peasant-girls or female mortals who take executive action in making such choices are often portrayed as active phallic women out to castrate or behead (often in a disowned and projected way through their fathers' actions as in Atalanta) the unpowerful, unintelligent suitors. When still, they can be seen as powerful eggs waiting only for the right sperm; prepared to watch the others die.

As represented in myth, the universality of oedipal problems shows that it is hard to allow for equal procreative partnership. Hand and genital form an early masturbatory omnipotent partnership that are essential in providing a preconception of intercourse but, if further psychosexual development does not occur, there is a problem in acknowledging the need for any other. Psychohistorically, birth comes from parthenogenesis. In such circumstances, the supremacy of a single-parent male omnipotent creator has been the definitive Western image.

If it is hard for an equal loving parental couple to be imagined or enshrined in myth by the physically and mentally normal population, what happens to oedipal fantasy and striving in the learning disabled and what, in particular, happens to disabled females? Whilst all girl and boy children struggle to make sense of their own creation those born with physical or mental handicaps have a harder task than average. However, the handicapped male often disowns his handicap by projecting it into the female who is then rejected. 'Why should I go out with normal man's leftovers?' asked one lonely self-disgusted man. The untreated female is then left with two places to project unwanted handicapped aspects into – her own body via self-injury and her child. The female therapist will inevitably become in the transference both the annihilating pre-oedipal mother who wishes to destroy her damaged baby and the handicapped therapist who cannot repair herself let alone help a patient.

CHILDREN OF A LESSER GOD

The film title *Children of a Lesser God* (in a film concerning deafness) poignantly evokes one aspect of the handicapped procreative parental image – an inferior sub-standard single-parent creator who makes people in his own handicapped image. Kali, Goddess of Destruction, Sexuality and Death or Euripides' priestess mother (Agave who dismembers her son Pentheus seeing only a wild animal) evoke the female flip-side, the infanticidal mother who produces damaged babies through her own murderous attacks on them or who kills or damages her normal babies. Parental couples, where it can be tolerated to recognize the couple, become either killing gods or transitional low caste deities.

Whatever the nature of the disability or handicap, patients share a similar problem. They have to contend with a primary condition, a reality, they cannot cure or alter: anatomy is indeed a major part in destiny. They also have fantasies about why they have such a condition. With nearly all such patients I have worked with there has been the fantasy that either a damaging act of parental intercourse caused the handicap (Sinason, 1993b), or their own violence inside the womb. In some cases there is 'faction' in which true knowledge of birth injury is mingled with the mother's own fantasy distortion and the child's own unique creation. For example, Angela, aged 8, said she got her cerebral palsy because 'I kicked my mummy so hard when I was inside her I broke my own legs and arms.' Her mother's pregnancy tales of this violent unborn babe who kicked, combined with actual birth injury and Angela's fantasy took a long time to unravel in psychotherapy. Andrea, aged 8 and with Down's syndrome, said 'I got this face because Daddy smashed my proper face in before I was born.' Two people coming together create a catastrophe in this fantasy and that makes connecting thoughts even more painful. It also hinders oedipal struggles.

Whilst we can easily find in our patients, colleagues and ourselves attacks on linking, it is crucial to consider the biological as well as the psychological origins of this. For some patients the attack began on the inside or the outside without their own psychobiological involvement, wish or permission. The 'inside story' (Raphael-Leff, 1995) involves uterine injury, chromosomal abnormality, birth trauma, anoxia, brain damage *in utero*, pre-birth VIMH (violence-induced mental handicap), malnutrition, foetal poisoning. As Ferenczi commented (1928):

> In the early states of embryonic development, a slight wound, the mere prick of a pin, can not only cause severe alterations in, but may completely prevent the development of whole limbs of the body, just as, if you have only one candle in a room and put your hand near the candle, half the room may become darkened. So if near the beginning of life, you only do a little harm to a child it may cast a shadow over its whole life. (p. 65)

Britton (1993) clarifies the normal development of the Oedipus complex in normal children. He comments that in the Oedipus myth there is the tragic phantasy of the infant Oedipus left to die while the parents sleep together encoded in the image of Oedipus left to sleep on the hillside by his mother. With handicapped children we have to consider the confusing overlapping between phantasy and reality.

For example, some children with severe epilepsy and learning disability are given beds in the parental bedroom because the fear that they might die in the night is so strong. This fear can be both realistic and/or a reaction formation against a death-wish to the child. The wish to abandon the handicapped Oedipus or oedipa is so powerful s/he has to be kept in a triangle to avoid murder. In some of these cases the child is almost used as a condom to keep the sexual parents at a distance. Where the parents have unworked-through primitive sexual guilt over their child's disability their own fantasy is projected on to the actual child who then sees himself/herself as a contaminated contraceptive.

With some patients the theme of damaging intercourse takes on a different emphasis. They are in the wrong place, the parental bed, the womb, because they are sexually perverted and therefore deserve to be killed, abandoned or moved to a hostile environment. Their disability itself is seen as a sexually perverse state that contaminates the host body (mother) and brings in an angry avenging phallus. Males and females in these situations refer to semen as 'pus' and vaginal secretions as 'slime'.

The fear of being in the wrong place can also be caused by not being wanted. When the mirror of mother's eyes says you are not the beautiful wanted baby but something disgusting, you lose your place in the world, your emotional legitimacy. Eyes look with disgust at the disabled baby and child and then phantasy persecuting eyes are seen inside the womb. Many handicapped children and adults feel that they are aliens from internalizing hostile stares. The reality of being stared at needs to be acknowledged before work can proceed on the phantasies around this. Egle Laufer's work (1993) on body image in late adolescence shows how hard the task is of integrating an idealized pre-pubertal image with a later one. Where there is deformity the task is even harder.

I am also aware of painful occasions all over the world in the last few years where a handicapped child did die from severe epileptic attack on a separate 'hillside'. In hospitals and homes all over the world now, not just in ancient Greece, handicapped children are abandoned. More poignantly, handicapped children, *par excellence*, accurately pick up real death-wishes. Bettelheim (1960, p. 110), in analysing Paul Celan's powerful poem 'Death fugue' and particularly the two lines 'Black milk of dawn we drink you at night/we drink you at noon death is a master from Germany' comments:

> When one is forced to drink black milk from dawn to dusk, whether in the death camps of Nazi Germany or while lying in a possibly luxurious crib, but there subjected to the unconscious death-wishes of what overtly may be a conscientious mother – in either situation, a living soul has death for a master.

Theoretically and clinically it is crucial to realize that fear of the murderous mother has a basis in reality as well as phantasy. This is hard for the handicapped girlchild, who, as with all females, stays linked to mother longest and who, with fear of abandonment as her greatest terror, faces impossible choices. She also has to bodily identify with mother as a female whilst struggling to individuate (Pines, 1982). As one multiply handicapped 6 year old with an abandoning father and abusive mother said: 'It's like the dolls inside dolls. They want to come out but if they do they will not be inside a mummy and they won't have a mummy' (Sinason, 1989, p. 43). That child knew it was safer to stay unborn with the illusion of a symbiotic link rather than face the mother's hatred.

I would now like to look at a clinical extract involving a 4-year-old unhandicapped girl who was a wanted and loved daughter. This provides a context against which the predicament of the learning disabled girl can be examined.

THE NORMAL VAGINA

Jeannette, aged 4, came to the therapy room holding on to her mother with one hand and proudly carrying a large carrier bag in the other. Once settled in the room she carefully took a large box out of the bag. The atmosphere was one of a grand unveiling. What she revealed was a jewellery box. It was covered in pink velvet. She stroked the velvet reverentially. When she opened the lid there was the sound of music and a little ballerina in a pink velvet dress pirouetted around. At the front of the box were two little drawers and inside them were beads, a necklace and a bracelet. Jeannette took them out with great care. 'Aren't they beautiful!' she whispered. 'They are my treasures.' Very carefully she put them away again, closing the drawers carefully, touching the ballerina's pink frothy tutu and then closing the lid. 'That's mine', she said, suddenly anxious and angry. 'You can't play with it. You've got your own!' 'Jeannette!', said her mother embarrassedly.

Jeannette, a loved 4 year old, was able to have a concrete representation of her own female inner space, her vagina. Although her primary fear was of having the inside of her body stolen by her mother or female therapist (Klein, 1921) in retaliation for such phantasies, Jeannette was also able to enjoy her female identification. Her mother was not of an envious nature and Jeannette was a wanted girlbaby. Within a relatively short amount of time the tensions between mother and daughter could be understood enough for change to occur.

Jeannette had a concept of a pretty pink place that was soft and velvety, attractive visually and tactilely and which had inner space for beautiful things – treasures. She also had a concept of me, her therapist, as a female who had a similar jewellery box and internal treasures. Freud (1900, 1913) understood that the casket, box, case or basket represented 'symbols of what is essential in woman'.

Whilst there are many complex issues to be thought about concerning such an apparently positive representation of the vagina, I hold that example in my mind as a contrast to the very different negative representations that I am faced with in working with sexually abused and learning disabled girls and women.

In examining my records of all my handicapped female patients over the last fourteen years the most disturbing finding is that only two were capable of representing their bodies solely by metaphor or symbol. Almost ubiquitous was the lack of metaphor, of representation. Almost ubiquitous was the need for presentation.

THE HANDICAPPED VAGINA: JILL

Jill (not her real name), aged 10, had Down's syndrome and a severe learning disability. She was referred for a psychotherapy assessment as a result of her compulsive public masturbating and hair-pulling at both school and home. Behavioural treatments, social skills lessons and sex education lessons had failed to make any impact. There was concern about sexual abuse.

In our initial meeting, before I could even introduce myself she threw herself into the seat opposite me, legs wide open, school knickers pulled aside with one hand whilst her left hand savagely masturbated her vagina. Her early pubic hair was visible and she had clearly developed breasts. With difficulty, I introduced myself. My speaking made no difference to her behaviour, but her eyes were fixed on me. I asked, 'I wonder why you want me to look between your legs?' At the sound of curiosity in my voice Jill felt allowed to have curiosity too. She looked at me with some interest and masturbated less forcibly. 'The medical word for that part of you is vagina but people say lots of different words,' I continued. As her face showed more interest I continued. 'I wonder if you want me to look at your vagina because it gives you an odd feeling you are not sure about, or pictures in your head or because you wonder if it is like mine.'

Suddenly, she stopped masturbating, sat bolt upright on her chair and asked, with a look of great concern and intelligence: 'Has my 'gina got Down's syndrome?'

There was an electric pause in the room while I gathered my thoughts together. Then I said: 'What a really good question. Because if your face looks different because you have Down's syndrome – how do you know if your vagina is the same?'

Whilst handicapped boys, in common with others, are able, if not blind, to see their penis, girls (Bernstein, 1993) cannot have such direct visual access. 'In addition to the visual difficulty she does not have complete tactile access to her own genitals.'

I told Jill that even though her face looked different her vagina was the same. There is a need for a straightforwardly educational comment at times. Where the phantasy has a life of its own such reality comments do not intrude but where the phantasy is created from lack of education it can be addressed quickly.

Jill wiped her hands on her dress with some discomfort and then wiped them on her hair, which was patchy because of her hair-pulling. I experienced sadness for her. I said she did not know where to put that wetness now she could think it was something all girls and women had, not just girls with Down's syndrome.

I added gently that she had hair on her vagina and that was what all girls and women had but most didn't until they were a little bit older. She held the sides of the chair and said, 'My sister hasn't and she is 11.' I said so she could be faster than her sister at some things. She suddenly grinned. Then she looked frightened and looked down at her breasts and looked at mine. Then she pulled her hair.

I said she was feeling pleased at becoming a woman and perhaps she was pleased she had breasts too. But then she got frightened I would be a jealous woman who didn't want her to have breasts like mine, or breasts that got bigger than mine and she got frightened I would steal them. Then, when she looked and saw her breasts were still there she was perhaps frightened I was cross with her for thinking I would be such a thief and she had hit herself.

Jill followed this with enormous concentration and relief. When I finished she laughed with pleasure. Then she wiped her hands on her dress and tried to wipe the few damp pieces of hair on her head. Having gathered herself together she turned to the toys.

She carefully picked up two dolls, one male and one female, and made them kiss. She held them close and looked very carefully at all angles of the kiss. I said she really wanted to get inside that kiss. She agreed. I said perhaps she wanted to see the moment where she was thought of when her mum and dad made her – perhaps she wondered how her handicap started. She nodded. She touched the girl doll's hair right down to its base. 'Gone wrong', she said, 'right from the root.'

I nodded. I said right from the root, the start, there was something that would give her Down's syndrome but there was also something right from the start that would let her think about these difficult things and try to understand them.

She put the dolls down and sat down on the chair again. She clasped her hands together so that they were like mine. She looked at me very carefully, her eyes settling on my left hand and looking for a ring. She then looked nervous and her right hand tentatively went to touch her hair. I said she was looking at my hand, perhaps to see if I had a wedding ring and she could not see one and that made her worry something was wrong with me and then she felt she had to attack her hair.

Clasping the ring finger of her left hand she very nervously said, 'Daddy doesn't want to marry me because I have got Down's syndrome.' She was the first patient I had worked with who made that comment and I was very moved.

In 'Moses and monotheism' (1939) Freud describes the common childhood fantasy of being kidnapped from Royal Parents by the common ones who bring you up! He considered this myth-making helped children to accommodate their changing disillusioned impressions of their parents. For many handicapped patients that important disillusionment is not possible and oedipal wishes can be similarly stymied. Daddy and the therapist, in the transference, remain distant gods, carefully kept at a distance to avoid the murderous projections that might rebound.

It was near the end of the assessment session and I found myself struggling with the appropriate interpretation. I was aware that she was considering me to be like her, ringless and handicapped, and that there was contempt in this projection. I was also aware that she was in touch with the terrible pain of being different.

I said it was almost time and we would meet again in a week and perhaps she felt I did not care about her because she had Down's syndrome and if I really cared I would carry on seeing her longer than I had arranged with her Mum and Dad. She grinned at that. I added, perhaps it could be the other way round too. She was not sure if I was any good if I wasn't wearing a wedding ring. Perhaps I was as handicapped as her. She looked shocked but then nodded with agreement. I then said it was time and as I opened the door to take her back to the waiting room she looked at me with deep interest and then sadly said, 'You have got children haven't you.'

I found that extremely painful, as always, when a handicapped female dares to consider me as a childbearing figure. There are a multiplicity of issues to be unpacked: the longing to have a child and the fear of having a handicapped child which is the disowned handicapped part of the patient; the hope for the female therapist to be normal and have normal children as well as the wish for the opposite. In this situation I felt that by interpreting her negative feelings for me as another handicapped person she was then freed to show appreciation that I had been motherly to her and then she could allow me my procreative abilities.

THE ABUSED HANDICAPPED VAGINA

Children and adults with learning disabilities are extremely vulnerable to sexual and physical abuse (Sobsey *et al.*, 1991). As I have itemized elsewhere (Sinason, 1993a) the impact of the handicap itself, obstructions to the attachment process, increased dependency needs, fear of being killed, communication difficulties, all join together to create extra vulnerability.

When Jane, aged 12, was able to say, 'Daddy hands nice. Make my Down's syndrome better', whilst demonstrating how daddy's hands went in her vagina, we were able to understand this more. 'What happens if Daddy's hands don't go in your vagina?' There was a long pause and she started rocking and biting her hand. I said that seemed a very painful thought. She began to scream. 'Kill me!' Then she huddled on her chair looking terrified of me. 'You think I am going to kill you – I am so cross with what you and Daddy do.'

She started slapping herself across the face. 'Daddy loves me', she kept repeating. I said she wanted her Daddy to love her especially when she was frightened her Down's syndrome would get worse if his hands weren't inside her. I added perhaps she was frightened I was going to kill her because she had been doing things with a Daddy that only a Mummy should do.

What could only be dealt with long into therapy, and after she was removed to a safe fosterhome, was her fear that I would kill her. Whilst all abused children are threatened with frightening physically abusive consequences if they tell, handicapped children *know* that people want to kill them and a threat is therefore even more silencing. Her fear of me was not only for oedipal reasons connected with the abuse. Far more painfully, like every handicapped patient I have worked with, she was in touch with a societal death-wish towards her. This makes the female therapist, *par excellence*, the annihilating pre-oedipal mother who will destroy.

HANDICAPPED PROCREATION: WOMAN PATIENT, WOMAN THERAPIST

I personally find the issue of abortion and procreation the most painful as a female therapist working with adult handicapped females. All the women I have treated, of whatever level of cognitive ability, have had an emotional understanding of the meaning of menstruation, pregnancy, abortion and sterilization. The issues are psychic minefields. Handicapped women hear on television and radio the cocktail chatter around terminations. 'As I am 40', one famous actress said on one such programme, 'I would have to be tested so I could terminate if the baby was handicapped.' I am not disputing at all the terrible consequences of bearing an unwanted baby. However, the lack of attention paid in such discussion to the thousands of handicapped people listening who face day-in day-out the abortion longings of society is of great concern.

Patients know that they 'slipped through' because no amniocentesis was booked (and that word might be the longest word several can say) or that they were masochistically endured as an act of religious faith or duty despite the death-wish against them. Even to consider pregnancy or childbirth means facing the internal phantasy of a death-threat and an external realization of one. The foetus, real or fantasized, is often the patient themselves as a child.

For six years I co-convened a once-weekly psychoanalytic group for learning disabled adults. It met for 1 hour 30 minutes a week and followed normal group psychoanalytic non-directive practice. For the first three years it consisted of five women and two female therapists. Out of the five women three had been raped. Then the group continued with a male co-therapist and expanded to include three male patients including one who, following childhood abuse, had become an abuser.

ADULT LEARNING DISABILITY GROUP

Here are the first year's main themes when the group consisted of women only. As can be seen, they powerfully illustrate the main gender themes of this chapter.

From Session 1, Lockerbie, disasters, crashes, terrorists, fear of parents dying. Fear of having children, how painful, being teased, split off acts of violence to friends under the influences of voices, man abusing a child, man beating a child, appearing in court, prisoners, fellow trainees who commit suicide, nice clever siblings and their children, fears of committing suicide, dirty men, disgusting toilets, nice mencap holidays, parents with cancer, mentally ill parents, abusive care workers, car crashes, physical injury, Hitler, abortions, dying relatives, unconsummated relationships.

In the beginning all conversation was in dyads between group members and myself or my co-therapist. It took twelve sessions for a linked juxtaposed series of monologues to exist and this extract shows why any intimate contact was so painful:

A: I had a dog that starved and was put down.
B: I had a pet that went blind.
C: My mother has got cancer.
D: When I was little I had to go to Great Normal Street Hospital. (Her version of Great Ormond Street Hospital. Like many handicapped patients she

enjoyed being in normal hospital with something physically wrong like other people).

E: I had a puppy that was put down.

It took forty sessions before the issues of cervical smears, amniocentesis, pregnancy and marriage could be mentioned, just before the introduction of a male co-therapist. It seemed that concretely, it was only when I was allowing the women to have access to a normal man that they could begin to consider their sexual issues.

It turned out that only one woman in the group had ever had a cervical smear. A used her intelligence in timing appointments for when she was menstruating so the smear could not be done. All the women feared how cold and hard the instrument would feel. We were able to slowly understand that since having a baby was the ultimate taboo it was easier for them to transform all sexual ideas of intercourse into something painful so that they could disguise their procreative wishes.

Session 40

B: I am going to family planning because I need to come off my pill and have something else and I do not want to make a mistake.

A: I am glad you are going to family planning, B, because abortion is terrible. I hate that word.

B: I agree

C: It is bad

D: The worst word is . . . is . . .

E: Amnio-

D: centesis

The killing word needed two people to carry it.

I said they all had very strong feelings that abortion was wrong and amniocentesis was wrong and they wanted families to be carefully planned and perhaps they were worried about me bringing in an unwanted group member who would then drop out and be aborted or make the group feel aborted. The group all nodded. I said we would have to think very carefully as to when a new member could join.

I had decided initially to take this issue into the transference with myself as the bad planner. I considered that it was not the right moment to raise their fear of my wish to kill them.

I then decided to take up another issue. I said there was another important subject for the group – not just avoiding having an unplanned baby but considering who might want to have a sexual relationship and might want – or not want – a baby.

C, D and E made clear they were terrified of having babies. It would hurt their bodies. They were also terrified of smears and of sex. B, who wanted a baby, said she did not like the cold metal thing going inside her for a smear. A, C, D and E all said they would never have a smear because it hurt. I said it was much easier to talk of what would hurt everyone than what might feel nice. Perhaps I had turned into some cold hard therapist who hurt everyone's insides and didn't want any of them to enjoy themselves.

C: (nervously) I like kissing and touching but I think anything else – you know – would hurt my insides and I know I could never bring a baby up. I – would not be able to manage.
D: If I knew, if I really knew I would be having a handicapped baby, like me, I would have an abortion.

There was a painful silence. I asked why and she replied very simply that she knew she would not manage a baby anyway and that would be even harder. E commented that kissing was disgusting so why even start. I said it seemed so painful to think they might feel a bit like their mothers felt when they were born – it seemed so painful to think of looking at a tiny handicapped baby – they would rather not even do things like kiss that didn't make babies happen.

There was then a discussion of tampons which C wanted to try. The others were frightened of that because it 'went inside' you but they were also fascinated and it proved to be a way of thinking about something inside their vaginas that they could consider.

A then brought up the topic of the burned soldier from the Falklands, Simon Weston, whose fiancée had married him despite his scarring. I said the group felt quite hopeful, despite their disabilities, that they were lovable. Perhaps having a male therapist about to join the group felt quite a battle but they also felt I did want them to be free to have their adult sexuality and was not keeping men away from them. There was laughter and agreement.

BABY AND WOMAN: MAUREEN

In the group of mildly to severely learning disabled women we can see how powerful the gender issues were. What about profound multiple disability where there is no verbal speech, adequate physical movement or literacy? How do gender issues appear in such circumstances – or do they?

Here is an extract of a session with a profoundly multiply handicapped young woman of 24 (Sinason, 1993b). I was to see her once weekly for six years until she died. She had no verbal speech, only a few signs, had blinded herself in one eye from her eye-poking, was doubly incontinent and had a history of abuse, abandonment and trauma. This comes from a session after two years.

Session 85

Maureen wheeled herself to the table, picked up a man and woman doll, a calf and a baby. Before I could comment on her feelings about couples and babies she threw them away, pulled her dress up, poked her vagina and wailed as a trickle of urine and menstrual blood came on to the floor.

I felt immensely sad and said, 'Maureen, it is your period and do you know, all the months you have seen me you have never wanted me to know when it was your period.' Her wailing stopped and she wiped her eyes and looked at me. I said perhaps Mary (key worker) going on maternity leave has made you think about your stomach and your period and how babies are made and whether you could have one. She nodded and then she cried. She wheeled back to the table and picked up a little baby doll and stroked its hair. Then she cried and dropped it. I said she was feeling awful, like a baby whose mother had left it because her own mother did leave her and now her favourite worker had left; but also like a woman without a baby who knows she is handicapped. She looked at me really sharply then pointed for the baby doll. I gave it to her. She put it down. Then she signed for a musical clock and listened to that and hugged it. Then she drew her wheelchair. Then she looked out of the window and looked round the room and looked at me and smiled. I said she enjoyed her music and being here with me and being able to see and draw and sometimes that made up for not being a mother with a baby or a baby with a mother. She nodded.

Maureen was to die a few months later. Her complex range of syndromes meant that her lifespan was very short. She showed me that with no verbal speech and hardly any physical or mental abilities she was amenable to meaning and insight. I attended her funeral.

CONCLUSION

Within the powerful context of treatment the therapist can be experienced as a range of personalities, ages, historical moments and sexes. The person seeking treatment is often reassured that whatever the sex or age of the therapist they enter treatment with, he or she will not preclude for them an experience of a sexual other. There is no doubt that our minds are capable of projecting myriad personalities on to the lent-out transitional space. However, to say there is no difference intrinsically in what the sex of patient or therapist is, is to enter a world of autistic sameness and denial. This is not to say that being of the same sex or the opposite sex is either an advantage or a disadvantage. It is to note the difference.

With learning disabled patients, many of whom have been abused, there are very specific gender issues. The extra dependency of the girlchild on the mother is exacerbated when developmental deficits impede autonomy and individuation. This increases fear of the abandoning annihilating mother. More painfully, the genuine awareness of parental depression, guilt or hatred over the child's disability exacerbates primitive fears of the pre-oedipal mother while the feeling of sexual damage often precludes gaining father as safe object. Same-sex identification is made harder with disabilities and existential loneliness is greater.

Pregnancy is the painful moment in which the unwanted learning disabled adult reperceives her baby experience and struggles against the psychic meaning of abortion by becoming asexual. The female therapist needs to help the patient to face these painful issues in the internal and external arena and then growth can occur. Difference, in the form of disability, is a difficult topic but needs to be faced.

With long term treatment there is a successful diminution of symptoms, including self-injury, an increase in linguistic and emotional ability and a greater courage in facing the real nature of the handicap.

NOTES

1 Linguistic note: The term 'learning disability' is currently used for what a few years ago was called 'mental handicap' or, slightly earlier, 'retardation'. The terms are changed every few years by a psycholinguistic process of euphemism (Sinason, 1993b) to avoid the pain of difference. In this paper the older term 'handicap' is sometimes used to symbolize the overarching nature of all the different kinds of disability.
2 This was a surprisingly difficult chapter to write. I finally realized that being the only trainee analyst with a chapter in this book led to an extra identification with my subject matter. I was the handicapped one out of whose pen or mind handicapped thoughts would come! Once I had understood that process I was able to finish.

REFERENCES

Bettelheim, B. (1960) 'Owners of their faces', in *Surviving and Other Essays*, Part I, New York: Vintage Books, 1980.
Bernstein, D. (1993) 'Female genital anxieties', in *The Gender Condundrum*, ed. D. Birksted-Breen, London: Routledge.
Britton, R. (1993) 'The missing link: parental sexuality in the Oedipus complex', in *The Gender Conundrum*, ed. D. Breen, London: Routledge.
Celan, P. (1971) *Speech Grille and selected poems*, trans. J. Neugroschel, New York: E.P. Dutton.
Ferenczi, S. (1928) 'The adaptation of the family to the child', in *Sandor Ferenczi: Final Contributions to the Problems and Method of Psychoanalysis*, ed. E. Balint, London: Hogarth, 1955.
Freud, S. (1900) 'The interpretation of dreams' *SE* 5: 354.
—— (1913) 'The theme of three caskets' *SE* 12: 292
—— (1939) 'Moses and monotheism'
Klein, M. (1921) 'The development of a child', in *The Writings of Melanie Klein*, London: Hogarth.
Laufer, E. (1993) 'The female Oedipus complex and relationship to the body', in *Gender Conundrum*, ed. D. Birksted-Breen, London: Routledge.
Pines, D. (1982) 'The relevence of early psychic development to pregnancy and abortion', *Int. J. Psychoanal.* 63: 311.
Raphael-Leff, J. (1993) *Pregnancy: The Inside Story*, London: Sheldon.

Sinason, V. (1989) 'Sexual abuse in psychotherapeutic settings', in *Thinking the Unthinkable: Sexual Abuse and Learning Disabilities*, eds H. Brown and A. Craft, London: Family Planning Association.

—— (1993a) 'The special vulnerability of the handicapped child and adult with special reference to mental handicap', in *Bailliere's Clinical Paediatrics: Child Abuse*, eds C. Hobbs, and J. Wynne, London: Bailliere Tyndall, pp. 69–87.

—— (1993b) *Mental Handicap and the Human Condition: New Approaches from the Tavistock*, London: Free Association Books.

Sobsey, D., Grey, S., Wells, D., Pyper, D. and Reimer-Heck, B. (1991) *Disability, Sexuality and Abuse: An Annotated Bibliography*, Baltimore: Paul H. Brooks.

Subject index

Author index